*Learning
Together*

Learning Together

A History of Coeducation in American Schools

David Tyack & Elisabeth Hansot

Yale University Press New Haven & London

The Russell Sage Foundation New York

Published with assistance from the foundation
established in memory of Amasa Stone Mather,
Class of 1907, Yale College.

Designed by Sonia L. Scanlon.
Set in Galliard type by The Composing Room of Michigan, Inc.
Printed in the United States of America.

Library of Congress Cataloging-in-Publication Data

Tyack, David B.
Learning together : a history of
coeducation in American public schools /
David Tyack and Elisabeth Hansot.
p.   cm.
Includes bibliographical references.
ISBN 0–300–04756–8 (alk. paper)
1. Coeducation—United States—History.   2. Public
schools—United States—History.   3. Sex differences
in education—United States—History.
I. Hansot, Elisabeth.   II. Title.
LB3066.T93   1990   89–78412
CIP

The paper in this book meets the guidelines
for permanence and durability of the Committee
on Production Guidelines for Book Longevity
of the Council on Library Resources.

10 9 8 7 6 5 4 3 2 1

For
Patricia Albjerg Graham,
friend and colleague,
whose qualities transcend
gender: integrity, compassion,
humor, commitment
to social justice, and wisdom.

⇒ *Contents* ⇐

⇁ *Acknowledgments* ↽

We are deeply grateful to the Russell Sage Foundation for sponsoring our study and for a stimulating year as scholars in residence. We especially wish to thank Eric Wanner, Peter de Janosi, and Alida Brill for making our association with the foundation so pleasant and intellectually invigorating. We are indebted to colleagues in three interdisciplinary centers at Stanford University for providing research support and forums for the exchange of ideas: the Stanford Center for the Study of Families, Children & Youth; the Institute for Research on Woman and Gender; and the Stanford Humanities Center. We thank the Rockefeller Foundation for a month of uninterrupted time for reflection and writing at the Villa Serbelloni.

One of the pleasures of working on this book has been the opportunity to discuss ideas with colleagues who have been generous in sharing their expertise in a variety of fields and candid in their criticisms. Without their assistance this book would have been much impoverished, but in mentioning their names we by no means suggest that they necessarily agree with our conclusions.

Several scholars gave us perceptive readings of the manuscript as a whole (in one or another of its incarnations): Larry Cuban, Kathleen Dalton, Carl Degler, Thomas James, Harvey Kantor, Susan Lloyd, Alison Prentice, Kathryn Kish Sklar, and Myra Strober. We are grateful for expert editing by Emily Boochever.

A number of other colleagues read portions of the text at various stages of its development and gave us excellent advice: Eric Bredo, Barbara Brenzel, Joan Brumberg, Joan Burstyn, Susan Carter, Geraldine Jonçich Clifford, Joseph and Wanda Corn, Julia Duff, Cynthia Fuchs Epstein, Mary Gluck, Barbara Heyns, David Hogan, Michael Katz, Linda Kerber, Susan Klein, David Labaree, Eleanor Maccoby, James March, Joanne Martin, Robert Merton,

John Meyer, Anne Miner, Theodore Mitchell, Marjorie Murphey, Nel Noddings, John Payne, Daniel Perlstein, Francisco Ramirez, Laura Rigal, John Rury, Maxine Seller, Leslie Siskind, Theda Skocpol, Kendall Stansbury, Catherine Stimpson, Richard Storr, Barrie Thorne, Jane Tompkins, Janet Viggiani, and Carolyn Williams. Our footnotes indicate some of our many other debts.

We have been fortunate to have the assistance of several first-rate research assistants on this project: Beverly Carter, Christopher Lyman, Susan Lynn, Sorca O'Connor, William Tobin, and Bette Weneck.

We thank the publishers for permission to use revised versions of articles published elsewhere: "Gender in Public Schools: Thinking Institutionally," *Signs* 13(1988): 741–60; and "Silence and Policy Talk: Historical Puzzles about Gender and Education," *Educational Researcher* 17(1988): 33–41.

In closing we wish to take special note of the encouragement and advice we received from David B. Truman at a critical stage of our research. He exemplifies for us the wise scholar and humane administrator. Our debt to another outstanding scholar-administrator, Patricia Albjerg Graham, is reflected in the dedication.

*Learning
Together*

⇒ *Introduction* ⇐

The known is the accustomed, and the accustomed is the
most difficult of all to "understand," that is to say, to
perceive as a problem, to perceive as strange, distant,
"outside of us."—Nietzsche, "The Origin of Our Conception of 'Knowledge'"

Anthropologists often make the familiar strange. Similarly, historians seek to solve the puzzles posed by the origins of the ordinary.
This book analyzes a practice that most Americans take for
granted: coeducation in public schools. It treats coeducation as the
major theme in a broader inquiry that asks why and how Americans educated not only sons but daughters as well. Carl Degler
observes that when one views American educational history from
the viewpoint of women, an issue "calls out for attention. It is the
decision to include girls in primary and secondary schooling on a
par with boys."[1]

Although coeducation has been an institutional fact in public
education since the early nineteenth century, both critics and advocates have been rare. To foreign eyes coeducational classrooms
often seemed strange and disturbing; to most Americans they
became a natural and unquestioned part of the educational landscape. But from time to time gender practices in schools have
become the focus of attention and debate. This happened largely in
periods when the everyday lives of women and men and cultural
beliefs about gender were in transition. In such periods, educational policy became a stage on which Americans argued in largely
symbolic but intensely serious ways about conflicting gender
ideals and the part schools should play in sustaining tradition or

1

creating a new pattern of relations between men and women. Amid all this policy talk, however, coeducational practice did not change substantially once it had been established. Thus, the history of coeducation must deal quite as much with constancy as with change.[2]

In seeking to answer the question: *Why coeducation?* we explore both rationale and explanation. Americans have justified and attacked coeducation, and this debate runs through the past into the present. But beneath this conscious discourse lies a complex and often unarticulated set of causes of coeducation that we examine here as well.

Coeducation in public schools represents an important example of a *gender policy* and *practice* in one major institution. What do we mean by these concepts? We see *gender* as a social construct, a set of cultural meanings attached to the biological division of the sexes. By gender *policies* in institutions we mean explicit rules that apply in different or similar ways to the two sexes; by institutional gender *practices* we mean customary arrangements, regularities of expected behavior crystallized into patterns that may or may not reflect official policies.[3]

Gender is a basic organizing principle in society, but the importance of gender distinctions may vary between societies and between institutions within any one society. Gender policies and practices in Sweden are different from those in Saudi Arabia. Likewise, gender has different salience in armies or unions than in old-age homes or elementary schools. These differences in institutional gender policies and practices may be studied in various ways: across time in the same institution—historically; in the same institution in different societies—cross-nationally; or in different institutions in the same society—cross-institutionally. In this book we analyze the institution of public schools historically. This is not a comprehensive history of public schooling—other topics and approaches would yield other perspectives—but we have found that focusing on gender does point up problems in some traditional interpretations of schooling.[4]

Through the analysis of coeducation we seek perspectives on two broader questions: How do schools look when viewed through the lens of gender? And how does gender look when seen in an institutional context? Underlying both questions is the fundamental issue of gender differences and similarities: to what degree have femaleness and maleness mattered in public schools, and why?

Speaking of women writers, Adrienne Rich has called for "re-vision—the act of looking back, of seeing with new eyes." Re-vision is also necessary in historical scholarship on gender in schools. Despite the useful pioneer work of scholars like Thomas Woody and Willystine Goodsell, historians have largely ignored gender policies and practices in education. That is changing: today historians of women are illuminating the educational experience of girls and women. But there is not much work that looks at both sexes and the relationship between them (in our view, research on gender, as on class, needs to be relational). Paying attention to gender reveals many neglected topics.[5]

Looking at schools through the lens of gender also compelled us to "see with new eyes" some familiar subjects. As we sought to understand the gender history of nineteenth-century high schools, for example, we became aware of a critical but largely ignored feature of these institutions: their small size, a characteristic vital in understanding how they operated. Likewise, in assessing to what degree reformers of the Progressive Era succeeded in differentiating schooling by gender, we have come to question a position that we, like many others, have held: that a vocational emphasis transformed public education. In other cases as well, we have found that inquiry into gender from an institutional perspective forces a reevaluation of interpretive frameworks in the history of education.

These are some of the questions we address in the chapters that follow:

- Who were the major advocates of the education of women, what arguments did they use, and how much opposition did they face?
- Why were the idea and practice of coeducation accepted so rapidly and with so little dissent during the first half of the nineteenth century, a time when Americans were busily creating separate cultural and economic spheres for men and women? How did Americans reconcile separate spheres for men and women with sexually mixed common schools for children?
- Why and how did coeducation spread in a highly decentralized system in which policy decisions about gender issues were normally made at the local level?
- Why did debate over coeducation not become conspicuous until the practice was already well established, and why did this debate focus on city school systems? Where and why did single-sex schools persist?
- How did beliefs about the similarities and differences of girls and boys shape gender policies and practices in schools?
- To what degree did gender policies and practices in public schools differ by class, race, and region?

• Why did groups of men and women seek to differentiate "identical coeducation" by sex during the Progressive Era? To what extent did these attempts actually alter coeducation?
• Why did the gender biases in apparently "identical" coeducation not become apparent to large numbers of people until the last generation?

One way to avoid taking so familiar a practice as coeducation for granted is to imagine that coeducation did not become the mainstream of schooling for boys and girls. One should not assume that what happened was the only possibility, once citizens had decided to educate their daughters. Consider, instead, several alternatives that can be projected from practices and beliefs that were common in the early nineteenth century. Americans might have chosen to give only a rudimentary education at home to their daughters, as indeed many did. They might have restricted secondary education of girls to private single-sex schools, a practice common in prosperous families in the Northeast and the South. They might have emulated the European practice of segregating the sexes in public schools; where this was done—in cities in the Northeast and South—such communities typically invested less in girls' schools and often restricted their curriculum.[6]

In practice the mixed, or "coeducational," schools did not follow a single gender pattern or a uniform institutional arrangement. There were many ways to educate boys and girls together under the same roof of the public school: to separate them in distinct rooms or on opposite sides of the classroom but give them the same course of studies; to offer them distinct curricula; or to mix boys and girls together in the classroom, teach them the same subjects, and subject them to the same set of rules and rewards. The last arrangement became over time the most common gender practice in public education; school people of the latter half of the nineteenth century called it "identical coeducation." But mixed schools remained a patchwork quilt of different gender patterns in many communities. Some districts practiced coeducation in the primary grades but not in grammar or high schools; others began coeducation at the top and extended it downward from the high schools to the grammar schools.[7]

The tangled history of gender policies and practices in public schools is not a unified tale of pathology or progress. In every period one can find what today would be called sexual bias, but discrimination is only part of the story. Schools may also have been unusual in their gender practices. To some degree they have been sheltered enclaves in which children and youth have been treated in ways that contrasted sharply with the lives of adult women and men. At the same time, societal conflicts about gender have entered gender discourse and practice in public education. Propelled by a millennial faith in schooling, yet driven by fears as well, Americans have made public education the repository of their hopes and anxieties about the gender order of the larger society.[8]

We suggest that the development of this variegated phenomenon called "coeducation" constitutes the central puzzle in the gender history of American public elementary and secondary schools. This book explores the emergence of coeducation and its career—contested but persistent—from the colonial period through recent years.[9]

Explaining Constancy and Change: Thinking Institutionally

The practice of coeducation became embedded in most public schools during the first half of the nineteenth century and then persisted despite a number of challenges and modifications. It became part of the standard grammar of the institution, accepted as one of the basic rules that governed its structure. Thus one phenomenon to explain is the origin and relative constancy of this organizational gender practice. At times, however, people did attack coeducation or seek to differentiate schools by sex; another task of interpretation is to account for change.

We focus primarily on the school as an institution. We could have directed our attention to individuals and their personal experiences in schools, as does much recent work by psychologists on sex-role socialization. We could have portrayed public schools as part of a seamless web of "patriarchy," or male-dominated society. Both of these approaches are common in scholarship on gender and education. But, we suggest, an institutional form of analysis, midway between the individual level and the societal, has a number of advantages. Because gender policies and practices became embedded over time in schools, an institutional and historical approach can illuminate which policies and practices were constant and which were transitory, which were hard to alter and which were malleable.[10]

The word *institution*—and even more the concept of institutionalization—has assumed protean shapes in the literature of social science. Without seeking a (probably nonexistent) consensual definition of the term, we employ the word "institution" in its traditional sense, to designate economic, political, religious, familial, educational, and other agencies that constitute distinctive arrangements in organizing society. In this view, institutions have goals, organizational structure, boundaries, and legal standing. Institutions also have histories with their own trajectories, internal dynamics, and relations to their environments. Organizations within any particular institutional sphere—such as education—may take a variety of forms (for example, schools may be public in control or private, working class or elite, and may differ in size and complexity, as do rural and urban schools).[11]

Using this institutional focus, we concentrate on gender policies and practices in schools. It is an open question whether an institutional analysis of some other topic in educational history—say, race relations—would follow a similar trajectory. Gender may be in some respects an idiosyncratic subject since it is often woven almost invisibly into the cultural fabric. But the turning points of an institutional history of gender in schools also intersect repeatedly with key events that shape education, such as the impact of major economic and political changes. The pattern of attempted gender reforms in public education, therefore, may illuminate more general processes of institutional change. Also, if there were comparable histories of gender practices in institutions other than schools, one could compare educational institutions with families, churches, and workplaces, for example. We suspect that if there were adequate gender maps of these institutions, one would find that gender was differently organized in each.

In recent years a number of scholars have criticized the views that institutions are merely passive products of larger social forces or simply neutral arenas for individuals and groups to work out their separate agendas. Instead, the "new institutionalists" argue, institutions (like schools) may strongly influence the behavior of their members and may have considerable autonomy and agency in setting and carrying out their own purposes (although, as we shall point out, schools have also been selectively responsive to their environments). Institutions have linkages with each other and mutual interactions that help to define the terrain in which they operate. As James G. March and Johan P. Olsen say, "institutions are actors in their own right." Of course, various institutions differ greatly from one another in their autonomy and in the degree to which they are buffered from their environments.[12]

The new institutionalists' approach applies directly to public education and helps to explain why schools often showed much continuity in practice amid shifting policy talk about gender. Public education played an important part in the allocation of prestige, money, status, and power, and thus was an arena for contests about who got what and about symbolic issues involving gender. As we shall point out, changes in society triggered demands for different gender policies in schools. But at the same time, schools showed considerable continuity in their basic institutional patterns, especially at the core of the educational process, the classroom. Once embedded, a basic practice like coeducation became part of standard operating procedures and deflected challenges. Sometimes schools had explicit policies governing gender relationships, but they also had organizational cultures in which many gender practices were implicit (often all the more powerful for being taken for granted).[13]

One way in which institutions perpetuate familiar gender practices over long periods of time is by distinctive *institutional socialization* of members. Acquiring appropriate gender behavior through institutional socialization differs from individual sex-role socialization. It focuses not on some generalized formation of gender roles, presumably established early in life, that translates uniformly from one context to another but on gender expectations that may differ in particular institutions. People are quite capable of changing their behavior and beliefs to match the expectations of others as they shift from one institution to another—say, from family to school to church to army. Gender lessons may also differ in formal and informal groupings in the same institution. Boys and girls typically segregate themselves in the informal groups of the school playground, for example, but teachers tend to mix them in classrooms where coeducation is the institutional norm.[14]

In the bureaucratized coeducational school that emerges in cities in the nineteenth century, for example, a child becomes part of an age-segregated group—a first-grade class—in which each student is only one among many, and similar tasks are assigned to each. The teacher is expected to employ the same standards of behavior, punishment, and reward for all. Pupils are supposed to learn not only to read, write, and do arithmetic but also to behave in an orderly manner in the group that forms the classroom.[15]

Students in such a school also learn an organizational curriculum: that the school is arranged in successive grades for pupils of different ages; that they need to demonstrate what they have learned; that adults such as teachers and principals have positions of authority; and that days, months, and years are scheduled into a mandated climb up the pedagogical ladder. Students compete to acquire the knowledge the school decrees worth learning. Thus the child learns the role of student and the official culture of the school.[16]

To understand the gender dimensions of this institutional socialization to school one needs to ask not only in what ways was gender salient but *how much* was gender salient—that is, to look not only at differences but also at similarities in the way girls and boys were treated. Both historical and current research reveals a variety of explicit gender differentiation in the way schools have been organized. Some official policies treated the sexes differently in coeducational schools. In high schools, for example, educators established separate vocational and physical education classes, enforced different dress codes, excluded pregnant girls but not their impregnators, and favored male sports. Like segregated black schools, single-sex girls' schools typically received less funding per pupil and had a more restricted curriculum at the secondary level than did white boys' schools. Employment policies and practices favored men over women.[17]

In addition to obvious sex-defined policies, investigators during the 1970s have discovered an implicit hidden curriculum of sex stereotyping in coeducational public schools. By portraying separate and unequal spheres for males and females, textbooks have reinforced the gender stereotyping prevalent in the larger society. Studies of classrooms and guidance offices have documented how teachers and counselors have treated boys and girls differently. Personal accounts of such schooling have illuminated the subjective effects of such school practices.[18]

No doubt such forms of sex differentiation have influenced how pupils experienced their gender as they passed through the school system. One should not assume, however, that sex discrimination marked all aspects of the curriculum or of organizational arrangements. We have discovered relatively few school-district policies that were gender-specific with regard to the core activities of the coeducational school: instruction in classrooms. In the rules governing such matters as admission to schools, promotion from grade to grade, curriculum, and rewards and honors, we have found little that distinguished boys and girls.

Institutional socialization in coeducational schools thus silently taught boys and girls that all students had similar institutional rights and duties and were subject to similar constraints and rewards. This second, hidden curriculum of organizational arrangements downplayed the salience of gender in school. Looking at gender through the institutional lens of the school, then, shows the multiplicity of gender messages the young received.

Thus far, we have suggested that an institutional approach may illuminate one part of the story of coeducation: the issue of constancy in gender policies and practices. But there is another part of the puzzle: explaining change, the origins of and alterations in coeducation. The institutional character of schools may help to explain continuities in practice, but schools were hardly hermetically sealed against the larger environment. Indeed, many school leaders prided themselves on adapting education to new conditions, while from the outside, lay activists lobbied for reforms in gender policies and practices. Throughout the story we tell, women and girls have been active participants in the campaign for educational opportunity.

In complex ways that differed by time and setting—for example, in rural versus urban districts—gender practices in the schools did change as society itself was transformed. As we see it, there was no automatic or simple correspondence between shifts in the political economy of gender relationships in the broader society and reforms in the schools. Instead, as changes occurred in the objective conditions of the lives of women and men or in the ideologies through which they interpreted the meaning of those transformations, individuals and groups sometimes translated their concerns into particular gender policies for schools. They then pressed these demands by influencing public opinion and through the political process. Some reformers appealed to traditional concepts of male and female spheres; others, to new concepts of gender justice.

Enacting new gender policies was only one stage in reform, however; they still had to be incorporated into the school. The gender changes that became institutionalized, that lasted, were often those that could be assimilated to the standard structure of instruction without disrupting it. Often such reforms ended up on the periphery of the school, not in the instructional mainstream, but they demonstrated that the school was doing something. And sometimes the intent of the reform became transformed as it was implemented.[19]

Change in gender policies and practices in public schools thus usually came about through a three-stage process of societal change, policy mediation, and institutional incorporation. The creation of home economics courses for girls provides an example. At the turn of the twentieth century, many Americans believed that new conditions—urbanization, the increasing employment of women, a rising tide of immigration—were producing a deterioration in family life characterized by symptoms such as increased rates of divorce and child mortality. As a remedy, reformers proposed teaching girls directly in schools to be better homemakers. Coalitions of women organized in clubs and professional associations lobbied legislatures and school districts to mandate programs in home economics. Edu-

Girls in cooking class in New York Public Schools learn American proprieties and feminine skills. (Jacob Riis, 1890s, Museum of the City of New York.)

cators installed home economics as a sex-segregated part of the curriculum in courses similar in structure to the rest of the instructional program. Such courses persisted and demonstrated that the schools were responding to a perceived problem, but they were marginal adaptations only.[20]

A number of other deliberate changes in gender practices followed such a pattern of initiation, enactment, and implementation. It would be a mistake, however, to assume that either change or constancy in gender policies and practices was necessarily the result of conscious decisions. Major shifts in gender relationships in the schools sometimes took place with minimal public discussion, while ardent debate sometimes produced little institutional innovation.

Silence, Policy Talk, and Gender Practice

Coeducation in public elementary schools came about in the first half of the nineteenth century gradually and for the most part quietly. Most justifications for and attacks on the practice appeared after the mid-century, when coeducation was already embedded. By contrast, some controversies left practice largely untouched. In the late nineteenth century, for example, doctors and psychologists claimed that coeducation in secondary education maimed the health of girls, but this did not stem the flood of girls into high schools. Critics complained that there were too many women teachers, but this did not halt the rapid exodus of men from the teaching profession. The King Canutes commanded, but the tide of coeducation did not stop.[21]

Policy discourse about gender in public education has taken many forms, some of which did have a real impact on practice. After the Revolution, for example, advocates of women's education played an important part in convincing parents to send their daughters to school (although many of them proposed separate rather than mixed schooling). By reconciling education with the separate spheres of the sexes, they defused conservative criticism. William T. Harris, while superintendent of schools in St. Louis in the 1870s, penned a persuasive justification of coeducation that gave city school leaders strong arguments for adopting coinstruction or for continuing what most of them were already doing. In the 1960s and 1970s feminists discovered and publicized the sex bias latent in coeducational schools and thus raised policy issues that had long gone unnoticed.[22]

Looking at coeducation in public schools through the lens of gender illustrates the complex relationships between silence, policy talk, and educational practice. Silence about major institutional changes in gender relations, attacks on coeducation with little practical effect, influential rationales, research on institutional sexism, reforms that had unintended consequences on gender relations in the schools, constancy in the basic forms of instruction in coeducational classrooms—these illustrate the need to analyze silence as well as policy talk, continuity as well as change.

In periods of rapid social change, gender relations have sometimes come into sharp focus and have been extensively discussed rather than ignored. On occasion, vigorous disagreement erupted about what was a just, natural, or God-ordained relationship between the sexes, and such controversies influenced rhetoric about schooling. In the nineteenth century, when traditionalists were determined to set sharp boundaries around the separate spheres of the sexes, critics claimed that coeducational public schools made girls too virile. In the Progressive Era, when feminists were pressing for the vote and greater opportunities in the economic and political world, conservatives worried that the schools were too feminine. In the 1970s reformers argued that the schools made the girls too feminine and the boys too masculine, thereby reinforcing sex stereotypes that restricted their opportunities both in school and later life.

Today there is vigorous disagreement about what constitutes a proper gender order in school and society. Some feminists urge educators to eliminate different treatment of the two sexes and to create gender-neutral schooling. They believe that such a nonstereotyped education will enlarge the aspirations of youth and cultivate competence in both boys and girls. Other feminists question whether a gender-neutral school is either possible or desirable. Coeducation as it currently exists, they claim, is male-defined and male-dominated. To integrate girls into such a system of male values and practices is to deny the worth of female experience, ethical outlooks, and cognitive styles. A better goal than gender neutrality, they believe, is education that honors both feminine and masculine qualities. Meanwhile, traditionalists hold with equal passion that schools should reflect and strengthen the separate spheres of men and women. Congress has both passed legislation to eliminate sexual discrimination in schools and considered a family-protection bill that would have reinforced traditional values in public education.[23]

The present period of self-consciousness about gender policies, however, is somewhat anomalous in the long history of gender policies and practices in public education. During most of that history, gender was rarely used as a root category of analysis in policy but rather was taken for granted. Only infrequently have Americans adopted explicit institutional policies about gender (as compared with the implicit policies represented by practice). Law is one place to look for formal policy; surely it reveals much about race, for example. But the educational provisions of state constitutions, state statutes, and court decisions dealt hardly at all with gender until recent years. In local district rules and regulations one finds few mentions of gender, compared to the elaborate provisions about age, proficiency, curriculum, and other matters that mark the boundaries or shape the content of schooling.[24]

The story of coeducation in public schools is in part one of silent change, of unintended results, of unlikely causes, of unheeded criticisms, and of hidden benefits and costs. Thus, the subject is replete with ironies and obscure transformations. The historian of gender in public schools, like Sherlock Holmes, needs to be aware of the importance of the dog that did not bark.

1

"Smuggling in the Girls"
Colonial New England

"In the early history of Massachusetts, and long after provision for Public Free Schools had been made," Horace Mann said in 1853, "it was a common thing for boys only to attend them. In many towns, the first improvement in this respect consisted in smuggling in the girls, perhaps for an hour a day, after the boys had recited their lessons and gone home." Harvard College, the Latin grammar schools that prepared young men for college, and most publicly supported town English grammar schools admitted males only. In the male-dominated public life of seventeenth-century Massachusetts, viewed from the top down by those who set policy, public schooling was not for girls.[1]

Although formal public schooling from the town grammar schools upward was initially a male monopoly, informal education and elementary literacy were not. From the beginning, women were teachers and girls learners. Both girls and boys were taught at home and in informal "dame schools" where they acquired the rudiments of literacy.

By almost imperceptible steps, and not by abrupt shifts in policy, the people of Massachusetts began to blur the sharp gender distinction between the formal public schooling that was open only to boys and the informal education that was available to both girls and boys. In the process, girls as students and women as teachers gained a foothold in public education. Thus, in colonial New England one may discern the faint institutional outlines of what would later become a coeducational "common school," or public elementary school.

13

By the middle of the eighteenth century, towns began to transform the private dame schools into "women's schools," which were held in the summer, often in the district school building, and which employed women at public expense to teach girls and young boys. When such basic instruction in reading and writing no longer satisfied girls, their parents sometimes "smuggled" them into the district winter schools taught by a man and attended by the older boys, usually paying the master to teach the girls at odd hours, before the boys came or after they left. These gradual steps toward coeducation made the integration of girls into common schools in the decades after the American Revolution seem part of a gradual evolution rather than a sharp new departure.

To understand this process, it is necessary to examine changing gender practices in two related institutions, the family and the church. Early segregation and later mixing of the sexes in schools, for example, paralleled developments in religious congregations. Originally the sexes were segregated in the meetinghouse, but by the eighteenth century it became increasingly common to seat families together in church. In the family, women came to play an increasingly important part in educating their children, a role that then expanded into public employment as teachers. In town after town, each with its own pace and political dynamic, the educational opportunities of girls began to widen.[2]

The Family as Educator

The family was a fundamental building block of the biblical commonwealth, bearing a close and reciprocal relationship to other institutions. A seventeenth-century preacher suggested that the borders between the family and other institutions were indeed permeable: "A family is a little *church*, and a little *commonwealth*. . . . Or rather, it is as a *school* wherein the first principles and grounds of government are learned; whereby men are fitted to greater matters in church and commonwealth."[3]

In this "school" of the family, parents were solicitous about the salvation of daughters as well as sons, and this required both girls and boys to read the Bible. In significant ways, the soul had no gender for the Puritans. Ruth Bloch writes that although "proclaiming female mental inferiority and insisting on the wife's duty to obey her husband (except when he violated divine law), Puritan literature tended to downplay qualitative differences between the sexes and to uphold similar ideal standards for both men and women." Laurel Thatcher Ulrich notes that Cotton Mather found "female as well as male virtues in the Godhead" and asserted "the spiritual equality of men and women and the essentially asexual nature of godliness."[4]

Laws made clear the parents' responsibility to educate all their children and called for compulsory education of all children, though not compulsory schooling. In 1642 the Massachusetts General Court ordered the selectmen of all towns in the colony to "take account from time to time of all parents and masters, and of their children, concerning their calling and imployment of their children, especially of their ability to read and understand the principles and capitall laws of this country," as well as to prepare them for some honest occupation. If parents or masters would not or could not so train their children, they might be fined or their children placed in other families. In 1648 the Puritans passed another law that required local officials to "have a vigilant eye over their brethren and neighbors, to see . . . that none of them shall suffer so much barbarism in any of their families as not to indeavour to teach by themselves or others, their children and apprentices so much learning as may inable them perfectly to read the english tongue, and knowledge of the Capital laws." The law also commanded parents and masters to "catechize their children and servants in the grounds and principles of religion."[5]

Ideally, the family was the guarantor of orthodoxy and a barrier against barbarism, the key educator of the next generation. Fearful of a declension from the ideals of Governor John Winthrop's "City upon a Hill," the Essex County Court in 1668 ordered the constable to list the names of young people who did not live in families, for they were the cause of "much sin and profanes" and "a great discouragement to most family governors, who consciently indeavor to bring up their youth in all christian nurture, as the laws of God and this commonwealth doth require."[6]

The governor of the family in Puritan society was the father, and on him in the early years of settlement fell the chief responsibility for the literacy and orthodoxy of his sons and daughters, for he was not only the head of the family but also usually more literate than the mother. Kenneth A. Lockridge estimates that in the years from 1650 to 1670 about 60 percent of men could sign their names to wills whereas less than a third of the women could do so. N. Ray Hiner observes that in the seventeenth century little attention was paid to mothers in tracts and sermons on the duties of parents and that "if the Puritan father had a relatively equal teaching partner, it was not his wife but his minister." The minister was the chief *teacher*, or "master," of his congregation, and the church was a school of godliness.[7]

Over time, however, women assumed a more prominent part in education. Gerald F. Moran and Maris A. Vinovskis argue that the early Puritans' reliance on fathers as instructors and catechizers of their children may have shifted as "males increasingly stopped joining the church . . . and the church's membership became feminized." They point out that "as women became increasingly literate, at least in regard to reading the Bible, and as they continued to join the church in larger numbers than males, ministers began to emphasize their role in the religious education of their children." They suggest that home instruction of girls may have produced more literate females than the percentage indicated by signatures on wills, for boys were usually taught to read and write and girls only to read.[8]

In enforcing laws on the education of children, the Puritans paid attention to girls as well as boys. In Watertown in 1670 a father was summoned before the selectmen for neglecting the education of his daughter and acknowledged "that the child had not been so well attended in the matter of learning as she should have been; did promise that he would be more careful for the time to come, that she should be learned in the knowledge of reading the English tongue." In their wills, parents made provisions for teaching their daughters to read and sew and their sons to read and write, indicating that they expected a higher standard of accomplishment for boys but were committed to at least a basic literacy for girls.[9]

Public Schools: Initially for Boys Only

Although both girls and boys were expected to become literate and pious, sharp gender distinctions appeared in formal schooling. By law, literacy was compulsory for both sexes, but attendance in public grammar schools was optional and open only to males who had already learned their ABCs well enough to read simple passages. To supplement informal instruction in the family, Puritan leaders passed laws requiring towns to create town schools. The most famous of these statutes was the Massachusetts Bay Law of 1647, which ordered townships of fifty or more families to "appoint one within their town to teach all such children as shall resort to him to write and reade, whose wages shall be paid either by the parents or masters of such children, or by the inhabitants in general." In communities of one hundred families or more, the town was also obligated to "set up a grammer schoole, the master thereof being able to instruct youth so farr as they may be fited for the university [Harvard]." The prologue of the law of 1647 reveals two of its purposes. Like the church and the family, the school was to ensure religious orthodoxy, for "saint seeming deceivers" (a reference to Anne

Hutchinson and the antinomian controversy that had shaken the colony) were making "false glosses" of the scriptures. Another purpose was to ensure a continuing flow of educated men so that "Learning may not be buried in the grave of our fathers in the church and commonwealth."[10]

Establishing what was religious orthodoxy and ensuring civil behavior was man's business; leadership was a male domain. Thus, it is not surprising that the "children" and "youth" who attended the town schools were almost entirely male, as were their teachers, at least until the eighteenth century. In a survey of the records of about two hundred communities in New England, Walter H. Small found only a handful of references to the education of girls in town schools during the seventeenth century, some of them ambiguous. A vote in the town meeting of Farmington, Connecticut, in 1688 expressed what was probably the consensus in New England about admitting girls to town schools. The town had allocated twenty pounds "for the maintenance of a school . . . for the instruction of all such children as shall be sent to it, to learn to read and write the English tongue." Apparently this raised a question about girls, for the town then declared that by "*all such* is to be understood only *male* children that are through their horn book." In 1680 the Hopkins Grammar School ruled that "all girls be excluded as improper and inconsistent with such a grammar school as the law enjoins and is the design of this settlement."[11]

Unlike home instruction or the private "dame schools," the town schools were part of the male public domain. Although they were required by colonial law, town schools were actually established by vote in town meetings. Individual towns differed in how well and in what way they complied with the requirement that they set up schools. Many towns ignored the laws entirely, especially the provision mandating the creation of Latin grammar schools when a community contained a hundred families. But the town school was, in theory if not in fact, a permanent institution independent of the person who occupied the office of teacher, unlike the colonial private schools, which were run as businesses by entrepreneurs.[12]

At first many towns located the district school in rented shops or rooms in houses, barns, and even blockhouses, but eventually they built schoolhouses. Erected by economy-minded citizens, these schools were typically small frame structures with small windows and large fireplaces that roasted the pupils nearest to them, while those farther away grew numb with cold. Typically they were equipped with sawn-plank seats and benches. Discipline was customarily harsh, and the usual method of instruction was memorization and recitation. Although some of the larger communities provided Latin grammar schools for youths who planned to attend Harvard, the vast majority of towns taught boys only such subjects as reading, writing, and arithmetic. Towns found it difficult to attract men into teaching and the turnover was rapid; approximately half the male Massachusetts teachers studied by Stephen Sellers taught one year or less.[13]

The Evolution of Dame Schools into Summer Women's Schools

In the century following the Massachusetts law of 1647 few girls won admission to the town English schools and no girls were allowed into regular classes in the public Latin grammar schools, but they did attend another type of educational institution that eventually became grafted onto the public school system. This was the dame school, the forerunner of the American public primary school.

Initially a form of child-tending and instruction privately subsidized by parents, the dame school slowly changed into a more public institution as towns began to pay "goodwives" to teach poor children. Over time the dame school was transformed into an official public summer school in which women taught young boys and girls of various ages. Finally, the dame school or woman's school became incorporated as the primary branch of a complex system of public education, as when Boston tardily adopted primary schools—conducted much like dame schools—into its structure of schools in 1818.[14]

The evolution of public primary education from the dame school of the colonial period was a grassroots development. Hence, its history is harder to trace than that of such institutions as the Latin grammar school that were created by legal decree. Kathryn Kish Sklar has observed in her study of twenty-five Massachusetts towns between 1750 and 1810 that public funding for primary schools for girls was most extensive where schooling "was not seen as a distinctly male enterprise, and the progression in education for both sexes seems to have been from the family outward." The gradual transformation of private dame schools into publicly financed summer "womens' schools" did not directly challenge accepted notions about the proper place of women in society. The whole process of institutional change took place in the glow cast by the reassuring image of a woman surrounded, as at home, by small children. It blurred two familiar institutions, the family and the school.[15]

The typical private dame school consisted of a few girls and boys under six or seven years of age meeting in the home of a woman who was paid a small sum by parents for supervising their children. She was expected to teach them to stay out of mischief, to mind their manners, to learn a catechism or short psalter, and to do simple tasks about the house, such as shelling beans. She often had to manage her own household while doing this. The "curriculum" was basic: learning the alphabet and a little spelling, mastering a few simple religious texts, knitting and sewing for the girls, sometimes writing for the boys, and perhaps a little oral arithmetic illustrated by numbers scratched in the sand of the floor with a stick. The quality of the dame school—like that of the town grammar school—varied widely with the character and talents of the teacher, but there is testimony about the excellence of many of the women who taught in them. In Northfield, for example, the wife of the smith taught little children for twenty-two weeks in the summer in her home. She was described as "a woman of great energy and versatility" who taught her own children so well that her daughter became a noted teacher of the next generation in the community.[16]

The dame school served at least two important purposes for colonial families. One was day care for young children: getting children out from underfoot and keeping them "out of fire and water" while adults did their work. This baby-sitting function of primary education is a largely overlooked but critical reason why parents during and after the colonial period sent their boys and girls to school. A Swedish traveler in the colonies observed that the parents of young children in the dame schools "probably realized that such little children would not be able to read much, but they would be rid of them at home and thought it would protect them from any misbehavior. Also they would acquire a liking for being with other children." Another purpose of the dame school was academic: to prepare boys for entry into the district grammar school by starting them on their ABCs and to give girls the basic literacy they would need to fulfill their religious and family duties. For the relatively few girls in seaport cities whose parents could afford to send them to private "venture" schools to learn ornamental subjects and perhaps to continue their study of the "English tongue," the dame schools also provided a base for further schooling.[17]

Presumably the public did not have an interest in baby-sitting—that was the parents' responsibility. But the town leaders did have an interest in securing the literacy of all children and in preparing boys for the district school taught by a master. In the seventeenth century most communities assumed that parents should either teach their young children themselves or pay for tuition in the dame school, but by the middle of the eighteenth century people were coming to believe that children could best learn to read in school. An increasing number of towns began to underwrite the primary education first of poor children and then of all girls and boys in summer schools taught by women.[18]

The towns generally bargained individually with the goodwives and widows who offered such services. There were several advantages in hiring women. They cost far less than men: women earned only a few pence per week for each child, a quarter to a half the amount paid a master. Good male teachers were hard to find, while many women were eager to teach, even in districts remote from the town center. In the mid-eighteenth century their demonstrated competence as teachers led town leaders to adopt new educational practices, each of which were small departures from tradition but which opened the way for the inclusion of women's schools as part of the public school system. Instead of the older practice in which parents bargained on an ad hoc and occasional basis with individual dame-school teachers, towns began to use part of the regular school appropriations to hire women to teach young children while continuing to employ men to instruct the older boys during the winter session. These women taught in their homes or in the houses of farmers in remote districts, sometimes moving from place to place to teach the children.[19]

It became increasingly common, however, for towns to hire women to teach in public school buildings during the summer, when costs were low not only because women were paid much less than men but also because the town or parents did not have to supply firewood—an important item in school costs. In Framingham, for example, the selectmen voted in 1755 that "women's schools should be kept at the five school houses in the summer season." This pattern of women teaching girls and little boys in the summer term—with men instructing the older boys in the winter—became standard practice and continued well into the nineteenth century.[20]

It was customary to require male teachers to be "approbated" by the minister or officials of the town, a primitive form of certification that stressed moral character and bestowed official sanction on the teacher. Slowly the practice began to extend to women teachers as well. This gave them a bounded authority to act in the public sphere, although control remained in the hands of men—a pattern that would continue to be the rule in public education. By 1789 when Massachusetts revised its school laws, it mentioned schoolmistresses as well as schoolmasters and required that both sexes be certified. As Sklar observes, such legitimations of women's public authority gave schoolmistresses "a new kind of prestige in their communities."[21]

This endorsement of women as teachers of the young and the consequent enhancement of educational opportunities for girls resulted in part from a changing appraisal of mothers as teachers of their children and as spiritual and moral guides in their families. As we have said, toward the end of the seventeenth century women began to assume a larger role in the church and in the training of their children. If mothers could be regarded as competent to teach their own children, it required only a small step to view them as desirable instructors and moral guides in the extended sphere of the school, especially since they were limited to teaching the young. Since both girls and boys were taught by mothers in the home, a coeducational summer school involved no disruption of established custom. The special virtues and talents of women as educators of little children would become a persistent theme of educational ideology in the early republic.[22]

The growing importance of women in schooling was matched by their increased prominence in religious congregations, a transformation evident in seating practices in churches. In the seventeenth century men and women were usually segregated on separate sides of the central aisle. Children sat together in a gallery or on the stairs, also separated by sex. Within this basic sexual division, members of the congregation were grouped by social status, as Barbara E. Lacey observes, with positions assigned by the seating committee to individuals "according to their age, office, and wealth; the oldest, most wealthy, and prominent members sitting closest to the pulpit." This practice began to change in the eighteenth century, as "rows of benches were gradually replaced by pews, and wives were seated with their husbands in pews. In some churches, children joined their parents in pews, but in most [until the nineteenth century] they continued to sit in galleries or in the back of the church." Lacey sees the new sexually desegregated seating arrangement in the meetinghouse as a sign that "the hierarchical family was giving way to an egalitarian one in which husbands and wives were equal partners, and shared the responsibility for family religious duties." She holds that "the woman's identity was no longer submerged in that of the husband, but rather it was given a status distinct and equal to that of her husband."[23]

Gender and Local School Politics

Local school politics played a part in the extension of educational opportunities to girls. Citizens in local communities argued about how to spend their limited school funds to best purpose, just as church members in the eighteenth century argued about whether seats in church should be assigned according to social status. As Sklar has shown, the local politics of education varied according to patterns of wealth in towns and by the degree of centralized control of school finances. Conflicts about how to allocate funds helped shape the education of girls. Because the records rarely mention gender, however, it is hard to tell how consciously the gender issue was framed.[24]

One key question concerned the proportion of funds to be expended on the boys' Latin and English grammar schools in contrast to the summer women's schools for young boys and girls. The Massachusetts General Court required the larger communities to establish Latin grammar schools to prepare boys for college as well as elementary district schools, but many towns dragged their feet. One legislator complained of a decline in the quality of the grammar schools, "which too many of our unlearned seem to be possessed with prejudice against." Citizens attempted to weaken or abolish the laws requiring the larger towns to found grammar schools; defeated in the legislature, they often went their own way in determining at the local level how to provide schooling for their children. The law permitted towns to finance public schools either by levying a poll tax on households or by requiring parents to pay "rates," or tuition, for their children. The former method tended to give the town's leaders the decisive rule in education policy, whereas the latter gave parents more influence in the allocation of funds and the education of their children.[25]

In a case study of Northampton, Sklar has shown that elite control of school affairs in that town restricted the opportunities for girls to obtain an education at public expense. Leaders in Northampton, which relied on poll taxes, invested a large proportion of its public monies in an expensive central boys' grammar school that was founded in 1687 and taught by a master. Not until 1759 was an outlying section of town allowed to establish a district school with poll taxes, and even then it was closely controlled by the school committee. Despite the pleas of citizens who wanted girls admitted to the public schools, the selectmen refused to use public money to educate females. This did not mean that the Northampton elite opposed schooling for girls; one of the leading opponents of tax support for the education of girls was the founder of a select private school for girls. What it did mean was that the elite families could prepare their sons for college at public expense in the Latin grammar school, while only those families who could afford to pay both private tuition and the local poll tax could send their daughters to private schools. Not until the 1790s, and then under a court challenge that asserted the town's duty to educate girls under the Massachusetts constitution, did Northampton schools admit girls. Similarly, it was not until 1789 that Boston permitted girls to attend the city's schools.[26]

Sklar's analysis of the town of Sutton illustrates how one community of middling wealth and decentralized school control chose to build its educational system, not from the top down, but from the bottom up, and in the process benefiting the girls. In Sutton the citizens paid for public schools not by a poll tax but by "rates" levied on the parents who sent children to school. This had the effect, Sklar writes, of "decentralizing the choices about who received formal schooling, and informally increasing the power of those families who actually sent children to school." The community did not have a mobilized elite to lobby for a Latin grammar school. Sutton did not establish a grammar school until 1793, two generations after it was legally required to do so. Instead, the townspeople focused their resources on inexpensive primary schools that were dispersed throughout the community. The families that paid tuition for the boys and girls and the district officials who oversaw the public schools believed that summer instruction was a desirable policy for girls as well as boys. The decision to invest in public primary education for both sexes gave the girls of Sutton opportunities unavailable in Northampton, where the allocation of funds favored only males. Teaching in summer schools also provided jobs for women, however poorly paid, that gave them a new public standing in the community.[27]

The first recorded action on education of the Sutton selectmen was a resolution applauding the founding of dame schools. It established first a "moving school" in 1732, that is, an itinerant teacher who traveled to teach in houses in the four districts of the town. Between 1732 and 1767 the town established fourteen district reading and writing schools (by the end of the eighteenth century it was paying those fourteen teachers less than one master's salary in the Northampton boys' grammar school). In 1767 the town records first mention "school dames" as part of the public schools and allocate one-third of the budget to pay them for teaching in the summer session. By 1773 the town was dividing the school fund equally between the coeducational summer schools and the boys' winter schools.[28]

Other towns as well paid women to teach coeducational summer schools by the mid-eighteenth century. In his study of teachers in four Massachusetts towns between 1635 and 1800, Stephen Sellers found that almost 15 percent of all teachers on the town rolls were women and that those towns began hiring females for the summer schools after about 1750. In the summer, when the older boys were needed on the farm, the school buildings would otherwise have remained unused.[29]

What went on in these summer schools? In her eighties Lucy Lane Allen recalled her days in a summer school in Scituate in the 1790s. "As the most we studied in school was reading, spelling, and writing, we had a good deal of time for [hand]work." The teacher stressed that the girls and boys "all should do their part toward family support," and in some respects the little school itself resembled a family. The devil found little work for the children, for their young hands were rarely idle, and the teacher never needed to use corporal punishment. The pupils all "carried sewing or knitting, and had regular stints." She and her sister made shirts for all the apprentices in her father's business. Manners and morals were at the heart of the curriculum. The older pupils read the Bible aloud every morning and the children imbibed theology and patriotism along with their *New England Primer,* Webster's spelling book, and the *American Preceptor.* When a minister or other august personage passed by the school, "the pupils would arrange themselves in a line and bow or courtesy all together."[30]

It is difficult, given the absence of written records of the process that led to the creation of coeducational summer schools during the colonial period in most communities, to penetrate the reasons why the citizens of towns like Sutton incorporated girls into publicly financed schooling. The steps from instruction in the home to the small private dame school to the public summer school of the sort that Lucy Lane Allen described were so gradual, perhaps, as not to occasion much comment. The summer school was cheap and provided useful supervision for young children in a busy agricultural season. It is possible that toward the end of the eighteenth century New England parents were more and more inclined to delegate to teachers and schools the religious duty of teaching young children to read, once their special province. It is also likely that parents in communities like Sutton saw economic advantages in the literacy of girls, as Sklar argues.[31]

The Rise in Female Literacy and the Demand for Further Education

Where girls gained access to public summer schools, the new educational opportunity probably increased the rate of female literacy. Literacy is notoriously hard to estimate in the absence of systematic surveys such as the U.S. Census (which had its own problems). The use of signatures versus marks on wills, deeds, and other documents as evidence of literacy in the colonial period leaves many questions unanswered. What was the rate of literacy among the poorest people, who rarely used such legal documents? Especially important in the case of women, who were often taught to read but not to write, how can one extrapolate from signatures or marks to the ability to read?[32]

Studies employing signatures on wills and deeds have reached somewhat different conclusions about the literacy of women, although all have found male signing rates higher than female. The most comprehensive of these, by Kenneth A. Lockridge, found that the percentage of men able to sign wills in New England rose from 60 to 90 from 1650 to 1795, whereas the percentage of women able to sign increased much less, from 30 to about 45. In Boston, however, where there were many private schools catering to daughters of prosperous families, he found that by the middle of the eighteenth century about two-thirds of the women signed rather than marked wills. Two studies of signatures on deeds in long-settled communities along the Connecticut River found substantially higher rates for women than Lockridge's overall averages. In Windsor, Connecticut, where the first schoolmistress began teaching a summer school in 1717, Linda Auwers found that about three-fourths of the women born between 1710 and 1739 were able to sign deeds, in contrast to 93 percent of those born in the 1740s. William J. Gilmore discovered that more than 95 percent of the men in the townships of Windsor District, Vermont, where schooling was well developed in socially connected communities, were able to sign deeds. In the last four decades of the eighteenth century, between three-fifths and four-fifths of Windsor District's women were also able to sign documents. These figures indicate discrepancies between the sexes but show overall a high rate of literacy for both men and women growing up in the middle of the century.[33]

Signatures on wills and deeds provide one kind of evidence of growing educational opportunities for women during the eighteenth century. Pressures to give girls further schooling beyond the meager fare of the summer schools are also a sign that gaining a little learning gave girls and their parents a taste for more. In the larger communities many prosperous parents chose to provide their daughters with more schooling, mostly in private "venture schools" but in time also in more ambitious and permanent private female seminaries. In some communities families also wanted their daughters to profit from the more advanced education provided in the boys' grammar schools conducted during the winter term.[34]

Until after the American Revolution, however, this grammar school instruction took place in sexually segregated settings. Here and there a town schoolmaster taught a small group of girls before or after the regular boys' sessions in grammar school or at noontime, usually for tuition paid by the parents but sometimes for free. The notion of little girls and boys going to school together had become commonplace by the late eighteenth century, but the idea of older children associating together in school did not appeal to many people. Small found that the towns that decided to offer an English grammar school education to girls in the late eighteenth century generally did so in separate schools, which cost less to operate and ran for shorter terms than those of the boys.[35]

The idea of offering a grammar school education to girls at public expense created controversy. In Plymouth, Massachusetts, a recommendation in town meeting to establish a female school taught by the grammar master aroused fierce debate. The prospect of well-educated women disconcerted some men. One said that the world was coming to a "pretty pass . . . when wives and daughters would look over the shoulders of their husbands and fathers and offer to correct as they wrote such errors in spelling as they might commit." When Boston considered creating girls' grammar schools in 1789, proponents and opponents took to the *Massachusetts Sentinel* to state their arguments. Opponents claimed that female minds were inferior, that educating girls would undermine the social order, and that servant girls would neglect their work and write love letters instead. Proponents of the plan, including a group of prosperous merchants and civic leaders who wanted better schooling for their daughters than was available in most private schools, argued that women needed education to discharge their duties as mothers and companions of their husbands, and that training in arithmetic would benefit widows forced to run a business.[36]

In colonial New England boys had access to all forms of education, both formal and informal, although their educational attainment differed by class. Initially, girls had access only to the more informal means of education in the family and dame schools, which provided only the rudimentary literacy demanded by Puritan religious principles. This situation changed over time as girls gained entry to town summer schools. But schooling for girls remained haphazard and limited during the colonial period.

The Revolution, however, created a new ideological climate that transformed the debate over the education of women. Reformers argued that schooling should be provided as a matter of right to all girls, not just to those few who were fortunate enough to have supportive, educated, and well-to-do parents. Mary Beth Norton writes that poorly educated women in the colonial period tended to regard their lack of schooling as a source of shame or a personal misfortune, not as a denial of a moral and civic entitlement. This demonstrates, she says, "how restricted were their self-conceptions and aspirations. . . . Only during the postwar years did American women begin to argue systematically that members of their sex should be better educated." In the early republic women and men began to debate in earnest why and how women should be educated.[37]

2

Why Educate Girls?

The Revolution created a fresh sense of possibility among the advocates of the education of women. The reformers of the revolutionary generation made a strong case that girls had a moral, social, and civic right to thorough schooling, not simply the rudimentary or frivolous learning they were permitted to acquire during the colonial period. During the early nineteenth century a resurgence of evangelical Protestantism gave new impetus and urgency to the conviction that the new nation required a new kind of educated woman. This emergent Protestant-republican ideology fused new concepts of gender and education to supply answers to the question: *Why educate girls?*[1]

This rationale took several forms. Employing ontological claims about the nature and being of woman, reformers asserted that woman was a person with the same moral and social rights as man. Emma Willard, for example, wrote that "reason and religion teach that we too are primary existencies . . . the companions, not the satellites of men." Advocates of education for girls refuted popular stereotypes about the mental inferiority of women. And they sought to convince citizens that practical benefits would flow from the schooling of girls.[2]

Proponents of schooling for girls believed that in a republican and Christian United States women had acquired new standing as persons and required a broader education to realize their ideal of feminine character. They often portrayed women in European societies as beasts of burden or as playthings of the aristocracy, not partners with men in creating republican virtue, as in America. Likewise, they believed that Protestant Christianity conveyed a special status and new duties upon women. Reports from missionaries abroad confirmed their opinion that women were grossly exploited in "pagan" lands, in sharp contrast to what they considered to be the privileged moral position and obligations of Christian women at home. The common-school crusader Horace Mann believed that the religious and civic standing of women in Victorian America represented a radical departure from their position in earlier times and in benighted societies. "Throughout the past ages of the world," he wrote, "the condition of woman has been degrading and demoralizing to her own sex, and dishonorable to the other. And even at the present day, the same unqualified affirmation may be made of the worst parts of the earth, and of many grades of society, even in the best." Women have suffered "servitude of body, nondevelopment of intellect, and depravation of heart. Only until within a period comparatively recent, have these facts of history been acknowledged, and the duty of reform been recognized."[3]

In 1851 the political philosopher Edward D. Mansfield declared it axiomatic that females and males have the same educational rights under a republican government. "It is the idea of moral right, founded in the nature of the soul, and derived from the Bible," he wrote, "which is the sole foundation of republican government, and the sole evidence that women have equal rights in the social system, and are equal partners in whatever benefits society might convey." Women and men were "equal before the law of God" in "all moral and social elements," he believed, and any differences they might display "in the physical system" or "in the political system" were irrelevant to their right to a full education.[4]

But what did equality of the sexes entail for the education of girls if it was "moral and social" and not economic and political as well? If girls gained an education similar to that of boys, would they not challenge the whole gender order of adult society? In a period when Americans were struggling to keep the sexes in their separate cultural and economic spheres, would not a rigorous education unfit young women for their separate destiny? Opponents and proponents of full rights for women agreed that education would disrupt separate gender spheres, although the former condemned the change in the status quo and the latter welcomed it. But most proponents of schooling for girls thought that education would simply make women more effective in their own domain.[5]

Alexis de Tocqueville observed that the "virile" education and considerable autonomy given to girls did not undermine marriage, disturb the separate spheres, or produce "weak men and disorderly women." He remarked, "In no country has such constant care been taken to trace two clearly distinct lines of action for the two sexes and to make them keep pace with the other, but in two pathways that are always different." He contrasted the independence of American girls with the sheltered existence of European girls, especially in Catholic countries. He was astonished "at the singular address and happy boldness with which young women in America contrive to manage their thoughts and their language amid all the difficulties of free conversation." Unlike French girls, sequestered in a "reserved, retired, and almost conventual education," American young women were exposed, he thought, to the world early and taught to control wayward impulses, to see but to shun vice and corruption.[6]

Tocqueville maintained, however, that when the American woman married, she found her youthful independence "irretrievably lost in the bonds of matrimony." So firm were the community expectations of the married woman that "she cannot depart for an instant from the established usages of her contemporaries . . . and she finds the energy required for such an act of submission in the firmness of her understanding and in the virile habits which her education has given her." Women in America, he believed, "often display a masculine strength of understanding and a manly energy" even though they scrupulously observe a division of duties with men. They preserve "great delicacy of personal appearance and always retain the manners of women although they sometimes show that they have the hearts and minds of men."[7]

Tocqueville portrayed, then, a discontinuity between the relative freedom of American girls in their youth and the restrictions of their adult life. By contrast, European women were more continuously sheltered. Curiously, he saw as "virile" the intellect that enabled young American women to submit to the constraints on their behavior required by the "bonds of matrimony."

What perhaps appears paradoxical today—an empowering of girls through an education similar to that of boys yet a subsequent closeting of women in their constricted domain—did not seem inconsistent to most proponents of the education of girls in the period from the Revolution to the Civil War. These advocates saw women as the equals of men—they had souls and a compelling civic responsibility—but considered them nonetheless as physically, morally, and socially different from men and destined to exercise their influence in different ways. In the process of justifying education for girls they articulated a new ideal of womanhood in which schooling was essential, but they also countered conservative opposition by demonstrating that this ideal did not challenge male dominance in the society as a whole.[8]

This rationale for educating women was largely the creation of middle- and upper-class writers. Many of them concentrated on promoting female seminaries, usually segregated by sex, in which girls could obtain an earnest and disciplined schooling not available in transient and ornamental private schools. They sought opportunities for girls comparable to those open to boys in public Latin grammar schools and in male private academies. It was more important to them that girls be educated than where they were educated.

Since the arguments of the proponents of education for girls were broad in character, however, they could be applied to schooling in general, not simply to one form, such as female seminaries. From the Revolution to the 1830s, educational institutions were fluid and heterogeneous: the lines between public and private institutions were blurred, for example, as were the distinctions between elementary and secondary levels. When the common-school movement gained momentum during the nineteenth century and public education became a dominant, more sharply defined institution, public-school advocates like Mann and Henry Barnard echoed these earlier arguments in favor of education for girls. Since two prerequisites for coeducation were the desire of parents to educate their daughters and a willingness of school boards to open the doors of the schoolhouse to girls, such rationales played a part in the rapid spread of coeducation. Barnard went so far as to say that if schooling had to be curtailed for either sex, it should be the males who left the classroom first, for boys "can more easily supply the deficiencies of school by improving the opportunities of self and mutual instruction." If girls, however, enjoy a thorough education, they "will, in the relations of mothers and teachers, do more to improve and bless society, and determine the civilization of the next and all future generations, than the male sex can do, however well educated, without the operation of women."[9]

The task of educated women was to buffer the effects of change on their families by being better wives and mothers. The generations living in the period from the Revolution to the Civil War witnessed major transformations in the political economy: the creation of a new nation, the first modern state; the expansion of commercial and industrial capitalism; increasing disparities in wealth and income; foreign immigration and enormous geographic mobility; and the most rapid pace of urbanization in American history. When speaking of boys, educators discussed how schooling would directly address problems created by these new conditions—for example, that it would mitigate poverty or help immigrants become assimilated—but when speaking of girls they focused almost entirely on their role in the home. Those who advocated the education of girls did not believe that education should respond to societal change by taking women out of the family (except for certain womanly jobs like teaching). The vast expansion in the education of girls from the Revolution to the Civil War thus provides a case study of major institutional change justified on traditional grounds.[10]

A New Nation, A New Woman

In the early republic Americans vigorously debated what constituted a proper education for girls. Reformers attacked the age-old notion that women lacked the intellectual capacity for schooling and the view that educated women were ridiculous bluestockings and old maids. Many writers argued that the new nation required a new kind of mother, educated not for show or selfish accomplishments but to raise virtuous and informed citizens. The Roman matron, not the coquette, became the cynosure—a woman who was sober, principled, efficient in doing good, a wise guardian of her children, and a worthy companion of her husband.

Linda K. Kerber suggests that in this version motherhood became a fourth branch of government. Just as both men and women had souls, so civic responsibility transcended the boundaries of gender. While women could not vote or hold office, they played a key part in the polity by educating their sons in civic virtue. "Let the ladies of a country be educated properly," wrote Benjamin Rush, "and they will not only [indirectly] make and administer its laws, but form its manners and character."[11]

Controversy about the education of girls took place in many forums and dealt with many issues, varying in tone from farce to sermon. One letter in a newspaper might claim that it was simple justice to admit girls to grammar schools along with the boys, while another might ridicule the learned woman as an Amazon of intellect. In college debates and in commencement ceremonies speakers pronounced on the intellectual capacity of women and disputed "Whether the Education of Daughters be not without any just reason, more neglected than that of sons." Student plays in secondary schools echoed fashionable drawing-room banter about whether advanced schooling turned young women into unmarriageable pedants. Sober opinions on the correct education of girls appeared in textbooks read by tens of thousands of pupils. Magazines printed disputes about the intellectual abilities of women, some claiming that there were few female geniuses and others arguing that it was amazing that faced with such meager opportunities any women had achieved eminence. From the pulpit ministers described the ideal of womanly character that should inform the schooling of girls. Novelists, playwrights, and poets took up the new theme of education for girls. Political commentators wrote tracts demonstrating that the new republican order required a different form of education for girls, while women activists argued that the new principles of republican liberty decreed a new status for women, not only in education but in all domains of their lives.[12]

One of the most outspoken advocates of educational equality was Judith Sargent Murray, who sought to use schooling to improve the condition of women. She was raised in a merchant's family and obtained a good education by studying with her brother as he prepared for Harvard in the 1760s. Married at eighteen, widowed, and later remarried to a Universalist minister, Murray attacked the presumption of male superiority on several fronts. She dismissed the biblical argument drawn from the fall of Eve by asserting that the first woman transgressed in search of knowledge, while Adam "was influenced by no other motive than a bare pusillanimous attachment to a woman!" Women did not lack brains but did lack instruction; their supposed deficits in reasoning and judgment arose simply because the "opportunity of acquiring knowledge hath been denied."[13]

Women's education, Murray argued, should not aim simply at enhancing their chances in the marriage market but should prepare them for useful occupations that could provide them with a decent income if they remained single or were widowed. Marriage should be a choice and not a necessity. The uneducated wife was condemned to frivolity in amusements and "experiences a mortifying consciousness of inferiority, which embitters every enjoyment" in her association with her husband. To those who would say "your domestick employments are sufficient," her reply was, "Is it reasonable, that a candidate for immortality, for the joys of heaven, who is to spend an eternity in contemplating the works of Deity, should at present be so degraded, as to be allowed no other ideas, than those which are suggested by the mechanism of a pudding, or the sewing of the seams of a garment?" Her ideal for women was not the dependent wife or fashionable maiden, but rather an educated and serious companion of her husband, a competent worker, and a mother who raised upright citizens.[14]

Benjamin Rush, a doctor and signer of the Declaration of Independence, gave a talk on "Female Education" to the visitors of the Young Ladies' Academy in Philadelphia in 1787 that was widely reprinted and gained considerable influence. Though less witty and radical than Murray, he agreed with her on many counts. A thoroughgoing utilitarian, he attacked merely ornamental education and preoccupation with fashion. "I have sometimes been led to ascribe the invention of ridiculous and expensive fashions in female dress entirely to the gentlemen," he wrote, "in order to divert the ladies from improving their minds and thereby to secure a more arbitrary and unlimited authority over them." He advised the young women of the academy to demonstrate that "the female temper can only be governed by reason and that the cultivation of reason in women is friendly to the order of nature and to private as well as public happiness." He wanted to train women in practical subjects so that they could "be the stewards and guardians of their husbands' property" and could "discharge the duties of those offices with the most success and reputation." He would have girls study "history, travels, poetry, and moral essays" as well as receiving "regular instruction in the Christian religion," favoring such earnest subjects over "the passion for reading novels that so generally prevails among the fair sex."[15]

Rush sought to adapt education "to the state of society, manners, and government" of the new republic. In America this goal mandated a new form of education for women and a new task for mothers: to understand the political system and to instruct "their sons in the principles of liberty and government." Unable to vote or participate directly in government themselves, they nonetheless had a solemn duty to ensure the perpetuation of the nation by raising children correctly, and to do this, they needed a thorough education.[16]

Rush feared that the vices and faulty political principles of Europe might infect the new nation, but he dreamed that "religion, liberty, and learning" might yet raise the country to unimagined "degrees of happiness and perfection." In this task educated women were to play a key part: "the opinions and conduct of men are often regulated by women in the most arduous enterprises of life, and their approbation is frequently the principal reward of the hero's dangers and the patriot's toils," he wrote. Besides, "the *first* impressions upon the minds of children are generally derived from the women." It was essential, then, that "they should think justly upon the great subjects of liberty and government!" While limiting their scope to the home, as wives and mothers, Rush nonetheless assigned women a civic role in creating a virtuous republic.[17]

The notion that women had an important public function persisted even though they could not vote or hold office. Horace Mann, for one, thought that women could serve the nation best by staying out of partisan politics and forming the political convictions of the young. Mann—who had taken his lumps in state and national politics—wondered why "any mortal who has ever lived within the roar and stench of that black and sulphurous lake" of partisan politics "should desire to see woman embarked upon its tumultuous and howling waters." Legislatures, he wrote, were "cabals . . . for intrigue and Machiavellianism on a magnificent scale." Women should be protected from such murk and corruption, just as they should be barred from joining the military or practicing the law.[18]

Women's true civic work was distinguished by "the intrinsic dignity and enduring importance of education" of the young in civic virtue, not "the ephemeral tinsel of political distinctions." The key to political stability was not the rough-and-ready forum of partisan politics but the home where mothers could train individual citizens to do right. Lasting reform would come not from politics, wrote Mann, but from improvement "in household training, in neighborhood proprieties and decencies, in public opinion generally"; and in these domains women reigned. Properly raised, every person in this atomistic view of the polity was a virtuous republic in miniature. The greed and conflict of partisan politics was the product of defective socialization. The proper instruction of children was thus the political, religious, and domestic duty of the well-educated woman citizen, a way to fulfill her feminine destiny.[19]

Rush had helped to create the Young Ladies' Academy to provide girls in Philadelphia with the sort of serious schooling they would need as republican mothers. In the last two decades of the eighteenth century such schools proliferated both in the seaboard cities and in smaller settlements inland. In the colonial period private teachers had sold their skills in "venture schools"—usually short-lived businesses that taught students subjects like music or fancy sewing. Serious-minded Quakers and Moravians had established some effective schools for girls, as had Catholic nuns. But both the demand for secondary schooling for girls and the number of schools mushroomed after the Revolution.[20]

Responding to this new market, a number of boys' academies opened their doors to girls, and separate female seminaries and "select schools" cropped up in communities across the more settled parts of the country, in the South as well as the North. A number of scholars who would later have eminent careers in other fields taught schools for girls: Noah Webster, lexicographer; Jedediah Morse, geographer; and Timothy Dwight, president of Yale. Some talented men—William Woodbridge, Caleb Bingham, and George B. Emerson, for example—devoted most of their professional careers to teaching young women. Ministers were often active in founding female seminaries, and some devoted a good part of their lives to the schooling of girls. The Reverend Joseph Emerson, for example, was an intense evangelical who taught and inspired Mary Lyon, Zilpah Grant, and other pioneers in women's education. They shared a common goal: to produce the new American woman.[21]

Mary Moody Emerson exemplified the Protestant-republican ideal of female character. "She gave high counsels," reads the epitaph on her tombstone in the Emerson plot in the Concord cemetery. "It was the privilege of certain boys to have this immeasurably high standard indicated to their childhood—a blessing which nothing else in education could supply." The daughter of a minister, born in 1774 on the eve of the American Revolution, Emerson was a self-taught intellectual who spent only a brief stint as student in a district school. When her brother William died in 1811, Mary moved into his house to help his widow raise six children. It was there that she began shaping the character of her nephew Ralph Waldo Emerson. "Scorn trifles, lift your aims; do what you are afraid to do," she urged. Deeply religious, independent of spirit, demanding of herself and others, she was, wrote Henry David Thoreau, "really and perseveringly interested to know what thinkers think." The new woman in the new nation was just such a person: rational and moral, not sentimental; austere and utilitarian, not frivolous; independent and competent, not passive. She was to transform the new nation by training the young aright, by giving "high counsels."[22]

The Evangelical Impulse

In the nineteenth century, many advocates of the education of women were activists in the evangelical religious movements that swept the nation in the first half of the nineteenth century. Religious doctrine sanctified their cause and legitimated a more active role for women in the churches, in social reform, and in education. It was inconceivable that women, whose souls were thought to be immortal, like those of men, and who exercised a formative influence on their children and their husbands, should not share in the benefits of schooling. Although most advocates believed that woman's destiny was to be a wife and mother, many recognized that an effective education might permit single women to pursue honorable careers as teachers. Through the abundant literature of advice to women in ladies' magazines, sermons, and books, women learned that childhood was a momentous time not to be "left run to waste" and that it was their primary duty to improve their sons and daughters in those impressionable years. The importance of this maternal task inspired a merchant in Illinois to give the then enormous sum of $110,000 to found Monticello Seminary:[23]

> One morning in 1830, while lying in my bed recovering from a severe sickness, my wife came into the room and made some remarks as she left. Our little daughter who had just begun to lisp a few words, caught the remarks, and while playing by herself on the floor, repeated them over and over for some time. This led me to reflect on the powerful influence of the mother on the minds, manners, habits and character of her children, and I resolved to devote a large part of my possession to the intellectual and moral improvement of women.

The most persuasive and influential justifications for women's education came from pioneer educators like Emma Willard, Catharine Beecher, and Mary Lyon, who created female seminaries whose curricula stressed intellectual achievement and moral character. Such reformers extolled a serious if not stern ideal of feminine character and called for "professionalizing motherhood." They wanted women to fulfill their feminine destiny but not to move outside their sphere. These pioneers were rarely parochial in their arguments, even when they sought to advance particular institutions.[24]

Justifications of women's education were closely interwoven with fundamental beliefs about God and religion, the nation and republican government, the changing character of the family, and the sexual division of labor in the economy. They reveal a whole system of beliefs about gender embedded in a broader Protestant-republican ideology and a millennial conception of American destiny. Mann drew on their thinking when he called on the educated woman to use her "divinely-adapted energies . . . in the work of regenerating the world" in accordance with God's design for America.[25]

Almost all advocates of female seminaries agreed that moral and religious education should guide women in the use of their new intellectual powers. Few could match the evangelical piety of Mary Lyon or her mentor Joseph Emerson, but most believed that knowledge was dangerous unless informed by religion. Many also believed that, religiously and morally, women were different from men—that is, better. "Our highest responsibility is to God, and our highest interest is to please him," wrote Willard;

"therefore to secure this interest, should our education be directed." Mothers well versed in religious doctrine were best fitted to teach a common, rigorous, and nearly gender-neutral morality to their sons and daughters, and to train them to be obedient, kind, truthful, industrious, and faithful.[26]

The feminine character shaped by such religious concerns was a stern and righteous influence on those around her. It was a mistake simply to train wives to please their husbands, Willard declared: it was the religious duty of women to help men keep to "their proper course" and not to accompany them in "their wildest deviations." Religious beliefs also sanctioned women's activism in rooting out "deviations" outside the home, through the temperance, missionary, and charitable associations they controlled and through the churches, in which they outnumbered men. Anne Firor Scott argues that although Troy Female Seminary existed "to educate women for motherhood and train some of them to be teachers, . . . in retrospect . . . the school can be seen to have been an important source of feminism and the incubator of a new style of female personality." She points out that there was no one litmus test of feminism, no one brand of "true womanhood."[27]

Educating the New Woman

The writings and speeches of Willard, Beecher, and Lyon are only the best known of a larger genre of prescriptive literature on the education of women created by the founders and supporters of girls' schools during the first half of the nineteenth century. Typically addressed to parents, potential patrons, donors, trustees, and religious associations of women and men, this literature linked ideology with institutional change by providing a broad-based rationale for advanced education for women and a practical template for such education. Broadcast through such educational publications as the *American Journal of Education,* the *American Annals of Education,* state common-school journals, women's magazines, and various associations' pamphlets, these ideas entered into the mainstream of educational thinking by the 1830s and became a powerful force behind the expansion of public and private schooling for girls.[28]

In the writings of Lyon, Beecher, and Willard there are important differences of emphasis—and occasionally of substance—but common themes do emerge. They agree on the ideal of female character: not the sentimental and dependent maiden but rather the competent, devout, principled woman, a fit companion for her husband and skilled nurturer and teacher of her children. They deplore the fact that most schools for girls were temporary, underfinanced, haphazard affairs that catered to the demand of parents for ornamental rather than basic instruction. Often the "faculty" consisted of one or two instructors who were forced to spread their efforts across many fields.[29]

Instead, as Kathryn Kish Sklar shows, Lyon, Beecher, and Willard thought that female seminaries should become well-endowed and permanent incorporated institutions with adequate facilities, several teachers who specialized in academic fields, careful standards of admission and grading of pupils, and methods of discipline and pedagogy calculated to lead rather than drive students to academic proficiency and moral beliefs and behavior. Embedded in this plan for permanent seminaries was a conviction that talented women could create for themselves a new autonomy as professional teachers of young women and provide a standard of instruction unavailable in most existing schools for girls. The moral function of the women principals in such schools resembled that of male ministers in the community at large. They could, in effect, preach to the girls and interpret moral law to them. And pioneer women educators shared a common hope that by offering expert training and creating a semi-autonomous female sphere, such institutions could professionalize the careers of their alumnae both as teachers of the young in primary schools and as mothers in their own families.[30]

The advocates of female seminaries argued that young women had intellectual capacities similar to those of men, abilities that they demonstrated by mastering many of the same academic subjects. Advocates of women's seminaries did not always agree, however, that male and female minds were identical. Speakers at the Young Ladies' Institute in Pittsfield, Massachusetts, for example, came down on different sides of that question. In 1846 Dr. Henry Tappan said flatly that "woman has the same mental constitution as man; there is not a power or faculty which belongs to the one, that does not also belong to the other." Seven years later, the Reverend Samuel Harris declared that "woman is not inferior to man, but she is different from him. . . . if . . . she has less of the logical, she has more of the intuitive; if less of the prudential, she has more of the spontaneous." But most agreed that for purposes of schooling, possible cognitive differences did not matter unless they might lead to a compensatory stress on reasoning for young women. There was general agreement that women's education had too often been superficial and showy, teaching them "to put on gaudy colors, and to flutter with due grace."[31]

Another common theme in the writings on women's education was the need to improve pedagogy. The leaders in secondary schooling for girls believed that instruction should be rigorous and systematic, but they criticized the mechanical method of instruction common in men's academies and colleges. Mere memorization and recitation killed interest and failed to develop reasoning and imagination. A number of teachers in female seminaries wrote textbooks demonstrating their new methods—Willard and Beecher foremost among them—and described their methods of teaching and discipline in leading educational magazines. Educators of girls were among the first to question the value of competition for place and medals and normally rejected corporal punishment entirely. In keeping with their belief that academic subjects should be solid and not ornamental, educators in female seminaries stressed fields commonly taught in male schools.[32]

In a study of catalogues of 107 girls' seminaries from 1830 to 1871, Thomas Woody found that in addition to the expected emphasis on English grammar and composition, over 40 percent of schools listed courses in ancient, modern, and U.S. history, while 34 percent offered courses in government (indicating that school directors were paying more than lip service to the notion that women were citizens); 83 percent in algebra and 79 percent in plane geometry; 59 percent in Latin grammar; 90 percent each in natural philosophy and in chemistry; and only 12 percent in ornamental needlework. Many schools paid special attention to the health of girls; 55 percent taught physiology, and 19 percent provided calisthenics (a favorite theme in Beecher's writings, as was domestic science, which many schools adopted).[33]

The purpose of such academically rigorous courses, advocates kept insisting, was not to produce showy pedants but sober and rational wives and mothers. This message was not lost on Elizabeth Stearns, a seminary student who wrote these lines in her copybook labeled "Depository of Valuable Sentiments": "Pedantry in a man is bad enough but in a woman is *still worse*. Few things are more offensive than to see a female, laboring to the uttermost to convince a company that she has received a good intellectual education. . . . vociferating about nitrogen, oxygen, caloric; then boasting her acquaintance with some of the greatest geniuses of the age; and at last of all entering into a stormy debate on politics or finance."[34]

Women advocates of female education wanted to reassure parents, donors, and trustees that secondary education did not produce such pedants but rather enhanced girls' chances of marrying well. Over and over again they reiterated their key argument that schooling would make young women better wives and mothers, adding systematic knowledge and utilitarian skills to their God-given talents in nurturing children. If the pioneers in women's education were ambivalent on the subject of marriage, they muted their doubts rather than expressing them in the salty rhetoric of Judith Sargent Murray. But like Murray, women educators wanted marriage to be a choice, not a trap, and thus wished single women to have an honorable alternative to matrimony (like teaching). Beecher wrote that a marriage entered into from necessity rather than from "pure affection" was a recipe for disaster and that early marriages were "productive of much of the unhappiness of married women, of many sorrows, sickness, and premature decay and death." Zilpah Grant, Lyon's able colleague at the Ipswich Female Seminary, rejected a marriage proposal after reflecting that she could never "be happy shut up with the candidate on shipboard."[35]

Links to Public Education

"Female seminaries might be expected to have important and happy effects, on common schools in general," wrote Emma Willard—a view shared by Beecher, Lyon, and many other pioneers in women's education. The seminaries' influence took several forms. First, their rationale for educating girls was echoed by the major common-school reformers and by advocates of public high schools for girls at the local level. Second, the seminaries demonstrated that there was a large public demand among girls and their families for secondary education and provided a model of curriculum and instruction for public high schools. Third, these pioneers articulated the standard case for hiring women as common-school teachers that was later used by leaders like Mann and Barnard. Fourth, their seminaries carefully prepared hundreds of women to teach long before the establishment of the more well known public normal schools. And finally, the women pioneers worked to improve public schools through their own activities and by encouraging their graduates to become advocates of common-school reform in local communities.

In an era of tumultuous change, the conservative rationale for educating girls reassured citizens that schooling would not disrupt but rather would bolster the separate gender spheres. The message that schooling led women back to the home better equipped to discharge their sacred duties appeared in speeches in local communities, in the writings of school leaders in the common-school movement, in magazines like Lydia Sigourney's *Godey's Lady's Book* and Sarah Josepha Hale's *American Ladies' Magazine,* in sermons, and in dozens of books of advice on child raising.[36]

The private female and coeducational academies became models for public high schools both in their mission and in their curriculum. For those citizens who were familiar with the attainments of the graduates of the best female seminaries, the question of woman's capacity to learn was settled. The foremost schools—those of Willard, Lyon, and Beecher, for example—were far more experimental in methods of teaching and discipline than the Latin grammar schools that prepared boys for college and more academically rigorous than many of the colleges that those boys attended. Some of the teachers in the first public high schools open to girls had taught in private girls' schools and introduced into public secondary education the subjects and methods used there. Public-school advocates wanted to attract the daughters as well as the sons of the "first families" to the public-school system, and modeling high schools on effective private seminaries was one way of showing local elites that public schools could equal private ones.[37]

In 1818, in her bold appeal to the New York legislature for public support of a female seminary, Willard advanced arguments for training and employing women as common-school teachers that would be repeated in substance again and again as teaching became preeminently a woman's occupation. She claimed that "nature" had "designed" women to be teachers of the young: "She has given us, in a greater degree than men, the gentle arts of insinuation, to soften their minds, and fit them to receive impressions . . . a greater quickness of invention . . . and more patience." Unlike men, women had "no higher pecuniary object" or ambition than to teach and "could afford to do it cheaper."[38]

Beecher argued a similar case in calling for a national normal school to train women to teach. Lyon saw teaching as a sacred cause for the evangelical young women she trained. Both women and men echoed these views, calling the sexual division of labor—in which women instructed the young—part of a providential plan. "A man, superintending a nursery of children, is like an elephant brooding chickens," wrote Mann. "That woman should be the educator of children, I believe to be as much a requirement of nature as that she should be the mother of children."[39]

In parts of the nation, particularly the Northeast, some communities had far more women than men. Educators, parents, and daughters began to realize, as David F. Allmendinger, Jr., notes, that many young women might marry late or remain single and hence needed to plan for a change in the traditional life cycle of direct movement from the parental to the conjugal family. They might experience a new period of relative independence between periods of subordination as daughter or wife. One solution to this problem was to train young women for a career that was increasingly open to them and compatible with marriage: teaching. Sanctified by religious and political values, teaching offered a meager but respectable livelihood for single women. But the public's conviction that marriage and motherhood should be women's ultimate destiny was so powerful that Beecher and others insisted that teaching was an ideal preparation for motherhood and that teacher-training programs were not seminaries for producing celibates. In a letter to Beecher, Lyon wrote that her hope for the redemption of America through female common-school teachers lay "in young ladies scarcely out of their teens, whose souls are burning for some channel into which they can pour out their benevolence, and who will teach two, three, or four years and then marry and become firm pillars to hold up their successors."[40]

Preparing women to teach in common schools linked the private secondary education of girls with public education. Willard, Lyon, and Grant began their careers at an early age as teachers in common schools. As Keith Melder has shown, the seminaries founded by Grant, Lyon, Willard, and Beecher were pioneers in training of teachers for the public schools well before Horace Mann established the first public normal schools. The total number of teachers prepared in these schools exceeded the number of graduates of public normal schools, at least into the 1850s. Beecher devised a plan for training and placing women teachers in the West and called for a nationally financed normal school to enable educated women to save their country through the proper instruction of the young.[41]

The four women were the centers of widespread networks of educated women and their male allies. Through these associates they placed their graduates in teaching positions and encouraged the creation of secondary schools for women and the spread of coeducational public schools. These women and their alumnae were pedagogical Jenny Appleseeds, planting schools across the nation. Anne Firor Scott has found that between 1839 and 1863 Willard's Troy Female Seminary offered tuition on credit to 669 young women; of these, 597 were sent out to teach. Between 1821 and 1872, 146 Troy graduates founded or administered a school. Allmendinger discovered that over four-fifths of the Mount Holyoke graduates from 1837 to 1850 taught, most of them for a few years before marriage, as Lyon had hoped. All told, Grant's and Lyon's Ipswich Female Seminary sent 88 teachers to the West and South, while about 40 found jobs in the Northeast. In 1867 academies in New York trained 363 men and 1,122 women as public-school teachers.[42]

The graduates of the female seminaries might not teach for a long period, but even when married they could still continue to improve public schools in local communities. So much attention has been devoted to the male state superintendents and common-school crusaders that the contribution of educated women in their local communities has been neglected, perhaps because they did not leave so many written records. Willard was in active touch with Troy alumnae through correspondence and widespread travel, and everywhere she went she encouraged graduates to take an interest in the common school.[43]

In 1840 Barnard enlisted Willard in his campaign to improve public education in Connecticut. He persuaded her to run for superintendent of schools in Kensington, where she won the election (even though women could not vote). She promptly set about training the women teachers and organizing the mothers of the town into a Female Association for the common schools. The association sought to ensure that all children attended school, to refurbish schoolhouses, to equip the classrooms with apparatus and books, and to monitor the effectiveness of teachers.[44]

Willard was careful to justify such actions as appropriately feminine. The Michigan superintendent of public instruction cited her precedent when he called on women not only to teach but to visit the schools and assist the children. All that was needed was some male encouragement, he wrote, for "benevolent females are usually modest and unassuming. If the proper authorities in towns and districts will invite their cooperation, they will cheerfully engage in this good work." He mentioned that in the Teachers' Institute in Oneida County, New York, Willard prepared two resolutions, one for the men and another for the women, that accomplished the purpose of assuring that males were still in charge and women remained "modest and unassuming." Willard asked the men to resolve that they would improve common schools by "inviting the ladies . . . to take such action . . . as may seem to us that they are peculiarly fitted to perform; and such as we regard as properly belonging to their own sphere in the social system." Women unanimously agreed to this resolution: "That if the men, whom we recognize as by the laws of God and man, our directors, and to whose superior wisdom we naturally look for guidance, shall call us into the field of active labor in common schools, we will obey the call with alacrity."[45]

While observing the surface proprieties of separate sexual spheres, Willard set a powerful example of self-respect and effective public service. Beecher, too, encouraged married women to work to improve local schools and founded several associations to focus their efforts. These groups, like the religious reform groups that multiplied among women, became the forerunners of the civic-minded women's clubs that pressed for public-school reforms in the progressive era.[46]

But there were members of the women's rights movement who demanded more than an education that merely prepared women for a limited destiny. Learning and literacy could be subversive. Instead of being trained to accept their place, some of the graduates of the new female seminaries—people like Elizabeth Cady Stanton and Susan B. Anthony—would come to claim that women deserved nothing less than full rights in all domains, in political and economic institutions as well as in the family or schoolroom, and to demand that they be taught together with men in coeducational institutions to realize their full potential as human beings.[47]

The arguments for the education of women that had the greatest public impact, however, mixed new claims with conservative gender premises: that girls were mentally as capable as boys; that they, too, had immortal souls and needed knowledge of God's will; that they could play a part in creating the civic virtue that was the basis of a stable and just republic; and that, above all, they required education to fulfill their careers as wives and mothers. The proponents of women's education reassured parents that schooling would make their daughters more marriageable and that education would not propel them out of women's sphere.

The advocates of education for women pricked the conscience of citizens about the education of their daughters, allayed their fears about the consequences of schooling, and argued for women's education as an investment in the character of the future generation. Indeed, those who believed that girls did not need formal schooling went on the defensive in the nineteenth century and were rarely vocal. The issue became not whether girls needed schooling but how to educate them.

3

Coeducation in Rural Common Schools

The entry of girls into public elementary schools in the first half of the nineteenth century was a gradual, decentralized, and obscure process. The paucity of records documenting debate about coeducation suggests that it was not a particularly controversial issue and probably was not even a considered act of public policy in most communities. But it was arguably the most important event in the gender history of American public education. At the time of the Revolution, only a few schools were open to girls. By the middle of the nineteenth century almost as many girls as boys were attending elementary public schools, or "common schools," as they were called. The vast majority of these—probably over four-fifths during most of the nineteenth century—were one-room schools in rural communities. In 1790 perhaps only half as many women as men were literate. A half-century later, largely because both sexes attended common schools, the literacy of men and women was roughly equal, at least in the North. By 1870 girls aged ten to fourteen had surpassed boys in their rates of literacy and academic achievement.[1]

Why and how did such major changes come about? We have no sharply etched answers. In chapter 1 we traced the origins of coeducational public schools in New England in the dame schools and women's summer schools. Admitting girls to the winter term of the district schools—as happened in rural communities after 1800 across the tier of northern states—could easily have seemed a small step, not a major policy change. We have also shown in chapter 2 that reformers developed persuasive answers to the question: *Why educate girls?* Convincing parents and school boards of the importance of education for women was one prerequisite for coeducation.

The published writings on the need to educate women, however influential they may have been, shed only indirect light on the question of why Americans created the specific kind of coeducational common schools that dominated the educational landscape. Another set of writings—educators' arguments on coeducation, which began to appear in the middle of the nineteenth century—are useful for illuminating why practical school people thought it better to educate boys and girls together or apart. But these dialogues appeared mostly after coeducation had already become an institutional fact in the rural schools that dominated public education. The mid-century controversy mostly concerned how to arrange gender relations in city school systems, which forms the subject of the next chapter.

During the first half of the nineteenth century, when coeducation was becoming the standard practice in the rural common school, Americans were mostly silent, so far as we can determine, about why they decided to educate their daughters and sons together in the one-room school. Silence about coeducation can mean many things, of course: that people simply took it for granted; that its rationale was so obvious as to not need stating; that the subject could so easily arouse conflict or embarrassment that the less said the better; or that the change was taking place so gradually that people didn't pay attention.

The adoption of coeducation seems to have been one of those major transitions in practice in which citizens moved gradually from *why* to *why not*. One point is clear: Most people who supported coeducation did not believe or hope, as did some feminists, that it would transform the separate spheres of adult women and men. Another obvious point is that coeducational public schools did not result from centralized state policy. Instead, they grew gradually from decisions made in tens of thousands of local school districts, usually with few records of debate on the question. By the middle of the nineteenth century, when reformers at the state level sought to regulate local school districts in order to make schools more uniform and effective, they largely took coeducation for granted. Indeed, Henry Barnard, commissioner of public schools in Rhode Island, in 1848 defined a district school as "a public school open to all the children . . . of both sexes."[2]

Given the relative absence of discussion about coeducation and the lack of explicit state or local policies during the decades when it became standard practice to educate boys and girls together in common schools, we need to rely in part on inference to explain the emergence of coeducation. One set of clues comes from examining the characteristics of common schools as institutions and their relation to the ecology of other institutions that surrounded them in rural communities, such as families and churches. In this chapter we argue that once parents had decided that it was appropriate to educate their daughters as well as their sons, they came to regard coeducation as the expedient and natural mode of schooling.

Coeducation was expedient because the population in the countryside was often highly dispersed and the average class size was small. Parents wanted schools that were within reasonable walking distance for their sons and daughters. To have created separate schools for boys and for girls would have greatly increased the costs, whereas educating them together in a common building under the same teacher was cheaper and more efficient.[3]

To be sure, economy alone was not enough to dictate integrated schools. Where people really cared about maintaining social distinctions, they often worked hard to preserve them through schooling. In the impoverished rural South, for example, the ironclad doctrines of white supremacy decreed that black and white schools be separate. But differences of sex had a very different valence from those of race. The fact that males and females had separate spheres did not mean that they needed to be physically separated in school, anymore than in family or church.

Coeducation seemed natural because the one-room school shared in some ways a set of gender relationships with two other familiar institutions, the family and the church. This gave the coeducational common school a kind of protective gender coloration. "The *beau idéal* of a good school," wrote an educator in 1855, "may be found in a well-ordered family, where the mother and father constitute the *head,* and the children, male and female, the *members.* . . . All this appears in harmony with the Divine administration. . . . In a well-ordered school, we find the male and female engaged as the teachers, only to carry forward and perfect the education begun by the parents." To mix brothers and sisters in the Sunday school, in the church, in the common school—as in the family—was natural, in accord with God's plan.[4]

Part of the "naturalness" linking coeducation to the family resulted from the tipping of teaching from a male to a predominantly female occupation. As girls were entering coeducational common schools, women were increasingly taking over as teachers in public education. In Massachusetts,

Table 1
Male Teachers in Public Schools, 1870–71

Division	Percentage
North Atlantic	26
South Atlantic	64
South Central	68
North Central	43
Western	45
United States	41

Source: U.S. Commissioner of Education, *Report for 1900–01*, p. 676.

women constituted 56 percent of teachers by 1834, a figure that jumped to 78 percent by 1860. In Vermont, they comprised 70 percent of teachers in 1850; in Connecticut, 71 percent in 1857. By 1870, women constituted 59 percent of all public-school teachers, but there were sharp regional differences in the ratio of men to women, as shown in table 1. The Northeast, which first established common schools, had the largest proportion of women teachers, and the South, which created them last and had a stronger tradition of single-sex schools, had the most men.[5]

The admission of girls into common schools and the employment of women teachers powerfully influenced one another. It is likely that parents would have been comfortable about sending daughters to classrooms taught by women, thinking them to be safe and congenial environments for girls. The rapid increase in the enrollment of girls, in turn, created both a greater demand for and a ready supply of teachers. Educated in the common school and sometimes beyond that level, young women constituted a large pool of potential instructors. People often justified the education of girls and the hiring of women teachers with similar conservative arguments.[6]

The Transformation of Female School Attendance and Literacy

The great mass of students in the nineteenth century attended schools in rural districts. In 1795, 95 percent of the population lived in communities with fewer than 2,500 residents, and as late as 1860, 80 percent of Americans lived in rural areas. At mid-century, the census counted 80,978 public schools but only 91,966 teachers, indicating that only a small proportion of the schools had more than one teacher. By then more than 90 percent of all pupils were attending public schools, and nearly all students were in elementary schools, as opposed to secondary or higher institutions (in 1840 the census reported that the ratio of school enrollment to the total population was 1:9 in common schools, 1:104 in secondary schools, and 1:1,052 in colleges). As late as 1883, the U.S. commissioner of education stated that the rural elementary school "is the only school that three-fourths of the people ever enter." He added that this rural "'common school' is and has been a 'mixed' school, in which boys and girls attend together."[7]

Most children, then, attended rural schools, but access to public education varied sharply by region and by race. In the South in 1850 the number of white children attending school was about half that in New England. Traditions of private schooling among the well-to-do were strong, and efforts to create public schools were sporadic and scattered. White southerners often favored separate-sex secondary private schools for their daughters and sons. Slaves were denied formal schooling—though they found other ways to educate each other—and nationwide in 1850 only 13.6 percent of free black boys and 10.8 percent of free black girls attended school.[8]

But by 1850 among northern whites the sharp gender disparities of a half-century before had so narrowed that girls and boys went to school in roughly similar proportions, as shown in table 2. Carl Kaestle has argued that much of the expansion of enrollments in common schools before the Civil War resulted from this inclusion of females. Since the figures include attendance in secondary and higher education, where males predominated, they exaggerate the sex disparity in common schools. By 1870 the gender gap had further narrowed until girls comprised 49 percent of all pupils in all public schools, and by then there was much less variation by region.[9]

Parallel to the entry of girls into public schools came a rise in the literacy rates of white females, especially in the North. Although it is notoriously difficult to estimate literacy, to determine how it is acquired, or to agree on what it means, it seems clear that there was a major improvement in the literacy of American women in the half-century following the Revolution. By the middle of the nineteenth century in most of the United States the previously large differences in literacy rates between the sexes had been nearly erased, well before the major increases in female literacy in most European nations.[10]

Table 2
White Males and Females Aged Five to Nineteen Attending School, 1850

Region	Male (%)	Female (%)	Difference (%)
New England	81.4	75.7	5.7
Middle Atlantic	66.1	59.6	6.5
North Central	61.4	55.8	5.6
South Central	44.3	39.0	5.3
South Atlantic	40.8	35.0	5.8

Source: U.S. Census Office, *Seventh Census* (Washington, D.C.: GPO, 1853). We have adapted a table in Maris A. Vinovskis and Richard M. Bernard, "Beyond Catharine Beecher: Female Education in the Antebellum Period," *Signs* 3(1978): 861.

Lockridge estimates that the literacy rate of white women in New England was only about half as that of white men in 1790, but the census of 1850 showed that these disparities in literacy between the sexes had been sharply cut by mid-century not only in New England but in other northern states. One must approach such census data on literacy with considerable caution, of course. There is good reason to question both the methods and the results of census figures on literacy in 1850. Since census enumerators simply asked family heads if each person was literate, there was some incentive on the part of families to deny illiteracy. There was no obvious reason, however, to overreport the literacy of daughters rather than that of sons, and hence the key point of convergence in literacy remains unaffected by the faults in the design or the execution of the census. In the South, where rates of school attendance were comparatively low, both the overall percentage of illiterates and the differences between white male and female literacy remained much higher than in the North. The percentage of white illiterates by state is indicated in table 3. Since these figures refer to all adults aged twenty or older, the changes in schooling that reduced female illiteracy in the older age cohorts probably began decades earlier.[11]

In 1870, census data on literacy became more valid and detailed than in earlier decades. Census takers asked two specific questions about each person—can he or she read, and can he or she write?—and only those who could both read and write were counted as literate. In addition, literacy was

Table 3
White Population Aged Twenty and Over
Who Were Illiterate in 1850

State	Female (%)	Male (%)	Difference (%)
Maine	2	2	0
New Hampshire	1	2	(1)*
Vermont	3	4	(1)*
Massachusetts	5	4	1
Rhode Island	5	3	2
Connecticut	3	2	1
New York	7	5	2
New Jersey	7	5	2
Pennsylvania	8	4	4
Delaware	15	12	3
Maryland	12	8	4
Virginia	23	15	8
North Carolina	36	22	14
South Carolina	16	9	7
Georgia	23	15	8
Florida	24	14	10
Alabama	24	14	10
Mississippi	14	8	6
Louisiana	21	12	9

Source: U.S. Census Office, Seventh Census (Washington, D.C.: GPO, 1853). The population of illiterates over twenty is divided by the population over 20.

*Parentheses indicate instances in which women were more literate than men.

broken down by age. In each of the major regions of the country, females between the ages of ten and fourteen were more literate than males, whereas the reverse was true of adults of the two sexes. These different rates of literacy for younger and older females indicated that the remaining gender literacy gap was closing. In addition, studies of the academic achievement of girls at that time found that they consistently outperformed boys.[12]

People can acquire literacy in many ways, of course, but most scholars agree that during the nineteenth century Americans found schooling the major path to literacy. And for the great majority of citizens, that education took place in one-room schools in rural districts. A study of families in

Table 4
African-American Illiterates, 1890, 1900, and 1910

Age	1890		1900		1910	
	Male (%)	Female (%)	Male (%)	Female (%)	Male (%)	Female (%)
10–14	41.9	37.7	33.5	26.8	21.7	16.1
15–19	45.7	39.7	36.7	27.2	24.9	16.0
45–54	74.8	87.1	59.3	77.8	38.9	56.3

Source: U.S. Census Reports, as compiled in *Negro Population in the United States, 1790–1915* (New York: Arno Press, 1968), p. 406.

agricultural communities in sixteen northern states sampled from the 1860 census underscores how high the rates of school attendance and literacy were for both sexes in farm families. Ninety-four percent of the husbands were literate, and 84 percent of their sons between the ages of ten and fourteen were attending school. Ninety-one percent of the wives were literate, and 82 percent of their daughters between the ages of ten and fourteen were in school. From both aggregated and individual census statistics it is clear that a major institutional change took place in the first half of the nineteenth century, opening the common school to girls as well as boys and sharply raising the literacy of women.[13]

Even more dramatic than the educational gains for white women was the revolution in literacy and school attendance that took place among African-Americans in the South after the Civil War. Black females showed more striking advances than males in the four decades from 1870 to 1910. Because of the ban on teaching slaves to read, probably about 70 percent of African-Americans in the South were illiterate in 1870. But even though impoverished and beleaguered by the caste system, black schools accomplished an extraordinary feat: by 1910, illiteracy for blacks aged ten years or over dropped to about 30 percent for both sexes (compared with 5 percent for whites). In table 4 the rates of illiteracy are broken down by age and sex (literacy was defined as the ability to write; those who could only read were classed as illiterate). As the table shows, older black women, born in slavery, had considerably higher rates of illiteracy than did men of similar age. For younger blacks the reverse was true: boys were more illiterate than girls at the turn of the century.

Table 5
African-Americans in School, 1900 and 1910

Age	1900		1910	
	Male (%)	Female (%)	Male (%)	Female (%)
5–9	23.2	24.2	40.2	42.3
10–14	50.6	57.0	65.6	71.5
15–20	15.0	19.8	23.8	28.9

Source: U.S. Census Reports, as compiled in *Negro Population in the United States, 1790–1915* (New York: Arno Press, 1968), p. 377.

A similar but somewhat less pronounced pattern of difference by sex appears in the 1900 and 1910 census reports on school attendance of African-Americans. The enumerators listed people as attending school if they had enrolled in any kind of school for any period of time during the school year. The vast majority of black children thus counted were in the lower levels of rural elementary schools or graded urban elementary schools, which were the only kinds of formal education usually available to southern blacks in their segregated and impoverished system. Among whites in 1910, 61 percent of boys and girls between the ages of five and twenty were in school; their rates of attendance by sex were nearly identical at each age level. By contrast, only 44.7 percent of blacks in that wide age group were in school, and their proportions differed by age and sex, as table 5 reveals.

From the start, during Reconstruction, the black common school was coeducational, and this feature enabled it to serve both sexes in what African-Americans called the "uplifting of the race." "Schools were established, not merely public day-schools, but home training and industrial schools . . . through the energy of the colored people themselves," wrote a black educator, Anna Julia Cooper. "These schools were almost without exception coeducational." This pattern of coeducation in black schools contrasted with the preferred pattern of sex-segregated schools for prosperous whites. Before the Civil War the white elite generally wanted private and sex-segregated schools for their children rather than the coeducational public schools favored in the North. After the Civil War, as public education became established in southern cities, whites often sought to preserve sex segregation as well as race segregation, although in rural areas, for reasons of economy and demography, white schools as well as black were usually sex-mixed.[14]

Poverty and a scattered population in the predominantly rural South certainly influenced the adoption of coeducation in black public education. But it also seems likely that the black common school was also based on two precedents: the cultural patterns of education carried over from black experience under the slave system, and the Yankee model imported by the northern teachers who flocked south to teach the freed people during the decade after the Civil War. As Thomas L. Webber has shown, slaves developed their own mixed-sex forms of education in the family, where both boys and girls often learned skills like cooking and crafts together; in their "clandestine congregations," which developed into the powerful institutions of the black churches; and in shared forms of work and play. James D. Anderson has documented how the ex-slaves, drawing on their past and their aspirations to share in the formal education that had been denied them, took the initiative in creating forms of universal education that bore the imprint of their own culture and values.[15]

Jacqueline Jones has demonstrated that the northern missionary teachers—"soldiers of light and love"—carried with them to the South the institutional form of the coeducational common school with its ideological underpinnings of Protestant-republican beliefs. Although in other respects black and Yankee cultures and individuals sometimes clashed, the principle that the black common school should serve both sexes became firmly institutionalized. It spread to the upper levels of black education as well, in industrial schools and colleges, as Cooper observed: "Funds were too limited to be divided on sex lines, even had it been ideally desirable; but our girls as well as our boys flocked in and battled for an education. Not even then was that patient, untrumpeted heroine, the slave-mother, released from self-sacrifice, and many an unbuttered crust was eaten in silent content that she might eke out enough from her poverty to send her young folks off to school."[16]

The male-female gaps in black literacy and school attendance present a puzzle. Given the lack of prior research on the subject, we can only suggest some tentative explanations for these disparities. Literacy may have had particular political significance for black men during the years of Reconstruction, when they were enfranchised and black women were not. As table 4 shows, older men, many of whom came of age during Reconstruction, were considerably more literate than older women. By contrast, black girls and young women outdistanced their male peers during the decades at the turn of the century when whites disenfranchised black men in the old slave states.[17]

Economic factors may also have played a part. Both black men and women were severely constrained by the low job ceiling that the caste system imposed, but the relation of jobs to schooling may have been somewhat different for the two sexes. It is possible that there was more demand for boys than girls in agricultural labor, and this may have kept more males out of school. In view of the dangers of sexual harassment for young black women in domestic service and the arduous nature of farmwork—the two most common forms of paid labor for black women—parents may have encouraged girls to persist in school. Cultural gender patterns in black families and communities may also have encouraged girls to continue their education. Girls had potent role models in black mothers who labored to ensure the survival of their families and to resist the degradation of black women under slavery and the caste system. As Jeanne Noble observes, "The social system of the Negro rewarded the enterprising, clever, ambitious woman" whether in the paid labor force or in voluntary or political activities; blacks did not draw such a sharp line between the spheres of males and females as whites. Enterprising black women, mobilized in clubs and in local educational politics, pressed hard to improve the miserable conditions of black schools and in the process may have raised the educational aspirations of female students, especially those from middle-class families.[18]

One of the few nonmanual jobs open to large numbers of blacks was teaching. Well before the twentieth century, school teaching tipped from being a predominantly male black occupation to a female one, even though after emancipation men had often been favored in schools under the control of black communities. This tendency changed as whites regained control of black school finance and governance. In 1890, the U.S. Census showed that 52 percent of black teachers were women; in 1900, 64 percent; and in 1920, 82 percent. No high educational attainment was required—in 1916, 70 percent of black teachers in Georgia and Alabama had certificates that represented a level of schooling that was lower than the eighth grade. The annual salary that country teachers received was often less than the $150 that it took to maintain a prisoner in a county jail. But the prospect of a teaching job—respectable and preferable to domestic or field labor—probably motivated substantial numbers of young black women to continue in elementary school. As high schools gradually opened for blacks in the

South in the twentieth century—the numbers grew from only 64 in the entire region in 1916 to 1,200 in 1932—girls vastly outnumbered the boys, and many of these young women became teachers. Originally, black men greatly outnumbered black women as college students. By the middle of the twentieth century, however, twice as many black women were graduating from black colleges as black men, and the vast majority of these women entered teaching at a time when standards for entry into the occupation were rising.[19]

An Institutional Portrait of the Rural Common School

The "district school" stemmed from colonial origins and spread rapidly across northern states as settlers on new frontiers transplanted the familiar institution. Sometimes sanctioned and promoted by state law, sometimes not, the district school was created by local communities. In sparsely settled areas it was sometimes the only public building and often the center of rural social, religious, and political life. The local citizens constructed the building; they chose the local school committeemen or trustees; they raised taxes or paid tuition to support the teacher and to heat and repair the building; they decided who would teach and for how long; and they determined what the curriculum would be. The district school was common in the sense that it was normally open to all the children of the residents of the district. The elected male trustees—there were usually three of them—were elected by the men of the district. The financing of the district school often blended state funds, local taxes, and private contributions from the parents of the pupils.

Control of the local school districts was highly decentralized, and the districts were by far the most numerous units of government in the United States. School trustees far outnumbered teachers. Even in relatively urbanized states, citizens favored decentralizing the control and location of schools so that each neighborhood might have its own district school. In New York, for example, the number of school districts jumped from 2,756 in 1815 to 10,769 in 1843. Each separate district usually had its own coeducational one-room school. Henry Barnard observed that "the practice has been almost universal in New England, and in other states where the organization of the schools is based upon the division of the territory into school districts, to provide but one school for as many children of both sexes, and of all ages from four to sixteen years, as can be gathered from certain territorial limits, into one apartment, under one teacher." State-level reformers like Barnard believed that it was pedagogically best to consolidate such one-room schools into union graded schools and to increase state control over education, but in the nineteenth century—and for that matter, the twentieth century—rural residents fought consolidation and standardization. They wanted the school nearby and under their eye and thumb.[20]

Both sparse settlement and a desire to economize on the costs of schooling pressured rural patrons toward coeducation once parents had concluded that they wanted to educate their daughters as well as their sons. In small communities many Catholic parish schools were also coeducational despite the church's demand for single-sex schools, suggesting that economic expedience often won out over gender doctrine and the sex-segregation common in Catholic schools in Europe. As we shall indicate in the next chapter, segregated boys' and girls' schools were common only in certain cities where they was a sufficient concentration of population and wealth to make that choice a feasible public policy. These urban districts included only a small fraction of the total number of students in common schools, and few of them chose to educate boys and girls apart.[21]

The schoolhouses varied according to the educational zeal, wealth, size, and age of the community. On frontiers they sometimes were rough log cabins with tiny windows, cavernous fireplaces, and splintery pine benches. Teachers in such schools struggled with leaky roofs, gaps in the logs that admitted wintry blasts, and the constant problem of keeping the fire going. The typical schools in settled neighborhoods were small clapboarded houses with built-in benches and desks lining three sides and a teacher's desk on a platform at one end. Small benches were placed near the potbellied stove for the younger children.[22]

Residents often argued at length about where to locate the school, for they cared about how far their children had to walk through winter blizzards or on muddy spring roads. But eager to save money, they often placed the school on land that was otherwise worthless, and to the dismay of reformers the rural people often neglected to build an accompanying outhouse. Sarah Josepha Hale ridiculed the decision of one community: "The only requisite was, to fix precisely on the centre of the district; and after measuring in every direction, the centre had been discovered exactly in the centre of a frog-pond. As near that pond as safety would permit, stood the schoolhouse."[23]

Into such schools flocked brothers and sisters of the families of the neighborhood. Pupils ranged in age from toddlers of two or three to young men and women of nineteen or twenty. Despite complaints from teachers and educational reformers, mothers often sent very young children to school along with their older siblings, there to squirm in discomfort on backless benches where their feet might not reach the ground. The little ones were sometimes expected to learn the alphabet, but a common reason for their attendance—as in the colonial dame school—was to get them out from underfoot so that their mothers could finish their work at home. Dean May and Maris A. Vinovskis estimate that as late as 1840 in Massachusetts "at least 10% of the children under four were in school statewide."[24]

The typical curriculum for the older children was reading, writing, arithmetic, and a mixture of geography and history. Students brought a variety of different textbooks from home, adding to the difficulty the teacher faced in grouping students of different ages and attainments for recitations. The standard method of learning and teaching was memorizing a passage or doing sums and then demonstrating that achievement orally to the teacher. The students could exhibit what they had learned also to parents and neighbors, who often came to the school to observe spelling bees, "declamations" (speeches), literature readings, and dramatic performances. This gave both sexes a chance to display their knowledge publicly. Girls as well as boys might win a spelling bee or recite an elegant composition, thereby demonstrating that they were, in a favorite word of the nineteenth century, "smart." As Barbara Finkelstein has observed, learning to read and write in such rural schools was a "process of communal exposure" in which children exhibited what they had learned in a "face-to-face community of oral discourse."[25]

The institutional character of the one-room school helps to explain why parents were willing to send both daughters and sons to learn together. The lines between the district school and the church were blurred, as were those between family and school. All three institutions—family, church, and school—were mixed-sex, and gender practices moved easily through the permeable membranes that joined the three social agencies in rural communities. Each institution shaped and legitimated the others.

With their small steeples and bells that summoned the pupils, schoolhouses often looked like small churches, and frontier families often held religious services in the school because there was no other public facility nearby. The teacher in the "weekday school" was often expected to teach in the Sunday school as well, and both might be conducted in the same building. The teacher, like the minister, was supposed to inculcate proper moral principles and ethical behavior in the children. Pupils read the Bible and sometimes recited their catechisms to the local minister.[26]

As we have mentioned, educators who justified coeducation in the latter half of the nineteenth century often claimed that training boys and girls together was God's plan, in school as in the family. The classroom, like the family, joined together boys and girls of different ages, who were often expected to help each other learn. In new settlements, where the pioneers had not yet erected a schoolhouse, a room in a home often served as a classroom. One observer wrote about the one-room school that "the pupils are brothers, sisters, cousins, and neighbors to one another; the kindly influences of the family continue beneficially during school hours; the stronger and older pupils protect those who are younger and weaker." Students in school did chores as they did at home. Boys split wood and tried to coax green logs to ignite or went to the well to bring back a bucket of water for the class. Girls assisted the teacher in sweeping and dusting the classroom and prepared an occasional community lunch on the potbellied stove. Sometimes children braided straw hats or did sewing and knitting at school as in their families. If not living at home, teachers often "boarded round" at the houses of the pupils, getting to know their scholars in the family setting. Often young teachers had trouble asserting their authority in the classroom because they were perceived more as older siblings or neighborhood companions than as public officials.[27]

In most rural communities the district school was a rather haphazard and occasional affair, subject to the values, power alignments, and whims of the local community. Class was held only during short terms of two or three months in summer and winter. Attendance was voluntary and irregular, and boys and girls frequently dropped in and out of school. The older boys were usually needed on the farm in the summer, and poor weather and illness kept children at home in the winter. By the nineteenth century, parents were largely turning over to teachers the task of teaching children to read, write, and compute, but schooling meshed only loosely with occupations. Young men learned vocational skills on the farm or on the job, while young women learned to keep house from their mothers. The day when the school would become a direct portal into sex-segregated occupations would not come until secondary education expanded in the Progressive Era.[28]

Women Enter Teaching in Rural Schools

What kind of people entered one-room schools as teachers? Overwhelmingly, teachers in rural areas were young, and this fact shaped both their pay

The formal portrait of a rural school showed the outside of the building, the teacher, the pupils and sometimes adult visitors as well. The need for abundant light and lengthy exposures meant that active children were usually posed as still lifes, in similar stereotypical ways. The photographs do, however, give clues about gender practices and customary self-presentation as well as the physical setting and buildings.

The first black school in Coconut Grove/Miami, Florida, 1896, held in the African Methodist Episcopal church and taught by the Reverend John H. Davis. It was common for African-Americans in the South to use their churches as schoolhouses. The boys and girls are dressed in their Sunday best and grouped more by size and age than by sex. (Historical Association of Southern Florida.)

The Canadian School in North Park, Colorado, in 1885. This pose is more informal than customary, showing boys and girls (side-saddle) lined up together on the horses that carried them to the log school, with a family dog completing the scene. (Colorado Historical Society.)

A sod schoolhouse in Logan County, Nebraska, with a woman teacher and her three pupils. The teacher lived in the building, which had a bed and cooking facilities. Such an arrangement harked back to the dame school of colonial days and exemplified the family-like character of pioneer schooling. (Nebraska State Historical Society.)

The wooden Watson ranch school in Nebraska, 1904, with a man as teacher. Girls and boys are grouped in separate clusters, and the school has two entrances, possibly one for each sex. While separate entrances, like separate cloakrooms, may initially suggest gender separation inside the one-room school, such clues do not necessarily imply that the teacher separated boys and girls in the single space to which the entrances led. In this respect rural schools differed, for example, from railroad stations in the South, where separate entrances led to rigidly separated waiting rooms for the two races. (Nebraska State Historical Society.)

and the degree of deference they received from the community. A legislator in Iowa commented that for both men and women "teaching is youth's work and can be done at *youth's wages* . . . the work of inexperience and hence done at the wages of inexperience." In their pioneering study of teachers in Massachusetts, Richard M. Bernard and Maris A. Vinovskis estimate that "the ages of most women teachers fell between sixteen and twenty-five." As late as 1900 the census found that the average age of women teachers was about twenty-five. The typical rural teacher's salary

An unposed later picture. Boys and girls rush out of school at day's end in Gee's Bend, Alabama, 1937. (Arthur Rothstein, FSA, Library of Congress.)

was comparable to that of a farm laborer or household worker, the chief competing occupations for young men and women in the countryside. In 1850 men teachers received on average $4.25 per week, and women teachers, $2.89 in rural schools. Both in and out of school, communities closely supervised the lives of teachers, who customarily took part of their pay in meals and lodging as they boarded around in the families of their pupils.[29]

As one might expect from their age, teachers had a very high turnover rate, so high, in fact, that Bernard and Vinovskis estimate that before the Civil War, one out of five women had at one time taught in Massachusetts classrooms. In the nineteenth century, teaching in rural schools was an occupation in which entry was easy, exit frequent. There was thus not much incentive to invest in lengthy or elaborate preparation. The vast majority of teachers probably had only a common-school education. Only in the cities were teachers likely to have special training for their work, and only there did large numbers of teachers stay in classrooms long enough to reach their thirties. The average tenure of women teachers in Massachusetts before the Civil War was 2.6 years. In Wisconsin in 1857 the average "career" of teachers was 18 months. An experienced educator estimated in 1870 that, for the nation as a whole, 40 percent of all teachers were beginners. In the early twentieth century Lotus Coffman found that in rural schools the typical length of service for rural teachers, both female and male, was two years. Such high turnover allowed local school boards easily to replace men with women or vice versa.[30]

Why did men want to enter this labor market? In rural areas a short stint of teaching in a winter school might be attractive to young men seeking to supplement meager cash income in a farming economy during the slack season. Many male teachers were college students working their way through school. Teaching was one of the few nonmanual jobs available in the countryside, and it could be a useful stepping-stone for a person eager to establish himself in a new community. If a young man wanted to get started as a minister, politician, shopkeeper, or lawyer, teaching gave him visibility. The job required almost no preparation, took only a few weeks out of the year when other work was dormant, and thus had low opportunity costs. But when states began to raise certification requirements and to extend the school term from a few weeks to several months, these halting steps toward "professionalization" began to drive men out of teaching, for the very marginality of the occupation had been one of its chief attractions for the easy-in, easy-out casual male teacher.[31]

Women had far fewer prospects for employment than men. Women could work in their own or neighbors' homes, but unlike the young men, they could not easily find other local work or migrate to the West or to cities. Even the low wage of teaching was attractive to women in cash-poor rural societies, for they could contribute to the family economy or perhaps save money for their own further education or for a dowry. In addition, it was a respectable and serviceable occupation, honored by high rhetoric.[32]

In rural communities the school committeemen who hired teachers faced few external constraints in their choice of teachers. The market for teachers was an open, competitive one, for until the late nineteenth century the state imposed only minimal standards of certification. Policy decisions about the sex of teachers were not made by the state, as in some other countries, but at the grassroots level. Local trustees bargained with young men and women for their services as if they were hiring a farmhand or house helper. They wanted the most effective instruction at the lowest price. Men cost more than women, but in many places the committeemen thought male teachers worth the additional cost because they thought men more capable of disciplining and teaching the older students. As the population of students in common schools burgeoned, however, school trustees worried about finding enough men to teach the children. One source of replacements was the growing group of young women who wanted to teach. But before hiring women teachers, local school boards needed to be convinced that they could do the job.[33]

Trustees and parents had preconceptions about the different talents of male and female teachers. Few questioned the superior skill and appropriateness of women in teaching little children; hence women came to dominate the summer sessions when the young pupils attended. As we have shown, in the late eighteenth century women teachers had already proved their mettle in teaching small children. A man who went to school in Westford, Massachusetts, in the 1780s commented that "a man teaching school in summer would have been thought entirely out of place." The superintendent of schools in Michigan agreed: "In visiting schools of small children taught by gentlemen, I have frequently been reminded of the condition of young children in the families of widowers." In 1841–42 women constituted 93 percent of all summer-school teachers in Massachusetts and 35 percent of the winter-school teachers. Women in Connecticut in 1839 represented about 80 percent of summer-school teachers and 23 percent of winter-school teachers. Henry Barnard observed that "the great ambition in many districts seems to be to have a 'man's school' in the winter, and a 'woman's school' in summer."[34]

The debate over hiring women to teach older children in the winter schools reveals much about the gender assumptions of the time and the institutional character of the coeducational common school. Male teachers often found the one-room school a battleground of muscle and wit. Women proved to be good disciplinarians, but they did so not by copying men but by using feminine appeals. At first, school boards thought that it might be inappropriate for "timid and delicate women" to preside over "large and rude boys." The Ware school committee in 1840 commented that "females are of too delicate a texture for the rudeness and consequential importance of boys fourteen, fifteen, and sixteen years of age. . . . there is a very natural feeling with boys of this age, that it is pusillanimous to *obey a woman*."[35]

Such doubts about the ability of women to control classes were understandable, given the prevailing harsh methods of discipline employed by many male teachers in winter schools and the rebelliousness of the boys. Men teachers, often close in age to their older pupils and not as large, frequently used corporal punishment to keep boys in line and sometimes were expected to lick them to show who was boss. The Vermont superintendent of schools complained that "the insubordination and rebellion of scholars" in winter schools was "encouraged by their *parents at home*" and sustained by the "hesitating, cowardly policy of the school committee" for fear of offending influential parents. Horace Mann reported in 1843 that large boys had "broken up"—sometimes by ejecting the teacher—over 300 schools in the five previous years. How could a frail woman cope with such a situation? citizens asked.[36]

The answer given by school reformers and by the women themselves was that they did not need to use the same methods of discipline as the men to tame the rowdy boys. A man was a challenge to the older boys in a way a woman was not, wrote a woman who taught in the 1840s. A male student "who would be constantly plotting mischief against a schoolmaster, because he was a 'man of his size' becomes mild and gentle, considerate and well-behaved towards a little woman, whom he could take up with one hand and carry out of the schoolhouse, simply because she *is* a little woman, whose gentle voice and lady-like manners have fascinated him." She concluded that the woman teacher "rules the turbulent boys in her school very much as the schrewdest and wisest of her sex rule men outside, by seeming not to do it." Deborah Fitts observes that the relationship between male teachers and the older boys was "competitive and expressed physically," while female teachers and male students had a relation "based on protection and deference."[37]

It was obvious that few older boys would choose to fight a female teacher, but was it true, as Horace Mann said, that chivalrous impulses would make them "respect a request from a mistress though they would spurn a command from a master?" In the late 1830s and 1840s stories in the popular press and many reports from school districts that had tried the "experiment" of hiring women in the winter term indicated that indeed women had proved to be good disciplinarians, although they shunned the harsh physical punishment often employed by males. They relied on the deference toward women that Alexis de Tocqueville had found characteristic of American males. The tale "Our Schoolteacher" told of schoolhouse mutinies against brawny and violent men teachers that ceased when "a little slip of a woman" entered the "den of lions." Her appeals to their conscience and courtesy—her "moral suasion"—tamed the wild beasts. In one of his annual reports Mann quoted from several communities whose experiences with replacing men teachers with women had been the same. One district reported in 1838 that one school had progressed only in rebellion until a woman took charge: "To see a school of 50 or 60 in this condition, taken by one of the gentler sex, and brought within a few weeks to willing, ready, cheerful, energetic performance of every school duty, was indeed surprising, and the more so as it was done by one of mild and gentle spirit, and apparently of physical force and courage scarcely to brave a mouse."[38]

A new pedagogical and moral order created by women teachers was a central theme in a book that was distributed free to eleven thousand school districts in New York. The author, educational reformer Alonzo Potter, claimed that female teachers had a "native tact" and an ability to "enlist the affections" of the pupils and the "good will of the parents." They would pay more attention "to the improvement of manners and morals in schools, since females attach more importance to them than men; and they have a peculiar power of awakening the sympathies of children, and inspiring them with a desire to excell." Potter said that the concern over women's ability to manage older boys was based on an antiquated notion of corporal discipline. "It is now admitted," he said, "that in the government of schools, moral influence should be substituted, as far as possible, in place of mere coercion. . . . the teacher ought to aim, first of all, to cultivate the higher sentiments of our nature, to awaken self-respect, and to induce the child to become a law to himself." And who, asked Potter, could govern through moral suasion better than women? "Their very delicacy and help-lessness give them a peculiar claim to deference and respectful considera-tion. . . . they are honourably distinguished from the other sex by warm affections, by greater faith in human nature, and in its capacity for good, and by disinterested and untiring zeal in behalf of objects that they love."[39]

The saintly image of women teachers was, of course, partly stereotype. There were female as well as male sadists in the schoolhouse. In Dedham, Massachusetts, in the 1820s one woman teacher punished two little girls for whispering by tying their thumbs to her chair for an hour, while another took to suspending delinquent small boys from the window, with the sash resting on their backs. One veteran pupil observed that "after ten or twenty years of strenuous teaching, a woman can become as hard-boiled as any man; in fact, some of them are that way when they begin. The worst cut I ever received from a switch in my boyhood, I took on the back of my bare calves from a woman teacher."[40]

The folklore about naughty boys turning into choirboys under the be-nign influence of women teachers was not to be trusted, a seasoned teacher warned novices. "We have all read any number of stories about hordes of ferocious boys," she said, "who have organized successful and successive rebellions, and ejected a long line of male dynasties from the professional chair, but who have been suddenly brought before you as gently as any sucking dove, by the apparition of a sweet-faced, low-voiced woman." It is true that sometimes "calmness and gentleness and firmness will work won-ders, where passion and violence have been only abbots of misrule," but don't "set your heart upon it."[41]

In many ways the new psychological strategies being urged on women teachers paralleled the advice being given to mothers in the profusion of books on raising children. The proposal to hire women teachers went beyond a desire simply to save money disguised in flowery rhetoric. As Fitts writes, the call for women teachers was an augur of "the emergence of a new understanding of teacher/student relationships. Proceeding on the assumption that women were psychologically more effective than men— better at managing children, more persuasive in promoting manners and morals, cleverer in their ability to elicit acquiescence to authority—reformers sought to transform classroom interactions by changing the gender of the teacher." Such taming of the wild beast in the boy would later be condemned by the mandarins of masculinity in the Progressive era as the "feminization" of the boy, not praised as the triumph of a new and superior pedagogical and moral order.[42]

How Salient Was Gender in the Rural School?

From written records about nineteenth-century country schools it is difficult to discover precisely what gender practices were common in these rural classrooms—for example, to what degree the sexes were separated in the one-room schools, whether the rules were the same for boys and girls, whether teachers treated the sexes differently, what the informal social patterns of interaction were between boys and girls, and whether they studied the same subjects in roughly the same way. State and local reports and the reminiscences of teachers and pupils rarely mentioned how gender influenced everyday routines in one-room district schools; perhaps people did not need to mention what was taken for granted. There is one major exception that we have already discussed: people did comment often on the discipline problems boys created and compared them unfavorably with girls. But in other respects the salience of gender in country schools is difficult to assess.

In any case, in appraising the occasional mentions of gender that appear in normative literature about schools, it is wise not to assume that prescriptions necessarily matched classroom realities. Consider, for example, the advice that boys and girls be segregated within the classroom. Geraldine Jonçich Clifford, who has read many hundreds of firsthand accounts of schools, maintains that "notwithstanding a literature that urged physical separation [of the sexes], teacher and student diaries suggest that practice departed widely from precept; separation was impracticable, and many Americans were just not that fussy about details." She concludes that most schooling below the college level in the nineteenth century "was not gender specific—despite some efforts to have it so."[43]

Sometimes reformers railed against gender arrangements precisely because they were common but in their view misguided. Across the country a common complaint of state superintendents was that local districts failed to provide two proper "places of retirement," one for girls and one for boys, each free of that bane of Victorian educators, grafitti. But in many poor districts, citizens thought it quite enough to provide one outhouse, as at home, for both sexes, and sometimes not even that. In the mid-1880s in Illinois, 1,740 schools had only one privy, and 1,180 had none.[44]

To take another example of gender prescriptions that were often ignored, state school reports regularly reprinted model plans of schoolhouses—often those provided by Barnard in his *American Journal of Education*—that generally called for two doors, one for girls and one for boys. This arrangement enforced a certain decorum among the pupils as they approached the classroom and provided a barrier of modesty for the sexes in coming and going and in hanging up their coats. In a loaded questionnaire distributed to all Connecticut districts, Barnard asked, "Do boys and girls enter the building by the same door?" clearly implying that they should not. But elaborate plans calling for separate entrances and fancy ornamentation, writes Wayne E. Fuller about midwestern districts, "were so out of touch with the plain life of the midwestern farmers and so far beyond their means that they were ignored as completely as the information on site selection." Not surprisingly, over four-fifths of the one-room schools pictured in Andrew Gulliford's copiously illustrated *America's Country Schools* have one door only. Some educational reformers wanted rural schools, like many urban ones, to have segregated playgrounds for boys and girls, separated by fences to protect supposedly fragile girls from the roughhousing of boys. In practice few rural schools had any designated playground at all, but pictures of boys and girls at recess show that in the late nineteenth century, as now, the sexes usually chose to play separately.[45]

It is likely that the one-room school of the nineteenth century was not so deliberately differentiated by gender as schools would become in the Progressive Era, especially at the secondary level. The nineteenth-century rural school was a more incidental part of the lives of children and less tied to vocation than the elaborated school systems of the twentieth century. Children attended for much shorter terms. The rural school, more casual in structure and limited in purpose, sought chiefly to convey a few basic cognitive skills and generalized ethical and civic beliefs.

In the twentieth century school officials wanted to consolidate and upgrade rural schools in order to give them the purported advantages of graded town schools. Believing that "the building will be a silent educator," the commissioner of school buildings for Minnesota pictured these three one-room-school plans. Figure A shows a school that was very common but, he thought, "ought not to be built"—it was too primitive and undifferentiated. Figure B reveals separate entrances and cloakroom-toilets for boys and girls but an undifferentiated space for instruction. Figure C represents a further stage in gender segregation; it includes separate spaces for manual training and domestic science. (S. A. Challman, The Rural School Plant *[1917], pp. 16, 101, 27.)*

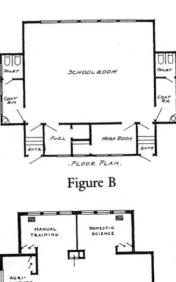

Figure B

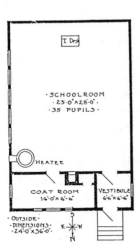

Figure A

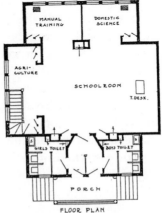

Figure C

Teachers, parents, educational leaders, and students had little desire to erase the gender distinctions that marked American society outside the school. Textbooks like those of William Holmes McGuffey clearly reflected the notion that males and females occupied separate spheres. In a proposal to engage teachers and parents in discussion of school matters, Warren Burton assumed that propriety in relations between the sexes should reign both in school and outside. He asked people to discuss in open meetings "how shall delicacy of feeling be cultivated, and propriety of conduct be maintained, between the sexes at school? and also in the neighborhood generally?" Alonzo Potter complained, for example, that the curriculum was insufficiently differentiated for girls and failed to prepare them for their "empire . . . over the family."[46]

But it is an open question as to how much gender differences actually marked pedagogical routines in classrooms. It is possible that other institutions and the messages conveyed by the general culture so firmly fixed the separate spheres of gender that citizens thought it unnecessary to treat boys and girls differently in school. Looking only for differences in the treatment of girls and boys can obscure similarities.

Inside the school, and under the supervision of the teacher, boys and girls worked together in learning to read, write, and compute, the basic tasks of the school. Age and proficiency were more important pedagogically than sex, and pictures of rural schools often show both boys and girls of similar size reciting together or putting arithmetic problems on the blackboard. William Ladd Taylor's portrait "The District School," for example, shows three older girls and two boys literally "toeing the line" of the board on the floor as they recite their spelling lesson, while a mixture of little boys and girls are hunched about the master's podium and older boys and girls, in separate pews to his left, whisper or study their lessons. In the district school's simple curriculum of the three Rs, there was little room for differentiation by sex in the curriculum. Girls sometimes learned to sew and knit under the supervision of a woman teacher. Boys, not girls, gave "declamations" when parents came to school to hear the public exercises of the students, for males, not females, gave political speeches. Some teachers assumed that boys and not girls needed to know the upper levels of arithmetic. But in general the curriculum was similar for both sexes. Although the lessons they read in their McGuffey Readers or in history texts assumed that the spheres of men and women were separate in the world outside the school, it is likely that inside the one-room school boys and girls were expected to follow the same rules, to learn the same subjects, and to be judged by similar standards.[47]

The District School, a painting by W. L. Taylor, 1900. (Library of Congress.)

Moral character was quite as much the goal of schooling as literacy and numeracy. The generalized virtues children were expected to acquire and display in school generally applied to both sexes. California reformer John Swett's handbook for common-school teachers includes a chapter called "Practical Lessons in School Ethics," which does not once differentiate by gender. The virtues he enjoined were universal, not sex-specific: for example, self-knowledge, self-restraint, temperance, honesty, obedience, punctuality, conscientiousness, impartiality, gratitude, friendliness, kindness, patience, frankness, seriousness, firmness, cleanliness, and courtesy. It was clear to Swett, however, that after the students left school, they were to display these virtues in domains sharply differentiated by sex. Swett added that "the life of the nation is made up of the mothers that guard the homes, and the men who drive the plough, build the ships, run the mills, work the mines, construct the machinery, print the papers, shoulder the musket, cast

School in
Sargent County,
North Dakota,
about 1904, with
elaborate stove,
school clock,
map, and bolted-
down factory-
built desks.
Children share
two-seater seats
with the same
sex but are
otherwise mixed
together. (J. H.
Hunter Forman,
North Dakota
State Historical
Society.)

the ballots." The contrast between "school ethics" and the opportunities awaiting the two sexes after their school years could hardly have been more sharply juxtaposed.[48]

Swett also believed that the two sexes expressed moral character in different ways. He wanted boys to experience the "refining, restraining, and humanizing influence" of girls and to be taught "to regard the female character as something pure and holy." Girls, in turn, needed to "respect manliness and manhood." All this could be done, he wrote, only in "a well-regulated school, where the boys and girls mutually educate each other." Swett thought that separate schools, not coeducational schools, undermined character. Sexual attraction, he recalled from his days in a rural school in New Hampshire, was innocent and benign: "My pleasantest memories of school-days are associated with the bright-eyed little girls who came to school in summer mornings, bringing May flowers and lilacs and pinks in their hands. I loved some of these pretty girls with all the fullness of boyish feeling. Nobody ever told any of the boys of our school that it was a sin to love them." It was these "farmers' girls, red-cheeked, barefoot too, and dressed in homespun, [who] taught us our first lessons of faith in the purity and nobleness of womanhood."[49]

Like the students, the ideal teacher was also expected to display such nongendered virtues as seriousness, cleanliness, and above all impartiality. Students and parents shared the conviction that the teacher should treat all

A three-teacher black school in White Plains, Georgia, 1941. Girls and boys are separated insofar as crowded conditions permit. (Jack Delano, FSA, Library of Congress.)

children alike—that the classroom should be a place where universal standards of conduct were honored and no favoritism was allowed. An experienced educator of teachers, Samuel Hall, observed in 1829 that "no complaint is more frequently heard, than that the instructer is partial—that he treats one better than another." He said that "in many schools . . . the small scholars are strictly governed, while the larger do nearly as they please." Forty years later, in Ashland, Oregon, a father wrote the teacher a note echoing Hall's concern: "I am vary sorry to informe that in my opinion you have Shoed to me that you are unfit to keep a School. . . . you Seam to punish the Small Scholars to Set a Sample for the big wons that is Rong." It is likely that students and parents would also have been aware of any partiality the teacher showed toward boys or girls, though educators and parents often considered different methods of discipline appropriate for the different sexes.[50]

Inside the school there was some segregation of the sexes, but the specific patterns are by no means clear. As Clifford said, one needs to distinguish prescriptions from practice, and evidence on practice is hard to find. Scattered descriptions and some pictures of rural schools suggest that early in the nineteenth century, and continuing in some schools well into the twentieth century—especially in the South—it was customary in some one-room schools to seat boys and girls on benches on opposite sides of the room, except when they recited in groups of similar proficiency. In this regime, one

Children putting on warm clothes for noon recess in Morton County, North Dakota, 1942. Girls and boys share the same cloakroom. (John Vachon, FSA, Library of Congress.)

form of punishment, especially for boys, was to send a pupil to sit with the opposite sex. On occasion, students protested being separated. The Vermont state superintendent reported in 1850 that in one district "two large boys . . . took offence because not allowed to sit with girls . . . and seized the teacher in an unguarded moment and dragged him out of the school. One of these boys was the son of the committee, and the committee, instead of dismissing the rowdies, dismissed the teacher." The town grand jury indicted and fined "the *young heroes*," however, thereby checking such "spirit of rebellion."[51]

In one village, school officials suggested that the delicacy of schoolgirls could be protected by erecting a barrier between the boys and girls to prevent eye contact, but this was ridiculed by the Cambridge School Committee in 1846: "As occasional glances were sometimes thrown across the aisle [separating boys and girls], it was seriously proposed by a most excellent citizen, that 'a squinting-board' should be erected between the boys' and girls' side of the house, to prevent any 'casting of sheep's eyes,' to the detriment of the morals of the school." The Cambridge committee asked: "What wise parent would be willing to send his children to a school, in which a squinting-board should not only separate brothers and sisters, and shut out from the two sexes the cheerful light of each others' countenances, but perpetually remind them that there is something degrading, something

A one-room school for Hispanic children with eight grades and two teachers in Ojo Sorco, New Mexico. Children appear to be divided by age but not sex. (John Collier, FSA, Library of Congress.)

vulgarizing, something to be ashamed of in associating together, and even in looking at each other?"[52]

In the late nineteenth and early twentieth centuries, when citizens began furnishing rural schools with better equipment, they often replaced the rough benches with bolted-down desks arranged in rows. The boys and girls faced the teacher's podium rather than facing each other. Pictures of these later schools often show children less separated by sex than the stereotypical arrangement of segregated male or female benches. In about two-thirds of the classrooms pictured in Andrew Gulliford's *America's Country Schools* children are clearly mixed by sex, in about a fifth they are loosely clumped by sex though not totally kept apart, while in only a few are they rigidly segregated.[53]

In nineteenth-century rural America, coeducation became established early as an integral part of the institutional structure of the common school. This gender practice grew to be so familiar and universal that it became, in Nietzsche's phrase, "the known, that is to say, what we are accustomed to, so that we no longer marvel at it." But in cities coeducation became the subject of much self-conscious debate.

4

Coeducation in
Urban Public Schools

Not until the middle of the nineteenth century did Americans begin to debate coeducation in public schools in earnest. For a variety of reasons coeducation became what a leading educational journalist called a "live issue" in policy talk, ending what had been a general policy silence. European visitors, often astonished to see teenage boys and girls together in the same classrooms, made Americans more self-conscious about coeducation; several surveys of coeducation by the U.S. Office of Education were explicitly designed to answer foreigners' questions and to defend the practice. The term "coeducation" itself appears to have entered these discussions in the 1850s as a synonym for the more common phrase "mixed schools." The dialogue focused chiefly on urban school systems. Even advocates of separate schools conceded that in the countryside the dispersed population made mixed schools expedient, if not inevitable, once parents had decided to educate both daughters and sons. In the cities, however, there was a policy choice, the protagonists argued. Density of population and comparative wealth made separate schools feasible, but which system was better, mixed or segregated?[1]

The mixture of different classes and ethnic groups in the cities raised one set of issues in the debate. Should girls attend separate schools to be shielded from the contamination—what one report called the "rude assaults"—of riffraff boys? Opponents of coeducation thought so, but their arguments against mixing boys and girls of different social classes provoked counterarguments that a common school should be open to both sexes as well as to all classes, nationalities, and religions.[2]

In some cities, middle- and upper-class parents claimed that their daughters needed to be protected against association with the sons of poor and immigrant families during what the parents regarded as a "dangerous" time of life. A number of educational leaders were concerned that unless the schools were segregated by sex, such prosperous parents would withdraw their children and send them to private girls' schools. The civilized upper classes everywhere chose separate sex schools, said the Boston superintendent John D. Philbrick: "It is precisely among those classes that the education of the sexes always has been, and continues to be, most exclusively unmixed." Separate-sex schools were common in the older cities of the eastern seaboard—Boston, New York, Philadelphia, and Baltimore—and in southern cities, and there the competition with private schools was most intense. To attract those families with the means to choose private or public education for their children, it was necessary to segregate the sexes, claimed some opponents of coeducation.[3]

Another set of arguments over coeducation concerned not what parents would think but instead what was bureaucratically and pedagogically prudent. The leaders, who were attempting to create a uniform system of urban education, were determined to leave no detail of planning to chance. They wanted to make a coherent policy decision about coeducation rather than muddling through with a patchwork of gender practices. They needed to decide how much to differentiate schooling according to the sex of the student.

These policymakers—especially the big-city superintendents—operated in a different institutional and political context than their rural counterparts. In the countryside, policy was usually informal and might shift with new school trustees or a new teacher. By contrast, the most influential city superintendents sought to create a hierarchical system in which there was a "uniformity of excellence," whether in gradation of schools, certification of teachers, design of school buildings, or curriculum. "The best is the best everywhere," said Philbrick, and urban school leaders carefully compared notes on what was indeed best. An innovation in one urban system was often rapidly adopted in others, especially in the new cities emerging in the West. Under such a philosophy of school management, in which centralized and uniform policy was the ideal, many leaders believed that gender practices should be planned and not allowed to drift. The debate on coeducation by these male administrators both rationalized existing practice and shaped gender relationships in the schools.[4]

We focus in this chapter primarily on the writings of school officials because we believe that they reveal actual changes taking place and because they provide important rationales for or against coeducation. But beyond the question of the institutional impact of their policy talk, we are interested in their substantive arguments, which often reflected contrasting views of gender relationships and educational goals. Commentators on coeducation addressed many key issues: whether it was wise to mix pupils of different sexes, social classes, and ethnic groups; what were the relative abilities and learning styles of boys and girls and, if there were differences, whether they were compatible or not; whether the two sexes should learn the same or different subjects; whether mixed or separate schools fostered better discipline; whether coeducation "de-sexualized" schooling or promoted immoral sexual behavior; and what was the proper relation between schooling and the later destinies of women and men.

These discussions, of course, did not take place in an institutional vacuum. Thus, it is useful to examine first the bureaucratic development of city school systems and the emerging sexual division of labor among adults who worked in schools.

The Institutional Character of Urban Schools

Urban public schools were only loosely linked with the heterogeneous social contexts of surrounding cities. Unlike rural schools, which were connected closely to families of relatively homogeneous background and often associated with neighborhood churches, school systems in large cities were far less anchored in other socially integrative institutions. Churches were frequently a source of contention rather than integration. In religiously pluralistic cities Catholics, Protestants, and Jews were often at odds about such basic questions as the use of the Bible in moral training. To some degree, schools stood apart from and even in opposition to the homes of many of the pupils.[5]

In urbanized Rhode Island, for example, Henry Barnard believed that "any scheme of school organization will be imperfect which does not include special arrangements for the systematic training of very young children." The reason was that in cities "many parents are sure to be found, who, for want of intelligence or leisure, of constancy and patience, are unfitted to watch the first blossoming of the souls of their children, and to train them to . . . all the virtues which wise and far-seeing parents desire for their children." The result of such defective socialization, he added, "is the neglect of all moral culture." Another educator observed that "in the open country the cooperative character of schools is strong and the influence of the family is prominent. In the dense city the public school stands more strongly as a token of authority, an ally of the police department."[6]

In the first half of the nineteenth century, before the institutional structure of urban school systems became standardized, city schools separated and mixed the sexes in a bewildering variety of patterns. They excluded girls entirely, educated them separately, taught them on separate floors of the same building with boys, or taught them together with boys in the same classrooms.

Boston schools illustrated all these choices. Its institutional structure was a mosaic of old and new organizational forms. Its primary schools, founded in 1818 and patterned after the rural schools, were small one-room schools for little boys and girls, taught by women and supervised by local male trustees. The city had intermediate grammar schools divided into a "reading school" and a "writing school." When Boston first opened these grammar schools to girls, it allowed them to attend only half the year in sessions separate from boys, but then it made this intermediate instruction separate but equal for girls. Boston continued its colonial Latin Grammar School to prepare boys for college and created a boys-only public high school in 1821. Under pressure from citizens demanding further education for their daughters, a separate high school was created for girls. As the city expanded its borders by incorporating nearby areas, it added some coeducational grammar schools. By 1857 Boston had 213 one-room coeducational primary schools scattered across the city; six intermediate, or grammar, schools that were coeducational, six for girls alone, and six for boys alone; and secondary schools that were completely segregated by sex. Given such a mélange of gender practices, it is no wonder that Bostonians were at the center of a storm of debate over coeducation in the latter half of the nineteenth century.[7]

Older cities in the Northeast, like Boston, did not start from scratch in creating city schools. They often dovetailed new forms of schooling into older ones, much as one might remodel a colonial house. Thus their systems commonly grew by accretion rather than starting from a new blueprint, as did those of burgeoning centers like Chicago or Portland, Oregon. The older cities of the Northeast inherited a pattern of education from the eighteenth century and often displayed incongruous mixtures of the old and the new, including diverse policies with respect to gender distinctions. But in the latter half of the nineteenth century, as the drive for a uniform system of urban schools gathered momentum, most cities began to adopt a standardized institutional pattern that differed from both the rural schools and the odd mixture found in Boston.[8]

The chief building block in this new institutional structure was the graded elementary school. Henry Barnard was a prominent advocate of this new method of classifying and instructing pupils. He thought that the mixture of proficiency levels in the large intermediate classrooms of cities like Boston or New York—sometimes exceeding two hundred students— was inhumane and inefficient. Instead, he and other reformers urged cities to create a new type of school in which students would be grouped by educational attainment—in short, "graded." A typical graded school divided pupils into eight classes of fifty to sixty students each, marched them up a curricular staircase at a regular pace, and examined them at the end of the year for promotion to the next grade.[9]

This institutional innovation swept the country. The graded school provided an institutional model well adapted to expansion; it was symmetrical, promised factorylike efficiency, and was easily reproduced cell by cell as cities grew at a staggering pace. By 1870 most urban school systems were organized into eight elementary grades (although the specific divisions into primary and intermediate grades differed). School boards in large cities usually hired superintendents to design a uniform curriculum, test pupils for advancement to the next grade, and create bureaucratic procedures. At the summit of the urban school system stood one or more high schools that had a curriculum progressing through three or four years. These secondary schools enrolled a tiny fraction of the pupils but were designed to give symmetry to the overall design and a goal for ambitious students in the lower grades. A competitive examination on the elementary curriculum governed admission to secondary education.[10]

While technically a part of the same state "common-school system" as the rural schools, urban schools were quite different structurally, and teaching in the city and countryside were in many respects different jobs. The school year in cities was often more than double that in sparsely settled areas. In 1842 New York City held school for forty-nine weeks; Chicago, for forty-eight weeks; and Brooklyn, Baltimore, and Cincinnati, for eleven months. In 1880 in thirty-two of the thirty-eight states, urban schools were open for more than 180 days, and in twenty-five states, for more than 190 days, compared with a national average of 130 days and a school term in many rural schools of only a few weeks. In the same year, cities spent $12.62 per capita on education, compared with only $3.28 in rural areas. Teaching was not only a full-time job in cities but also paid from two to three times more than weekly salaries in the countryside. City teachers were generally older, better educated, and more experienced than those in one-room schools.[11]

During the middle of the nineteenth century city after city decided to replace male teachers with women. As a result of this deliberate policy, by 1890 women held 92 percent of the teaching jobs in all cities with populations exceeding ten thousand. The sexual division of labor in city school systems contrasted with the more informal gender choices made in small rural districts, which hired female or male teachers in an open labor market. Some of these urban districts were enormous by the standards of the day: in 1890 the city of New York employed 3,706 teachers, more than the total number employed in twenty-one individual states and territories. City school systems were among the first public bureaucracies to create a rationalized sexual division of labor, complete with sex-designated jobs and fixed separate and unequal pay schedules for women and men.[12]

A researcher for the U.S. Bureau of Education concluded that when school boards discussed employing women in the 1840s and 1850s, "unquestionably the original motive was economy in nearly all cases. The records show that very clearly." Providence, Rhode Island, illustrates how teaching was converted from a male into a female occupation in one of the older cities. In 1836 the Providence school board decided to hire two "female assistants" at a salary of $175 per year to replace the male "ushers" (assistants to the male masters), who were paid $300. The "masters," forerunners of school principals, were paid $600. The board reported that "the ushers were not at once removed, but whenever vacancies occurred in the place of ushers, they were filled by two female assistants. . . . In the course of a year or two, all the ushers having resigned, female assistants were employed in all the grammar schools of the city." In Baltimore a roughly equal number of male and female teachers taught in the separate-sex schools of the city until 1848, when women teachers began being placed in the boys' schools; from then on, women rapidly replaced men. In St. Louis there were 5 men and 5 women teachers in 1844, but 20 men and 108 women by 1858. In Cincinnati in 1840 there were 21 men and 38 women teaching in 1840, and 34 and 108, respectively, by 1850. In the newer cities arising in the West, such as Portland, Oregon, school boards usually emulated eastern practices and hired mostly women as teachers.[13]

In many cities, female graduates of the high schools constituted an inexpensive pool of prospective teachers well trained in the district's curriculum. In addition, where cities had coeducational schools—and most did—a classroom guided by a woman teacher seemed a safe and compatible environment for girls. Coeducation and the transformation of teaching into a woman's job went hand in hand and reinforced each other.

When cities changed their large ungraded grammar classrooms with male masters and assistants into a graded system with mainly female teachers, the gender transformation became written into official school policy and frozen into salary scales that favored the men. From 1850 to 1900, women teachers in urban schools as a whole earned only about one-third the weekly salary of the men. In the big cities school boards generally did not bargain individually with teachers, as did trustees in rural districts, but fixed the price of employees by sex and bureaucratic function. In Cincinnati, for example, in 1862 a male high-school principal earned $1,500 a year; his male assistants, $1,080 to $1,188; and female assistants, $630 to $900. In the elementary schools male principals earned between $1,068 and $1,152; male assistants, between $717 and $807; and female assistants, between $240 and $540.[14]

In this way a rule-based sexual division of labor arose in city schools: women practically monopolized the lower grades, while men worked in the higher grades and as managers. This sex segregation of women on the lower rungs and men on the upper rungs of urban school bureaucracies was not simply the unplanned outcome of ineluctable economic and cultural forces, although such factors obviously played a part. It was, as we have said, mostly the result of deliberate institutional policies adopted in cities during the middle of the nineteenth century.[15]

Men did not leave the system entirely as teaching turned into a predominantly female occupation but remained in formal control of the system as superintendents and principals. In the early stages of the graded elementary school, the job of principal was given to a man, who was to be chosen "with special reference to his ability in arranging the studies and order of exercises of the school, in administering its discipline, in adapting moral instruction to individual scholars, and superintending the operations of each classroom, so as to secure the harmonious action and progress of every department."[16]

When teaching in the graded school became women's work, the nature of the job itself changed. Although advocates of coeducation sometimes compared the urban school—with its male head, female teachers, and mix

In many cities school systems created special "normal," teacher-training, classes in high schools or separate vocational schools to prepare teachers. Often the curriculum of the normal school was precisely calibrated to the public-school course of instruction. In these pictures of "stretching and yawning" (exercises to relax the body and counteract tension), for example, the normal school students learn to do what grade school pupils are expected to do. For the most part, male administrators planned the curriculum, while the women teachers were expected to carry out their superiors' design to the letter. These photographs were taken by Frances Benjamin Johnston in Washington, D.C., in 1899. (Library of Congress.)

A class of normal-school students learns a botany lesson they will teach in the elementary grades. A solitary male student sits in the center of the room.

Grade-school pupils do their
"stretching and yawning."

Normal-school candidates for
teaching learn to stretch and yawn.

of boys and girls—to a family, in its operation it was more like a factory. Planning and supervision of instruction became the duty of the male administrators, while the female teachers, like their pupils, were to toe the line. A former teacher, Mary Abigail Dodge, called such accountability without power "the Degradation of the Teacher," and she wrote a sardonic book attacking the presumption of male administrators and the accretion of bureaucratic regulations that constrained the freedom of women to teach. Everywhere the cities were moving, she wrote, "in the direction of more supervision, more machinery, more complication. The tendency is not to put more brains inside the school-room, but more offices outside."[17]

The presence of a man as principal and the pedagogical standardization found in graded classrooms eased the fears of school boards about the ability of women to control the boys despite the gradual shift from corporal punishment to milder methods of discipline. An official in the U.S. Bureau of Education observed that the older pattern of teaching children of varying abilities in nongraded schools posed severe problems for the teachers, who were expected to keep the pupils quiet while they heard successive groups of students recite different lessons. In the graded school, by contrast, he wrote, "at least half the pupils are engaged in reciting at the same time. Each pupil is on the alert lest he be called upon suddenly; if he is not in the section reciting, all his thought must be given to preparation for the next lesson. His time is fully occupied. That of itself is of the greatest value in discipline." As a result, he concluded, in a graded school "a weak woman with reasonable tact can now do the work which formerly required a bully."[18]

The male superintendents and principals linked the schools to the male-dominated power structure of the community and to the male school boards. Since women were generally subordinate to men in the larger society, some people assumed that they would be more likely to obey male bosses than the more independent schoolmasters. In 1878 a writer declared that "women teachers are often preferred by superintendents because they are more willing to comply with established regulations and less likely to ride headstrong hobbies." The opinion lingered that the firm hand of a male principal was necessary for proper pedagogical order, but actual experience in employing women suggested that this was a myth. Women teachers proved to be quite capable of controlling their classes. In 1891 an English commission asked the U.S. commissioner of education and eight big-city superintendents the question, Does the work of women teachers "require supplementing by men?" Six of the officials said no, and the other three argued not that women needed help but merely that it was good for students to have both male and female teachers. In his reply, the New York superintendent stated simply that "each teacher is responsible for the instruction and discipline of her own class."[19]

Women teachers did sometimes resist dictation by male supervisors and organized to improve their condition. Toward the end of the nineteenth century women themselves moved increasingly into positions as principals of elementary schools, where they usually supervised only women. By 1905, in cities with populations greater than eight thousand, 62 percent of the elementary-school principals were women. In Philadelphia, the school board grew so concerned about the lack of male teachers—and hence local male candidates for principalships—that it created a normal school restricted to males.[20]

In the case of women, as opposed to the men who became urban administrators, people continued to assume that teaching was not a lifelong career but a temporary stage in the life cycle between the parental family and the conjugal family. Even Dodge, who was single and attacked the stereotypes that "degraded" women, argued that the qualities that made women good teachers also made them effective mothers, and vice versa. "I venture to affirm, that the ranks of silly, characterless, inefficient wives and mothers have never been recruited from the ranks of successful school-teachers," she wrote. Women teachers' low pay and lack of power stemmed in part from their relatively short tenure, which in turn resulted in part from the common practice of dismissing them when they married. But many single women and widows did make teaching a long-term career, and disproportionately from their ranks came successive waves of militant women who protested unequal pay, stifling supervision, and powerlessness.[21]

In northern cities white men had a far more opportunities for employment other than public-school teaching than did white women. When the job of master became that of schoolmistress, white men could either seek another job or stay in the school bureaucracy as teachers in the upper grades or as administrators. To the degree that the job of primary teacher became labeled as female, men were probably deterred from even applying for positions in the lower grades.

By contrast with urban white men, black men in southern cities had very few choices of white-collar positions. For African-American men, teaching in the segregated black schools, despite its relatively low pay, offered a steady salary in a respectable occupation. During Reconstruction, when blacks exercised some control over their schools, black men often taught in southern cities. But when whites regained control over their dual urban systems, they often replaced black teachers with white women—often those who had scored badly on certification tests and hence were not considered fit for white schools. Blacks protested that they should have black teachers for their children, and they often succeeded in obtaining them. But the white school boards and superintendents chose to hire black women, not men, as teachers. It is likely that the whites who controlled the black schools considered black women teachers less threatening to the racial caste system, less likely to serve as models of the full citizenship they were determined to deny to black men. In 1890 in cities with populations of ten thousand or more, black male teachers represented only 14 percent of black teachers in South Carolina; 18 percent in Georgia; and 9 percent in Mississippi.[22]

In the racially segregated schools of southern cities, race divided the school systems in two. In every part of the nation there was also a sexual division of labor in educational employment. But as cities bureaucratized their systems, they faced a key question: Should students be educated together or divided by sex? Should students in theory be interchangeable parts and not treated differently according to their sex? On the one hand, the ideal of the common school decreed that public education should deliberately mix different kinds of people in order to create a unified nation of people who shared similar civic values. Also, the new forms of bureaucratic instruction—batch processing—depersonalized students and, in theory at least, treated them not as boys or girls, Catholic or Protestants, rich or poor, but as pupils in the third grade or the algebra class. For purposes of educational classification, such categories as age or proficiency seemed more relevant than gender or the social characteristics of their families. But, on the other hand, in a society that struggled to keep clear the separate spheres of the sexes, did it make sense to educate boys and girls identically through a system of coeducation?

Anatomy of a Controversy: Charlestown, Massachusetts, 1848

In 1848 the school committee of Charlestown, Massachusetts, in its search for "greater perfection and uniformity in our school system," decided to reorganize its city schools. It had just created a new coeducational high school and was in the midst of rebuilding some of its grammar schools and changing district boundaries. But most important, the committee decided to make the entire system coeducational, mixing the sexes in the three grammar schools that had previously taught boys and girls separately.[23]

A group of 176 residents of Ward 1 protested the shift to coeducation. As parents of children in the Harvard Grammar School, which had formerly been an all-girl school, they had objections of a "strong, serious, and decisive character" to combining boys and girls in the same rooms. They petitioned the trustees to reverse their decision and to hold separate classes for the two sexes. The school board responded by appointing a subcommittee to investigate. The members asked the parents to write a letter detailing their objections to coeducation and requested that the masters of the grammar schools comment on discipline and morals in mixed schools and indicate whether coeducation should be continued. They posed similar questions to three masters in the Salem schools.[24]

The protesting parents appealed to tradition. A mixed school was "a variation from a known, well-tried and well approved method of instruction in cities and other places of dense population." Coeducation might be necessary in the countryside, but in Charlestown it was "uncalled for by any consideration of economy, convenience, or good order." They invoked the principle of separate spheres for the sexes. It was foolish to train girls as if they were to be, "like boys, our future engineers, navigators, merchants, legislators, and governors." Instead, they should be prepared "for those duties of life, to which they must inevitably be called."[25]

Above all, they feared what might happen if their daughters associated with low-life boys. Girls from eight to fourteen were at a "dangerous" time of life, during which they required "that watchful care, that attention to sexual differences, that jealous guarding of mental and physical purity, which, it is believed, cannot be had in a Mixed School." Coeducation exposed girls to "rude assaults by writings, allusions and intercourse, which no vigilance can fully prevent." True, some girls were "guilty of using improper terms and expressions," but they had "little influence with their own sex, unless countenanced and encouraged by rude male companions." Those girls inclined to be "vicious" were more easily corrupted in the presence of boys. And, most important, by being exposed to a miscellaneous collection of the opposite sex during "a period when the mind receives its deepest impressions" and sexual impulses begin, youth might make the wrong choice of "worthy and suitable companions." The parents warned that "a mistake at this period, which care and prudence may prevent, often becomes a source of lasting misery."[26]

The six teachers in the Charlestown grammar schools disagreed with the citizens from the Harvard district. Their perspective was that of the classroom. All said that the mixture of the sexes produced greater restraint and decorum and thus fostered easier discipline and better "order and government" in the schools. "The society of the sexes at school," said one, "will serve, I have no doubt, to modify the deportment of each, mutually inciting both to habits of neatness in their personal appearance, and rendering them more circumspect and chaste in their language and manners." Four teachers said that coeducation produced better morals, one was undecided, and another thought morality a problem, though he believed that if boys and girls were to be in the same building they should be "in the *same* room also." None of the teachers, then, wanted a change back to separate schools.[27]

The subcommittee of the board visited the Salem schools because that city was in some ways similar to Charlestown and had introduced coeducation earlier. Three masters from Salem grammar schools gave more diverse testimony on mixed schools than that of the Charlestown teachers. One was on the fence about whether coeducation influenced the industry and morals of pupils, but he preferred teaching single-sex classes because different methods of discipline and instruction worked best for the two sexes. Another said that girls might soften and refine the boys, but that the boys coarsened the girls. He requested the Salem school committee to put up a partition between the boys' and girls' sections so that he could use different methods of discipline with them.[28]

The third Salem master had a totally different opinion. He was so convinced of the favorable influence of boys and girls on each other that he placed them side by side at the same double desks. He said that "this mode of seating pupils secures to us the double advantage of placing together children of dissimilar propensities, habits or tastes, and also of placing together the different sexes; the object of which is to stimulate what is good, or to repress what is evil." And that, he asserted, "in fact is the actual result as found by experience, [so] that I have no desire to return to a separation of the sexes to different rooms, or to different parts of the same room." He declared that coeducation had come to stay in most of New England, and added: "If the sexes must be separated at school, why not be uniform, and carry this separation into churches, coaches, railroad cars, and even to the very streets themselves?" (pp. 16–18).

Charlestown school-board members Charles W. Moore and George P. Sanger, who wrote the majority report of the subcommittee, took the side of the parents who wanted to reinstate separate schools. They rejected the idea that discipline was better in mixed schools. If, in a mixed school, a boy and a girl were to commit the same offense, a teacher might be accused of partiality if he did not punish them in the same way; "while if he makes the flesh of the girl tremble under the rod or the ferule, he is liable to be charged with undue severity." Likewise, they dismissed the idea that the more diligent girls would stimulate the boys to learn more: "In the same proportion that the boys are helped, the girls will be injured," for "where the good scholars help the poor ones, the poor ones are a drawback and a weight upon the advancement of the good ones." But for Moore and Sanger, the key objections to coeducation were the ones raised by the parents: that the future destinies of girls and boys were so different that they should be educated separately and that in big cities coeducation threatened morality. To the common school came "children of every grade and . . . subject to all sorts of influences at home"; girls should be protected from "contamination" and sexual innuendo coming from vulgar and obscene boys (pp. 16–18).

Seth J. Thomas, the dissenting member of the subcommittee, objected especially to this thinly veiled prejudice against poor and immigrant families. The worry of the petitioners that their daughters might be attracted to boys of a lower class if exposed to them in school, he wrote, constituted not only a rejection of coeducation but of the premises underlying public education. "The objection is an attack upon the common school system," he declared; "it strikes at the root of that system; it will last as an objection while that system lasts." The petitioners were demanding "a more select association" instead of the social mixing that undergirds the common school, Thomas wrote. They deplored "the 'lasting misery' which may come from a companionship—perhaps an alliance—with the 'unwashed'. . . . the law has provided that these schools shall be public and common. . . . the rich and the poor, the high and the low, the polite and the vulgar, all have an equal right in them" (pp. 18–19).

Some of the same families that objected to common schooling of girl and boys sent their daughters to dancing schools, he observed, "there to meet boys, and where they meet under far less restraint, too, than in our grammar schools" (pp. 18–19). They did not object to this way of ensuring that girls and boys would mutually improve each others' manners and dignity. In the carefully supervised mixed class, moreover, boys and girls tempered and fostered each others' moral development (pp. 5–8).

Thomas also ridiculed the accusation that coeducation would not prepare girls for their feminine sphere but rather would train them for men's work. The curriculum in mixed grammar schools and single-sex schools was the same. It was surprising, he wrote, that "these gentlemen should, just at this moment, have awoke, after so long a repose, and for the first time discovered that the study of reading and writing and arithmetic and spelling and English grammar and geography and American history and composition, in the grammar schools, tended to defeat the object of a good education, and that there was a serious project on foot of the school committee to make of their daughters, engineers, navigators, and members of the legislature" (pp. 31–32).

The curriculum for boys and girls was the same for good reason. No one could predict precisely what either boys or girls would do in later life. Girls might become schoolteachers, in which case they needed a thorough academic training. They might do housework, but even the petitioners would not "seriously urge that as a reason for introducing the study of housework into the grammar schools, as a means for fitting them for such duties." The real purpose of education for all children was not to train narrowly for vocation but to "develope the mind, to draw it out, and give it a scope and balance and strength" (pp. 31–32).

There were also "psychological" reasons, Thomas declared, why boys and girls learned more effectively together than apart. "Girls, as a general thing, receive impressions into the mind more readily than boys; boys subject these impressions, when received, to a severer criticism in the understanding. . . . the union of the two in the same class will benefit both; for it will give aptness to the one and strength and solidity to the other. There will be mutual emulation; the progress will be more rapid" (pp. 28–29). That has been the result, he said, in the one grammar school that was coeducational, where children improved in learning as well as in deportment.

Thomas's final argument was perhaps the most telling one for those who wanted to standardize the system into a unified bureaucracy. He argued that if the school committee agreed to change the Harvard school back into a sexually segregated institution, other parents would soon insist on coeducation, inducing contending factions to barrage the committee with contradictory demands. The way for the committee to decide was not to respond just to political pressures, for that would produce chaos, but to determine by principled arguments whether separate or mixed schools were pedagogically and morally best (pp. 28–29).

In its report for 1848 the school committee admitted that coeducation was controversial and sought to be conciliating, but they basically accepted Thomas's position. They had "availed themselves of the opinions" of pedagogical experts, they said, and declared themselves "not unmindful of the opinions and wishes of the large class of our own citizens, who feel deeply interested in all matters connected with the educational interests of their children, and the prosperity and usefulness of our public schools." They had "deliberately formed" their decision to mix boys and girls "with a full conviction that if parents generally will second the measures decided upon by the committee, the schools will be placed in a higher sphere of usefulness to the children, of both sexes, than they have heretofore sustained" (pp. 33–34).

The Charlestown schools, the committee said, had exemplified "nearly all the varieties of school organization": coeducational primary schools; a mixed high school; and among the grammar schools, one that taught one sex only, one that taught both girls and boys but in separate rooms, and one that was fully coeducational. After full discussion of the "different merits" of these diverse gender arrangements and "the intellectual and moral influence exerted by them upon the young," the committee found itself "irresistibly led" to the conclusion that mixed schools were best (pp. 33–34).

The committee went well beyond the pedagogical claims to assert that "the separate school system for each of the sexes appears to be entirely at war with the whole social organization of society." "We do not find [the separation of the sexes] in the organization of Sunday Schools or Primary schools," the committee declared. Everywhere "in all the social gatherings of the young, whether in the domestic circle, in parties of pleasure, or in rural or other excursions, it is desired and expected that both sexes will be brought together to participate in, and add to the enjoyments of the occasion." People in all civilized quarters recognize the power of women "to refine and soften the feelings of man and promote his welfare and happiness. . . . Shall, then, our schools be the only places where this influence is to be excluded, and school days . . . be marked as the only period in life, at which the bringing together of the sexes, can have no agency in purifying and elevating the character and condition of the social compact?" In any case, "by the proposed arrangement of our schools, the children of one family will be brought together in the same room, and under the influence and instruction of one set of teachers."29

The school committee did not believe that coeducation, which mirrored the gender mixing of social life, should lead to equal opportunities in economic and civic life for women and men. The school committee argued that high-school studies needed to be "modified according to the sex and advancement, and to some degree, the future destination of the pupils." Boys, but not girls, studied Greek as preparation for college, learned double-entry bookkeeping, and gave political "declamations." Boys needed to be prepared for commerce, agriculture, the mechanical arts, and college; girls were to cultivate their minds and morals with "practical views of the duties and obligations of life" in order to radiate "purity of thought, manners and conversation" in their domestic circle. The liberal educational policymakers of Charlestown who decided that girls and boys be educated together were hardly proposing a revolution in the status or opportunities of adult women.[30]

The Case Against Coeducation

The controversy in Charlestown foreshadowed most of the arguments over mixed schools that appeared in the educational journals and reports of school officials in the next half century. As in Charlestown, advocates of separate schools in other cities often wanted not only to keep the sexes strictly separate but also to preserve class barriers. They wanted to protect "delicate" daughters from "coarse" boys. The principal of the elite Girls' High and Latin Schools in Boston wrote, for example, that in homogeneous towns and small cities coeducation might work well, "for there the conditions approach in simplicity the conditions of family or neighborhood life. In large cities, however, the case is different. The population is not homogeneous, the families represented in the school are not known to one another, the numbers brought together in a single school are much larger, and the proportion of coarse natures among the pupils is apt to be somewhat larger." He did not need to explain that "coarse natures" was a euphemism for the targets of class and ethnic prejudice among parents.[31]

San Francisco was almost alone among western American cities in separating the sexes in graded schools. Its superintendent argued that parents wanted separate schools because there were so many ruffian boys in the city. Mixed schools might work in small communities, but "in a large city like San Francisco, where many of the children receive much of their daily education in the streets, and within the sight and under the influence of infamy and crime, parents have objections to placing delicate and refined daughters in the same class with rude and depraved boys, which all the beautiful theories of the optimist cannot overcome." He said that a few persons "who think that the highest type of manhood and womanhood can only be developed by the coeducation of the sexes" opposed the separation of boys and girls, "yet it has received the commendation and approval of nearly every parent and teacher interested in the prosperity of our public

schools." One former San Francisco teacher who became state superintendent, John Swett, disagreed with what he called the "Pecksniffian morality-
men" who wanted separate schools in the city. "There are some," he wrote,
"who have no faith in the purity of either sex; they believe in total depravity
to the letter. . . . That the tendency of educating boys and girls together is
to excite improper and impure thoughts, I deny." Did France, where the
schools were separate, have a higher standard of sexual morality than the
United States?[32]

The "beautiful theories of the optimist" about the value of mixing all
children in the common school were less prevalent in the South than in the
North and West. White boys and girls in Southern cities were more often
taught in separate schools than white children from other parts of the
nation. In Memphis, in 1870, the superintendent quoted the San Francisco
report on separate schools and claimed that "the separation of the sexes into
separate departments, when practicable, will be found to popularize the
city schools, and tend to preserve and cultivate the refinement of the
pupils." He substituted male for female teachers in one school he deemed to
be "an improper and disagreeable location for a female teacher." Some
Memphis schools may have been a bit rough: a regulation of the school
board required all pupils "to avoid all profane and indecent language,
intoxicating drinks, tobacco, and the carrying of deadly weapons."[33]

The racial caste system complicated the decision to coeducate the sexes
in southern cities, especially at the secondary level. Philbrick observed that
"generally, in the Southern states, the high schools for white pupils are
unmixed, while those for colored youths are mixed." Is this "through
ignorance or design"? he asked rhetorically. The white school boards and
administrators who controlled the white and black city schools had a different standard of sexual propriety for the two races. White females, relegated
by men to a pedestal, supposedly needed the protection that came from
isolation; black women, exploited by white men and stereotyped as pas-
sionate and available, needed no such buffering from males. Southern railroad stations, wrote a black woman protesting this degradation of her
sisters, "have three waiting rooms, and the very conspicuous signs tell the
ignorant that this room is for 'ladies,' and this is for 'gents' and that for the
'colored' people." In similar fashion, white girls and boys were often segregated in school, but very rarely were black boys and girls.[34]

Segregation by sex and segregation by race were linked in the minds of
some southern leaders. In a New Orleans case protesting separate schools
for blacks and whites, the court held that the common precedent of separat-

ing boys and girls in public schools could be used to justify racial segregation. "The state," he wrote, may be of the "opinion that it is better to educate the sexes separately, and therefore establishes schools in which the children of different sexes are educated apart. By such a policy can it be said that the equal rights of either sex are invaded?" The important principle was to provide "equal school advantages," for "equality of rights does not necessarily imply identity of rights."[35]

The judge did not say that gender segregation was not state policy in Louisiana but left to the discretion of local school boards (even in New Orleans, where the white schools in the city center were single-sex, the district schools in outlying areas where the population was scattered were coeducational). Nor did the "separate-but-equal" principle explain the fact that in southern cities not only black schools but also those for white girls often received substantially smaller public funding than the schools for white boys. Separate was rarely equal for girls anymore than it was for blacks.[36]

Class as well as race complicated the decision about coeducation in urban districts in the South. In a number of southern cities officials reported that they separated white boys and girls because of public opinion—probably meaning opinions expressed by those with political and economic power. Single-sex private schools were the traditional form of schooling for well-to-do southerners. In a region where prosperous white families customarily sent their children to private schools, public school officials wanted to persuade well-to-do families as well as poor families to send their children to the public system.[37]

The Washington, D.C., schools had both mixed and separate classes for pupils in 1850. Although the school board conceded that some citizens believed that coeducation exerted a "salutory influence," it concluded that "the general desire of the people of the city" was to separate boys and girls "in the more advanced schools of the city." By 1871 the superintendent reported that the policy of separating the sexes in schools and on playgrounds was observed except in districts on the outskirts of the city where there were too few children to make the segregation of boys and girls practical. In Savannah, Georgia, the superintendent used negative language similar to that in reports from Memphis and San Francisco about "enthusiastic supporters" of coeducation and claimed that "the practical tendency in our large cities is more and more to separate the sexes."[38]

The Savannah superintendent was wrong. Apart from the South, the only other place where sexually segregated public schools were common was in the Northeast, where elite private education was also generally for one sex only. Even there separate public schools for boys and girls were coming under attack. In the process the advocates of sexual segregation were forced to state their case.

In 1890 in Boston advocates of coeducation challenged the separatist policy of the board of education, taking advantage of the fact that the city was contemplating building new schools. At that time, said a committee appointed to look into the question, only 36 percent of boys and girls attended mixed classes, and Boston, for all its claims to educational leadership, "hampers more than any other city the rightful advance of girls, and lessens the refining influences on boys by this separation of the sexes in our schools." The committee surveyed the Boston teachers and studied practices in other cities. Almost all the urban superintendents and educators contacted favored coeducation. One woman in Milwaukee replied in surprise: "Your inquiry strikes a Wisconsin man or woman as would an investigation into the advisability of allowing men and women and boys and girls to occupy the same pews in church."[39]

There was a predictable split among the Boston teachers: those who taught in separate schools tended to favor the practice, while those in coeducational schools preferred the mixed schools. Of the 254 opponents of coeducation, 231 taught in separate classrooms. Overall, 58 percent of the masters favored mixed schools and 7 percent were undecided. The opinions on coeducation expressed by the educators in Boston in many ways echoed the arguments heard in Charlestown forty years earlier. The key objections remained worries about sexual morality (concerns about "adolescent appetite" enflamed by "flashy novels and bare-legged theatricals"); the exposure of pure daughters to coarse boys and the possible loss of their maidenly delicacy—an example of "democracy run to riot"; and the need to discipline and teach boys and girls in ways appropriate to their sex. After this concerted effort of the coeducationists to revive the issue, and after widespread support of mixed schools in the press and community, a divided school board voted to postpone its decision, ostensibly because of uncertainty about the source of funds to reorganize the schools.[40]

Philbrick, for many years the superintendent of the Boston schools and an expert on urban education, had perfected his case for separate schools through years of navigating the tempest in the Boston teapot. He said that coeducation might be expedient where there was no practical alternative and insisted that he believed in equality of education for both sexes. But he maintained that "difference is compatible with equality of value and equality of excellence." The real questions to answer were whether the different natures and destinies of the two sexes should require different forms of schooling and whether good morals and manners were better fostered in single sex or mixed schools. Scientists had proved, he said, that the differences between the sexes were "radical and fundamental . . . and that progress is impossible without accepting and respecting in education this difference of sex." Foreign authorities all agreed, he said, that separate schools are best for morals and instruction.[41]

The Case for Coeducation

Philbrick, however, was out of step with his colleagues elsewhere. Most American authorities disagreed with him, whatever the European educators might say. William T. Harris, the most influential advocate of coeducation in his generation, both as superintendent of the St. Louis schools in the 1870s and later as U.S. commissioner of education, told a Norwegian educator that Philbrick "stood almost alone among our ablest writers on education in his opinion [in favor of separate schools]. The Boston schools under his charge educated the sexes separately. It may be that his experience in that city had undue influence on his opinion."[42]

The controversy in Charlestown had anticipated most of the positive as well as the negative arguments about coeducation. This suggests that the issues of the debate were already alive in the culture before they became widely publicized. To the leaders of urban schools, however, settling the question of coeducation in practice became increasingly important as Americans moved forward with planning and building urban graded school systems in the second half of the nineteenth century. In the United States there was no national ministry of education to decree uniformity in local school affairs. State governments passed laws on racial but not on sex segregation or integration. Such policies were decided by local school boards, although in many cities professional superintendents played an important role in defining the issues. These leaders exchanged ideas in national forums like the National Education Association. Much of the similarity among city schools across the nation stemmed from the tendency of urban systems to copy each other and from an emerging consensus on policies among the professional leaders. Thus, the debate on coeducation was of more than theoretical interest; it also influenced practice. And in that debate there was a clear winner: public-school officials who wrote on the subject overwhelmingly favored mixed schools. By the 1890s there was a firm consensus among school administrators that coeducation was best both in policy and practice.[43]

In the 1850s coeducation became a common topic of discussion in state teachers' associations and in the reports of state superintendents. In 1857 the Michigan superintendent of schools made a survey of all "union schools," or large graded buildings, in the state. All officials who commented on coeducation approved the practice. Combining the sexes permitted larger and better graded classrooms, they said. Uncouth and unruly boys became more gentle, while girls became less "coyish and simpering" and more self-reliant and energetic in character. In other states, also, teachers' organizations were endorsing the principle of coeducation. More than five hundred delegates to the Ohio State Teachers' Association, for example, unanimously voted for mixed schools in 1851, while in Pennsylvania in 1854 the teachers' organization endorsed a report approving coeducation written by its chairman, J. P. Wickersham, and James Thompson.[44]

In their justification of coeducation, Wickersham and Thompson raised two questions that would continue to dominate the discussion of mixed schools: whether "the object of educating each sex is the same," and, if so, whether coeducation was the best means of attaining that end. They argued that the education of women had been grossly neglected in the past, but they refused to discuss whether women should enter the professions or politics or other male domains as a matter of right. "We claim only for her, as a woman, that she has a right to perfect her nature—to cultivate and ennoble all her God-given faculties." There are differences in "the relative mental capacity of the two sexes," they said, but these were not sufficient to require a different curriculum. Whatever their rights in other domains, women did clearly have a right to an equal education, and that meant the same education: "Governments have no right to make a difference between the sexes in making provision for their education. . . . for purposes of development and discipline the same studies should be pursued and to the same extent."[45]

Wickersham and Thompson asserted that both experience and theory justified coeducation. They observed that mixed schools were almost universal in the countryside and that about half of the secondary schools were coeducational. They knew of no instance in which a school district had changed from mixed to separate schools, "while changes to [coeducation] are constantly occurring." Educators were coming to agree, Wickersham and Thompson wrote, that coeducation "renders school government more easy, acts as a stimulus to study, facilitates the introduction of graded schools, causes more refined feeling and a more healthy moral influence to pervade the school, [and] enables the sexes to form a more just estimate of each other."[46]

One argument against coeducation rapidly evaporated: the notion that girls were not so smart as boys. Once girls had actually been admitted to coeducational classrooms, they did at least as well as boys, and often better. In 1852 in Dedham, Massachusetts, the school committee complained that in one school "girls of ten years old are advanced well in their studies, and boys of sixteen years old are advanced but little beyond the alphabet." In the same year in West Cambridge the school trustees urged the boys to "show a little more energy in their recitations and ambition to keep up with the female portion. The misses have rather taken the lead here. We have no objection to this; for we believe that females should have as much school education as males, but we should be pleased to see a little more spirit and energy among the boys. One reason why this difference to such a degree exists here, is that many of the lads are employed at home during the summer months, and attend only in the winter."[47]

Urban educators developed elaborate examinations to rank students and promote them from grade to grade. They rarely published the results of these by sex in the lower grades, but when they did, girls generally did better than boys. In Washington, D.C., in the 1870s girls tested notably better than boys in English grammar and spelling and about the same in arithmetic (one year doing worse; the next, better). Because nineteenth-century Americans assumed mathematics to be a male preserve, the subject was thought to be a major obstacle for girls, but several reports indicate otherwise. The principal of the coeducational Woodward High School of Cincinnati wrote in 1859 that visitors often asked if "the girls equal the boys in the severer branches, such as Geometry." The answer was clear, he said: on the mathematics exam the eight girls averaged "86 [and] 37/176 per cent., whilst that of the ten boys was 85 [and] 21/23 per cent." How could one contest such exactitude? His message: "Similar advantages give similar results."[48] In 1873 New York City educators reported the percentages of girls and boys earning excellent or good marks in reading, writing, and arithmetic in grammar schools listed in table 6.

In his reports for the St. Louis schools in 1869–70 and 1872–73, Superintendent William T. Harris wrote the classic summary of arguments for coeducation—one that recapitulated the earlier discussion and became the most widely quoted and influential rationale thereafter. When Harris

Table 6

Proficiency of Boys and Girls in New York City Grammar Schools, 1873

	Reading		Writing		Arithmetic	
	Excellent* (%)	Good* (%)	Excellent* (%)	Good* (%)	Excellent* (%)	Good* (%)
Boys	21	63	36	51	22	50
Girls	51	46	56	40	27	55

Source: New York City School Board, *Annual Report, 1874,* p. 223.
*Only the grades "excellent" and "good" are given. Two other categories were also listed—"fair" and "indifferent"—and the totals amounted to 100 percent.

republished his report almost four decades later, he wrote in a preface that he had had "no occasion to modify" his views in the meantime. Indeed, his argument became the conventional wisdom on the subject.[49]

Prior to 1858 only the primary schools and high school of St. Louis had been mixed. In 1858 one of the grammar schools became coeducational, with the other grammar schools gradually following suit. Harris, whose experience included both mixed and separate schools, believed that he had an excellent vantage point from which to compare the two systems. Economy and better classification of students had been the intial motives for introducing coeducation in the high schools and for extending the practice to the grammar schools, he wrote, but experience demonstrated other, more important advantages. Coeducation improved the educational process for both sexes.[50]

Discipline and instruction improved as a consequence of mixing the sexes, not because boys and girls were similar, Harris argued, but because of a tempering of their differences. "The rudeness and *abandon* which prevails among boys when separate, at once gives place to self-restraint in the presence of girls. The prurient sentimentality, engendered by educating girls apart from boys,—it is manifested by a frivolous and silly bearing when such girls are brought into the company of the opposite sex—this disappears almost entirely in mixed schools. In its place a quiet self-possession reigns." Likewise, mixing the sexes in the classroom merged boys' and girls' different mental abilities and tastes, resulting in better learning for each. The unbalanced nature of instruction in separate schools shifted in coeducational classrooms as the sexes interacted. "Where the sexes are separate," Harris said, "methods of instruction . . . gravitate continually toward extremes that may be called masculine and feminine. The masculine extreme is mechanical formalizing in its lowest shape, and the merely intellectual training on its highest side. The feminine extreme is the learning-by-rote system on the lower side and the superfluity of sentiment in the higher activities." Only if girls and boys have each "other as a counter-check" will "educational methods attain completeness. . . . More rapid progress is the consequence, and we find girls making wonderful advances even in mathematical studies while boys seem to take hold of literature far better for the influence of the female portion of the class."[51]

Harris also held that the psychological and sexual development of both boys and girls benefited from their association with one another. He turned the argument about the sexual threat of mixed schools on its head: separate schools threatened virtue more than coeducational ones. "The girls confined by themselves develope the sexual tension much earlier, their imagination being the reigning faculty and not bridled by intercourse with society in its normal form. So it is with boys on the other hand." But when boys and girls had the opportunity to "meet on equal terms in academic work—each sex testing its strength against the other on an intellectual plane in the presence of the teacher"—sexual tensions gave place to a "de-sexualized" atmosphere in which "the standard of admiration [shifted] from mere external charms of person to the spiritual graces and gifts which lie deep in the character." Any "tendency toward indecency" was likely to be checked in coeducational schools by "the crossfire of watchfulness which made intrigue far more difficult to keep secret." Harris believed that when "the brothers and sisters and other relatives and intimate acquaintances of the pupil attended the same school, and every act was scanned from two points of view—the boys being participant in boys' gossip, and the girls being participant in girls' gossip, and the barriers being removed within the precinct of the family, parents could not fail to have a more faithful account of their children than when isolated in different schools." As a result, "brothers and sisters mutually protect each other from shame."[52]

Harris went well beyond the bureaucratic justification of coeducation on grounds of economy and institutional convenience to insist that pedagogically and morally it was best to teach boys and girls together. In 1882, city school superintendents' responses to a survey by the U.S. Bureau of Education indicated that a large proportion of his peers agreed. Of the officials who explained why they had adopted mixed schools, fifty stated the practice was "beneficial," adding such comments as, "The result is a more harmonious development of both sexes." Only fourteen replied that either economy or convenience was the chief motive. Seventy claimed it was "natural" or "customary," suggesting that coeducation had simply become an unquestioned norm. Many of the replies mixed these arguments. But only five "gave justice to both sexes as the prime reason for coeducation." Again, most educators did not advocate "identical coeducation" as a means of opening opportunities to women in all domains of life after they left school.[53]

The National Council of Education was an elite group of school leaders within the National Education Association. Its function was to decide complex policy questions. In 1890 the members heard their Committee on the Education of Girls render a verdict on coeducation in public schools. Despite the opinions of a few conservative dissenters, mostly from the big cities, both theory and practice confirmed the wisdom of coeducation, said the committee. William T. Harris had shown the advantages of mixed schools "in such a masterly way as to attract the thoughtful attention of educators not only in our own country, but in Europe as well." Coeducation led to better discipline, more balanced instruction, and a healthier psychological and sexual development of both boys and girls. Women had proved themselves equal to men in intellectual capacity, and the apocalyptic fears that study would undermine their health had been shown to be "groundless."[54]

The notion that studying the same subjects together would make women mannish and coarse and men less strong and courageous, said the committee, "will soon be numbered among the infinite host of dead theories that lie strewn all along the path of human progress. There seems to be no natural antagonism between strength and refinement, or between vigor and delicacy." Through their complementary abilities and qualities, boys and girls would improve each other's characters and minds. Accordingly, "the course of study for the sexes should, in all grades of schools, be identical." The committee concluded, "The question of coeducation in every grade of schools in this country, in its practical aspect, is settled." Although "individuals may deny the soundness of the theory, . . . the public mind is made up, and it is not likely to be shaken in its convictions."[55]

A year later, the U.S. Office of Education did a survey of coeducation that corroborated the committee's view that the question was more or less settled in practice in American schools. The superintendents of forty states and four territories answered the questionnaire. Twenty-eight states and three territories reported that all their public schools were coeducational,

In 1899 a superb professional photographer, Frances Benjamin Johnston, took hundreds of pictures of pupils in the schools of Washington, D.C., to illustrate the "new education" (or what became called "progressive education") as part of the United States exhibit at the Paris Exposition of 1900. The posed pictures gave a vivid, idealized vision of one major school system. More important for our purpose, they open a window unobtrusively on common gender practices in the capital, for illustrating gender differences and similarities was not part of Johnston's agenda. (The photographs are deposited in the Library of Congress.)

In a sex-separate class, boys learn woodworking from a male teacher in a shop for manual training.

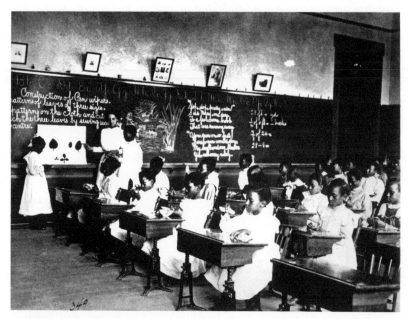

A woman teacher shows black girls
how to sew pen-wipers.

Primary school children confront
tortoises at the zoo in a field trip
supervised by their teacher. Girls
and boys are mixed together.

Pupils learn about Indians through examining artifacts. Seated boys and girls are separated by row but are more clustered by sex near the exhibit and the teacher.

The teacher watches students carry out a project to measure and record the dimensions of the sidewalk. Boys and girls hold the same tapes and both record the results in notebooks.

In this class, mapping their measurements and studying a plan of the city streets, a girl and boy cooperate in locating the school on the map. The sexes are mixed within as well as between rows of seats.

Boys and girls gather together around a sand table in this project in physical geography.

As the teacher dissects a heart, children of both sexes gather about the table to watch.

In this portrait of a more traditional class, with children holding their hands in their laps, the seating is sex-mixed but the boys tend to cluster more at the back of the classroom.

On a field trip to the art museum, there is more opportunity for children to mix with their same-sex friends (note the two girls at the right holding hands and the boy in the center putting his hand on the shoulder of his pal).

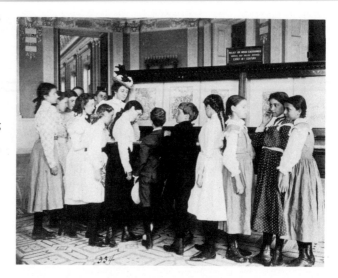

except for two cities that had some separate schools. The remainder practiced coeducation except in a limited number of schools in certain city and town districts. Replies from superintendents from 628 cities, including almost all the largest urban areas, indicated that only 41 had any single-sex schools, and in only 13 of these were all grades separated by sex. The cities practicing sexual segregation were in seventeen states, eleven of them in the South; the others were chiefly in the Northeast. As in the 1883 survey, administrators declared themselves overwhelmingly in favor of coeducation.[56]

Coeducation and Life after Schooling

In the early 1890s most public-school leaders, like those in the National Council of Education, took it for granted that public schools should be coeducational and that the curriculum should be substantially the same for both sexes. In these discussions, the advocates of coeducation sometimes came close to suggesting that the common school might become a utopian island in which differences of gender might be ignored, however firmly they determined opportunity in the larger society.

This did not mean, however, that these educators thought of coeducation as the portal into full rights for adult women. When they referred at all to "woman's rights," male educators generally rejected the notion that women should enter man's sphere or said they preferred to talk only of women's educational rights. Thomas H. Burrowes, for example, argued for identical coeducational education for both sexes and said that "the theory of our social institutions is that of general equality amongst all the members of society." He deplored, however, the "extremism" of those who demand that woman should be prepared "for all the duties of the opposite sex" and who assert "that it is her right to assume and discharge those duties in life." Even those educators who compared the present opportunities of women favorably to an earlier "savage" state of society and called for equal education generally assumed that women should use their training in traditional domains, for instance, as teachers of the young in families and schools.[57]

The discussion of coeducation and its effects on adult life was not limited to the circles of American professional educators, however. Some of these other voices were more conservative or more radical than those of mainstream educational leaders. One attack on coeducation came from an influential physician who declared that coeducation—and indeed, any form of serious mental work for girls during adolescence—was dangerous because it endangered the most important adult function of women, motherhood. In the 1870s, Dr. Edward H. Clarke insisted that girls who competed with boys in coeducational schools were losing their health because adolescence was a period when their reproductive organs, not study, should absorb their vital energies. Clarke's key tract went through eleven editions and had an impact on public opinion, as we will show in chapter 6.[58]

Other conservative opponents of coeducation resorted to theological arguments and ridicule. They feared that coeducation might blur the God-ordained differences between the sexes; it led in their imagination to an absurd adult sameness. Coeducation was based on false premises, wrote three critics in Pennsylvania. "God has made the sexes unlike; why seek to change them?" they asked. "Coeducation would re-form their minds, without reference to the inherent difference of their natures. It would attempt to mould in the same pattern, materials not only different in kind, but intended for different uses. The attempt would be useless, impious, and injurious to both."[59]

While claiming they supported the education of women in and for their sphere, the conservatives attacked and ridiculed leaders in the women's rights movement, whom they saw as "strong-minded persons, who vainly try to subvert the laws of creation." Imagine, they wrote, a coeducational Yale. Here pass flush-cheeked young men and women smoking cigars. There, on the playing field, are football players of both sexes, the women wearing "Bloomer dress." Under an elm sits a quiet group: "Ah! 'tis only a kind-hearted Bloomer, instructing a few of her male friends in the art and mystery of dressing a doll."[60]

Advocates of woman's rights were undeterred in their quest for coeducation by such religious attacks and caricature. They wanted girls to be educated with boys for reasons that went well beyond better pedagogy, greater economy, or more precise bureaucratic classification—the usual arguments advanced by school leaders. They believed that separate schooling would rarely be equal, given the male bias of those who controlled school systems. Mixed schools would allow the sexes to know and respect one another and would ensure an equality of funding and instruction rarely available in girls' schools, especially at the secondary level, either in public high schools or female seminaries. Caroline H. Dall argued that women "will never be thoroughly taught until they are taught at the same time and in the same classes [as men]"—in effect with boys as hostages to make sure that the facilities and curriculum were equal. Feminists focused especially on higher education—the Seneca Falls Declaration of 1848 had declared that man "has denied [woman] the facilities for obtaining a thorough education, all colleges being closed against her"—but also pressed for coeducation in public schools.[61]

Leaders in the woman's movement claimed that equal schooling should not simply lead women back to the home but should open to them any occupations and activities available to men. Coeducational schools should equip young women to work in a variety of jobs, to participate politically, and to become the equals of males in all respects. Dall wrote that man's right to an education gave him "the right to a choice of vocation." If the logic of that was correct, then the same should apply to woman: for her, too, "the moment society conceded the right to education," it conceded the right to use her educated abilities in any domain she chose. How could man give identical coeducation to both sexes, and then, in the language of the Seneca Declaration, monopolize "nearly all the profitable employments"? Women teachers like Susan B. Anthony raised these questions in educational organizations, eloquent speakers like Elizabeth Cady Stanton gave speeches on coeducation across the nation, and writers like Dall sought to use equal and mixed education as an argument for opening a full range of opportunity to women.[62]

Foreign visitors to the United States were often astonished to find boys and girls—even in their adolescent years—studying together in school. Here was a nation that had no established church, no nobility, no standing army—and little gender segregation in public education below the college level. They sometimes wondered if educational opportunities for young women—far greater than those found in Europe—translated into a challenge to gender distinctions in the broader society and adult life. These foreigners' reactions made some Americans self-conscious and occasionally defensive about why they were coeducating youth. The American influence was also felt on the other side of the Atlantic: European proponents and opponents of mixed schools, both of whom tended to be more vocal about the issue than Americans, drew on their impressions of U.S. schools to support their arguments.[63]

Some foreign commentators (upper-class Englishmen, in particular) feared that coeducation would feminize the boys or overstress conscientious girls or simply stir up sexual desire. A French educator, Marie Dugard, was amazed at the "sight of youths of 16 to 18 years, almost men, working, chatting, and enjoying daily comradeship with young ladies. . . . [It] confounds all [a Frenchman's] ideas. He is astonished that such an ideal should have sprung up in the healthy American mind, and he does not dare to think of the results, so opposed do they seem to his moral sense." Even foreign observers who approved of coeducation and educational equality for girls often expressed surprise. Visiting the Hartford High School in the 1840s, a Swedish commentator, Per Siljestrom, wrote that the school "presents the strange spectacle (strange as regards our habits and ideas) of girls and boys of the ages of 15 and 16, assembled in a common school-room under the guidance of female as well as male teachers."[64]

The voices of foreign observers, feminists and their foes, and medical men like Clarke stirred debate in the United States over coeducation in the latter half of the nineteenth century, but it was not until the Progressive Era and the rekindling of interest in differentiation by sex among professional educators that the practice of coeducation would be seriously challenged in the schools, especially in secondary education. The optimistic view of the National Council of Education in 1890 that the issue of "identical coeducation" was settled was to prove premature.

5

The Rising Tide
of Coeducation in the
High School

Many of the pioneers in creating public high schools believed that the sexes should be educated separately, and in the early years often regarded public secondary education for girls as an experiment. Most early advocates of the high school could not foresee, and probably would not have approved of, what actually happened. In the last three decades of the nineteenth century four facts were becoming clear:

1. Public secondary education was overwhelmingly coeducational. In an 1882 survey, only 19 of 196 cities reported that they had separate-sex high schools. By the end of the century, only 12 cities out of 628 reported that they had single-sex high schools.[1]

2. With few exceptions, girls and boys studied the same subjects. The curriculum was not significantly differentiated by gender.[2]

3. Girls at least equalled and often outperformed boys in their academic studies.[3]

4. Girls substantially outnumbered boys as both students and graduates of high schools, accounting for 57 percent of the students and 65 percent of the graduates in 1890. In 1889 the U.S. commissioner of education estimated that only about one-quarter of the students in the high schools of the ten biggest cities were boys.[4]

114

Trying to understand why high schools developed such gender patterns is like fitting together pieces of a complicated jigsaw puzzle.

An important part of the story is the institutional character of public high schools. The early history of the high school is still obscure, though conservatives relish nostalgic images of a golden age, with dignified temples of learning in which the teachers were scholars, the pupils were studiously preparing for college, the academic mission of the institution was simple and strong, and the public was well satisfied with its creation. There were a few privileged high schools that achieved this ideal, but, as a whole, public secondary education during the nineteenth century was diverse, controversial, and ambiguously connected with the larger society.[5]

Urban educators developed bureaucratic visions of high schools as the capstone of a meritocratic and unified urban school system. They expected a competitive high-school entrance examination to pressure elementary-school administrators to standardize their curricula and to stimulate the ambitions and industry of talented students. They hoped that the high school would rival in quality the best private academies so that prosperous parents would enroll their children, but thought it should also be the people's college, a place where the children of janitors were welcome, too.

Despite hopeful rhetoric, most high schools were small and short of funds and hence had tiny faculties and limited curricula. Few young people attended them, and these were disproportionately from middle-class families. A high percentage of students, particularly boys, dropped out.

One reason for the shortage of students was the lack of a demonstrated connection between high-school studies and later life. Only a small proportion of public-high-school students were preparing for college. Although educators considered high-school attendance a reward for diligent work in the lower grades, boys often regarded secondary education as irrelevant to their futures, for they could obtain a variety of white-collar jobs without going to high school. The situation was different for girls. They had few opportunities to do nonmanual work. The late-nineteenth-century high school enrolled mostly native-born and middle-class students and thus seemed a safe haven for the proper urban girl, a place to spend one's adolescent years preparing to be a better wife and mother. In addition, the high school was a gateway for many young women into teaching careers, one of the few white-collar jobs open to women at the time.

Educators had good organizational reasons to adopt coeducation in high schools. In most cities, the elementary schools were coeducational, and mixing the sexes in the high schools maintained the symmetry and uniformity of the system. Girls performed better than boys in the lower grades, and it would have been a denial of meritocratic principles to forbid their admission to secondary schools. Besides, the number of students in high school were so paltry that creating separate-sex secondary schools would have been prohibitively expensive. Indeed, one might argue that in most places high schools could not have been justified economically if girls had not populated the classrooms.

The inclusion of girls in coeducational high schools, then, might be explained as the logical product of ideology (republican equality and preparation for the female sphere), economy (the financial necessity of coeducation in small schools), and organizational development (the high school as the upward extension of a coeducational bureaucracy). But this would be too neat. Because high schools were contested ground in politics, the path of their development was not straight and logical but winding and shaped by conflicting public opinions. In a series of case studies of the creation of secondary schools in diverse cities we trace this winding path, looking first at school districts that chose to educate girls in separate high schools and then at the movement toward coeducation.

There were King Canutes who commanded the tide of coeducation in the high school to stop, but they were ineffectual. European critics aimed volleys against coeducation, but apart from eliciting explanations of the practice from officials like the U.S. commissioner of education, the attacks had little effect. For a variety of reasons, school people found coeducation not only institutionally expedient but pedagogically desirable in high schools as in the primary and grammar grades. For their part, leaders in the woman's movement applauded coeducation in secondary schools and colleges, for they saw mixed schools as a necessary step toward the emancipation of women. They recognized that American coeducational high schools gave large numbers of girls access to secondary schooling far beyond that available in any European nation, where secondary education for girls was usually separate and vastly inferior to that of boys.[6]

M. Carey Thomas, president of Bryn Mawr College, argued that "only by having the schools and universities coeducational can we assure the girls of the world of receiving a thoroughly good education. There is not enough money in the world to duplicate schools and universities for women, and if we could duplicate them, they would soon become less good." It had been "a fortunate circumstance" for girls, she wrote, that the United States in the nineteenth century "was . . . sparsely settled; in most neighborhoods it was so difficult to establish and secure pupils for even one . . . high school that girls were admitted from the first." And equally fortunate, she said, was the fact that women secured positions as teachers in high schools, for their presence strengthened the claim of girls to coeducation.[7]

A Diverse and Controversial Institution

In contrast with the one-room rural school and the urban graded elementary school, which were fairly well defined, from its origins in 1820 throughout the nineteenth century the public high school was an institution in search of identity and coherent purpose. In some communities the high school was simply a room in a grammar school where older scholars might pursue the elementary curriculum at a somewhat more advanced level. Such an institution was essentially an extension of the grades beneath it, an upward projection of the common school. In some of the larger cities, by contrast, the high school was housed in a palatial building that symbolized its separate and elite status, offered a rigorous classical curriculum, and sought to distinguish itself from the grammar school. Most high schools probably fell somewhere between these two extremes.

Public high schools appeared almost exclusively in cities and larger towns, for people in the countryside lacked the concentrated population and tax base necessary to sustain secondary schools. Although urban elementary schools mushroomed, high schools grew only slowly. In 1873 a survey of high schools in 536 cities showed that on average only 4 percent of all pupils in those cities were enrolled in high schools, with a range of 2 to 6 percent. Except in a few of the largest cities, high schools were small; the average urban high school in 1873 had only eighty-five pupils and three teachers. High schools prepared few graduates for either college or specific vocations, except for teaching, although there is some evidence that employers did use high-school attendance as a sorting strategy in hiring boys. Attrition was very high. Students, especially males, opted out or dropped out in droves; probably over two-thirds of them did not graduate.[8]

Public high schools were controversial from their very beginning and throughout their development, in part because their constituencies and purposes were multiform. Even their advocates had different visions. Some used the traditional republican rhetoric: high schools would train virtuous citizens and principled leaders. Others regarded high schools as an upward extension of the public school system that would prepare students for white-collar employment. Still other high-school promoters wanted to attract the children of the wealthy and thereby gain support for public as opposed to private schooling.[9]

Many urban school superintendents saw high schools as meritocratic institutions. They developed competitive examinations for entrance into the high school that served as a template for the grammar-school curriculum. Grammar-school masters felt pressure to teach to the test since the examination results were often listed by school. In Chicago a newspaper called this entrance exam a form of academic "Olympic games." High-school promoters often argued that this competition for entrance motivated grammar pupils to excel, making the whole system more efficient. In most large cities educators added "normal departments" to high schools in order to train young women to teach the standardized curriculum in the approved manner, thereby further bureaucratizing the whole system.[10]

College officials had their own vision of an effective high school: one that would effectively prepare students to meet the requirements for admission to higher education. In the Midwest, state universities took the lead in accrediting high schools and shaping their curriculum to assure a steady flow of qualified students. Disenchanted with the hodgepodge of secondary-school curricula, Harvard's Charles William Eliot called the high school the "gap" between the elementary schools and the colleges and worked to upgrade precollegiate instruction.[11]

The opponents of the high school were even more diverse than the proponents. Issues of social class often arose. Working-class critics of the high school complained that it attracted chiefly the children of the prosperous and thus was an elitist institution. Studies of the social origins of high-school students do show high proportions of middle-class students— typically two-thirds or more—and relatively few from the working class. David Labaree, for example, has found that in Philadelphia students from middle-class backgrounds "outnumbered the working class at the high school by a ratio of two to one, [although] in the city as a whole workers outnumbered the middle class by a margin of three to one." Sensitive to the criticism that high schools were elitist, educators broadcast stories of friendships between working-class students and children of the wealthy in the high schools. A principal in Newburyport, Massachusetts, wrote about two girls walking "with their arms closely entwined about each others' necks. . . . [one was] a daughter of one of our first merchants, the other has a father worse than none, who obtains a livelihood from one of the lowest and most questionable occupations, and is himself most degraded." In Boston the principal of the boys' high school declared that "some of our best scholars are sons of coopers, lamplighters, and day laborers."[12]

Critics of the high school asked why taxpayers should subsidize the teaching of subjects like Latin and French. Sometimes citizens challenged in the courts the legality of instructing pupils in subjects beyond the common-school curriculum, as in Michigan's Kalamazoo case of 1874. In revising the California Constitution in 1879, the Workingmen's Party in California tried "to exclude high schools from the school system of the State" and to discourage their growth. The Oakland high-school principal fought the Workingmen's notion that "free schools should instruct in the elements only, and that anything further should be left to private enterprise." The rapid development of the economy demanded that youth be trained in advanced subjects, he argued, and, in turn, these "changes in our relations to the material world have rendered our social and civil relations more complex. . . . Permit the coming generations to grow up in ignorance of all those principles which underlie good government . . . and [workingmen's protest] will be the muttering thunder which precedes the tempest."[13]

In some communities opposition came not from those on the bottom of the social structure but from those on top, the rich. They claimed that the high school gave unfair competition to private schools by providing free secondary education and argued that high schools spoiled workers. A conservative newspaper editor in Portland, Oregon, remarked in 1879 that the high school graduated "whole regiments of sickly sentimentalists: young gentlemen unused and unfit for work." School leaders countered by showing that graduates did go on to work, college, or useful lives as wives and mothers. The Oakland principal reported that at a meeting of the alumni of the high school in 1880 no graduate could be found who was "an example of the so-called pernicious effects of over-education."[14]

Countering the claim that the public high school invigorated and unified the common school, some critics objected that it diverted funds away from the elementary schools and brought an undesirable centralization. Especially in times of retrenchment—in the periodic panics of the nineteenth century—the high school struck many people as a costly luxury. In addition to the expense of the public high school, other critics objected to the grand plans of the professional educators. As Carl Kaestle has shown, much of the educational politics of the nineteenth century was a contest between localists and centralizers, between those who wished to retain local control and those who wished to create unified systems. As a symbol and instrument of centralization, the high school became a lightning rod for those who opposed the bureaucratization of the schools.[15]

Given such controversy, it is perhaps surprising that the high school took hold as firmly as it did in the nineteenth century. It is possible, however, that the very ambiguity of the high school's purpose and constituency may have shielded it. By claiming that the high school might be all things to all people, its advocates blunted attacks and coopted the uncommitted.

Conflict over gender policies occurred in some communities, but in general these were less potent sources of controversy than the charge of class bias. The high school was originally designed for boys and indeed was regarded by some observers as a distinctly masculine institution, yet girls became model students who outperformed boys in a system that prided itself on being meritocratic. In a period when citizens strenuously maintained separate ideological and practical spheres for men and women, both sexes learned a similar curriculum. Many foreign observers of American high schools regarded coeducation and the predominance of female students as the most distinctive—and disturbing—features of American secondary education. Relatively few nineteenth-century Americans, however, worried about the implications of the number and performance of female high-school students for a society which decreed separate and unequal opportunities for the sexes in adult life.[16]

At the time of the origin of the high school, it was by no means clear, however, that coeducation would become the standard gender practice. Americans had more qualms about mixing teenage boys and girls than about educating younger children together. But by the early 1870s about nine out of ten public high schools were coeducational. In the modal high school at that time, teachers were about equally divided between men and women. Although some policymakers called for differentiation of high-school studies by gender, they failed to have much impact until the twentieth century.[17]

Although the term *coeducational public high school* came to designate a particular type of institution after the Civil War, each word in the phrase was ambiguous in the antebellum period. A separate school was straightforward enough: it meant that only one sex attended classes in a school building. Prior to the 1820s, girls had been excluded from the sole form of public secondary education, the old Latin grammar schools. The first high schools open to girls were generally segregated by sex. Only a relatively few cities, however, chose to educate girls in separate buildings. A more common practice was to house both boys and girls in the same building but to separate them on different floors or in different "departments." Even when separate boys' and girls' departments were abandoned—in part because it was so expensive to teach small numbers of boys and girls in separate classes—the sexes were often segregated in study halls, required to use separate entrances, cloakrooms, and playgrounds, and allowed to mix only when reciting in academic classes. In some cases, certain courses of study were open to only one sex—for example, the normal (or teacher-training) program for girls and the classical course that prepared boys for admission to college. But as fears about the consequences of coeducating adolescent boys and girls faded, girls and boys generally studied the same subjects side by side in their regular classes in high schools, just as in primary and grammar schools. This came to be the generally understood meaning of *coeducation*.[18]

Like the word *coeducational*, the term *public* carried many meanings in education in the first half of the nineteenth century. Eventually it would designate a school that was free, supported by taxation, and controlled by clearly designated public authorities (usually a mix of state and local). Until the 1880s, however, the majority of secondary schools could not be described as public using these criteria. These "private" schools usually had self-perpetuating boards of trustees, charged tuition, recruited and selected students from a geographical area wider than the public school districts, and operated under charters that gave them authority as private corporations invested with the public interest. They far outnumbered public high schools. In Ohio, for example, there were ninety-three academies chartered before 1850, thirty-two seminaries, thirty institutes, and fourteen private high schools; only nine school districts had received legislative mandates to found public high schools. In some parts of the country, states gave private academies public funds. In New York the state subsidized the education of students preparing to become teachers, while in Illinois academies received funds from federal land grants. The charters of some academies specified that the trustees should be elected by the voters of the towns where they were located. As the public-high-school movement gained momentum, many towns simply incorporated academies into the public school system as high schools. Even in public high schools students often paid tuition, private benefactors provided endowments, and admission was highly selective, based on stiff entrance tests.[19]

Similarly, the name *high school* was ambiguous. The universe of secondary education, of which public high schools formed a part, included a variety of institutions, whose diversity is reflected in the multiplicity of names given to secondary schools: academy, classical school, English school, institute, grammar school, union school, college, select school, seminary, boarding school, graded school, and many permutations of these and other titles. The educational specialist of the U.S. Census complained as late as 1893 that the term "high school" designated a multitude of types of institutions and levels of instruction. Some high schools in the larger cities were elite academic institutions that competed with the best private academies, while in Tennessee a "high school" was defined by law as grades six, seven, and eight of the common school.[20]

Because of scanty records and the ambiguity of the term "public high school," it is impossible to determine the exact number of high schools during the nineteenth century. One can only guess how many high schools existed before the Civil War; one reasonable estimate is that there were 321 high schools founded before the Civil War, over half of them in Massachusetts, New York, and Ohio. After the establishment of the U.S. Office of Education in 1868, federal officials tried to remedy the lack of statistics by collecting data from state and local officers. But their work, and that of the U.S. Census, produced conflicting results. The 1870 census counted 1,026 high schools in thirty-two states. In 1873 the U.S. commissioner of education reported 536 urban high schools in one table, but in another table summarizing the results of his survey of all "secondary schools," public and private, he listed 944 institutions, only 136 of which we estimate to be public high schools (75 of these were in the North Atlantic states and 13 in the North Central).[21]

People disagreed about whether the high school was growing from the top down—modeled on colleges or elite academies—or from the bottom up from the common school. Philadelphia's Central High School was a prime example of the munificently equipped large urban high school: it had an elegant blue marble facade, an Ionic portico, and an expensive astronomical observatory. By contrast, in many communities the high school was often just another classroom in a graded union school, where a small number of students studied the advanced common-school subjects under the guidance of a single teacher. The superintendent of schools in Washington, D.C., argued that the city needed a high school because in the grammar schools there were many pupils already studying advanced subjects: "There is a small, incipient High School, in some cases of quite vigorous growth, protruding from the top of each of our Grammar Schools." As late as the 1890s, only 9 of the 59 high schools in Connecticut had their own building, and only 38 of the 258 in Illinois, yet these were relatively advanced states. The costs per pupil of secondary education varied greatly by locality, but generally they were considerably higher than those of the graded elementary schools, largely because the teachers' salaries were higher and the pupil-teacher ratios smaller than in the lower grades.[22]

Although high schools were a hodgepodge, some educational leaders sought to articulate a common definition of the high school and a vision of its potential. Henry Barnard was one of the earliest and most influential of these advocates. In his 1848 report as superintendent of the Rhode Island schools, he described a high school as "a public or common school for the older and more advanced scholars of the community . . . [with] a course of instruction adapted to their age, and intellectual and moral wants, and, to some extent, to their future pursuits in life." He continued: "It would be a mockery of the idea of such a school . . . if the course of instruction pursued is not higher and better than can be got in public schools of a lower grade; or if it does not meet the needs of the wealthiest and best educated families, or, if the course of instruction is liberal, and at the same time the worthy and talented child of a poor family is shut out from its privileges by a high rate of tuition." Barnard walked a fine line: the high school was to be an academically elite school fit for the first families, but it was not to be restricted by social class.[23]

To justify public support through taxation, "the advantages of such a school must accrue to the whole community," he wrote. The public high school would make the lower grades more efficient by removing advanced scholars who required extra time and attention from teachers and by rewarding the hard work of talented students who wished to continue their education. The high school was not for all: it was to be a meritocratic institution with strict entrance examinations and academic standards. Its influence would reach down into the lower schools by forcing the standardization of the curriculum and offering an opportunity for the ambitious. A well-ordered high school, said Barnard, would not only attract the wealthy away from private schools but would place "the privileges of a good school . . . within the reach of all classes of the community, and will actually be enjoyed by children of the same age from families of the most diverse circumstances as to wealth, education, and occupation."[24]

The school should teach boys subjects directly useful in later life in a wide array of occupations, such as "navigation, book-keeping, surveying, botany, chemistry, and kindred studies, which are connected with success in the varied departments of domestic and inland trade, with foreign commerce, with gardening, agriculture, the manufacturing and domestic arts." But Barnard also wanted pupils to learn "astronomy, physiology, the history of our own state and nation, the principles of our state and national constitutions, political economy, and moral science." The result would be "such a course of study as . . . shall prepare every young man . . . for business or college."[25]

The high school, in Barnard's eyes, was not for boys alone. It would be open to girls as well but would prepare them for a much narrower sphere. Barnard argued that "the great influence of the female sex, as daughters, sisters, wives, mothers, companions, and teachers, in determining the manners, morals, and intelligence of the whole community, leaves no room to question the necessity of providing for the girls the best means of intellectual and moral culture." In their rationale for secondary education for girls, Barnard and other advocates of coeducational public high schools borrowed freely from Beecher and Willard.[26]

In the plans of Barnard and his fellow reformers, the urban high school occupied a pivotal position in relation both to other educational agencies and other school-related institutions. They believed that the high school should unify the lower schools and motivate students to work harder and continue their education. As a citywide institution, the high school would link together isolated districts, Barnard claimed, and lessen the "estrangements which now divide and subdivide the community." Because it trained some students in subjects required for college admission, the high school also connected city systems to higher education. By educating boys in skills useful in white-collar jobs, high schools were connected with the labor market. And secondary education offered girls from the urban middle class a place to spend their teenage years productively preparing for marriage and motherhood, thus reinforcing the family and the traditional female sphere in the home.[27]

Despite the blueprints of educators like Barnard, who sought to create institutional coherence in the high school and win broad support for public secondary education, in practice high schools remained contested terrain, ambiguous in purpose and diverse in character. To analyze the politics of gender policies and practices in the high school, we look at some cities that segregated by sex and some that chose the path of coeducation.

Separate-Sex High Schools

Most scholars agree that Boston created the first public high school. It was for boys only. Called the English Classical School when founded in 1821, the institution was renamed the English High School when it moved into its new quarters in 1824. For almost two centuries the Boston Latin School had prepared boys for college, but in 1820 a group of prominent citizens decided that another kind of school was necessary, one that could "furnish the young men who are not intended for a collegiate course of studies, and who have enjoyed the usual advantages of the public schools, with the means of completing a good English education to fit them for active life or qualify them for eminence in private or public station." Such a school, advocates claimed, would round out the system by providing boys with the kind of practical training they could at that time obtain only in academies. A subcommittee of the school board composed of "men well known as among the most eminent of the Town, and representing the mercantile, clerical, legal and the journalist professions" recommended the creation of the school, which offered a three-year course of studies. In the first year pupils studied arithmetic, geography, history, English, and bookkeeping; in the second year, those subjects, plus algebra, geometry, natural philosophy (or science), and "natural theology"; and in the third, most of those subjects together with practical applications of mathematics, including navigation, surveying, and "astronomical calculations."[28]

Although the boys' high school was housed in an expensive three-story building and had a large, well-paid staff—costing what was for the time an exorbitant $31 per pupil—it failed to attract many students. No more than 90 boys applied for admission in any year from 1822 to 1828. Seventeen years after the school was founded, the entire enrollment was only 104. In addition, the attrition rate was very high; few boys continued to the third year, when the practical applications of mathematics were studied. From a beginning class of 65 in 1822, only 3 graduated, and the largest number to complete the three-year course of studies until 1828 was 17.[29]

Why did so few boys enter the high school and so many leave before completing the course of studies? Some of the boys, no doubt, left because they were unable to meet the academic standards of the school (in Philadelphia's Central High School the best predictor of graduation was the grades the boys earned). But it seems clear that a large proportion of the school leavers in Boston were not pushed out and did not drop out but left to go to work, whether of their own volition or as a family decision. The Boston school board explained high attrition in the boys' high school in this manner: "The parents of scholars are able to find places to put them out as apprentices, or in counting houses." They may thus be seen as "opt-outs" rather than "push-outs" or "drop-outs." The subcommittee did not consider the low demand or high attrition rate a sign of failure on the part of the school, for it declared that the "High School for boys . . . in every respect has been successful and popular."[30]

If there were relatively few applicants and high attrition, and if the major goal of students was to secure a good starting job, why did boys attend the school at all, and why was the community willing to support such an expensive institution? The observations of the Providence school committee on Boston's high school offer clues to this puzzle. They pointed out that admission to the high school was a "reward of merit" given only to the "most deserving scholars of each Grammar School." Those who showed the most "diligence and good conduct" (note that academic achievement was regarded largely as the product of character, not intelligence) then went on to the high school—and left in droves! The Providence committee did not see this as an anomaly but as a proof of the value of the school "both to the community and the individual." Their report for 1828 states: "Sixty or eighty boys enter it annually, but such is the demand for clerks from this school, though in such a city there are always abundant applications for such situations, that in no case did a greater number than eight or ten complete the whole course." In other words, the chief function of the high school was not so much to teach knowledge needed on the job but to sort out those who displayed "diligence and good conduct." Admission to the high school signaled to employers in a large and somewhat anonymous labor market that these boys were meritorious; merely being selected for the high school gave boys an edge in securing the best jobs in a competitive labor market. Their "credential" was thus more their character than their knowledge, and admission to the high school was their certificate of diligence and good conduct.[31]

The fate of Boston's High School for Girls, which opened in 1826, was far different from the one for boys. From the start, secondary education for girls in Boston was considered a tenuous "experiment," and it "failed" by becoming too popular among the girls and their parents. In 1825 a Unitarian minister and advocate of education for girls, John Pierpont, urged the Boston school committee to create a high school for girls, arguing that women's influence as mothers and wives justified their receiving an education "if not equal, at least bearing a near and an honorable relation, to that of men." He claimed that the "more sprightly girls" in the upper grades of the grammar schools were "in danger of falling into habits of mental dissipation." The school would not cost much, he said, and would repay the investment by training teachers for the primary schools.[32]

Pierpont's proposal passed the school committee unanimously and aroused no public dissent. It was especially popular with parents of girls, many of whom had previously paid for private schooling. On the day of the entrance examination 286 candidates sat for the test, far more than the 120 the school committee had predicted. It decided to raise the minimum age and standards so that only 133 could enter the school. In an effort to economize, the committee hired only one teacher—Ebenezer Bailey, a talented Yale graduate—at a salary 25 percent less than that paid to the masters in the Latin school and boys' high school, even though he was responsible for three times as many recitations. Bailey was expected to teach all 133 girls in a complex three-year curriculum in crowded temporary quarters. There was no pretense that the separate boys' and girls' schools were equal: the cost per pupil in the two male secondary schools was three times that of the Girls' High School.[33]

In August 1826, a subcommittee of the school committee concluded that the "experiment"—despite all the handicaps under which the students and Bailey labored—had exceeded "the most sanguine expectations." The girls were highly motivated, their attendance was excellent, and they did better on the citywide high-school exams than the boys. No girl indicated that she wished to withdraw. Indeed, the subcommittee estimated that in the next year 427 girls would apply. The mayor, Josiah Quincy, was alarmed at this potential flood of girls into the high school. "Girls are not like boys," he explained, for boys have their minds on "some particular trade or profession" and girls do not. In Quincy's opinion, the school was probably attracting too many middle-class girls whose parents viewed advanced schooling as an attractive way to fill the teenage years of their daughters, though perhaps not their sons', and who were reassured by the "selective" and "exclusive" character of the school that their daughters would associate only with proper classmates (that is, there would not be an unseemly mix of classes and ethnic groups).[34]

The very success of the Girls' High School proved to be its undoing. Robert P. DuFour has shown that the school's chief foe was Quincy. As mayor, Quincy convinced the city to spend millions of dollars widening and cleaning its streets, modernizing its fire department, building a new water system, and erecting the new Quincy Market, but he claimed that providing adequate secondary schooling for all the girls who wanted it would drain Boston's treasury (the first appropriation for the school had been $2,000).[35]

As chair of a subcommittee of the school committee, Quincy outlined his reasons for discontinuing the school. He rejected the argument that "one sex should have the same [educational] advantages as the other." Adolescent boys and girls faced different futures: the boys entered the paid labor force, while the girls had no such opportunities and therefore found attending the school "very attractive." There was no danger of boys' flocking to the male high school. By contrast, Quincy predicted, as many as 1,400 girls might seek to enter the high school, requiring new buildings and an estimated expense of $10,800 annually.[36]

Quincy thus claimed that providing the same educational opportunities to boys and girls would produce quite different results; the girls would benefit more than the boys. To Quincy and a majority of the school committee, such an outcome was unacceptable. They rejected the idea of making the girls' entrance exam tougher, thereby limiting the size of the incoming class. That would only produce ill will in the families of the daughters who failed the test. A meritocratic examination system and a free but exclusive school made sense for boys since they were preparing for "professions and pursuits" where special talents were required. But meritocracy made little sense for girls, whose destinies were far more circumscribed. While the cost of the boys' high school might be justified by the return to the city and the individuals in economic terms, the social benefits from secondary schooling for girls seemed less concrete. It was better to keep the "sprightly" girls in the grammar schools with the other pupils, where they could raise the quality of education for all, and to allow them to continue in the higher branches of education there for an additional year. This argument appealed to male teachers who were unhappy about having their most promising girls leave to go to high school.[37]

The teacher of the Girls' High School, Bailey, and others were dismayed by Quincy's argument. Far from being a failure or impracticable, said Bailey, the school was succeeding on all fronts: it was providing teachers for the primary grades; it was demonstrating the usefulness of the monitorial system whereby the students taught one another; and it was improving the grammar schools by increasing the zeal of the students to do well on the entrance test. The financial argument was false, for the city was quite capable of supporting the school, and the notion of limiting places in the high school to those who passed the examination had been accepted as fair in principle. Bailey asserted that the review of the school and the decision to kill it were "managed" by the hostile mayor. The school committee proved unresponsive to such arguments, however, and the school was closed in 1827 after only two years of operation. It was not until 1852 that Boston would again create a secondary school for girls, one that was limited at first to preparing teachers for the elementary schools.[38]

Beginning in the 1840s and 1850s, a number of other large seaport cities in the North Atlantic and southern states, like Boston, created separate high schools for girls: Portland, Portsmouth, Newburyport, New York, Philadelphia, Baltimore, Charleston, and New Orleans, for example. In almost all these cities the grammar schools were sex-segregated, not coed-ucational. Issues similar to those in Boston were raised in many of these communities. Male school-board members worried about expenses if too many girls wanted to continue their schooling. They questioned whether secondary schools were needed for girls since their sphere was the home. They wondered about how to preserve girls' femininity.

Still, the political pressures from the parents of girls and the advocates of women's education were great enough in these cities to force the school boards to establish separate girls' high schools. As in Boston, the girls' demand for entrance was powerful and their performance impressive. In Philadelphia, where the only high school was for boys, the principal and teachers of the boys' school conducted "Saturday classes" in high-school subjects for the female teachers and older grammar-school girls of the city. The principal was astonished to find that although the classes were held "at the very inconvenient hours from 12 to 2 of Saturday," they were "thronged entirely beyond my ability to give them adequate instruction." In Newburyport, 55 percent of girls graduated from the separate girls' school, in contrast to 20 percent of the boys in a parallel institution.[39]

One way to convince school boards that it was both politic and cost-effective to educate girls in high schools, given their apparently ravenous appetite for schooling, was to recommend preparing girls to teach in the primary grades. School boards argued that the increased pedagogical effi-ciency of the educational system as a whole would justify the expense. In Charleston, Louisville, and New Orleans, the primary purpose of the girls' high schools was training teachers; in Charleston boys paid tuition, where-as girls did not, perhaps because girls were being trained as future school employees. In cities where the sexes were separated, the "normal high schools" for girls were usually established well after the boys' schools, but Washington, D.C., presents an interesting exception. There the girls had a normal school before the boys had a high school, despite repeated requests from trustees that Congress establish a high school with two departments, one for boys and one for girls. As late as 1876, the school trustees were still complaining that "girls have the Normal School, but boys pass no higher than the Grammar School. . . . Boys sometimes have cause for thinking they are ill-used. Let there be an equality of sex."[40]

Educators in single-sex high schools made it clear that secondary educa-tion must not create any change in the established sphere of women. The Baltimore superintendent, for example, stated that the girls "are in prepara-tion for a different sphere of life. . . . The circle of their operations may be circumscribed by the domestic relations, but their influence for good or evil is scarcely less limited than that of the other sex." Propriety forbade "their entrance upon the arena of public action . . . but in the quiet seclusion of home and at the hearthstone they begin the work for weal or woe at the very foundation of human character."[41]

Baltimore prided itself on the feminine climate of its girls' high school: "With a view of securing more perfectly, a ladylike deportment on the part of the pupils . . . the retiring compartments have been greatly enlarged, neatly fitted up, and placed under the charge of the first assistant; a lady eminently qualified to exert a wholesome influence over the pupils in this regard." By listing the occupations of the students' parents, however, which showed that most were self-employed craftsmen and others of modest position, the school board tried to demonstrate that the "ladylike" pupils were not members of an elite. The school sought to project a tony image without being socially exclusive.[42]

In most cities that segregated schools by sex, the early history of the high school illustrated the distinct and often subordinated educational status of women. In such places girls were at first simply barred from secondary education and then grudgingly admitted by cost-conscious school boards to separate schools. Girls were typically offered a curriculum narrower than that offered the boys. In cities like Boston, Baltimore, and Philadelphia, parents complained repeatedly after the Civil War that the curriculum in the girls' high schools was not equivalent to that of the boys' high schools and did not prepare girls for college. Separate high schools for girls continued throughout the nineteenth century in some cities, and the girls' institutions were rarely equal to those of boys. In Louisville, Kentucky, for example, the per-pupil cost of the white girls' high school in 1902 was the same as that of the coeducational school for blacks—58 percent that of the academic high school for white boys.[43]

The Origins of Coeducational High Schools

Cities that segregated high schools by sex, however, were not typical of public secondary education in most of the nation, especially after the mid-century. The cities that pioneered in creating coeducational high schools were mostly small or medium-sized cities in the Northeast and cities of every size in the Midwest and Far West, and their school districts usually had already adopted coeducation in the lower grades. School boards that established coeducational high schools confronted many of the same issues as those that built separate secondary schools for boys and girls, but they interpreted them differently. They welcomed the strong demand from girls for advanced schooling, and they tended to see this as a way to fill sparsely populated high-school classrooms, not as some demographic and fiscal time bomb. As we have shown, relatively few boys were interested in going to high school. In 1866 a Massachusetts educator observed that boys had to be convinced to attend high schools, but girls did not: "While there is need of constant and vigorous efforts to secure the higher education of boys,—to inspire boys themselves with a generous ambition for intellectual culture, and to make parents see the utility of providing for their sons an education above that which is merely elementary,—with girls the case is wholly different." In the United States, he said, "everywhere girls are thronging the higher grades of educational institutions. It is the fashion; the spirit of the times. There are in this commonwealth upwards of a hundred High Schools, and there is no doubt that of the pupils attending them two to one are females."[44]

School boards realized that creating separate schools for each sex would be prohibitively expensive, except for the largest cities (the Louisville school board complained that only 8 percent of its pupils attended high schools but 20 percent of the district budget went to those institutions, largely because of the "maintenance of separate schools for the two sexes"). The small size of high schools, then, was a key factor in the decision to coeducate. The favorable experience of commingling older boys and girls in the grammar schools, together with the ideology that rationalized the practice, provided further precedent, especially for those who viewed the high school as an upward extension of the common school. Sometimes the legitimation of coeducation ran the other way around: in Charlestown and St. Louis, as we have seen, the high schools were coeducational before the grammar schools. Typical state legislation authorizing high schools did not differentiate by sex. A Massachusetts law of 1827, for example, required that all communities of five hundred families or more should provide schooling beyond the elementary level "for the benefit of all the inhabitants thereof."[45]

This law had a checkered history of enforcement. Some communities shifted back and forth between separate to coeducational high schools. Lowell, for example, formed a high school for both sexes in 1831, and at first boys and girls occupied the same room. They were separated when the town built a new school in 1840, although they continued to recite together in some classes. In 1852 the male and female departments were abolished and the school divided instead into an English and a classical course. In 1827 Springfield opened a small high school for boys, but after the reorganization of its system in 1848, Springfield High School became coeducational. Worcester combined its separate boys' and girls' high schools into (in the language of the Massachusetts Law of 1827) "a school for the benefit of all the inhabitants of the town" that was "open to scholars of both sexes." In some cases where the sexes were separated into different "departments" of boys or girls in the same building, school boards moved to mix the sexes and to create curricular tracks such as a classical or English course of studies. In Springfield the principal of the high school applauded the new system of classification by subject rather than sex as a step toward pedagogical efficiency. The general trend in high schools in the state of Massachusetts, Alexander Inglis found, was to merge separate sex schools.[46]

Across the Charles River from Boston, the Cambridge school committee complied more thoroughly with the inclusive language of the law of 1827 than did Boston under Mayor Quincy. The Cambridge committeemen had a far different view of the educational rights of girls from the grudging attitude of the Boston school board. In Cambridge the first high school was for girls only. When it became apparent that the girls in separate-sex schools in Ward 1 were more advanced in their studies than the boys, they "were placed under a classical instructer, and their school was denominated the Female High School." In 1845 the parents of the boys of the ward asked for the creation "of a High School for boys, that the boys might have equal advantages with the girls, but that the two sexes be still kept in distinct schools if the proposed arrangements might be made without uniting them." The school committee found, however, that only 10 or 12 boys wanted to attend a high school.[47]

Rather than having two separate-sex schools that combined both grammar and high-school instruction, the committee decided to mix the sexes in distinct grammar and high schools. In their report for 1846 they argued that the schools were flourishing, that the boys were acquiring better manners and refinement of mind, and that the girls were gaining a new "dignity of character." The committee stated that whatever distinctions needed to be made in instruction to accommodate the differences in the sexes could occur in coeducational classrooms. The next year the committee reported that it was "exceedingly *gratified*" with the progress of the coeducational high school, and in 1852 they read a lecture to Boston: "In Boston there is no public school for girls corresponding to the Latin and English High Schools; and the want of such an institution, though supplied for the wealthier classes by the excellent private schools . . . is still felt deeply by those who cannot afford to pay the prices for tuition." The system of equal rights in Cambridge, the committee asserted, "is wiser, more republican, more philosophical. The object we have aimed to accomplish is to train up both sexes equally."[48]

A Swedish educator, Per Siljestrom, described gender practices in coeducational Hartford High School. The building was a three-story brick structure equipped with a library, science apparatus, two classrooms fifty feet square accommodating 120 pupils, and a large hall on top for public declamations and readings (similar to assemblies in later high schools) and calisthenics for the girls. Siljestrom noted that girls and boys entered through separate doors, had their own cloakrooms, and sat on opposite sides of the classrooms. Such architectural distinctions probably reflected contemporary concepts of sexual propriety and formally signaled a social separation, especially at those points where the school opened to the larger world. Otherwise, boys and girls were treated the same. Boys and girls, wrote Siljestrom, "are upon quite an equal footing, and in the recitation rooms [small rooms attached to the main classrooms] you may see classes composed of both sexes." He concluded that "there can be no doubt but that this system of allowing boys and girls to receive their education in common, must tend to refine the manners and morals of the school, while at the same time it must exercise a great influence on the position of women, not only as regards education, but also afterwards in society." Both boys and girls had a choice between an English course and a Latin course, each lasting four years.[49]

The majority of the high schools founded in the new states of the Midwest and Far West followed the coeducational pattern of Cambridge and Hartford rather than the separate-sex model of the larger coastal cities. Anna Tolman Smith observed that in western cities the promoters of high schools were less likely than educators in the large eastern cities to try to save money by excluding girls, relegating them to separate and inferior high schools, or relying on private institutions to provide them with a secondary education. In cities in Ohio, for example, "the right or expediency of giving girls equal school advantages with boys seems never to have been questioned." There, she said, the "prominent citizens, county officers, educators, superintendents of common schools, and governors" allied to create efficient systems of schools, "attracting the patronage of the better classes by the certainty of superior advantages for their children, and opening to the poorest child access to the whole realm of knowledge, 'not as a charity, but as a right and without humiliating conditions.'" Smith's interpretation is somewhat too optimistic: there was some conflict in the Midwest over the founding of high schools, but coeducation was early established as the standard practice.[50]

In Cleveland, for example, controversy arose over the first high school, founded in 1846 and at first open only to boys. It was an institution, said the mayor, from which might "issue the future Franklins of our land." The next year dissidents in the city council attacked the high school, questioning its legality and protesting its cost. They lost their battle against the high school, but in the process one of the chief opponents made a motion in the council to admit "girls equally with boys." In 1854 all curricular restrictions on the girls were abolished, and the principal reported that "the first class of girls permitted to take the full course in mathematics stood considerably higher, on the average, than the boys."[51]

In Cincinnati separate-sex high schools gave way in 1851 to two new coeducational institutions. By 1854 the superintendent reported that mixing the sexes had worked so well that he was recommending that "the plan be more generally resorted to in the District Schools, especially in the higher grades. It will secure to both male and female departments greater facilities of classification than they now have, and the good results known to flow from a judicious division of labor." Parents who wanted to have instilled in their daughters both "maidenly modesty . . . and . . . self-reliance . . . can best secure these results in *mixed schools*." The principal of the Woodward High School agreed: Not only were the girls the intellectual equals of boys but, he said, "every year confirms my opinion that as God made us male and female to be in each other's society, in the family, the church, and all other social circles, so he would not have us separated in school."[52]

In the 1850s the Chicago school board and superintendent, like those in Ohio cities, were looking eastward and concluding that a high school was "eminently essential to complete the machinery of education" as the city's schools became bureaucratized. By 1852 the case for urban public high schools was becoming as standardized as the school desks and textbooks, and each new city to propose secondary schools borrowed arguments freely from its predecessors. In 1856 Chicago's common council, responding to the school board, passed an ordinance establishing a coeducational high school. Superintendent William H. Wells was proud that "no other city in the Union has so early in its history manifested such liberality in the endowment of a High School for both sexes." He contrasted Boston's and

Philadelphia's late and grudging attention to the secondary education of girls with Chicago's equal treatment of the sexes. The new Chicago High School had a fine Athens stone building with ten classrooms, five teachers, and four courses of study—classical, English, classical and English, and normal. Girls had access to all the courses, but boys were not admitted to the teacher-training course. Wells was right in claiming that Chicago was more even-handed and liberal toward girls than the cities with separate high schools. Chicago, not Boston or Philadelphia, was following the standard pattern of gender practice in high schools. By mid-century coeducation was becoming the norm.[53]

The High School through the Lens of Gender, 1870–1900

We began this chapter with four observations: that high schools were coeducational, that girls and boys studied mostly the same subjects, that girls equalled or outperformed boys academically, and that girls outnumbered boys as students and as graduates. We now return to these characteristics and ask how they connected with the nature of the high school as an institution during the period from 1870 to 1900 when the high school became rapidly institutionalized. We also look briefly at how the high school connected with the workplace and the life cycle of girls in the family to explore why there were fewer male than female students.

High schools of this era had small enrollments and high attrition. One should be cautious and skeptical in using almost all nineteenth-century educational statistics, and nowhere more so than in analyzing the very ambiguous institution called the high school. But by using federal, state, and local sources, one can make create a rough statistical portrait of public secondary education. Consider, for example, the report on city high schools in 1873 cited in table 7.

This table captures some of the essential institutional features of the modal public high school in 1873: it had a small enrollment; its teaching force was tiny and balanced between men and women; and it enrolled only a tiny fraction of the students attending public schools. Averages can of course mask variability. The census of 1870 makes it possible to group the average size of high schools by states, the more urban states having the larger schools: six states had an average high school enrollment of 35 to 50 pupils; fourteen states, an average of 51 to 100; six states, an average of 101 to 150; and three states, an average of 151 or more.[54]

Similar high-school characteristics were apparent in census statistics col-

Table 7
Statistics on Urban Public High Schools, 1873

Number of Schools	536
Average Number of Pupils per School	85
Average Daily Attendance per School	62
Percentage of All Urban Public School Students Enrolled in High Schools	4
Average Number of Teachers per School	3
Percentage of Female Teachers	53

Source: U.S. Commissioner of Education, *Report for 1873,* pp. xliii–xliv.

lected in 1890 and 1900. In 1890 the number of students in high schools represented only 3 percent of the number in elementary schools. The average number of students in public high schools was 80 in 1890, and 86 in 1900. The typical high school had 3.6 teachers in 1890, and 3.4 in 1900. Women constituted 58 percent of high-school teachers in 1890, and 50 percent in 1900. But again, it is useful to compare the sizes of high schools in different sizes of communities. In 1903 the statistics on high schools were disaggregated in a way that permits comparison of cities with populations greater than eight thousand, in which the average number of pupils was 355 and the number of teachers was 12, whereas in communities smaller than eight thousand, the average number of students was 52 and number of instructors was 2. Clearly such differences of scale greatly influenced what the high schools could offer their students and how they could group them for instruction.[55]

High schools continued to have a high attrition rate. In 1889–90 graduating seniors constituted only 11 percent of high school students. In Wisconsin only 6 percent finished the course of studies; in Ohio, 8 percent. In Chicago there were 2,699 ninth-graders, but only 731 twelfth-graders. Nationally in 1890, graduates of all secondary schools, public and private, accounted for only 3.5 percent of all persons seventeen years old. And as in the early years of the high school, few of the students were preparing for college—only 14 percent of the total high school population.[56]

Low enrollments and high attrition meant that, during the nineteenth century, high schools, like the colleges of the time, faced a shortage of qualified students. It is true that in some cities, like Boston, citizens were worried that if secondary education was opened to girls, the ensuing flood

Table 8
Boys and Girls Enrolled in Certain High School Subjects, 1900

	Boys (%)	Girls (%)
Physics	19.5	18.7
Chemistry	8.2	7.4
Physiology	28.0	27.0
Physical Geography	23.6	23.2
Algebra	57.0	55.8
Geometry	27.0	27.7
Latin	47.1	55.8
Greek	3.7	2.6
French	6.6	8.7
German	13.4	15.0
History	36.1	39.6
Rhetoric	37.5	39.2
English Literature	40.7	42.9

Source: John Francis Latimer, *What's Happened to Our High Schools* (Washington, D.C.: Public Affairs Press, 1958), p. 149.

of scholars would bankrupt the school treasury. This was, however, a minority viewpoint. Middle-class parents of girls were among the high schools' most ardent supporters, and girls from such families could arguably be seen as the mainstay of the institution. By filling more than half the seats in most high schools, these girls helped to refute the charge that high schools were unpopular and too expensive because they were too small. By the latter half of the nineteenth century, most people agreed that girls could profit from an extended education, and schooling for them did not need to meet a severely practical test. An academic education could well fit them for their work in later life as teachers, wives, and mothers.

The size of high schools also helps to explain why both boys and girls studied the same, largely academic curriculum in coeducational classrooms. In a school of sixty to ninety students and only two or three teachers, it was simply impossible to offer separate classes for the two sexes or to provide a sexually differentiated course of studies. Educators found it expedient to mix the sexes as a way of achieving better classification of students by subject as well as by age and proficiency, as in the grammar school.

Even though few students prepared for college, the curriculum of high schools was primarily an academic one, and it was pursued by both girls and boys. Table 8 indicates the percentages of girls and boys who enrolled in these basic subjects in 1900—figures that do not differ markedly from data gathered in 1890. Individual school reports showed the same general pattern of similar course enrollments among girls and boys in coeducational schools.[57]

Despite the dominance of such academic subjects, pursued jointly by girls and boys, the curriculum included some courses or divisions of a more vocational nature. Foremost among these from an early period were the special normal departments that prepared girls to teach in primary schools in the cities. By the end of the nineteenth century some high schools began to include business and commercial courses, which were generally taken by both sexes (in 1900, for example, about 11 percent of both boys and girls enrolled in business courses). Some schools introduced courses in manual training and home economics. Even these courses were not entirely sex-segregated, again probably because some high schools were so small that it was difficult to schedule and staff separate courses. In 1900, 0.5 percent of the boys and 6.3 percent of the girls took home economics, while 5.2 percent of the boys and 2.4 percent of the girls took manual training.[58]

High-school promoters justified the institution on meritocratic grounds, and this, too, helps explain why girls were welcome. The grammar schools were coeducational; to pass the high-school-entrance test was the ambition of both sexes. According to the common rationale for coeducation in the lower grades, girls and boys encouraged in each other a more ardent and balanced form of academic achievement—an argument also applied to the high school.[59]

From the start, girls proved that they could meet the meritocratic standard for admission to high school and could perform at least as well as the boys in their courses. Already accustomed to the superior work of girls in the lower grades, superintendents also found that girls carried off more than their normal share of scholastic honors in high schools. In the Somerville, Massachusetts, high-school girls were usually the valedictorians, for example. In St. Louis, academic records for the period from 1870 to 1885 demonstrated that girls did slightly better than boys. In 1900 the superintendent of the Kansas City school system reported by sex on the rate of failures in different courses in the high schools. Although boys constituted only 36 percent of the students in the four high schools of the city, they accounted for 43 percent of the failures in mathematics, 50 percent in

These photographs of high-school classes in Washington, D.C., taken in 1899 by Frances Benjamin Johnston, portray the more favored schools: the moderately large and well-equipped "people's college" of large cities. Many "high schools" in small cities were little more than an extra room attached to a graded school. Except for a dwindling number of separate-sex high schools, especially in the Northeast and the South, public high schools at the turn of the century were coeducational and mixed the sexes in academic classes, though usually not in manual training. (Library of Congress.)

Formally dressed boys and girls seated side by side sketch a model in an art class, surrounded by casts of classical statues.

A "professor" (the name often given to male high school teachers) lectures students on the wonders of the brain in a biology class. Girls and boys sit in separate rows.

A girl and her male teacher perform a chemistry experiment while a mixed class watches and takes notes.

Boys learning
to operate
machinery like
lathes in the
boys' vocational
high school.

African-American girls in an upper
grade of elementary school in a
cooking class. Home economics
became a prominent subject in
secondary schools for blacks.

Boys doing experiments in a physics laboratory.

foreign languages, 49 percent in science, and 44 percent in history and related subjects. A study of failure rates by sex in Indiana cities and rural schools concluded that "the boys are much less successful than the girls. The difference in the per cent of failures varies for the different subjects, but in practically all instances the per cent of failures and also the per cent of conditions is noticeably higher for the boys than for the girls. In many cases it is more than double. Even in mathematics the girls show a slight superiority."[60]

As the phrase "even in mathematics" suggests, educators were surprised that girls did well not only in literary subjects—often gendered as feminine in a society that seemed to reserve high culture for women—but also in mathematics, a field typically gendered as male. Hence, when educational researchers began to collect evidence on the performance of girls in mathematics, they were surprised to find that females did well there, too. In 1903 Edward T. Thorndike and a superintendent of schools administered a test to twenty-eight boys and forty-nine girls in a high school in Albion, Indiana. The test itself showed a marked male bias: of twelve mentions of gender, eleven referred to men or boys, while the problem situations were typically masculine. Nonetheless, they reported, the girls did about 5 percent better than the boys. Suspicious of their results, they made the surmise—comforting to males—that probably the more able boys had already left school (an odd kind of school where the leavers were smarter than the ones who persisted).[61]

High school was one environment where effort paid off for young women, even though success in high-school studies did not generally translate into enhanced opportunities in later life. Competitive entrance examinations to normal classes and a competitive examination to qualify for teaching jobs strengthened the meritocratic underpinnings of the high school and justified the expense of creating high schools in the first place. Normal training classes firmly linked the high school to the improvement of the whole system in a meritocratic way and motivated girls to do well in high school in order to obtain a job after graduation.[62]

Of course not all girls aspired to teach. For most girls the high school years probably represented a moratorium between the parental and the conjugal family, a safe and productive way to spend youthful years, free from the dangers of the workplace and rich in cultural and human associations. In the Victorian era, middle-class parents in cities increasingly viewed the adolescence of girls as a time of special promise and jeopardy, and a whole literature emerged on what Joan Jacobs Brumberg has called "the iconography of girlhood." Jane Hunter has found that the diaries of schoolgirls were full of positive allusions to their classmates and school experiences.[63]

Despite educators' rhetoric about the high school as "the people's college" and their desire to prove that it served a cross-section of the population, high schools continued to attract mostly the sons and daughters of what was broadly called the "middle class"—professional people, shopkeepers, clerks, skilled laborers, and the like. The class composition of high schools no doubt varied according to the character of the community. In Erie, Pennsylvania, for example, the high-school principal claimed that over half his pupils came from homes where the parents had property assessments of less than $500, and in Adrian, Michigan, the principal found more children of farmers, railroad employees, and widows than of businessmen or professionals. But Selwyn Troen has found that in St. Louis in 1880, 80 percent of the sons of professional fathers and 64 percent of the sons of white-collar workers between the ages of thirteen and sixteen were in school, compared with only 32 percent of the sons of unskilled workers. In Philadelphia that same year, 46 percent of the students in Central High School came from what David Labaree calls the "proprietary middle class" (or "occupational groups that are self-employed") and only 3.5 percent from the unskilled working class.[64]

·LI|E·

FOR THE BENEFIT OF THE GIRL WHO IS ABOUT TO GRADUATE.

The cartoon pictures the young woman's domestic destiny when she graduates. Asleep after burning the midnight oil over her book, she dreams that an army of pots and pans, a stove, and washing and scrubbing utensils is marching toward her armed with signs like "HAVE YOU ANY IDEA WHAT I AM?" (*Life* magazine, 1900; Library of Congress.)

Because the high school was basically a middle-class institution and employed both female and male teachers, middle-class parents could be confident that a coeducational high school was a secure environment for girls who were no longer needed to help about the home in many urban households. Meeting boys in such a controlled setting and obtaining the cultural capital deemed appropriate to young women may have enhanced their daughters' standing in the marriage market. Indeed, contemporary observers of the high school claimed that more and more middle-class girls attended school because it was "the social thing to do." Sara Burstall, an English educator, wrote that high-school graduation could give girls "a certain social advantage." In 1894 the Atlanta schools reported that alumnae from its girls' high school were "adorning the highest ranks of society in the state."[65]

Boys faced a different kind of decision than girls did in choosing whether to attend a public high school in the years from 1870 to 1900. For boys going to school meant forgoing paid employment. They had a much wider array of white-collar and skilled jobs to choose from, even as teenagers, and less stigma was attached to young men's work than to most of the jobs young women could obtain. The high-school principal in Alameda, California, lamenting that only 30 percent of his students were boys, wrote that "this undesirable condition can be accounted for by the fact that boys of High School age have a strong desire to earn money and get a start in the world, while girls as a rule have not this impulse and are encouraged to continue their studies by pride, ambition, encouragement of parents, and in many cases by the desire to prepare themselves as teachers."[66]

Boys often found a quicker educational route to their goals than attending high school. Public-school leaders complained, for example, that private business schools that offered a short course of practical subjects were draining off boys from the more academic high school. Indeed, in 1890, 64,163 young men were attending such schools, almost three times the number of young women. Likewise, among boys who planned to go to college in 1900, almost 35,000 bypassed high schools by attending the "preparatory" departments of colleges and universities, outnumbering girls there three to two. One can explain the relative absence of boys from high schools in part as a function of their greater range of choices or the pressures to go to work or college at an earlier age.[67]

At the turn of the century, however, the dearth of boys in high schools—increasingly referred to as "the boy problem"—came to be explained as the result of the "feminization" of public education. Some doctors and psychologists now worried that the high school was too masculine for the health of the girls, while others depicted the high school as too sissy for boys.

6

King Canutes Attack the Perils of Coeducation and Women Teachers

The rising tide of coeducation in the high school did not go unchallenged, however natural and expedient it may have seemed to most school people. Chief among the King Canutes who would command this tide to stop were two men who claimed the authority of science and attracted much public attention: Dr. Edward H. Clarke of Harvard Medical School, a specialist in nervous disorders who had written an influential book entitled *Sex in Education* in 1873, and G. Stanley Hall, president of Clark University, a flamboyant psychologist. Both men argued that there were such fundamental biological differences between adolescent girls and boys that they should be taught separately and in different ways. By the early twentieth century the attention of many critics of coeducation shifted from the dangers of masculinized high schools for girls to the alleged "feminization" of boys in coeducational classrooms taught by women teachers, who were denounced as "the woman peril" by the new mandarins of masculinity.[1]

Identical coeducation, Clarke and Hall claimed, was a slippery slope leading to disaster. They conceded that women could learn the same difficult subjects that men mastered; young women's performance in secondary schools and colleges had conclusively demonstrated this fact. The problem was not girls' lack of mental ability; rather, it was the physiological effects of hard study on them. Academic competition with boys in coeducational institutions, they argued, would interfere with the development of girls' reproductive organs. By overloading their brains, girls not only ruined their health but threatened to bring about "race suicide" among prosperous Anglo-Saxons. At a time when people were fascinated by the Darwinian doctrine of the survival of the fittest and worried about whether women were adequately fulfilling their traditional domestic roles, such arguments added an apparently scientific sanction to the doctrine of separate spheres of the sexes. Clarke and Hall went well beyond the traditional theological, social, and political grounds for separatism by claiming a biological polarity of the sexes. Hall undercut the case for biological polarity, however, by claiming that sex identity was plastic and shaped by conditioning. The anxiety both demonstrated about strengthening the traditional gender order indicated that maintaining the separate spheres was becoming increasingly hard cultural work—femininity and masculinity were hardly to be taken for granted but rather required conscious buttressing.[2]

However fanciful and retrograde their theories may appear in the 1990s, at the time many influential people took Clarke's and Hall's writings and speeches seriously enough to welcome or challenge them. Traditionalists regarded Clarke and Hall as useful allies. Advocates of woman's rights, by contrast, considered the two men to be reactionaries bent on denying educational opportunities to women. Opponents of Clarke and Hall recognized that the prestige of science joined to the entrenched power of males could undermine the educational gains women had already achieved and threaten coeducation, which they considered vital to opening opportunities in both secondary and higher education. Critics also realized that Clarke and Hall had a conservative social agenda: they were struggling to keep women in their "natural" place as wives and mothers and to prevent them from challenging men in public arenas. Clarke and Hall did not affront only advocates of women's rights, however. By attacking the rationale for coeducation elaborated by school leaders like William T. Harris, they provoked Harris and other educators to counterattack.[3]

Although most of the nineteenth century debate over coeducation in secondary schools and colleges focused on the supposed damage to women's health and worries about their departure from their proper sphere as wives and mothers, at the turn of the twentieth century men began to worry about the effects of coeducation on boys. Clarke asserted that the nineteenth-century college and high school were basically masculine environments in which girls lost their health and distinctively feminine characteristics by competing with males on foreign territory. Hall continued to repeat this charge, but he also became concerned about the effects of coeducational high schools on boys as well. In classrooms where women taught and girls outnumbered boys, males were becoming "feminized." Thus he saw coeducation, paradoxically, as too virile for the girls and too feminine for the boys.[4]

Hall was hardly alone in asserting that the high school was being transformed into a feminine environment. This observation had become a familiar lament among other mandarins of masculinity who wrote in the popular and professional magazines. These critics thought that the high schools must be flawed indeed if girls did better than boys. The chief target of their attack was women teachers. Only slightly less culpable than the women teachers were the girls who had the gall to shame boys by outperforming them in their studies. The advocates of a more masculine high school wanted to rid the curriculum of its sissy tinge, hire more men teachers, and in some cases to abolish coeducation itself by resegregating high schools and making them fit places for boys. Women teachers came under attack from both male administrators and teachers inside the schools who protested the "feminization" of their profession and commentators outside the system who worried about a decline in masculinity in the society as a whole.[5]

A great deal of policy talk about the evils of coeducation in the high school was ventilated in the years from 1873 to 1920, in contrast to the relative silence that greeted coeducation during the first half of the nineteenth century when it became embedded in common schools. Rosalind Rosenberg argues that it was no accident that Clarke's attack occurred in the 1870s. "The idea that woman's mind was limited by her body was as old as antiquity," she notes, but never "was that idea more fervently held or more highly elaborated than it was in America after the Civil War." More and more young women were entering the labor market in industry and commerce, women's reform groups were attacking urban problems, the woman's movement was gaining momentum in its demand for political and economic rights, and women were demanding entry to higher education on a par with men. "Because the home no longer defined the limits of female activity and women were joining the men in the outside world, however marginally," Rosenberg writes, "many Americans believed that the need to draw a clear line between appropriate male and female activities had become acute."[6]

Criticism of coeducation arose in part because of changes in the objective circumstances of men's and women's lives, especially in the range of educational opportunities open to young women and the transformation of teaching into a woman's job. Different people interpreted the ideological meaning of these changes in quite different ways. Liberals felt compelled to counter conservatives' arguments; here and there the attacks of traditionalists may have diminished educational opportunities for women. But overall, the rhetorical assaults did not deflect basic trends in gender practices in education. Young women continued to flock into high schools and colleges, coeducation expanded, and by 1920 almost nine out of ten public-school teachers were women. Thus the case of the King Canutes illustrates that while talk about gender may have generated more talk, it did not alter practice much.

Ovaries and Algebra

Clarke claimed the high ground of science in his attack on the identical coeducation of girls and boys, but he also had a political agenda. A professor and overseer at Harvard, a friend of the university's president, Charles William Eliot, and a determined foe of coeducation there, he firmly opposed the educational demands of women's rights advocates and their male allies, whom he called "the bulls of female reform." He stressed the biological basis of female destiny and denied the validity of women's demands for full opportunities in all domains of life, regarding competition of the sexes in the public sphere as damaging to the future of the "race." Following Darwin, Clarke asserted that through evolution males had become more specialized in functions, while women remained less differentiated; thus, biology defined social roles as well as reproductive capacity. "Differentiation is Nature's method of ascent," Clarke wrote. "We should cultivate the difference of the sexes, not try to hide or abolish it." Science proved to be a double-edged sword in the battle over educational opportunities for women, however. In the twentieth century pioneer women psychologists clearly perceived the sexual stereotypes and distortions in the work of Clarke and Hall. These women scholars demonstrated that research could be used to clear away the underbrush of misinterpretations created by their male predecessors.[7]

Clarke was not only concerned about gender. Ethnic and class biases also shaped his vision of the ideal society and underlay his fears for the future. In a speech to the National Education Association in 1874, Clarke declared that the duties of educators were "first, to secure the perpetuation of the

[Anglo-Saxon] race in America; and, secondly, to provide for the survival of the fittest here also." It was clear that his focus was not women in general but the "Anglo-Saxon" native-born women of the middle and upper classes, those who constituted the vast majority of young women attending secondary schools and colleges. As his critics were fond of pointing out, when Clarke talked of the dire effects of steady work on young women, he was not referring to the black women who labored in the fields or the daughters of immigrants who toiled in factories or as servants in prosperous homes. He had in mind the effects of academic labor on the fertility of elite Anglo-Saxon girls. He feared that native-born women might become less fertile, while immigrants of Irish and other stock were producing large families that would ultimately threaten the dominance of the "Anglo-Saxon race."[8]

A fundamental physiological difference divided young women from young men, Clarke asserted. During the teenage years girls were developing their reproductive organs, and "periodicity" was basic to the "nature of the female." Believing, as many scientists did, that there was only a limited amount of "forces" available for the development of the different parts of the body—a biological misinterpretation of the law of conservation of energy—Clarke held that if blood was channeled to the brain, it was not available for the development of the reproductive organs. If girls had to compete intellectually with boys, with no allowances made for their menstrual periods or special needs, the result would be "monstrous brains and puny bodies, . . . flowing thought and constipated bowels"—in other words, mastery of algebra at the expense of the ovaries. Identical coeducation was the worst kind of instruction; by emulating boys academically, girls would lose their health and might become sterile.[9]

The only way to ensure the proper development of the female reproductive organs was to educate boys and girls separately, instead of in the masculine atmosphere of the coeducational school. Girls should have schooling that was adapted to their "periodicity" and to their future lives as wives and mothers. He believed they should receive monthly rest periods, work a third less than boys on their studies, pursue a less demanding curriculum, and above all be spared the threat of competition with boys. Such competition could lead only to the masculinization of women, the production of freaks who would lose their feminine qualities and even the ability to bear children. "Identical education of the two sexes is a crime before God and humanity," Clarke declared, "that physiology protests against, and that experience weeps over." Another physician put it this way a decade later:

"Why should we spoil a good mother by making her an ordinary grammarian?"[10]

Clarke's book, *Sex in Education,* published in 1873, provoked intense interest and controversy. In thirteen years it was republished seventeen times, and in the university town of Ann Arbor two hundred copies were snatched up in one day. The psychological effects of the book on some academically ambitious girls and their parents were no doubt substantial. Thirty-five years after the book was issued, the president of Bryn Mawr College, the supremely confident M. Carey Thomas, recalled how she and other intellectually ambitious young women "did not know when we began whether women's health could stand the strain of education. We were haunted in those days by the clanging chains of that gloomy little specter," Clarke, whom she called a "woman hater." Was it true that women could succeed in advanced schooling only at the expense of their health and their future prospects as full human beings?[11]

Advocates of women's rights were appalled by Clarke's contentions, because they threatened to undermine the striking gains women had achieved through coeducation and their chance to enjoy larger opportunities in the public sphere. Anna C. Brackett, one of Clarke's most perceptive critics, argued that just when the academic success of the girls had been settled by their achievements, "the opponents of higher education for women . . . have within a few years shifted their ground." No longer able to claim that women were intellectually inferior to men, "they have taken up their new . . . assertion that women are not able physically to pursue a thorough and complete course of study." She deplored the assault on coeducation, for she believed that "for the masses, coeducation and higher education for women are practically one and the same thing." The issue of girls' health was basically simple, she wrote: "We have only . . . to learn the laws of physical health, and to obey them, and the whole matter will be set at rest."[12]

But the challenge to women's rights went beyond the physical effects of study. Men wanted to restrict women's opportunities to shape their own lives: "There is a perpetual effort to readjust her claims, to define her position, and to map out her sphere, and these boundary lines are arbitrarily drawn at every conceivable distance from the centre." By contrast, Brackett observed, "we do not hear constant discussions of men's sphere and men's education." Unlike women, "each man is left very much to work out his own career, without the responsibility of the whole sex resting on him." A man is "at liberty to make mistakes in his medical practice, to blow up steamboats by his carelessness, to preach dull sermons, and write silly books, without finding his whole sex put under ban for his short-comings."[13]

One reason that Clarke's book had such impact on public opinion was that for decades even the staunchest advocates of advanced education for girls had worried about the effects of hard study upon the health of girls. Antebellum advocates of the education of girls, like Catharine Beecher, Mary Lyon, William B. Fowle, and Dio Lewis, were also pioneers in physical education. They argued that schoolgirls too often taxed their brains without developing their physical strength. Unlike boys, who were expected to play and do hard physical work, girls were too often pale and delicate in health because they failed to exercise or eat a proper diet. Slaves to fashion, they led overactive social lives and wore clothing that was too tight, heavy, and constricting. The solution to the problem of poor health, these advocates claimed, was not to lessen the academic demands on girls but to provide them with a healthier regimen of exercise, eating, sleep, and dress.[14]

From Clarke's point of view, these were mere palliatives and did not address the chief problem: that a girl had a finite amount of energy. If this vital force was drained away from the creation of the reproductive organs in order to feed an overactive brain, her basic physiological development and future health and happiness were at stake. Critics responded to Clarke by questioning the accuracy and representativeness of his case studies and by gathering new evidence on the health of young women attending secondary schools and colleges. These studies generally showed that young women were about as healthy as young men, healthier than their sisters who did not attend college, and healthier than a sample of employed working-class girls (one writer pointed out that Clarke himself was forced to leave Harvard temporarily because of ill health).[15]

The controversy aroused by Clarke stimulated the demand for physical education programs for girls. Both high schools and colleges and universities in growing numbers introduced calisthenics and other forms of supervised exercise. It was common, for example, for high schools to hold exercise classes for girls in the largest recitation room or auditorium well before gymnasiums became common. But despite refutations of Clarke and the new awareness of the importance of physical education for girls, which in many regions preceded the arrival of physical education for boys, the argument that hard study undermined the health of girls continued to pepper both popular magazines and professional journals.[16]

The public-school leaders who responded to Clarke generally dismissed his arguments, in part because to have accepted them would have alienated their chief source of pupils in coeducational high schools. The only big-city administrator to wholeheartedly endorse Clarke's views—and call for separate high schools for boys and girls—was Boston's superintendent, John Philbrick. William T. Harris, then superintendent of St. Louis schools, attacked Clarke on two grounds. The first was philosophical: Harris denied that "the mind with its culture is subordinate to the organization of the body," a belief that he decried as "materialism." For him biology was not destiny; the "culture of the rational mind," he wrote, "is the privilege of every human being, whether male or female" and must not be limited by physiological doctrines that could easily turn into "fanaticism."[17]

Harris's second argument was practical and probably carried more weight with his peers. He asked what Clarke's "law of periodicity" meant for school organization. Clarke opposed "identical coeducation" because it taxed girls to keep up with the work during their menstrual periods. "Stated in plain school language," Harris observed, "classes imply regularity or persistence in work, and this is injurious to girls between 14 and 20 years." Irregularity in attendance was in fact a serious problem in public schools of all kinds, he admitted. But how could any school, even one for girls only, arrange a course of studies to accommodate monthly absences of the students? "When one can point out a plan for a girl's school, wherein the organization is such that three-fourths of the class do not suffer by the constant absence of one-fourth of the class, he will have discovered a new organization, which wise educators will hasten to adopt, even for boys' schools." But that was moonshine. In the St. Louis high school, he said, the girls had slightly lower average rates of attendance than the boys (88.7 versus 93.6 percent), but their average academic performance was higher (85.4 versus 84.4 percent). The only way to satisfy Clarke's objections would be to "adopt a system of individual instruction for all girls between the ages of 14 and 20. It would practically shut out from a fair education nine-tenths of the entire sex, and the remaining tenth, lacking the discipline of class work, would not acquire a thorough education."[18]

Most public-school critics of Clarke agreed with Harris that the doctor's preoccupation with menstruation and his educational prescriptions made little sense. His interpretation, said one, was based on the pathologies of a few young women and had little to do with everyday school life. Next, suggested a reviewer in *National Teacher's Monthly*, Clarke might attack "co-dancing, co-praying, co-sleighing, and coquetting."[19]

Most public-school educators ignored or rebuffed Clarke, largely because their experience of coeducation did not substantiate his views and because they could see no practical way to answer his objections to the education of adolescent girls. During the very years when the debate raged, girls continued to pour into coeducational high schools, which suggests that they and their families were not deterred by the supposed health hazards of a secondary education. But Clarke's ideas did not disappear. They resurfaced in 1905 in a controversial chapter entitled "Adolescent Girls and Their Education" in G. Stanley Hall's book *Adolescence*.

Hall was convinced that secondary coeducation was a serious mistake for girls, because they were different from boys "in every organ and tissue." The "whole soul" of woman, he wrote, "is best conceived of as a magnificent organ of heredity, and to its laws all her psychic activities, if unperverted, are true." The proper education of girls would "keep the purely mental back and by every method . . . bring the intuitions to the front." "Biological psychology," wrote Hall, "already dreams of a new philosophy of sex which places the wife and mother at the heart of a new world and makes her the object of a new religion and almost of a new worship, that will give her reverent exemption from sex competition and reconsecrate her to the higher responsibilities of the human race . . . where the blind worship of mere mental illumination has no place."[20]

Hall summarized a half-century of "scientific" studies—almost all of them conducted by men—that demonstrated that the biological and social differences between men and women were crucial. To ignore these differences in education could only produce societal disaster. He restated the familiar case that women needed to concentrate in adolescence on the harmonious development of their reproductive system and emotional nature. "I have never met or read a physician, if he is not a feminist, who does not hold that at times girls should metaphorically be turned out to grass," Hall wrote, "and lie fallow, so far as strenuous intellectual effort goes." Both in school and adult life women should avoid competition with men and concentrate on their sacred domestic functions.[21]

Hall went beyond Clarke by actually sketching an ideal separate school for girls. It should be set, he wrote, "in the country in the midst of hills," where the young madonnas could rest during their menstrual periods; sustain their health through proper exercise, diet, and sleep; learn the domestic skills they would need as wives and mothers; learn to please through good manners; and study religion, nature, art, history, and literature. At the center of his utopian school was a "healthful, wise, large-souled, honorable, married and attractive man."[22]

The polarity of the sexes, then, was a major theme of Hall's book and one reason for his opposition to coeducation during puberty. Not surprisingly, his chapter on girls became the target of vitriolic attack by feminist educators such as Willystine Goodsell. M. Carey Thomas observed that "now we know it is not we, but the man who believes such things about us, who is himself pathological, blinded by neurotic mists of sex." But Hall was not only interested in preserving the femininity of girls and protecting them from a "masculine" school environment. He and many others at the turn of the twentieth century were equally concerned about the virility of boys. With no apparent care for inconsistency, he warned that the coeducational school also feminized the boys.[23]

The Woman Peril and the Mandarins of Masculinity

In 1914, Adm. F. E. Chadwick gave the fear of feminization a name: "the woman peril." Chadwick did not mince words. Women teachers have "had so evil an effect upon the manhood of the country, on the qualities that go for the making of the masculine character, that it is more than full time to consider most seriously this great and vital question." In spite of "all the claims of the feminist movement," men must "do the main work of the world: build and handle steamships and railways, command armies and fleets, fight our battles, tunnel our mountains and make our steel." No woman can adequately train the "force of character" necessary for men because "the masculine and feminine natures are as far apart as the poles." Therefore, to subject a boy to women teachers "at his most impressionable, character-forming age is to render violence to nature"; it can only "result in a feminized manhood, emotional, illogical, noncombatitive."[24]

For some time before Chadwick's emotional outburst, critics had been complaining about the declining number of men teachers and the predominance of girls in public high schools. Their targets were women teachers and female students. The women were feminizing the boys, they accused, and the girls were shaming the boys by outperforming them in academic competition. Boys suffered the indignity of failure because girls matured earlier and were better adapted to the "feminized" curriculum and the schoolmarms who taught them. The critics proposed to stem the tide of women teachers in the schools, attract and retain more men, and make the school a more masculine environment. If the schools were not made fit places for boys, disaster lay ahead.[25]

Nineteenth-century defenders of coeducation like Harris had claimed that mixing boys and girls in the same classroom blended the qualities of the two sexes to the benefit of each. They accepted the separate spheres of adult men and women as a given and showed little anxiety about disturbing those spheres by teaching boys and girls together. Men like Clarke had attacked the coeducational high school and college as masculine and competitive arenas that injured girls; they feared coeducation would make the women of the Anglo-Saxon "race" unfit for their duties as mothers.

By the turn of the century, however, the terms of the debate over the sexual character of the institution had shifted as critics began to call for the buttressing of the masculine side of the great sex divide. Chadwick was more vehement than most opponents of the "feminized" high school, but his polemic on the woman peril was only one of many that appeared in professional and popular magazines. During all this policy talk, however, the actual character of the high school changed far less than the ideological controversies that mirrored adult fears and hopes.

Why this concern for masculinity in the coeducational high schools at the turn of the twentieth century? By then, critics had turned virility into an issue of unprecedented urgency. They believed that educators would have to labor to reproduce a differentiated gender order rather than being able to take it for granted. In part this new self-consciousness may have resulted from a perception that formal schooling counted for more in shaping young men since they were now staying longer in school, had less exposure to the world of work, and saw less of their fathers than their rural counterparts in the nineteenth century. But the emphasis on virility was also part of a larger reorientation of American culture in the 1890s, as John Higham has shown.[26]

During the nineteenth century some critics of the high school, particularly self-made businessmen, had attacked the unreal and bookish character of the institution and declared it irrelevant to success in a male world. Mark C. Carnes argues that in the Gilded Age boys rebelled against maternal supervision and relished fiction that portrayed autonomous young men making their way in the world (the most famous of the books that glorified the "bad boy," Mark Twain's *Huckleberry Finn*, was considered so subversive that some libraries had banned it). But in the 1890s, these minor currents of protest against a proper, pious upbringing and decorous schooling became a wave of glorification of the self-consciously masculine life. As Joseph F. Kett observes, "the word 'manliness' itself changed meaning, coming to signify less the opposite of childishness than the opposite of femininity." In the very years when boys were becoming more dependent, spending a greater number of their adolescent years in school and away from their fathers, commentators were touting the strenuous life, sports, and the need for sexual differentiation.[27]

Higham interprets the rise of competitive athletics and enthusiasm for outdoor activities as clues to a larger reorientation of American culture in the 1890s: "It was everywhere a hunger to break out of the frustrations, the routine, and the sheer dullness of an urban-industrial culture. It was everywhere an urge to be young, masculine, and adventurous." This spirit took the forms of nationalism and imperialism, a popular lust for contact sports, and a boom in physical fitness. The fiction of the time equated nature with virility, adventure with masculine action, while the popular press and music glorified jingoism and athleticism. No one symbolized more "the whole gladitorial spirit" than Theodore Roosevelt: "He loved the great outdoors, the challenge of sports, the zest of political combat, the danger of war. He exhorted women to greater fecundity. He brought boxing into the White House and contributed immensely to its respectability."[28]

Since male Americans were subjected to a such a barrage of demands for macho behavior, it is not surprising that many of them were disturbed by the suggestions of foreign visitors that American boys taught by women in coeducational schools were in danger of becoming sissies. One English educator wrote that "the boy in America is not being brought up to punch another boy's head, or to stand having his own punched in a healthy and proper manner; that there is a strange and indefinable air coming over the man; a tendency toward a common, if I may so call it, sexless tone of thought." Hall, an American pioneer in the study of sexuality, aroused further anxieties by asserting that sexual identity itself was an achievement shaped by circumstance and not a fixed characteristic. Research on pathologies demonstrated the plasticity of sex, he asserted. Even those who denied that women teachers constituted a "peril" accepted the notion that sharply distinct sex identities were desirable; John Dewey, for example, reassured his readers that American boys were not "mollycoddles."[29]

While men were exhorted to become more virile, women were urged by critics of feminism to become less so. The prospect of women acquiring the vote and entering male professions aroused deep anxiety in the masculinity camp. Some male educators reacted to the "woman peril" with contradictory fears. Critics claimed that women teachers were biologically and culturally so different from men that they could not understand or properly shape the character of boys. Women were so docile that they could not foster aggressive masculinity. But at the same time the opponents of militant women leaders in education argued that women were losing their femininity by competing with men on equal terms in occupations and even demanding an equal role in politics.[30]

Male educators deemed this new militance of women a personal threat, for women teachers were becoming more aggressive in some cities. In Chicago, for example, critics called Margaret Haley and her allies in the all-woman teachers' union the "lady labor sluggers" because of their aggressive tactics, and in New York fourteen thousand women teachers banded together to secure equal pay for equal work. Women educators also competed with men for administrative positions and offices in professional associations. If women teachers were politicized and militant, they were unfeminine and challenged the natural gender order of education in which men ran things. After women teachers elected Ella Flagg Young president of the National Education Association in 1911, an educational journalist complained that the women took "the bit in their teeth and ran away, smashing the carriage." When Young became superintendent of the Chicago public schools in 1909, she declared that "women are destined to rule the schools of every city. I look for a majority of big cities to follow the lead of Chicago in choosing a woman for superintendent. In the near future we shall have more women than men in executive charge of the vast educational system."[31]

Male educational leaders had not always been so apprehensive about women teachers. Barnard and Mann enthusiastically endorsed them, in part because they were supposedly obedient to male supervisors. As St. Louis superintendent in the 1870s, Harris justified the employment of women as teachers and approved the principle of equal pay for women and men teachers. In 1891 Harris, then U.S. commissioner of education, and the superintendents of eight cities told an English educational commission that women teachers were quite as effective as men in "giving intellectual training" and "in maintaining discipline and order."[32]

But in the 1890s more and more leaders began to worry about the replacement of men by women, a trend that Harris attributed to low salaries and the fact that the job was "coming to be considered a woman's business." Harris reported in 1891 that many schoolmen believed that "the increasing femininity of the schools" was a principal reason for the "already noticeable decrease in the proportion of boys in the higher grades." In Philadelphia and Chicago the school boards lamented the decline in the number of men teachers, particularly in the high school. Philadelphia created a normal school for men only. In teaching older students, "the man teacher, understanding the boy nature as no woman can, becomes needed," wrote the board, "to make the instruction attractive, efficient, and thoroughly educational from a manly standpoint, and to fit the pupil, in the true sense, for the duties and responsibilities of his rapidly approaching manhood."[33]

Men who did remain in teaching—about 10 percent overall in most urban school systems and no more than 50 percent in most high schools— sometimes found their own masculinity and force of character questioned. Like high-school boys so outnumbered by girls as to feel "stray and lonesome" in many of their classes, men teachers also felt anomalous even though men dominated school systems as administrators. They often banded together in all-male teacher associations in the larger cities and formed educational fraternities such as Phi Delta Kappa. Willard Waller observed that men sometimes reacted to the unflattering stereotypes of male teachers by becoming overly hearty, much as a minister might try to prove himself a regular fellow.[34]

In 1904 the Male Teachers' Association of New York City publicized the arguments that had been circulating in professional circles about what was later called the "woman peril." The purpose of their report was to justify hiring only men to teach boys over ten years old and to pay them at a higher rate than the women teachers. Women's true profession, they claimed, was marriage and motherhood, and public employment of "so large a body of unmarried women teachers . . . is diminishing the extent, power, and influence of the home." Women might "endure the strain [of teaching], but are there not signs that their greatest and best physical powers are being broken?" Was it not clear that "the differentiation of the sexes indicates a differentiation of vocation"?[35]

Beyond biology and sociology, were there not pedagogical reasons for employing only men to teach older boys? The New York male teachers replied with a resounding yes. "Men teachers," they claimed, "are necessary as ideals for boys. . . . If it is granted that a boy should, during his school life, gain above all true, sterling, manly character, then we are left to aver that he must come under the immediate control of its only embodiment—a just, capable, and devoted man." They claimed that male teachers were "less mechanical in instruction than women. . . . Women prefer to follow, and are willing to do without knowing any reason for such action." Women feminized the curriculum by stressing "the softer and more showy arts at the expense of the hard essentials." They were squishy and sentimental in discipline, using "the boy's feelings . . . as a constant and immediate lever for all actions." By contrast, men teachers appealed to boys "through the notions of right and justice." Men, they concluded, should be paid more as teachers because they were not doing the same work. The woman teacher "works as a woman, and after all cannot quite undo her true, womanly self."[36]

Not surprisingly, the women teachers of New York were incensed at this self-serving and insulting report by their male fellow teachers and reacted in ways alien to what many men thought was their "true, womanly" nature. Under the leadership of Grace C. Strachan, a district superintendent, they rapidly organized in an association and successfully lobbied the state legislature to obtain a law guaranteeing equal pay for equal work. They also argued that women, like men, should be allowed to teach after they married and had children.[37]

Criticism of women teachers became for a time a spectator sport in popular and professional magazines. The accusations against female teachers contained various catch-22s—women were damned if they did and damned if they didn't. Women undermined the prestige and permanence of the profession because their rate of turnover was high, yet in many communities they were required by law to resign when they married. But if they stayed single and remained in teaching, they became old maids and suffered nervous exhaustion and emotional dry rot (or what one commentator called "the withered heart"). Single women teachers rapidly degenerated after the age of twenty-eight, said one expert on the female psyche. If they were true females and not militant "lady labor sluggers," they feminized all with whom they came in contact, including possibly even the male teachers. A feminized school was particularly noxious for adolescent boys, who needed male challenge in academics and beneficent head-bashing on the playground. The effects of the feminization of the school reached well beyond education to infect the whole cultural life of a society, critics asserted. Men, busy with affairs of state and their work, left culture to the women; in the process culture became "feminized," undisciplined, and timid through association with female teachers.[38]

G. Stanley Hall joined this woman-teacher-bashing with relish and argued that females spoiled boys by sparing the rod. "Devoted teachers often wear themselves out in coaxing, rewarding, and coquetting with parents, to keep bad boys decent, when a single dose of Dr. Spankster's tonic would do the business with celerity and dispatch, for in the moral world there are situations in which the rod is a magic wand that can still work miracles." The result of feminine "sugary benignity" was either an overly docile boy or a rowdy potential juvenile delinquent. "Is there not something wrong with the high school boy," Hall asked, "who can truly be called a perfect gentleman, or whose conduct and character conform to the ideals of the average unmarried female teacher?" Boys must pass through a "raw period" of revolt in order to move to "virile manhood," but that restless time when boys have their own distinct "tastes, interests, plays, games, and ambitions" must be controlled and tempered by male teachers. Like the New York male teachers, Hall was suggesting that women teachers practiced a different philosophy of education, one that eliminated corporal punishment and used more "progressive" teaching methods, one whose forms of moral suasion were more relational than abstract. In these traits he saw not an advance toward a more enlightened pedagogy but female weakness inappropriate for boys. The way to adjust secondary education to the fundamentally different natures and needs of boys and girls was to have separate and different forms of schooling for each.[39]

Hall expressed sentiments that were popular in an age that exalted virility in anxious rhetoric. That prime minister of masculinity, Theodore Roosevelt, wrote to Hall to approve his "sound common sense, decency, and manliness. . . . Over-sentimentality, over-softness, in fact, washiness and mushiness are the great dangers of this age and this people." Americans must keep "the *barbarian virtues*," he wrote, for a "nation that cannot fight is not worth its salt." He applauded Hall's stand on corporal punishment. An editorial in the official Wisconsin state educational journal also agreed with Hall that discipline had become too soft as a result of "the invasion of our schools by women." Men coerced nonconformists, while women jollied them along—that was their nature. Everywhere one could "see boys in our schools who are going to the bad mainly because they do not come under the hand of a strong man anywhere in their school course. Nothing but masculine vigor, not too much repressed, will properly impress such boys and turn them from their evil ways."[40]

Many people apparently believed that male and female teachers were fundamentally different. A speaker at the National Education Association reported testimony from 543 men and 488 women on "the teacher who did them most good." He stated that 81 percent of the men and 50 percent of the women responded that this teacher was a man. Women were cited, he said, for "personal kindness, self-reliance, and social help," exemplifying purity, refinement, and the "lady-like" qualities, whereas men teachers embodied "masterful strength and masterfulness in relation to vitally significant things"—courage, vigor, and the ability to lead.[41]

Although the mandarins of masculinity won public attention for their cause and kept on bashing women teachers, their opponents entered the fray to defend the women and to deny the claim that coeducational high schools feminized boys. Popular magazines such as the *Ladies Home Journal, Muncey's Magazine,* and *Arena,* as well as educational periodicals like *School Review* and *Educational Review* published rebuttals to articles by men like Chadwick and Hall. Many writers came to the defense of women teachers, claiming that it was absurd to think that they undermined the virility of boys. In a popular article John Dewey echoed the arguments for coeducation developed by Harris in the 1870s, stressing its beneficial effects on morals and manners and the positive intellectual results of merging the somewhat different learning styles of girls and boys. An editorial in *School Review* ridiculed the idea that certain subjects were "feminine," reminding readers that in the nineteenth century Latin was "regarded as entirely inappropriate for women—it would render them masculine," while in the early twentieth century some considered Latin too feminine. A pioneer in the professionalization of physical education, Luther H. Gulick, drew on his knowledge of boys' sports in New York City to disprove the accusation of foreign observers that boys had become effeminate. Over the past twenty-four years, he wrote, "I have not observed that the American boy has become less strenuous, courageous, resolute, enduring, indifferent to pain, in connection with these sports during these years." Neither the friends nor the foes of coeducation disagreed on one key point, however—that boys should be boys and that the sexes should be clearly differentiated during the adolescent years in activities like sports and vocational training.[42]

One educational researcher, Edward L. Thorndike, decided to test the notion that women teachers drove the boys out and that men would keep them in. Using statistics on high schools in 1906, he concluded that the ratio of men teachers made essentially no difference in the proportion of boys. An increase of two-thirds in the number of men teachers was accompanied by an increase of only 2 percent in the number of male pupils. He found also that in the larger schools, a higher proportion of male teachers was associated with a lower rate of graduation for boys. He supplemented his cross-sectional study of 1906 with a historical investigation of changes in the sex composition of staff and students in 1896. He found there, too, that "the addition of men teachers has made very little difference, and very likely none at all, in the proportion of male students." Thorndike's research, published in the premier education journal, did not quiet the debate about the woman peril, however, for the controversy fed on basic fears that had a life of their own. Thorndike himself had doubts about whether it was wise to have so many women teachers.[43]

The rank and file of teachers and administrators probably thought that the attacks on women teachers and the coeducational high school violated pedagogical common sense. When Hall suggested in a speech to the National Education association that separate education was preferable, three high-school principals responded; two of them defended coeducation, and the third said it was often the only feasible solution, although some distinct treatment of the sexes was desirable. Frank Sheldon Fosdick from Buffalo dismissed Hall's ideas out of hand. "Some things are so axiomatic in their very nature that they require neither proof nor defense," he said. "Such a one is 'coeducation in the high school,' which has so commended itself to the people of our country that 98 per cent. of the public high schools . . . are coeducational, and 93.6 per cent. of all the pupils in all our secondary schools are receiving their education where boys and girls meet together on a common level." He had yet to see a feminized boy or a masculinized girl, he asserted. Instead, "the charm of tenderness that is inborn in the girls, balancing the strength of true manliness that is imminent in the boys, conduces to the production of a complete, perfect manhood and womanhood." Emulation between boy and girl, each supplementing the qualities of the other, created a more "well-rounded intellectual development." There were mental differences between the sexes, but there were greater ones within each gender. The call for a separate course of study for girls and boys might make sense as "physiological reasoning," but, quipped Fosdick, "to a practical man a request for female bread, female salad, and female pickles would be equally forceful."[44]

Policy talk about ovaries and algebra or the woman peril flourished in public forums, but those debates did not have much effect on institutional practice. The dire warnings of Clarke and his colleagues did not stop the rising tide of girls pouring into coeducational high schools. Likewise, the palaver about the woman peril did not stop the ratio of women teachers from increasing. During the first two decades of the twentieth century, when the debate over feminization was at its height, the percentage of women teachers rose sharply from 70 percent to 85 percent in the public schools as a whole. Those who advocated increasing the percentage of male teachers failed to persuade school boards to hire more men, in part because women high-school teachers were paid a modal salary that was about two-thirds that of men even though they had more years of education and almost the same number of years of experience. Table 9 indicates sex ratios of teachers and students in high schools from 1890 to 1920, a period of explosive growth in public secondary education, when the number of students grew ninefold, from about 202,000 to 1,857,000.[45]

Because of the uneven quality of educational statistics—only about

Table 9

Sex Ratios of Teachers and Students in Public High Schools, 1890–1920

	Women/Teachers (%)	Female/Students (%)	Female/Graduates (%)
1890	58	57	65
1900	50	58	63
1910	55	56	61
1920	65	56	61

Source: U.S. Bureau of Education, Biennial Survey of Education, 1918–20 (Washington, D.C.: GPO, 1923), p. 497.

three-fifths of high schools reported in 1890, for example—one should not make much of minor variations by decade, which may be artifacts of data gathering rather than accurate trends. But overall, it is clear that girls continued to outnumber boys as students and graduates (although boys began to make modest gains in the twentieth century). After a dip in the 1890s, women teachers captured an increasing share of the coveted positions in high schools.

Thus, coeducation continued as the basic way to organize gender relations in the high schools, as in the elementary grades. The opinions of the King Canutes on the effects of "identical coeducation" on girls revealed anxieties about the ways in which education seemed to be altering traditional patterns of family life, while the hue and cry about "the woman peril" and the alleged decline of masculinity revealed ideological concerns about keeping gender roles distinct for boys as well. In the Progressive Era, these concerns fueled attempts to differentiate coeducation in order to cope with "the boy problem" and "the woman question."

7

Differentiating
the High School
The "Boy Problem"

In *The Saturday Evening Post* in 1912 William D. Lewis, a high-school principal, described how high schools cheated boys and what should be done to remedy the boy problem. The hero and the victim of the article was Rogers, a star football player. The scene opened with the fans praying "to the great god Mars for a victory that meant a celebration in assembly next day." The quarterback made a fake run to the right and threw a pass to Rogers, who caught it in a blaze of glory. Then the triumph aborted: " 'Take him out!' commanded the principal. . . . He has no right to play in this game—and he knows it!" From the bleachers came catcalls, yells, and groans. The principal "had issued a challenge to the public sentiment of the school that required as much nerve as it does to storm a breastwork." Rogers's crime? He had "failed to make the academic standing required of athletes in all self-respecting schools."[1]

"What's the matter with Rogers?" yelled the cheerleaders. And that was indeed the question, said Lewis. Why was it, he asked, "that with every incentive to keep up, some of the squad is always behind"? Asking such boys to do the traditional academic work of the high school was like trying to make an elephant waltz. "They are boiling over with energy, and no amount of future reward, even in a football game, will make them very keen on the scent of a crooked construction in Caesar or a knotty quadratic unless they see how the trail leads to their own dens."[2]

The academic high school of 1912, Lewis thought, was still designed for "socially and mentally homogeneous sons of American parents," students who were eager to learn and focused in their ambitions. But in fact the pupils who entered its doors were "as heterogeneous as an election-day crowd," and many of them had little sense of direction or willpower. Boys came from grammar schools where their teachers and the principal knew them well and kept their noses to the grindstone, but when they entered the more anonymous and academically oriented high schools, boys like Rogers circled from puzzling class to class, earning low marks and losing self-esteem until they dropped out to work. For some boys the traditional college preparatory subjects made sense, but for the vast majority a more practical curriculum was the only way to focus their interest and tap their abilities. Not algebra but business mathematics, not Virgil but woodworking, not ancient history but the workings of the local political machines—these were the subjects that would keep the new kind of boys interested and able and willing to remain in schools, Lewis asserted.[3]

The episode of Rogers on the gridiron and Lewis's interpretation of his high-school experience illustrated both the nature of the "boy problem" and educators' solutions. Much of progressive education can be understood as a campaign to better fit schooling to boys, particularly those who seemed non-academic in inclination or ability. Basically, the boy problem was that boys did not do as well in school as girls. At the turn of the century a large number of educators and researchers piled up evidence on the massive rates of "retardation" (or grade repetition) and "dropouts" (a term that seems to have been coined sometime about 1900) among "hand-minded" boys, many of whom were of immigrant background. Educators experimented with segregating boys and girls in academic courses in order to adapt instruction better to presumed sex differences. They created vocational tracks for boys from blue-collar families and wanted to make schooling in general more relevant to work by stressing the "life career motive." They also sought to instill a more masculine tone and temper in the schools, in part by co-opting the informal interscholastic athletics that the boys themselves had created.[4]

Male educators thought that public schools must be defective if girls did better than boys. There was a great gender disparity between success in school and success in later life, observed a high-school principal in Chicago in 1910: "The valedictorians of the high school graduating classes are almost always girls; but in after-life, whether in universities or in life occupations, boys have not shown themselves wanting." It was striking, he wrote, that "the Great Business College of Life has conferred its highest degrees upon many a boy who has been marked a failure in high school when compared with the average girl."[5]

The chief target of the King Canutes had been identical coeducation. Although they failed to halt the progress of coeducation, in the Progressive period at the turn of the twentieth century more and more educational reformers came to agree that schooling should be differentiated, not identical, for boys and girls. Coalitions of reformers sought to translate broad-based gender concerns into new educational policies. As educators incorporated these changes into coeducational schools, to what degree did the reforms remain at the periphery of the system rather than penetrating the coeducational core of the schools?

The Rationale for Differentiation

The principle of designing different kinds of education for students of diverse backgrounds and destinies distinguished the ideology of "social efficiency" in the Progressive Era from the older aims of the common school. The institutional character of public education changed as well in the early decades of the twentieth century. Reformers sought to keep students in school for much longer periods of time, added new courses and curricular tracks designed to calibrate education to "life," and created complex new bureaucratic structures in urban districts. Infusing this wave of organizational innovation was an almost millennial faith in the ability of the redesigned school to correct even the most intractable social evils, including the challenges that a new urban and industrial order posed to a traditional set of gender relationships.[6]

Educational crusaders of the mid-nineteenth century had argued that public schools should be common in two senses: they should include children of all classes, ethnic groups, and religions, and both sexes; and they should expose all students to a standard curriculum that would ensure not only literacy and numeracy but also a common set of political and moral values. Thus they designed an institution that was to be in most respects the same for all—unisex, uniclass, unicultural, and unipurpose—even though citizens' paths diverged in adulthood.[7]

In practice the public schools of the nineteenth century fell far short of such an ideal. They tended to reflect the values and interests of the white, Anglo-Saxon, Protestant, middle-class males who, by and large, founded and ran them. Blacks were often excluded and almost always shortchanged in resources. Some religious and ethnic groups resisted what they saw as a nativist and Protestant bias in the school curriculum. Working-class children often received far less public schooling than children of higher status. Girls at first were excluded from some public secondary schools and faced, as we have shown, various other forms of unequal and differential treatment. Because local communities varied enormously in wealth, so did the quality of their schools. But usually these forms of discrimination were not part of a conscious design to differentiate schooling to fit different kinds of pupils, and in many places the common schools approximated the ideal of similar treatment for all children.[8]

The idea that a common schooling would suit all pupils seemed absurd to many reformers of the Progressive Era. A one-size-fits-all education seemed to them rigid, inefficient, inhumane, and unscientific. Instead, responding to the demands of a new industrial society, the social engineers of the new pedagogical order wished to adapt schooling to presumed differences in students' abilities, interests, and destinies in later life. This is what they meant by the slogan "social efficiency." They believed that a redesigned and expanded school could solve a myriad of social problems: how to assimilate millions of immigrants, restore the primacy and health of family life, mitigate the evil effects of industrialism and dampen class conflict, and ease the transition from school to work. They wanted to create a school that would deal with the whole child and the whole society and believed their goals could be achieved through a carefully differentiated program.[9]

To accomplish this task, reformers relied heavily on a new "science" of education that justified differential treatment on apparently objective grounds. They tried to calibrate schooling to students' abilities and likely future destinies. They devised intelligence tests and ways to appraise vocational aptitude and interests, at times referring to these as properties of individuals and at others as attributes of collective groups (sexual, ethnic, racial, or socioeconomic). As institutional solutions to differences of academic ability, gender, class, race, and ethnicity, they proposed grouping students by I.Q. scores, guiding them onto different curricular tracks, establishing specialized vocational high schools (sometimes divided by sex), offering elective courses that appealed to different groups, and introducing new required subjects such as home economics and manual training or physical education classes. Americans were generally ambivalent, however, about a the central issue: whether a differentiated school system should simply offer more choices to individuals or should actually channel certain groups into what educators regarded as appropriate tracks and programs.[10]

Reforms that produced segregation of students by social class, academic ability, and ethnicity aroused controversy. Some advocates of vocational training and guidance believed that one could predict the future work of pupils with some accuracy from the class background of their parents. The development of I.Q. testing during the second decade of the twentieth century convinced many educators that differences of "intelligence" were so great that students should be grouped by ability and steered into academic or trade-training programs in high schools. But the notion that educators could predict the vocational destinies of students from their class backgrounds and plan the curriculum accordingly offended those who perceived in such differentiation a thinly veiled antidemocratic attitude. Some questioned the scientific validity of intelligence testing and regarded tracking with suspicion. Many citizens rejected as arrogant ethnocentrism the campaign to "Americanize" the children of immigrants. And blacks and their white allies continued to fight the separate and grossly unequal education that characterized the caste system of the South and the second-class status of blacks in northern schools.[11]

Differentiation by gender, by contrast, aroused relatively little dissent. Whereas Americans were reluctant to talk about class differences, especially in education, they freely discussed gender distinctions. All but a handful seemed to take it for granted that the sex of children not only would but should shape their opportunities in life. Although educators of the Progressive Era presumed that boys should have a wide choice of careers in later life, most agreed that girls should find their major life's work in one: marriage and motherhood (perhaps after a brief detour into a woman's job). Some reformers worked to adapt the curriculum better to boys, while others sought to adjust schooling to girls. Women school reformers, both lay and professional, did not want the girls to be ignored amid all the attention being paid the boys; they called for programs in home economics, hygiene, girls' physical education and athletics, and vocational training— all in sex-segregated classes. Differentiation of instruction by gender created new specialists, both women and men, within school systems— coaches, health instructors, vocational teachers, or deans of women, for example—who had a vested interest in expanding their sex-segregated domains.[12]

Differentiation by gender in the Progressive Era was not based, for the most part, on presumed cognitive differences between the two sexes. It relied, instead, on the doctrine that boys and girls needed to be prepared for different futures. Test designers knew that girls and boys performed about the same in academic work (though girls had the edge in grades), and since the major purpose of intelligence testing in schools was to predict academic performance, psychologists balanced test items so that scores did not differ much by sex.

Women psychologists in the early twentieth century found that many of the supposed mental differences between men and women were illusory. An able cadre of scholars like Helen T. Wooley and Leta S. Hollingsworth demolished fanciful male interpretations of innate sex differences like those of Hall. They explained later lack of achievement in the "Great Business College of Life" not by differences in genes and temperament but by social constraints and discrimination; reverse the job opportunities and home responsibilities of the two sexes, they said, and one would have an interesting experiment in the correlation of gender and "success." A major developer of school I.Q. tests, Lewis Terman, agreed with Wooley that "mental tests have at last vindicated woman's claim to intellectual equality with man. As far as the *average* ability of the sexes is concerned the question has received a final answer. Among psychologists the issue is as dead as the ancient feud as to the shape of the earth."[13]

What might male educational leaders have concluded if girls had performed worse than boys in school and had dropped out in larger numbers? They might have explained such trends in terms of lesser female intelligence and stamina, but they did not choose that explanation for the boy problem. "On the whole," wrote Wooley in 1914, "girls have stood better than boys in measures of general intelligence. So far as I know, no one has drawn the conclusion that girls have greater native ability than boys. One is tempted to indulge in idle speculation as to whether this admirable restraint from hasty generalization would have been equally marked had the sex findings been reversed!"[14]

Those who wrote about the "boy problem" assumed that the cause of male academic failings lay not in male genes but in a defective school system. At the turn of the century reformers were eager to correct those faults.

The "Boy Problem"

The "boy problem" was not imaginary, even though much of the rhetoric about it was inflated. Nineteenth-century educators had often pointed out that girls learned to read earlier, won higher marks, served more frequently as class valedictorians, and created fewer disciplinary problems than boys. The higher ratio of girls in secondary schools had provoked earnest discussion well before the Progressive Era. The Massilon, Ohio, school board complained in 1858 that "our young men do not remain long enough in the High School. They generally leave before completing the course of study; accepting the first offer to engage in business, though unfitted both in age and accomplishments to assume the responsibilities of active life." Pointing out that girls outnumbered the boys, the board observed that "the mothers of the next generation will be more thoroughly educated than the fathers. For this, perhaps, posterity may be thankful."[15]

In the first decade of the twentieth century, anxiety over male dropout rates reached a crescendo as "posterity" became less thankful about the comparative advantage of girls and more concerned about male attrition than they had been in the past. Several well-publicized surveys of promotion and graduation rates illuminated the gender gap. In a study entitled *Laggards in Our Schools,* Leonard P. Ayres found that 17 percent more girls than boys completed elementary school. Table 10 shows the uneven distribution of pupils by grade level and sex in urban school systems in 1907. Almost half of all students were lumped in the first three grades, while only 1.2 percent were in the fourth year of high school. Sharp gender contrasts complicated this skewed distribution by grade level. In the first three grades boys outnumbered girls because they were held back more often. In the fourth and fifth grades the sexes were approximately equal. But thereafter the gap widened steadily until girls constituted 61 percent of the students in the twelfth grade and the boys only 39 percent.[16]

Table 10 masks considerable variability in sex ratios and dropout rates by social class, nationality, and locality. Social class was a critical factor in school performance and retention for both boys and girls, but as John Rury has found, fewer working-class boys than working-class girls continued in school, suggesting that males dropped out more often to go to work. By contrast, ethnicity seemed to play a larger role in retention for girls, perhaps because of different cultural attitudes toward female education. Although girls vastly outnumbered boys in high schools, in some immigrant groups—those from Austria-Hungary, Poland, Italy, and Russia, for example—more boys than girls attended high school. The persistence of boys in high school also varied a good deal from city to city in the early twentieth century. Out of 100 boys entering Boston high schools, for example, only 10 reached the senior year, whereas half the white boys in nine Georgia

Table 10

Grade Distribution by Sex in 752 Cities of 4,000+ Population, 1907

	Girls (%)	Sex Gap (%)	Total Population of Boys and Girls in Each Grade (%)
Elementary Grades			
First	48	4	19.0
Second	49	2	13.7
Third	49	2	13.2
Fourth	50	0	12.2
Fifth	50	0	10.6
Sixth	51	2	8.9
Seventh	52	4	7.1
Eighth	54	8	5.1
Ninth*	52	4	1.0
High School			
First year	56	12	3.8
Second year	58	16	2.5
Third year	59	18	1.7
Fourth year	61	22	1.2

Source: U.S. Commissioner of Education, Report for 1907 (Washington, D.C.: GPO, 1908), II, p. 580.

*Ninth year reported separately in 143 cities.

cities and one-third of those in Kansas City, Missouri, became seniors.[17]

There were also important racial differences in the proportions of boys and girls enrolled in high school. There were very few black secondary schools in the South, and this severely limited opportunity for both sexes to continue their education. But as table 11 shows, the disparity between the sexes was much greater for blacks than for whites (even though few commentators on the "boy problem" mentioned this fact). A major reason why more black girls than boys attended high school was that attendance enhanced their chances of entering what was becoming a chiefly female occupation—teaching.

Table 11
Female High-School Students by Race, 1898–1928

	White (%)	Black (%)
1898	57.8	68.1
1908	57.4	66.0
1918	57.0	67.9
1928	51.6	62.0

Source: U.S. Commissioner of Education, *Annual Reports* and *Biennial Surveys.*

During the period from 1900 to 1930, the proportion of children be-tween the ages of ten and fifteen in the paid labor force dropped dramat-ically from 25 percent of the boys and 10 percent of the girls to 6.4 percent and 2.9 percent, respectively. This decline in child labor resulted from a complex set of causes still not fully understood. Compulsory schooling laws and child labor laws played a part, but as Harvey Kantor points out with regard to California, "the rise in attendance began before the passage of stiffer legislation and it continued to outdistance the requirements of the laws." Increased educational requirements for some jobs, rising family in-come and decreasing numbers of children, and concern about sheltering children during adolescence may all have influenced the shift from work-place to school. But crucial to the transition were changes in the workplace itself, where technological changes had eliminated many jobs that children had performed and where new white-collar jobs in the tertiary sector cre-ated a new demand for further schooling.[18]

The major decline in child labor, resulting in the gradual movement of child workers from dead-end jobs into the schools, mitigated some of the worst evils publicized by the humanitarian reformers, but the addition of working-class children to the upper elementary grades and to secondary-school rolls challenged educators to adapt the system to the newcomers. The percentage of fourteen-to-seventeen-year-olds enrolled in school in-creased sharply and steadily from 6.7 in 1890 to 51.4 in 1930. During most of that period, however, the vast majority of these young people were attending elementary schools, not high schools. As late as 1930, after decades of effort to reduce the rate of "retardation" (or holding pupils back in grade), only 64 percent of fourteen-to-seventeen-year-olds in school were in grades nine through twelve, and the secondary-school enrollments that year were only 17 percent of the total public-school roster. Even though most young people in school were still in the elementary grades, proposals to differentiate schooling by gender usually bypassed the elementary grades and focused instead on the high school.[19]

In professional meetings and in the educational journals administrators and researchers argued about the precise dropout rates and ratios of boys to girls, but they agreed that attrition was a critical problem. Educators defined truancy primarily as a male problem, in part because male truants were more visible on the streets than truant girls, who often worked at home, and in part because boys were much more often arrested as delinquents. Some of the studies that linked child labor in dead-end jobs to leaving school did attend to girls as well as boys. But most of the male educators writing on dropouts assumed that academically inclined girls were already doing well in comparison with boys, and if less talented girls left school to help at home, such a decision seemed socially and economically acceptable unless they went to work in factories or other blind-alley jobs. As a result, when these educators discussed the reasons for the boys' poor performance and high dropout rates, and remedies for the situation, they largely ignored the girls.[20]

"Anyone whose duties give frequent opportunity for high school visitation cannot fail to be struck by the fact that the boys are conspicuously absent in nearly all high-school classes," wrote two educators. "It is not an infrequent experience to find a good-sized class with not a single boy, while a class with twenty girls and two or three stray and lonesome boys is fairly common." They warned that "if we are not to have a comparatively ignorant male proletariat opposed to a female aristocracy, it is time to pause and devise ways and means for getting more of our boys to attend high school." Educators began to talk about boys as a disadvantaged minority in need of compensatory education.[21]

One of the favored tools of the new "science" of education was the questionnaire. University researchers, superintendents, state officials, and principals, in their efforts to understand why boys quit the upper grades of elementary school and high school, began looking to administrators, teachers, and (sometimes) pupils for clues. The answers to questionnaires tended to be mechanical, in part because the categories were predetermined and because the researchers often signaled correct replies. Studies also tended to downplay the role of economic necessity in leaving school to go to work and underestimated the degree to which families needed children's and wives' wages. Urban working-class families often could not make do on the father's wages alone.[22]

Administrators, teachers, and students gave somewhat different reasons for the boys' dropout rates. Administrators gave most weight to the desire of boys to earn money or the "commercial ideals at home" or to peer attitudes that stressed work over schooling. They said that boys were more often "lazy" or "ashamed not to pass" than "mentally incapable." They ascribed less importance to students' dislike of school; interestingly, in view of the talk about "the woman peril," they did not place much blame on women teachers. Like administrators, teachers focused on the appeal or necessity of work and also stressed the laziness more than intellectual failings of dropouts. Students told a different story: they ranked dislike of school first, "services required by family" second, and "ill health" third.[23]

The most interesting study of dropouts used a more open-ended and revealing technique than the questionnaire. William F. Book asked 961 students (718 girls and 243 boys) in English classes across the nation to write an essay on the reasons why students quit high school. They were told that their teachers and principals would not see the compositions. So full and frank were the replies, Book said, that "it was as if the writers had been waiting for years to unburden their minds of certain things which they had never been given an opportunity to express." Book grouped their replies into three (in fact overlapping) categories: the lure of work outside the school; the individual characteristics of pupils, such as ill health or laziness; and attitudes toward school work. The students reacted to both the pull of the outside world and the push of dissatisfaction with their school life.[24]

Over 90 percent of the students stressed the attraction of paid work, either as a way to contribute to the family economy or to gain financial independence. Both boys and girls wrote that this motivation applied mostly to boys, who enjoyed a far wider range of alternative occupations than girls and thus paid higher opportunity costs for remaining in the classroom. Here are some of the boys' comments:

Boys in high school feel too big to ask their parents for money so drop out of school to go to work.

Some boys think, and they cannot be convinced otherwise, that it is a perfect waste of time and energy to spend four years in a high school which could be, as they say, more profitably employed in getting a start in life.

One reason for so many boys dropping out of school is that some parents think when a boy gets enough education to be able to work problems he must go to work and help support the family. The girls stay in school until they graduate because they can't do much to earn money until they get a good education.

Girls put a somewhat different spin on boys' eagerness to work:

A boy don't care for books like a girl.

They think if they could work and make their own money they would be more like men and treated so.

Boys think it looks babyish to be in school studying with girls when they might be making money, getting started in life, and making something of themselves.

Boys are naturally conceited. When they reach a certain age they think what they don't know is not worth learning.[25]

In their themes the students often claimed that high school demanded very hard work, harder than they would find outside in the paid labor force or at home. Thus, some students equated going to work with laziness. As a sixteen-year-old girl put it, "school means hard work and I feel discouraged enough sometimes to just drop out myself. It is nothing but study, study, study from morning to night." About dropouts, another girl wrote: "They are too lazy to persevere, too indolent to work and get tired of their teachers always scolding them." A boy observed: "The reason why so many drop out of school is not because circumstances compel them to do so, but because a little solid work bores and frightens them." Girls were critical of the boys' lack of perseverance, claiming "boys lack the patience of girls", or "they don't have the grit to win out." Less than 1 percent of the students mentioned lack of intellectual ability as a cause for quitting school. But almost a fifth identified ill health as a reason for leaving—always attributed to girls, not boys, perhaps because this was a more culturally acceptable reason for females—and this they connected with the work load as well as an overactive social life and lack of exercise:

They broke down from over study.

Had home duties which with the work of the school proved to be too much.

It (school) is like the struggle for existence. Only those mentally and physically strong can survive.[26]

In this struggle for survival, many wrote, students became discouraged by low marks and by unsympathetic or confusing teachers. While recognizing the pull of the labor market, the appeal of a cash income and fine clothes, and the character defects of their fellow students, the pupils put much of the blame for attrition on the teachers' lack of empathy and skill and a boring and irrelevant curriculum. Suppose a boy "gets one or two D's in his first term," wrote one boy, speaking of "personal experience with one of my chums. . . . His strongest inclination is to throw down his books and say: 'Hang the stuff! I can't do it to save my neck! I can't, and I never can do it so there's no use trying.' "[27]

Some boys, instead of dropping out of school, constituted another kind of "boy problem." They formed a counterculture of male students who resisted the school and regarded it as a place designed for sissies and girls. One principal described such a subgroup of boys as "the gang" or "the loafers," students who were "typical of nearly every high school in the country." These boys delighted in turning on the fire hose in the hallway and were interested in fraternities, sports, mischief, and girls—in that order. Clearly they were not attracted by the kind of academic program the school offered, which they disparaged as female.[28]

In her study of Greenwich Village in New York City during the 1920s, Caroline F. Ware described how working-class boys—mostly of Italian and Irish background—formed an anti-school male counterculture similar to the English "lads" more recently analyzed by Paul Willis. "Along with the necessity of being foul-mouthed, tough, and playing to win," Ware wrote, "boys were under social pressure to hate school and all forms of school activity. . . . Pressure from other boys was sometimes so strong as to warp an actual desire and liking for school into the general pattern of rebellious hatred. Girls, by contrast, could safely like school, and often played school on the stoops."[29]

Working-class young men, Ware found, "spent practically all their leisure moments in public and in company. It was as unheard of that boys should do chores around the house, other than running errands, as that girls should not. . . . They were, consequently, constantly exposed to the strong pressure of public opinion." Peers demanded that they "avoid signs of refinement or culture. It was all right to be educated, but not to act in

In the Chicago public schools in the 1920s boys were appointed as "junior police" and expected "to ensure domestic tranquillity" by breaking up fights on the playground. (*Chicago Report for 1924*.)

speech, manner, or etiquette as if education had made any difference." In school the boys were exposed to a middle-class curriculum that was designed to "Americanize" them and did not impart "the values recognized in the local community." As a result, the world portrayed in the school seemed unreal and contained little "to command the interest and respect of the local boys."[30]

But more than that, the school represented to the boys an environment that violated their codes of masculinity. The local public schools in the Italian neighborhood were segregated by sex, and in the boys' school there was continual warfare between the teachers and the students, often accompanied by corporal punishment of the boys and smutty remarks and behavior in class (in a sex-education lecture on the "evils of self abuse," one boy defied the teacher by masturbating in the back of the classroom). The Italian-American girls, by contrast, were more willing students, Ware reported. "The home training and neighborhood experience of the Italian girls produced fewer attitudes that were unpalatable to the teachers . . . and many of the things which the girls' school taught were things which the girls wanted to learn—such as manners and etiquette—or were especially designed for their needs—such as sewing."[31]

In proposing remedies for the "boy problem"—to combat the anti-school male counterculture, male underachievement, and the high dropout rate—reformers attempted to change the school system, which they could control more easily than the student's economic or psychological circumstances. A few educators proposed to challenge the long tradition of coeducation by separating the sexes in academic subjects.[32]

Experiments in Segregating Academic Subjects by Sex

In the Progressive Era some public-school educators believed that the "science" and logic of gender differences dictated that boys and girls should be educated separately in academic courses as well as in peripheral fields like vocational, sex, and physical education. They regarded sexual segregation as a promising form of compensatory education for boys, which was their central concern, although they also believed that separate classes would benefit the girls as well. They came to view presumed gender differences of aptitude, intellectual and social maturation, temperament, interests, and learning styles as inhibiting learning, not assisting it. Such reasoning directly contradicted the influential argument of William T. Harris that coeducation was desirable because the different intellectual styles of boys and girls complemented each other.

If girls had the edge over boys academically, and each sex had different interests and ways of knowing, these reformers asked, was it not wise to segregate the sexes in academic subjects? They did not argue for separate schools—coeducation was too firmly fixed for that—but rather for separate boys' and girls' sections in certain required subjects like English and mathematics. They also devised electives that would appeal to boys or girls only.

One of the most highly publicized experiments in limited segregation of a coeducational school began in 1904 in Englewood High School in Chicago. The principal, J. E. Armstrong, found that boys not only constituted less than a third of the graduates but also performed far less well than girls: 20 percent of the girls but only 2 percent of the boys held a grade average of 90 or better. Coeducation might have social advantages, he admitted, but academically it hurt the boys during adolescence. One reason was that boys were "one to two years less mature than the girls of the same age, and so unable to approach the work with the same degree of seriousness and willpower." As a result, he proposed that in the first two years of high school the boys and girls be taught separately in certain subjects, even though they were grouped together in some courses and in study halls and assemblies.[33]

Segregation encouraged teachers to adjust instruction to the different interests, traits, and learning styles of the two sexes, Armstrong argued. In the boys' English classes, for example, teachers could select texts that appealed to boys and require them to do their compositions in class under supervision as "assistance to the weak will-power of the boy." Since males allegedly had less verbal memory, they needed "devices" like "tables that appealed to visual memory." Boys had some academic strengths, not just weaknesses, he believed, and in separate classes the teachers could take advantage of these. Boys like studying "the causes that underlie great historic movements" and did "more original work in mathematics." In the boys' science classes the teachers stressed experiments, observation, and logical reasoning. Girls, by contrast, were presumed not to be interested in mathematical or scientific abstractions and experiments; therefore, teachers in all-girl classes in those subjects should draw connections between those subjects and domestic life. In the subjects in which girls traditionally did better than the boys, such as English or languages, the teachers could increase the academic demands to challenge the girls' supposed verbal fluency and greater willpower and diligence. Where possible, Armstrong sought to give pupils teachers of their own sex. Sex stereotypes about the presumed deficits and abilities of boys and girls thus underlay his experiment in sex segregation.[34]

Armstrong was pleased with the results: more boys stayed in school and received better grades. Grouped together instead of forming a lonely minority in classes composed chiefly of girls, and free of the competition from more mature female students, the boys "responded to the treatment" splendidly, Armstrong reported. The enrollment of boys increased from 34 to 38 percent of the total roster during the first three years of the experiment. Whereas the girls of the unsegregated class of 1905 had a grade average well above that of the boys, the boys of the class of 1909, who had attended segregated classes, received slightly better grades than the girls. Armstrong admitted that one could not really compare the ability or achievement of the two sexes, since the work of the two groups was not identical, but teachers may have picked up the message that their principal wanted them to give boys higher marks.[35]

Not surprisingly, given the purpose and the results, Armstrong found that men teachers and boys overwhelmingly favored the experiment, while women teachers and girls were more divided in their opinions. When Ella Flagg Young, an associate of John Dewey and a firm advocate of coeducation, took over the superintendency of the Chicago schools, she opposed the experiment. Englewood High School again became coeducational in 1910.[36]

Another experiment in sex segregation in a formerly coeducational high school took place at the Broadway High School in Seattle in 1915. The school was chosen by the school board because it was the largest, having 287 classes, and thus provided the greatest flexibility in classification. The Seattle principal, Thomas Cole, shared Armstrong's assumptions about sexual differences and was also pleased to find that the boys' grades improved substantially under the new regime. Teachers were divided in their evaluation, twenty-four being in favor and seventeen opposed. A physics teacher said the new system was better because he could omit "much of the most difficult part for the girls" and could cover more challenging topics with the boys. Others thought that students felt freer in class discussions and found the work more suited to their interests. But several teachers commented that much had been sacrificed by eliminating coeducational classes, especially the sexes' different contributions to each other's learning. A teacher who had two daughters in the school complained that "I feel a distinct loss to them."[37]

Again, objections to the experiment came largely from girls and their parents. Cole later recalled that opposition arose from the PTA and the Federation of Women's Clubs, perhaps because the plan was designed primarily to solve the "boy problem" and seemed to offer little to the girls, who received lower grades while the boys' marks rose. Furthermore, girls were given a watered-down curriculum in science. But the most important reason that the experiment was terminated, apparently, was that it was more expensive than coeducation, even in a large school.[38]

A number of other districts decided to experiment with sex-segregated academic classes. In Riverside, California, all secondary classes were segregated in 1911. South Bend, Indiana, divided all its eighth-graders into distinct boys' and girls' classes in 1913. Boys and girls in Everett, Washington, attended sex-segregated classes in all eight elementary grades and in most high-school classes beginning in 1912, based on the view, said the superintendent, that "there is enough difference in the way the minds of boys and girls attack a subject to classify them separately."[39]

Most experiments in segregating academic instruction by sex in formerly coeducational schools fizzled, even though in places like the large Englewood and Broadway high schools they were tried under favorable conditions. There were practical and ideological reasons for this failure. Segregation sometimes was more costly and required a large student body for efficient classification. There were relatively few high schools that had large enough enrollments to permit the kind of sexual segregation found in Chicago and Seattle. In 1904 more than one-third of all high-school students attended schools with only one to three teachers; more than one-fifth, schools with four to six teachers; and more than two-thirds, schools with one to ten teachers. Such schools simply did not have sufficient population to segregate boys and girls in academic work, even if they wanted to do so. But many educators, students, and parents were also ideologically committed to coeducation. While coeducation continued to be the standard form of gender organization in the schools, experiments like those in Chicago and Seattle still revealed much about the worries and assumptions of the male administrators struggling with the "boy problem."[40]

Providing sex-typed academic electives was a more common and less controversial strategy; they were not imposed from the top and were therefore less likely to arouse local dissent. Instead, electives seemed to offer choices to students and their parents, and, in a consumer society, choice seemed beneficial. If boys and girls chose different electives, that was considered normal, even desirable—not, as later critics would accuse, the baneful result of different sex conditioning. Some reformers argued that the number of required courses should be reduced to allow more time for electives. A common candidate for such elimination was algebra so that girls would not have to undergo the "soul-destroying" task of learning so alien a subject. As electives expanded and girls were no longer required to take so much mathematics and science, the disparity between male and female enrollments increased. Table 12 shows the drop in female enrollment in certain courses in California between 1895 and 1915. In 1895 both girls and boys generally took the same courses in all subjects; in effect, the courses offered were so limited in number that practically all of them were required. In 1915 there were more electives and fewer requirements.[41]

Some school systems created special science electives for girls. In 1915 the high school in San Jose, California, offered a course in physics for girls, in which the students learned about the mechanics of plumbing, vacuum cleaners, and sewing machines; the principles of sound "underlying the art of music"; and the properties of light as they applied to "the illuminating power of wall surfaces, the efficiency of lamps, and a comparison of colors." Thus instructed, they were hardly prepared for college courses in science or engineering, but this did not seem to bother high-school curriculum designers.[42]

A few districts differentiated the content of courses for boys and girls in other fields as well. Some English teachers tried to select different readings to suit the tastes of boys and girls. Girls were thought to be particularly interested in the emotions and adept at detecting metric form in poetry,

Table 12
Excess of Boys over Girls in Enrollments in
Certain Subjects in California, 1895 and 1915

	1895 (%)	1915 (%)
Algebra	4	6
Geometry	1	7
Trigonometry	14	34
Physics	2	20

Source: Millicent Rutherford, "Feminism and the Secondary School Curriculum, 1890–1920," Ph.D. diss., Stanford University, 1977, p. 151.

whereas boys preferred adventure and action. The assumption underlying this idea of social education was that women and men had fundamentally different roles to play. A survey of fifty leaders of the National Council of Education reported in 1930 its consensus that the school should foster a sexually differentiated ideal of "home membership": "The man to provide the income; to be in the home when practicable and help in training the children. The woman to buy wisely; to manage the home so as to preserve the family morale; to preserve her own health and bear children intelligently; to train the children wisely."[43]

That the man was "to provide the income" was taken for granted at the time and justified the decision to create for boys, but not girls, a range of opportunities in vocational education. One solution widely proposed for the "boy problem" was to connect the school with the workplace.

The "Life Career Motive" and the Vocational Education of Boys

School was irrelevant to work, as many students and adult reformers agreed. Public education was too "bookish" and out of touch with the workplace that beckoned youth. The older, more casual education consisting of a few years in elementary school and then on-the-job training on a farm or in a trade, store, or factory was obsolete, vocational educators believed. Researchers documented how boy laborers drifted from one blind-alley job to another and predicted that young workers would become an unskilled, disaffected, and restive adult labor force.[44]

Working children, said the reformers, were alienated both from school and from work. Over and over again young workers told social investigators how much they hated school. The Milwaukee schools in 1922 offered to pay child workers an average daily wage of seventy-five cents if they would come back to the classroom full-time. Only 16 out of 3,000 young people took up the offer. But child workers usually held low-paid, repetitive, and often unhealthy jobs: lacquering canes in a hot, stuffy Chicago attic; packing cigarettes; pasting boxes; or picking slate out of coal on a fast-moving chute. The turnover of young people in such dead-end jobs was staggering. The transformation of adult industrial work—the deskilling of labor, the rise of massive factories, the centralization of control and profits in huge trusts, and dangerous and oppressive working conditions—produced much worker resistance. Like the young, adult workers changed jobs frequently. Many of them joined unions, went on strike, and were attracted to radical organizations like the IWW and the Socialist party.[45]

Where should Americans turn to in a social crisis of such magnitude? The establishment of vocational programs in the public-school system attracted a strange mixture of manufacturers, union leaders, settlement house workers, economists and other social scientists, university educationists, humanitarians, and change-minded school people. Their motives and proposals differed, but together they agreed that the path to salvation lay through the school and in the process mapped different courses for the two sexes.[46]

Taking up the slack created by the decline in family nurture and apprenticeship training in an urban-industrial society, the school was to imbue students with a "life career motive" that would motivate boys to stay in school and give shape and substance to their learning. This middle-class concept of career, leading from the formative years through adulthood, permeated the thinking of many vocational educators. They wanted not simply to retain students in school and to smooth the transition between schooling and work but to revolutionize public education. Preparing boys and girls differently for their separate "careers" was a key goal of this revolution.[47]

Advocates of the "life career motive" dreamed of a smoothly meshing and meritocratic transition between school and workplace, in which the talents of the individual would be matched to the job, to the benefit of the economy as a whole. They believed that a new science of education and astute analysis of the labor market, coupled with proper vocational training and guidance, could assist pupils to find their proper niches in the workplace. Psychologist Edward L. Thorndike wrote in 1913 that "through the knowledge of the science of human nature and its work in the industries, professions and trades, the average graduate of Teachers College in 1950 ought to be able to give better advice to a high school boy about the choice of an occupation than Solomon, Socrates, and Benjamin Franklin all together could give."[48]

The proponents of vocationalism held that the process of selecting an occupation and preparing for it in school would motivate the individual and make the wheels of progress spin with less friction. Adding vocational courses and tracks to the academic mainstream would diversify the curriculum to fit new kinds of students and contribute new choices of studies and future vocations. The rhetoric of choice and "career" blurred the class and gender character of the tracks thus created; was it not more democratic and pluralistic to give boys and girls a range of options?

But as vocational education developed in practice, effective choice was severely constrained, for most advocates of vocational education and guidance also prided themselves on being social realists and on knowing what was best for pupils and society. Real choice was possible for white boys of appropriate talent. The range of male choices was broad: in St. Louis the school district produced a guidance pamphlet called "Trades Open to Boys" that described over one hundred distinct crafts, while hundreds of other white-collar and professional occupations were also open to white males. Girls, by contrast, had few vocational options either in school or the labor market. Most vocational educators believed that girls were destined to become homemakers, and if they prepared for paid work, it was typically confined to a narrow range of sex-typed and short-term jobs. The job market had few niches for blacks, and hence they should only be prepared to do menial tasks better. And reformers assumed that all but a gifted handful of working-class white males would find themselves in blue-collar occupations.[49]

These white working-class boys, not the middle class, were the main focus of attention for most vocational educators. The architects of vocationalism did not give much thought to preparation for white-collar jobs, either in the forms that had been common in the nineteenth century—teacher training for girls or clerical training for boys—or in the commercial education tracks that became popular in the early twentieth century. The debate about vocational education for males centered on the industrial work force. One advocate of vocational training thought the notion of "equality of educational opportunity" only an "academic and philosophic abstraction." The proper goal, he said, was "an *equilibrium,* a balancing of educational opportunity. . . . An equilibrium of opportunity implies that grade of reward commensurate with capacities, whether those capacities are of the endowments of nature, of the acquisition of training, or of the fullness of family coffers." Vocational education should become "consciously selective" in order to fit "the square industrial worker into the square industrial hole, the round industrial worker into the round hole, the triangular worker into the triangular hole."[50]

Looking back, it takes some effort of the imagination to understand why Americans of diverse backgrounds and ideologies—employers, labor unionists, and humanitarian reformers—placed such faith in a vocationalized school. How could a few courses in shop skills and vocational guidance really remedy the momentous dislocations brought on by industrialism? Was it plausible that attending a continuation school for a few hours a week would really provide young workers with significant career opportunities? The rhetoric vastly outstripped the reality; the means, the ends. But such overpromising has been characteristic of much of American educational reform, especially when outsiders have attempted to use schooling to solve structural problems. Debate and political gestures have often focused on the schools because education has been one of the few clearly public agencies available for the symbolic reformulation of intractable issues. Thus vocational education may be regarded as part of this ongoing and intensely serious drama.[51]

To what degree did American public education actually become vocationalized, fulfilling the hopes of the reformers? To what degree did vocational education succeed in differentiating schooling according to the different work destinies of boys and girls?

Despite all the policy talk about vocationalizing the school, we suggest that the actual changes failed to qualify as a revolution and that vocational courses remained on the periphery of the basic system of coeducation. In the first place, the nineteenth-century high school had not in fact been so divorced from vocations as it was alleged to be, and the Progressive Era therefore did not represent so sharp a turning point. From the first high school in Boston onwards, Americans expected secondary education to pay off occupationally, at least for boys, although admittedly the talk about jobs heated up in the twentieth century. Second, the great majority of students were enrolled in elementary schools, where there were few explicitly vocational courses or programs. Differentiated preparation for careers was limited to secondary schools, and until the 1930s high schools enrolled far fewer working-class than middle-class students; most working-class young people were not even in secondary school during the first three decades of the twentieth century. Third, secondary students generally spent much less time in vocational courses or tracks than in academic courses. Fourth, to the degree that students did prepare directly for vocations in high school, as opposed to preparing for college, they overwhelmingly and not surprisingly chose commercial courses and white-collar occupations rather than the industrial courses that were the keynote of reformist rhetoric in vocational education. Fifth, industrial education, found mainly in large cities, though marginal even there, failed to realize the hopes of its advocates; it was not notably successful in preventing working-class students from dropping out of school or in placing them in the jobs for which they were trained.[52]

From its origin, the high school did serve as a portal to respectable jobs for boys, even when they dropped out to take positions in commerce or other urban white-collar work. As in Boston, employers sometimes used admission into high school as a criterion in screening job applicants, because it implied that a boy was likely to be industrious and academically competent. Skill in ciphering and handwriting, proper spelling and diction, a record of punctuality and obedience to rules, middle-class appearance and decorum—these were assets in a clerical job as in school. Toward the end of the nineteenth century, many public schools added subjects like bookkeeping or mechanical drawing to train boys for mid-level jobs in commerce or technical positions. The high school also led through college or university to professional and managerial occupations. The "life career motive" no doubt inspired many of the boys who did remain in the "bookish" schools of the nineteenth century. The same was true of many girls who enrolled in normal programs in city high schools. Supplying teachers for the common schools had been a compelling argument for admitting girls to high schools. In 1900, 46.3 percent of the female high-school seniors in St. Louis, for example, were in the normal course of study.[53]

Most programs to vocationalize education focused on high schools rather than elementary schools, although only a relatively small percentage of public-school students attended secondary schools until the surge of enrollments in the 1930s. The vast majority of fourteen-to-seventeen-year-olds were enrolled in grade school until at least 1920; in that year, only 10 percent of all public-school students were in grades nine through twelve. And many of the students in elementary school did not even graduate from the eighth grade before they went to work. In 1917 the U.S. commissioner of education reported that 68 percent of students in elementary school were

This picture of a classroom about 1900 (place unknown) depicts boys doing woodwork while girls in the same room do sewing and cooking. A male teacher supervises the boys, a female teacher the girls. Such forms of manual instruction for both sexes were generally not considered to be vocational but rather to train the hand, eye, and habits of useful industry. (Library of Congress.)

in the first four grades and only 6 percent were in the eighth grade. One study of girls who had applied for working papers showed that 65 percent had not reached the seventh grade.[54]

To what degree did elementary schools segregate boys and girls to prepare them for vocations? Probably very little in the formal curriculum of the rural schools, and these constituted a very large segment of American public schools well into the twentieth century (although, informally, boys did "male" tasks about the schoolroom and girls did "female" ones). In some cities, educators proposed that schools should take over functions formerly performed by farm families, such as teaching girls to cook and sew and boys to handle tools. The advocates of such handwork in elementary schools, however, usually did not justify it on economic grounds as training for specific work; rather, they stressed its value in developing latent mental powers and good habits. Despite much talk about the pedagogical and

A boy in a vocational school in New York City in the 1930s has disassembled an automobile engine. (*New York Report for 1934–35,* p. 135.)

moral benefits of homemaking skills and manual training, a survey of thirty-six cities nationwide in 1890 revealed that only 2 to 3 percent of students were actually taking those subjects.[55]

In the twentieth century, however, it became common practice to offer, and even require, manual training and domestic skills in the upper grades of the elementary school. Such classes were generally segregated by sex, although sometimes not (on occasion, in districts unable to hire special teachers, the regular classroom teacher taught both sexes together in manual and domestic arts in the same room). Often the classes in manual training were introduced first, and the work in domestic skills was added later as a way to occupy the girls while the boys were in shop. Instruction in sewing and cooking might be construed as preparation for the vocation of homemaker, but manual training for boys rarely aimed at the specific job training that was the goal of advocates of industrial education.[56]

In the high school, where educators hoped to offer specific preparation for jobs and thereby to retain boys who might otherwise drop out of school, students hardly flocked into industrial and agricultural courses, two fields subsidized by the federal Smith-Hughes Act in 1917. By 1930, only 4.6 percent of boys in urban schools were enrolled in specialized trade and industrial programs (and many of these boys were students at the specialized trade high schools found in large cities). In rural communities, 13

Table 13
Boys and Girls Enrolled in Manual Training, 1900, 1910, and 1928

	1900 (%)	1910 (%)	1928 (%)
Boys	5.2	21.4	24.7
Girls	2.4	1.0	0.2

Source: John Francis Latimer, *What's Happened to Our High Schools?* (Washington, D.C.: Public Affairs Press, 1958), p. 150.

percent of boys between the ages of fifteen and eighteen studied agriculture.[57]

Beyond such federally targeted subjects—often taught in separate trade schools—boys did take courses in handwork in comprehensive high schools, but it is hard to be precise about enrollments. Statistics for the period are often incomplete and should be used with caution. Also, labels for courses were continually changing. One cannot be sure of the content of a subject called "manual training," for example; in most schools it was probably simple woodworking of the kind taught in the upper grades of elementary school, but in others it might have provided training for a specific trade. Table 13 lists enrollments by sex in manual-training courses.

A survey in 1934 divided enrollments in manual-vocational courses into fifteen categories, ranging from the general "manual training" to courses in printing, welding, and automobile mechanics. Over half the male enrollments were in two courses: mechanical drawing (13.2 percent of boys took this subject) and manual training (12.6 percent). Next in line were woodworking (4.2 percent), general shop (2.4 percent) and printing (2.2 percent). The remainder of specialized vocational courses each attracted less than 1 percent of high-school students. Of course, an individual student might take several courses, so that one cannot add up separate course enrollments to arrive at a total number of students taking shop courses. Another way of estimating the salience of shop courses is to calculate their enrollments as a percentage of all courses taken. In a study of five California cities during the period from 1917 to 1922, Kantor found that only 2.5 to 5.9 percent of all course enrollments were in shop.[58]

Beyond the rudimentary introductory courses in manual training or mechanical drawing, then, trade and industrial courses reached few boys, despite the hopes of educators who wished to attract, retain, and place male students in specialized blue-collar occupations. Questions arose about how effectively vocational programs prevented dropouts and whether they actually promoted mobility into skilled jobs. Secondary students and their families generally believed that high school should lead to white-collar jobs in any case, whatever their social origins and no matter how unrealistic their expectations.[59]

This desire to enter white-collar occupations helps to explain the striking success of one kind of vocational education largely neglected by the advocates of vocational schooling: commercial education. Unlike home economics or trade education, commercial education appealed to and enrolled both sexes, and its expansion reflected a market demand from students and their families. In large numbers, boys took business and commercial courses even though they became outnumbered by girls when certain clerical occupations became stereotyped as female.[60]

To put American vocational education in perspective, it is useful to compare it to European secondary education. Not only did a far larger proportion of American fourteen-to-seventeen-year-olds attend high school than their European peers, but most of them were also enrolled in comprehensive schools, where there was a wide choice of courses and few institutional rules to constrain the market system. Although capitalist groups like the National Association of Manufacturers (NAM) and some educators wanted to create a separate set of vocational high schools, with a different administration and curriculum from college-preparatory high schools, labor unions and most educators wanted instead to include vocational training as part of comprehensive secondary education under the same school boards that directed the rest of the public educational system. The latter group won, even in cities like Chicago and New York where a concerted attempt was being made to create a dual system.

"There is little formal stratification in the U.S. national system," Richard Rubinson observes, "compared with other countries where formal rules stratify schooling into different status streams." In Europe only a small percentage of students is "admitted to academic secondary schools that lead to universities and then to high-status occupations." Most students enter separate vocational schools that "are terminal points, not linked to advanced education. . . . Such tracking decisions typically occur at 10–12 years of age, based on performance on a national examination, and the number of positions is determined by formal rules."[61]

In American comprehensive high schools, by contrast, the institutional rules segregating pupils are far less rigid. There are different tracks—college-preparatory, general, and vocational—but there are academic course requirements common to the different programs, and no single test or set of quotas determines admission to the tracks. Students may switch tracks and decide late in their school careers to seek admission to higher education. As Rubinson notes, class factors shape the choices of individuals about which courses they take, and class bias may influence the advice students receive about programs, but the American system does not have official institutional rules, like those in Europe, "that effectively ensure class segregation." The result is more of a pedagogical market economy than one in which the state, by its mandates, commands streaming.[62]

In such a market economy of secondary schooling, it is not surprising that most boys bypassed training for blue-collar work and opted instead for college-preparatory or commercial education that offered them a better chance to enter the white-collar and professional sector of the job market (which was expanding at a rapid rate during the twentieth century). Although the efforts of vocational educators from 1890 to 1930 aimed at reducing the blue-collar dropout rate through trade and industrial training, students and their families nonetheless tended to think of high schools as gateways to white-collar employment. The rhetoric of vocational purpose suffused the statements of educators during those years and perhaps reflected and reinforced the common tendency of American families and students to justify schooling in terms of higher future income and enhanced occupational opportunities. But the route to the best jobs continued to lie through the coeducational academic high school.[63]

If the goals of vocational education seem in retrospect disproportionate to the results obtained, and if the high schools retained much of their white-collar flavor, still the adoption of vocational education helped defuse the external criticism of the schools that emerged in the Progressive Era. At least symbolically, the attention paid to working-class boys and the creation of a distinctively male and "hand-minded" niche in the curriculum showed schools to be responsive to the "boy problem" and the public's general anxiety about what was happening to the adult male work force. Vocational tracks also served an important internal organizational purpose for educators, for they now had a new place for working-class students who were alienated by the traditional curriculum. There were also other ways to demonstrate the masculinity of the high school and to entice a potentially disruptive counterculture of boys into the institutional framework of the high schools. One of these was competitive athletics.

"Bashing Heads" and Staying Healthy

In one domain schools did become associated with masculinity, even for boys in an anti-school counterculture: they became bases for athletic competition. In one New York school in 1909 the principal put "the most troublesome and backward boys" into one class and placed it in charge of an excellent basketball player, a woman teacher. She took her class of tough boys to the gymnasium for an hour every day. The result: "An incorrigible class was brought to the gymnasium; a tired but tractable class left it." The New York superintendent wrote, "Many instances have come to my notice where big, strong, incorrigible and 'stupid' boys have been stimulated by the opportunity to represent their schools, and [by] the anxiety of their school mates, to work hard enough at their lessons to obtain the coveted 'B' in proficiency." Sports tamed the unruly boys, and educators learned in time to tame sports. Athletics proved useful not only for keeping the boys in line but also for winning public support for high schools that had been tainted with femininity. For those who equated masculinity with contact sports, the football contest was a reassuring spectacle.[64]

As Jeffrey Mirel has shown, students themselves were the originators of that lasting and pervasive "reform," high-school athletics—a rare instance in the history of educational change. It was they, not the school authorities or outside adult reformers, who first organized interscholastic teams in sports like football or baseball, free of the supervision of adults in the school. No doubt many of these adolescents were copying the collegiate varsity sports that emerged in the last two decades of the nineteenth century. Athletic competition between public schools did not become a fully accepted and integrated part of public education until the second or third decades of the twentieth century in most communities. By then educators had learned some of the institutional as well as individual benefits of sports; athletics helped them solve some pressing problems, including how to retain the boys and foster their loyalty to the school.[65]

School athletics did not evolve from school-sponsored physical education—or "physical training," as it was often called—but rather from the independent games that children played during recess or after school. Like those games, school athletics were sex-segregated, voluntary, and, initially at least, played for fun. By contrast, most programs in physical education were controlled by school officials, conducted by teachers in coeducational classrooms in the elementary schools, compulsory, and designed to improve the health and academic performance of pupils, not to entertain them.[66]

Few rural districts or small towns had this kind of standardized physical training. Recess in open yards gave children plenty of opportunity to run about and let off steam; children also walked to and from school and played and worked hard after class. In dense cities, by contrast, the health of working-class children suffered because they had few safe places for active play or outdoor labor; the typical tenement homes were crowded and often unsanitary. In school they were expected to sit stiffly and silently in over-crowded classrooms, subjected to rigid discipline and routinized recita-tions. To improve the health and posture of these children and to foster better discipline and instruction by periodically relieving nervous tension, some urban school systems introduced compulsory calisthenics as a regular part of the curriculum. The usual first step was to hire a director of physical training—most often a woman—to train teachers to conduct these exer-cises with their boys and girls.[67]

"It must be distinctly understood that school gymnastics are not recre-ation," wrote the director of the Washington, D.C., program of physical training; "they are school work." If one had "many instructors, few chil-dren, large grounds, and much school time," she said, one might use games as physical training and adopt a more informal regime. But actual condi-tions in city schools were far from ideal. Classrooms were crowded, the schedule was jammed, schools often lacked playgrounds, and only the reg-ular class teachers were available to guide the pupils in their prescribed physical exercises. Thus, in coeducational schools, compulsory physical training was perforce coeducational.[68]

In many cities, physical training was rigidly programmed like the work in mathematics. The teacher led the girls and boys in prescribed maneuvers with Indian clubs, wands, and dumbbells. In Washington, the teachers even led the students in prescribed exercises in yawning and stretching. Despite an earnest interest in the educational value of play, increasingly voiced in the early twentieth century (sometimes amid incredulous reactions from traditional school people), formal gymnastics probably remained the main type of physical training offered. In most systems, gymnastics formed part of the identical coeducational curriculum of elementary schools, for both boys and girls had health problems, and neither the resources nor the inclination existed to differentiate this basic instruction by sex. Only in high schools was physical training—usually calisthenics—segregated by sex, and there it was often required only of girls, in part because of the fear that study might undermine their health.[69]

Few resources were available for physical education. In a survey of phys-ical education in 555 cities in 1904, J. H. McCurdy found that less than a

These are pictures of physical education, calisthenics, recess, and interscholastic competition in Washington, D.C., taken in 1899 by Frances Benjamin Johnston. They illustrate the gender differences between these different forms of activity. (Library of Congress.)

Boys of different ages at their separate recess in a grade school engage in a variety of games (like leap-frog in the foreground).

A male physical education teacher coaching a boys' basketball game in a high school class.

Boys' track teams in competition
supervised by male coaches, with
an audience of boys.

quarter employed physical education teachers or had gymnasiums. In all,
the cities had only 291 special teachers, 65 percent of them women and 35
percent, men. The programs that did exist had been established as a result of
lobbying by women's groups, doctors, parents, and educators concerned
about the health of schoolchildren. The demand for coaches in sports, by
contrast, came from the boys and educators determined to gain control of
interscholastic contests. In these 555 cities, over 80 percent had football
teams and 70 percent had baseball teams. For the most part, students
initiated such interscholastic athletics, managed the teams, and paid their
own coaches, even in cities that had physical education teachers. "In fact,"
wrote McCurdy, "it would appear in many cases that these competitive
sports have grown up without the cooperation of the school authorities or
[physical education] director, you might say almost in spite of them." These
student-run athletics, said McCurdy, were threatening to get out of hand.
More men teachers and physical education teachers were urgently needed to

An outdoor coeducational calisthenics
class in a grade school.

prevent "the evils arising from the presence of athletics in the high schools
without adequate supervision."[70]

What were these evils? Many educators considered unsupervised sports
competitions "injurious to studious habits and a prolific source of rest-
lessness, disorder, and rowdyism" as well as serious physical injuries. Varsity sports produced "neglect of the many for the few." Denied official
school sponsorship or supervision, and determined to win, adolescent athletes sometimes co-opted "ringers," or non-students, to play for the school,
bent the rules, and played with a violence that resulted in smashed noses
and broken legs. Some teams in New York were composed totally of non-
students, and the athletic heroes were often truants. Often the teams met
secretly and generated more betting, said one critic, than horse races. Work,
not play, was the activity appropriate to school, thought many citizens.
"The statement, 'Athletics is an evil,'" wrote one advocate of sports in
1923, "was prevalent in the talk and writings of those who were alarmed by

the fact that boys and girls are physical and are so by nature. This was the age of damnation . . . of all athletic activities wherever found." Educators condemned competitive sports "with enthusiasm and vigor." But the students themselves, he said, "craved to participate in athletic activities" and organized and played their games "as secretly as possible."[71]

The pressure from boys who wanted to compete in sports and from fellow students and community fans who wanted to watch them proved irresistible in most communities. Responding to such demands and realizing the institutional advantages in interscholastic athletics, high-school leaders eventually decided to adopt competitive sports as part of the school program—as long as they could control the enterprise. Wisely managed, athletics could help solve the problem of male dropouts, provide a safe outlet for adolescent energies, create school spirit, reverse the image of high schools as a feminine domain, and win community support for expanding the scope and functions of secondary education at a time when educators dreamed of using high schools to solve a whole array of social problems.[72]

In 1902, at the annual meeting of the National Education Association, one speaker proposed several topics for his fellow high-school principals to discuss. The first subject was "School Athletics." They spent their whole time on that, for they found it "full of life and interest." The group of principals, who represented more than twenty states, concluded "that the real boy and girl can be reached most effectively through properly regulated athletics." School athletics, said Principal W. J. S. Bryan of St. Louis, "is a question of practical importance, because it has not been called up from the realm of the imagination, but has arisen in the life of nearly every secondary school. . . . The existence of athletics and their forceful if not forcible entrance into the life of secondary schools has been regretted by some, because they seemed likely to disturb the calm serenity of the school, and often did prove a disquieting influence." Because of this distrust, athletic events "were for some time left severely alone, if they were not openly discountenanced and discouraged."[73]

"Left to themselves," Bryan said, "the youth displayed a lack of judgment which older heads and mature years might have contributed had there been proper sympathy with youth and a right appreciation of the opportunity afforded for helpful suggestion and wise direction." Many people were beginning to agree that sports were "not sinful or subversive of good" but a natural outgrowth of the energies of the young and a useful part of the total educational program. Boys had a natural "fighting instinct," thought many educators, and that urge would find an outlet, licit or illicit. Boys, wrote McCurdy, "have with instinctive discernment selected the sports requiring courage, manliness, and physical vigor." Athletics properly controlled by school authorities and by local and state athletic leagues enhanced the students' alertness, manliness, health, self-control, obedience to authority, sense of school spirit, and "loyalty which may be used in other connections as well." Educators often compared athletic contests to war and, by implication, drew a connection between male citizenship and military duty.[74]

The largest and one of the most elaborate programs of athletic competition between schools developed in New York city during the first decade of the twentieth century. In 1903 the public schools appointed a physician, Luther H. Gulick, as director of physical training. Like the reformer Jacob Riis, he was convinced that the city was failing to develop "social morality and good citizenship in the young," particularly in the boy who, "blindly reaching out to express [his] social instinct . . . finds himself thrown upon the street and the corner, with scarcely any activity open to him in crowds, save those of an illegal nature." To satisfy the boy's "gang instinct" in a productive way, Gulick proposed the creation of the Public Schools Athletic League.[75]

The league did not become an official part of the school system until 1914, mainly because the school board was unwilling to bear the cost of the program and persisted in regarding sports as voluntary rather than as an integral part of schooling. But the league did build on a tradition of interschool sports competition that had started in the 1890s. It received funding from some of New York's most famous—or infamous—entrepreneurs, men like John D. Rockefeller, J. Pierpont Morgan, William K. Vanderbilt, and Andrew Carnegie, while newspaper magnate William Randolph Hearst contributed trophies for the champions. Gulick kicked off the new program with a huge meet in Madison Square Garden, in which more than one thousand boys from many different schools competed. By 1921, more than one hundred thousand boys were taking part in the competitions, while four hundred teachers volunteered their time as coaches. The city's newspapers applauded the sports program and gave it much publicity. President Roosevelt became an honorary vice-president of the league and declared that "every boy who knows how to play baseball or football, to box or to wrestle, has by just so much fitted himself to be a better citizen." Gulick claimed that the work of the league and the rapid rise of sports elsewhere proved that the charge that American boys were becoming effeminate was bosh. "Ninety-five per cent of all high schools in America support football teams," he wrote. "No game affords better opportunity for the display of manly power than does football." In the light of such facts, how could English observers say that sports were becoming "progressively ladylike"?[76]

Educators came to see competitive athletics as an ally rather than a foe in their campaign to solve the "boy problem." What they originally perceived as an arena of anti-intellectual rowdies became transformed in their thinking into a stimulus to academic achievement and the building of manly character. Little of the competitive masculine athletic ideal corresponded to the prevalent image of girls. For girls, sports developed good health and a spirit of cooperation. The new ideal of manly character achieved through competitive athletics appealed to school administrators and to a large segment of the public. The vast majority of the superintendents polled by McCurdy believed that properly supervised competitive athletics would enhance public education. Success in games generated good press for the schools and aided public relations. As Joel Spring has noted, school athletics soon became an enormously popular spectator sport and began to occupy more and more space in the sports pages of newspapers.[77]

Male interscholastic sports fulfilled an important symbolic function by asserting the masculinity of the public schools. In this sense, sports directly addressed the "boy problem" and justified investments in elaborate gymnasiums and playing fields. The boys on the gridiron or the diamond and the men who coached them became culture heroes—proof that the high schools were not "feminized."

But still the idea that boys were at a disadvantage in the educational system did not die. Indeed, until the 1960s, educators would continue to lament the "boy problem." They would rediscover periodically that boys had more reading and discipline problems and more learning disabilities, and performed less well in school generally than girls. On the other side of the coin, people tended to assume that girls were doing fine in school. When reformers turned to the "woman question," they were discussing female destiny more than compensatory pedagogy.[78]

8

Differentiating the High School
The "Woman Question"

"Whether we wish it or not," M. Carey Thomas wrote in 1908, "the economic independence of women is taking place before our eyes." The changes amounted to a "stupendous social revolution," she believed. "Women are one-half of the world, but until a century ago . . . women lived a twilight life, a half life apart, and looked out and saw men as shadows walking. It was a man's world." Now that "women have won the right to higher education and economic independence," she declared, "the right to become citizens of the state is the next and inevitable consequence of education and work outside the home. We have gone so far; we must go farther. We cannot go back."[1]

"What ought women to be?" That question never "occupied so large a place in thought as it does today," asserted one advocate of vocational guidance for girls in 1919. "In familiar discussion, in the press, in the library, on the platform, the 'woman question' is an all absorbing topic." The Progressive Era was indeed a time of transformation in the lives of many women. They agitated for the vote and won it in 1920. The percentage of women aged fourteen and over in the paid labor force jumped from 18 in 1890 to 25 in 1910, a ratio that persisted until 1940 amid important shifts in the distribution of women in the labor force. Vastly increased numbers of young women completed high school and college and entered jobs newly opened to women, such as clerical positions. Militant working-class women and their elite allies fought for higher pay and better working conditions. Collectively, in their clubs and reform organizations, many middle- and upper-class women enlarged the narrow confines of women's sphere to include the reform of society. And there were significant changes in the family. Increasing numbers of married women worked; by 1920 they constituted 23 percent of gainfully employed women. Conversely, those women who gained professional positions often remained single; only 12 percent of professional women were married in 1920. Increasingly, couples chose divorce rather than continuing unhappy marriages.[2]

Feminists and their opponents vigorously debated the meaning of these changes. As Carolyn C. Lougee observes, controversy "over the education of girls is a key to understanding social conflict." A new political economy of gender and new forms of family life seemed to be emerging, full of promise to some and threatening to others. Activists in the "woman movement" in its various forms—political, economic, and social—hoped to define a more ample scope for women's lives, while their conservative opponents wished to preserve woman's traditional sphere and functions. Both this broader ideological conflict and changing objective conditions of women's lives shaped educational policy, especially with regard to training girls for adult duties. As in the case of the "boy problem," reformers devised educational solutions to bring about their own versions of a preferred future. Various groups with different agendas lobbied for better vocational education for girls, for training in home economics to improve family life, and for sex education.[3]

Not all the changes in school gender practices during the Progressive Era were decreed from on high by adult reformers, however. To the degree that the schools offered a range of electives, parents and students themselves shaped the curriculum through choices that often differed by sex. Girls flocked into commercial education, for example, and greatly increased the demand for sex-typed courses in secretarial and clerical work. A whole array of extracurricular activities sprouted alongside the formal curriculum, nourished by student interest as well as school sponsorship, and providing in many cases sex-segregated niches that reflected peer values and aspirations for of future adult gender roles. Both boys and girls developed their own separate peer cultures that helped shape their responses to the official culture of the institution.

As semi-autonomous institutions, schools responded to the demands for change in differing ways and in differing degrees. Some reforms appeared visibly on the periphery—demonstrating that the school was reacting at least symbolically to outside reformers—but how profoundly did educators respond to the larger agenda of the activists in the woman movement and their opponents? To what degree did the basic form of coeducational instruction remain intact despite the new policy talk and the campaigns of reformers?

Women's Work, the Family, and Enfranchisement

"In the decades before and after the turn of the century," Robert W. Smuts observes, "the employment of women was a major public issue." This controversy over paid work for women engaged a wide spectrum of opinion. On one end were feminists like those in the National Women's Trade Union League (NWTUL) who lobbied for equal and coeducational trade education in all fields. They claimed that women should be free to choose and enter virtually any occupation, even those traditionally held only by men. Economic justice was a central aim of militant women union members and of increasingly well educated women who wanted to pursue professional careers. Activists argued that anything less than full equality of the sexes in the workplace was stifling for individuals and unjust in principle. "It cannot be repeated too often," Eleanor Flexner wrote, "that for women working a ten- or twelve-hour day, whose earnings were almost half those of men, whose lives were often bounded by the sweatshop, and whose relation to their employer lacked any safeguards to personal dignity or job tenure, 'equal rights' was a question of more than education or getting the vote." Such women workers also needed "better pay for their labor, security from fire or machine hazards or the unwanted attentions of a foreman, and a chance to get home to their domestic tasks before complete exhaustion had overtaken them."[4]

At the other end of the spectrum stood the conservatives—both men and women—who believed that schooling should not prepare women for paid work but rather for their duties in the home. Woman's place was in the home, and employment elsewhere was treason to her God-assigned duty and her unique biological and moral functions. A woman who competed with men in the marketplace demolished the separate spheres of the sexes and endangered the family. A husband or father who permitted his wife or daughter to work outside the home demonstrated his own incompetence as breadwinner and master of his home. Many male trade unionists argued that the displacement of craftsmen by poorly paid women workers would undermine men's status as wage-earners and fathers while it unsexed the women.[5]

The influx of women into the paid work force and the movement of a few into male-dominated occupations triggered concern about what was happening to the traditional family. Conservative critics claimed that the opportunity for an independent career was causing many college-educated women to shun marriage altogether or to refrain from bearing children, thereby leading to "race suicide." They blamed working mothers for ill-bred, unhealthy, or delinquent children. They argued that women's employment produced more divorces. When women found that they could support themselves, they no longer behaved as their husbands' respectful dependents. And conservatives contended that factory work, in particular, injured women's morals and led to an increase in prostitution. Many feminists interpreted the changes in the family quite differently. They believed that financial independence through employment gave wives greater equality in marriage or the opportunity to find fulfillment in careers as single women, that the increasing availability of divorce promised to liberate women from oppressive husbands, and that new forms of child care and housekeeping needed to be invented in order to give women a fair chance to develop their talents and lead full lives.[6]

Controversy over women's work and the family also intersected with the debate over women's political enfranchisement. In 1894 Mary Putnam-Jacobi wrote in *"Common-Sense" Applied to Woman Suffrage* that the employment of women created new reasons for giving them the vote. No longer were they working only "in the personal service of father or husband," and no longer could it be assumed that men so preempted the economic sphere that they could represent women politically. Furthermore, women who now worked in factories needed political power in order to protect themselves through effective legislation. A New York working woman, Rose Schneiderman, ridiculed a state senator who feared that women would lose their charm if they would vote. "We have women working in the foundries, stripped to the waist, if you please, because of the heat," she said, yet "the Senator says nothing about those women losing their charm. . . . Surely these women won't lose any more of their beauty and charm by putting a ballot in a ballot box once a year than they are likely to lose standing in foundries or laundries all year round."[7]

Although some of the leaders of the woman suffrage movement tried to enlist militant working-class women in their cause, the key organizers and spokeswomen were from the middle and upper class. Some of the latter sought to reassure male politicians that the vote would not "unsex" women; on the contrary, enfranchised women, through their purity of motives and moral actions, would cleanse politics in a fit of social housekeeping.

This message came across clearly in a magazine article written by high-school students in San Jose, California: "Are your city's politics dirty? Pitch in and clean them up! To destroy this great evil we must grant women suffrage, so that the standard of politics may be elevated by the purity of woman's vote." In 1890, one suffragist declared, "Woman is the teacher of the race; in virtue of her motherhood she is the character-builder; she forms the soul life. . . . It is not part of woman's work to contend with man for supremacy." By magnifying the generic virtues of "woman" (as opposed to the pluralistic qualities of "women") such leaders tried to link the cause of enfranchisement with a traditional ideology of womanhood, family, and woman's sphere.[8]

In the debate of the "woman question" agitating the nation in the Progressive Era, how did educational policymakers respond to the issues of suffrage, women's work, and the family? The leaders of the educational establishment—city and state superintendents, school-board members, university professors of education—were overwhelmingly men. Their periodicals and meetings largely ignored woman suffrage at a time when it was a lively controversy. Their silence, in all likelihood, implied not support of the vote for women but rather a desire to avoid controversy or doubts about the wisdom of enfranchisement. Millicent Rutherford surveyed four leading national educational periodicals and the *Addresses and Proceedings* of the National Education Association for the years from 1890 to 1920. She found only two direct discussions of women's suffrage: the National Education Association's "Ratification of Suffrage Amendment" (the NEA ranks consisted almost entirely of women by that time, but the leadership was in the hands of men) and an article in 1909 in *Educational Review* that reported the defeat of state campaigns for suffrage and concluded that sensible women did not want the vote anyway.[9]

In contrast with male educational leaders, women educators gave substantial support to female suffrage movement. Many of the leaders of the campaign for the vote for women—like Susan B. Anthony and Carrie Chapman Catt—had served stints as teachers. At the 1908 National Suffrage Convention, about a third of the participants had taught at some time. The woman suffrage movement proved to be a powerful educative agency for society, raising basic issues about the political economy of gender. But unlike another women's social movement—temperance—it seems to have had little direct impact on civic instruction in the public schools other than stressing that women shaped the character of the young and might serve as civic housecleaners. A woman principal argued in 1906 that disenfranchised females "must have a training for citizenship," but her concept of educating the girl for citizenship was a depoliticized version of social feminism. "Enlist her interest in all civic questions," she said; "lead her to espouse the cause of right and justice, and to become the champion of the weak and helpless; to assert her prerogative of home-maker, care-taker, and peace-maker." The girl should recognize, she continued, that "while her chief responsibility is toward the small circle immediately about her, she owes something to her fellows; and thus develop in her a larger sympathy which will tend to develop in her the impersonal side."[10]

In the leading education journal, a conservative woman, Annie G. Porritt, made some dire observations on the consequences of having disenfranchised women teachers give civic instruction to boys. What were the results, she asked, of "putting the training of our citizens and voters" and leaders "into the hands of a class [women teachers] that consists of individuals who in the full sense of the word are not citizens, and who have no part or lot in the politics and government of the country"? Perhaps the same as befell Greece and Rome when they turned over the education of their young men to slaves: a failure "to measure up to the traditions of their free forefathers." It was no surprise that the best men in the United States, trained under the "feminine influence" of their mothers and teachers, abandoned politics to "the ward heeler and the party boss." In England, by contrast, the governing class, trained by men in separate-sex schools, regarded running the government "as the highest earthly desire of the ripened mind." The solution Porritt proposed was to abandon coeducation and to train boys in their own schools for "politics and the larger life of the nation" and not to give girls "a training which would tend to unfit them for their own sphere, and probably to make them utterly discontented with it."[11]

Porritt portrayed the women teacher as someone caught in a catch-22. If she is a "womanly woman," she does not care about politics and "is extremely unlikely to teach civics well." But if she is informed about the civic weal and cares deeply about it, she is bitter about her own disenfranchisement and "is likely to disturb and unbalance the course of instruction she gives to boys and girls, and . . . to advocate theories which no believer in the purely masculine government for the nation could indorse." Another solution to the dilemma of the voteless teacher, Porritt suggested, was to give her the franchise. This unrealistic remedy, inconsistent with the rest of her conservative analysis, she defended thus: "The strongest believer in masculine government might be willing to bestow the franchise on the teachers of his boys, not for their own sake, nor in response to any demand arising out of the needs of their sex, but as part of the necessary preparation to fit them to train and educate the next generation of voters."[12]

The males who dominated educational policy did not generally seek to use education to alter the sexual division of adult labor in the economy— or, closer to home, in the schools themselves. Men resisted direct competition from women in schools as in other economic sectors. Male school boards usually hired only women as primary teachers in graded schools and reserved top administrative positions for men; only in high schools were the numbers of male and female teachers nearly equal. In addition to this sex segregation, salary schedules discriminated against women who performed the same work as men. Male school boards often dismissed women teachers when they married or became pregnant. Women educators fought all these types of sex discrimination in public education.[13]

Rather than supporting equal job training and employment opportunities for women, leaders in public education generally subscribed to a nostalgic ideal of domesticity. Educational policymakers hoped that home economics would arrest the perceived disintegration of American family life. Male school administrators proved responsive to the demands of women lobbyists for home economics programs, but they usually turned a deaf ear to feminists who objected to the view that women should basically be prepared for a "career" in the home, while boys were trained for a host of adult jobs.[14]

Public schools did little directly to counteract sex discrimination in employment. As the economy shifted toward the kinds of white-collar jobs for which high schools prepared students, however, schooling began to pay off for girls: the jobs women secured correlated strongly with their level of education. But their choices at each level—blue-collar, white-collar, and professional—were highly restricted, even though a few women were to be found in almost all occupations. Although commercial training led mostly to sex-segregated jobs, it was an important avenue to economic opportunity for women during much of the twentieth century. Commercial education, however, was not the product of the kind of self-conscious gender reformism that inspired the home economics programs or the quest for coeducational trade instruction. Rather, it resulted largely from changes in the demand for white-collar labor and girls' own choices of electives.[15]

In 1890 poorly educated women as a group were most likely to be in the paid labor force; by the mid-twentieth century it was those with higher levels of education. As Geraldine Jonçich Clifford argues, education itself was one of the forces that prompted more and more young women to try their hand in the paid labor force, "both by contributing to ego development and by raising the level of 'wants' that can be met only by increased earnings." The relation between schooling and jobs for women, she notes, was highly complex. While schooling did not pry open many doors in the male sector of the labor force, completing school did provide significant advantages to young women prepared to enter those sectors of white-collar employment that were opening to them. Sex-specific vocational instruction played only a small part in the process of integrating girls into the labor force, for most of their education took place in coeducational academic classes.[16]

Training Girls for Trades and for Commerce: Failed Reform and Success in the Shadows

From one perspective, public schooling had always been vocational for women. Schooling, claimed the common-school crusaders, made women better mothers. These nineteenth-century reformers regarded women's education as a moral duty, and when they spoke of a female vocation, they generally meant a sacred calling and not a paid job. If society invested in the "human capital" of women, the payoff came not in the paid labor market but in the nuclear families managed by women. The products of their labor, according to this Victorian model of educated motherhood, were healthy, literate, knowledgeable, moral, and disciplined children and a well-run home. Schooling contributed to this goal by inculcating the three Rs and morality in mothers-to-be. It also prepared some young women to be teachers, whose aims were thought to be similar to those of mothers.[17]

Common-school reformers expected girls to learn homemaking skills from their mothers and other women. This was the typical pattern on the farm, where almost half of all Americans lived as late as 1890 and where women labored hard even if they were not paid for it. A girl might be taught to clean house, care for her brothers and sisters, cook and sew, tend a kitchen garden, milk the cows and churn butter, and do laundry for the family and hired hands. In the Progressive Era, amid the changes wrought by urbanization and industrialization, educators like John Dewey idealized this kind of rural training for work. Indeed, when reformers proposed vocational education for agriculture, they tried to keep Americans down on the farm by reinforcing such traditions in the school.[18]

This idyllic picture of women's work and education in farm families hardly matched the reality of the lives of black women in the rural South. Most of them lived in desperate poverty, and many of them had to work alongside the men in the fields hoeing or picking cotton. Out of a total of 2.7 million black girls and women over ten years old in 1890, more than one million worked for pay, approximately half as agricultural laborers and half as domestic servants. Apart from teaching and laundering, these were practically the only occupations to which the caste system of the South assigned black women. Factory work in the South was almost entirely reserved for whites.[19]

Life on the farm was also far from idyllic for many millions of poor white families who tilled the land. They left the countryside in droves to find work in cities, as did successive waves of European peasants who migrated to America. The single, young, and minimally educated daughters of such families constituted the majority of women in the paid white work force in 1890. In the cities they took jobs typically associated with housework: domestic service, laundry work, food processing, making cloth and clothes, teaching, and nursing. Non-working-class families in 1890 tended to keep their single daughters at home to protect them, writes Robert W. Smuts, from the taint "of the harsh world of work" and to prove that the father "was capable of providing for all of his family's wants."[20]

In the early twentieth century, a number of social investigators, many of them women, made detailed and poignant studies of the conditions under which these young urban women worked, especially child laborers. These girls and women might spend nine or ten hours a day pasting labels on boxes, tending the bobbins in a cotton factory, punching holes in shoe leather and inserting laces, stitching collars, or stuffing olives in bottles. In a cigarette factory, during a ten-hour day young women "caught" and examined from 130,000 to 150,000 cigarettes. The pace of such work was often nerveracking, and the workplace was often baking hot in summer and cold in winter, dimly lit, and fetid in atmosphere. Workers generally learned rapidly how to perform these unskilled jobs and received very low wages. When women worked in the same factory with men, they generally did different tasks and were paid far less.[21]

Leaders of the National Women's Trade Union League (NWTUL) believed that an egalitarian form of education in the skilled trades—coupled with protective legislation, suffrage, and unionization—could improve the lot of working women. The NWTUL was an unusual organization that combined unionized women workers with a group of elite reformers concerned about the lives of women in industry. Jane Bernard Powers observes that "educational equity was a major theme in their writings and speeches. They believed that young women should have access to the same training and educational opportunities as . . . young men and that one of the major reasons for women's depressed status in the labor market was their lack of access to skilled trades." At the league's convention in 1913, its president, Margaret Dreier Robins, asked the delegates "to see to it that we demand coeducation in every trade; and that in this new development of our public school education the girls be given from the beginning the same chance as their brothers." The NWTUL must see to it, she added, that girls as well as boys enjoy the "same chance and opportunity for self-respecting self-support and for training in intelligent knowledge and mastery of their respective trades."[22]

Leonora O'Reilly—a union activist, NWTUL member, and teacher in a New York trade school for girls—believed that vocational training for work should not perpetuate gender stereotypes or the existing sexual division of labor. She told a commission preparing legislation on vocational education for Congress that if girls wanted to hammer nails and boys to sew, that was fine. She and the NWTUL objected to the notion that girls should be trained for the "vocation" of homemaking. Home economics should be part of a general not vocational education, they believed, one that should be made available to both sexes. By offering girls the chance to acquire skills in well-paid crafts, coeducational trade schools could challenge the monopoly of male unions over the best jobs. Women worked in printshops, for example, but they were relegated to menial and low-paid work. If they acquired the skills necessary in male crafts and were not trained for female occupations alone, they would have a chance to integrate the workplace and to make a living wage.[23]

The actual development of trade education for women dashed such radical hopes. Those who shaped policy in public education—and perhaps the majority of Americans—were deeply ambivalent about the notion of women in the paid work force, especially in factories. They might tolerate the idea of young women preparing themselves for temporary positions prior to motherhood, but not for careers, especially if those careers threatened the dominance of men in the workplace. Critics of vocational training for girls were reluctant to face the educational implications of the fact that many women were already long-term paid workers. A third of women over fifteen years old were single in large cities nationwide, and many of these women were forced to support themselves. Married women were increasing their numbers in a wide array of occupations, and more and more married as well as single women were staying in the labor force for long periods of time. A study of over 800,000 women in cities with populations over 50,000 found that more than half the women in several key occupations were over thirty years old. Women in most fields followed a flat trajectory of work; a girl might enter a factory at age fifteen and still be a "girl" at forty.[24]

Conservative attitudes about women's place and staunch union resistance to women's presence in male trades subverted the ideal of equal coeducation in skilled blue-collar jobs. Indeed, educators thought it a virtue that vocational classes and programs were sex-segregated, for this established at least part of school as a masculine domain and showed that secondary education reflected the institutions of adult life such as the workplace and family. As in the case of blacks, most educators believed the vocational training and guidance of women should be "realistic"—that is, should be adapted to the limited employment opportunities awaiting white women or blacks. As a result of this "realism," the range of curricular choices, funding, and facilities for white boys in vocational education far exceeded those for white girls and blacks.[25]

There were very few trade schools that prepared girls for blue-collar jobs. In 1916 there were only 11 separate-sex public vocational schools for girls, and these largely focused on women's work such as the garment trades and home economics (black girls' courses often trained them for domestic service and laundry work). In 1910, out of 193 trade schools, only 26 admitted girls. In 1920 there were only 5,913 young women in federally subsidized trade or industrial schools and only 9,575 in 1930. Trade education did little to enhance the earning power of young women, for many of the skills needed in women's factory work could be learned on the job in any case. In addition, few parents or girl students saw much point in investing time in secondary school in studies that would only lead to blue-collar work.[26]

One form of vocational training for girls, however, attracted hundreds of thousands of girls and responded directly to changes in the job market. It received no federal support from the Smith-Hughes Act and was largely ignored by vocational education lobbies. This success in the shadows was commercial education. Strangely, classes that prepared women for the two most common white-collar occupations for women—teaching and commercial work—were largely taken for granted in the Progressive Era. Winifred Richmond argues that it was "just because business education is so well established" that "we hear less about it, and do not regard it as a live issue in the sense that we do industrial training or training for the home."[27]

Business education did have its critics, however. Academically inclined educators (the "culturalists") attacked it as superficial, while the proponents of home economics resented the competition it presented. Since business education prepared students for white-collar jobs, the social reformers and trade-school advocates thought it did not really address the needs of the blue-collar worker. Because commercial education soon became a predominantly feminine domain, those concerned about increasing the proportion of boys in school found it problematic. And conservatives who wanted young women to become worthy mothers rather than employees predictably worried that the office would appeal more than the home.[28]

The origins of commercial education reached well back into the nineteenth century, when it was aimed primarily at boys. City high schools offered students courses in bookkeeping, penmanship, and commercial arithmetic or geography, as well as academic subjects that enhanced their value to employers. Even elementary schools added courses in bookkeeping in the eighth grade, partly to keep boys in school by offering them something presumably practical. But these public-school programs faced tough competition from private business schools, run by businessmen for profit. By 1890 students in private commercial schools represented more than a quarter of the total number in all public and private secondary schools. It was clear that there was a strong market for such commercial education among parents and students. Public educators responded to this consumer demand—most of it probably from middle-class families—by expanding student enrollment in business courses almost ninefold between 1900 and 1934, when they reached almost 4.5 million.[29]

In the twentieth century, sex ratios in commercial courses in public high schools changed dramatically as young women found their way into the greatly expanded and transformed market for office jobs. In 1900, about half the students enrolled in business and commercial courses in high schools were young women. By 1922, they accounted for 63 percent in bookkeeping, 76 percent in shorthand, and 70 percent in typing. In 1900, there were about 100,000 women in clerical jobs, and by 1920, about one million. By 1930, stenographers and typists were the third leading occupation for women and clerks, the fourth.[30]

The consolidation of corporate capitalism and the expansion of governmental bureaucracies vastly multiplied the demand for workers in the tertiary, white-collar sector of the economy. Whereas male secretaries and clerks had once performed a variety of skilled tasks and often treated their jobs as useful apprenticeships for higher-level business positions, twentieth-century clerical jobs became increasingly specialized—a woman might work as a private secretary, file clerk, receptionist, typist, bookkeeper, and so on—and many of them became routine and dead-end. Labor in business occupations was also sexually segregated; women were assigned to "women's work" such as typing and kept at the lower levels of the occupational ladder. Managerial jobs for men increasingly required education beyond the high school, but commercial classes continued to prepare women for their work in the "pink-collar ghetto."[31]

From a modern viewpoint, such women's work may appear deskilled and unrewarding, but to young women at the time it represented a significant expansion of the job opportunities open to them. Offices had once been portrayed as places of spittoons, cigars, and men's talk, but their image changed as women established their presence there. Indeed, women were credited with making the office, like the coeducational classroom, a more civilized place. Office work generally offered higher pay than factory work, a chance to wear smart clothes, a cleaner and healthier workplace, and an occupation glamorized in the women's magazines. Some women climbed a ladder of opportunity—within the female sector of office work—leading to positions as personal secretaries. As Jane Bernard Powers notes, for working-class parents and girls, "clerical work represented economic and social mobility, and it seemed to be a vast improvement over factory work." A mother in Middletown phrased her husband's attitude in this way: "He don't want the girls to go into no factory work if he can help it." George Counts found that in Bridgeport, Connecticut, 88 percent of working-class high school girls chose the commercial course of studies. Whereas first-generation Italian-American families in New York often urged their daughters to leave school to go to work at an early age, by the second generation girls were staying longer in school, in part to prepare themselves for white-collar jobs in the massive clerical labor force of the city.[32]

Clerical work, particularly the more highly paid secretarial jobs, also became a respectable way station before marriage for middle-class, native-born young women, providing for the first time a significant alternative to teaching. A definite class and ethnic bias operated in the hiring of office and sales workers. John Rury points out that "in 1920 nearly one out of four native working women were employed as clericals, . . . only one in twelve immigrant women, . . . and fewer than one in a hundred black working women." By 1930, more than 90 percent of women in these white-collar jobs were native-born (but by then this group no doubt included a large number of second-generation immigrants). Because appearance and bearing were important, a school in Chicago that prepared young women of foreign parentage for office work stressed skin and hair care, poise, and proper clothing. One of the students wrote: "Among all other things I have learned, the most important things are manners, . . . never to say anything that is not just lady-like and courteous." For some, the contrast between life in the office and life in the home created conflicts. "At work a girl's in a light, attractive office among well-dressed people," said one female office worker. "She hears and speaks English only. Her betters treat her with respect and speak to her like a countess. She's called 'Miss,' and is asked how she feels and what she thinks." At home, however, "her parents speak crudely to her. They pounce upon her if she expresses an interest in a new hat. If she mentions a ball, they tell her to dance with the laundry."[33]

Unlike the abortive attempts at urban trade education for girls, commercial courses were widespread in all types of communities and ranked among the most popular of school subjects. One reason for their popularity was that they lent themselves to the traditional forms of pedagogy and fit the institutional structure of the typical high school. The most popular subjects—bookkeeping, shorthand, and typing—were relatively cheap and easy to start up. In California in 1915 four out of five high schools offered typing and shorthand, and by 1920 these subjects were among the top three (along with English) in enrollments. But even in commercial tracks, young women still took about 70 percent of their courses in academic subjects.[34]

As Susan B. Carter and Mark Prus note, one reason why girls took business subjects was that employers were less willing to give them on-the-job training than they were to boys, on the assumption that young women would not work for long periods of time and thus repay their investment in training. Young women were therefore expected to enter the work force with skills already in hand. For this reason, clerical training had a direct payoff for women, although only within the restricted domain of a sex-divided labor market.[35]

Although girls vastly outnumbered boys in commercial courses in the twentieth century, boys did continue to enroll in substantial numbers, as shown in table 14. Unlike home economics or trade education courses, most commercial education remained coeducational. Because the labor market was largely segregated by sex, and many educators believed that schools should prepare students directly for their later careers, coeducation in this area of the curriculum disturbed advocates of sex differentiation in commercial subjects. But as John L. Rury notes, a survey of 112 schools in

Table 14
Boys and Girls Enrolled in Commercial Subjects, 1928

	Boys (%)	Girls (%)
Bookkeeping	7.6	12.0
Shorthand	3.6	13.9
Typing	10.1	22.6

Source: John Francis Latimer, What's Happened to Our High Schools? (Washington, D.C.: Public Affairs Press, 1958), p. 150.

1917 found that 98 percent of them did not differentiate commercial education by sex. For all the efforts to match schooling to the workplace, in instruction in commercial courses the schools remained more gender-neutral than the adult business workplace.[36]

Commercial education was a success because parents and students—especially girls—wanted it. Unlike trade education, it aroused little controversy about class distinctions or unequal opportunities. In its origins and development, it was not the creature of social reformers but rather an expression of middle-class aspirations. It won the support of parents and attracted their children to secondary school. Driven more by the desires of families and the needs of employers than by the command of educators, commercial education represented a market-driven innovation in education.[37]

Home Economics: Social Salvation and White Sauce

By contrast, home economics was openly ideological. Even though it may have produced mostly white sauce and stitched seams, it promised social salvation. The campaign for home economics programs in public schools became a broad-based social movement in the early twentieth century, drawing on a traditional set of values about women's proper sphere and enlisting the support of hundreds of thousands of women and highly placed men in Congress, state legislatures, and local school boards. Well-organized lobbies managed to give bureaucratic form to what was in the beginning more a crusade than what it became—an organizational appendage. The proponents of home economics wanted the field to go far beyond

In the Business High School in Washington, D.C., boys as well as girls studied typing in 1899. Commercial education had not yet become heavily identified as a female field. (Frances Benjamin Johnston, Library of Congress.)

In Bishopville, South Carolina, in 1939, girls filled the typing class. (Marion Post Wolcott, FSA, Library of Congress.)

the training in cooking and sewing that had been the staples of some schools in the nineteenth century—the female equivalent of manual training for boys—and to become the science of household management and child raising. In their campaign for domestic science, women's groups drew on decades of successful experience as organized school reformers in their local communities and in national groups such as the Women's Christian Temperance Union (WCTU).[38]

Advocates of home economics linked their cause to a comprehensive analysis of the "woman question." They claimed, as Rury says, that proper homemaking was more than women's natural vocation: "it was a cornerstone of the modern social order." They argued that urbanization and industrialization had disrupted the traditional family apprenticeship of young women, many of whom went to work at an early age and no longer centered their aspirations and activities in the home. Home economics held the key, they thought, to solving societal problems. Mothers who knew the principles of nutrition and hygiene could reduce the high rates of child mortality and improve the health of their children. Trained to be prudent consumers and managers, they could mitigate the effects of poverty. Attentive and skilled wives would attract men out of the saloon and into the family by cooking tasty meals and making the home attractive; in the process, they would lower the rising rate of divorce. A Republican senator asserted the "the country is fast awakening to the fact that probably 50 percent of all divorce would have been avoided had the girls been good cooks, good homemakers, and good mothers." By making homemaking into a profession based on science, home economics would dignify the occupation, attract back those women who had fled the home for outside careers, and stem the drop in the birthrate of native-born women. In the process, home economics would also give women the knowledge they needed for municipal housecleaning, for making the larger urban environment safe for their families.[39]

As Powers notes, the designers of home economics programs did not want merely to adapt schooling to "woman" as a generic group. They also believed that home economics should differ according to the race, ethnicity, and class of women. They believed that instruction in proper homemaking would help to "Americanize" immigrant women and their families and thus hasten their adoption of correct standards. Vocational courses would train girls—immigrants, young black women, and Latinas, in particular—for domestic service and thereby help alleviate "the servant problem" (the number of domestic servants dropped by almost one-quarter between

1910 and 1920, and members of the General Federation of Women's Clubs [GFWC] complained about the ignorance and lack of skills of the women they could hire).[40]

Although much of the case for home economics was congenial to those who held traditional views of woman's place and worried about threats to family life, there were many feminists who regarded its aims and consequences as problematic at best and atavistic at worst. Activists in the NWTUL feared that home economics would divert attention away from the task of securing economic justice for women in the workplace; they preferred to think of home economics as general education for girls and boys alike. In 1914 Mary Leal Harkness launched an attack on home economics in the pages of the *Atlantic Monthly*. What prompted her ire was a newspaper article by a vocational educator who said in effect that " 'the problem of girls' education is simple . . . since what you have to do is merely to train them to be home-keepers; to teach them the details of the management of the house and the care of children, and not to despise domestic duties.' "[41]

Why, asked Harkness, "does every one know that the vocation which is sure to delight every girl and in which she is sure to succeed (always provided, of course, that she is given the proper "practical' training in her school-days) is housekeeping and the rearing of children" when the careers of boys require so much deliberation? This prejudice reeked of the twaddle of the "woman's page" of the popular press. "The idea that literature is properly created male and female is no less absurd than the idea that there is one education of the man and another of the woman." There is no more reason to teach every woman to cook, she wrote, than to teach every man to milk a cow. That some women should cook and sew well is desirable, but the attempt to redirect the education of girls in one direction is based on a false premise "that one-half of the human race should be 'educated' for one single occupation, while the multitudinous other occupations should all be loaded on the other half. The absurd inequality of the division should alone be enough to condemn it." Both men and women should be "home-keepers," and both should have access to the same education and the same range of jobs outside the home. She thought it stupid and vicious to demand that "a woman must choose between marriage and a career."[42]

Such dissenters were rare, however, and most advocates of home economics were women, not patriarchal men who wanted to keep them in their place. Proposals to train young women in domestic economy had their antecedents in the writings of such pioneers of women's education as Catharine Beecher and Emma Willard, who wanted wives and mothers to have expert autonomy within the home. The key proponents of the twentieth-century campaign for home economics were organizationally sophisticated and politically astute women educators in the American Home Economics Association (AHEA), founded in 1908 and led by Ellen Richards, and the GFWC, whose membership was approaching one million by 1910 and which had branches in forty-six states. Composed mostly of middle- and upper-class women, the GFWC was a federated organization that set policy at the national level and influenced the federal government, lobbied at the state level for legislation, and pressured educators to implement home economics at the local level.[43]

Members of the federation, some of them married to congressmen, testified at the hearings on the Smith-Hughes bill in favor of including home economics in school curricula and increasing appropriations for the subject. Senators and representatives echoed their arguments in debate on the bill. In local communities like San Jose, California, they successfully petitioned men on school boards to install home economics programs. The members of the AHEA articulated the goals of the reform, designed the new programs, and lobbied effectively for home economics in the Congress and state legislatures. In the process, they built a bureaucracy of federal, state, and local supervisors and teachers of home economics and created careers for themselves and other women. But all of this would probably not have been possible if their arguments had not been compelling to male legislators, school board members, and administrators, as Powers observes. A U.S. senator expressed the consensus this way: "We believe that at a certain stage of progress the pathway for the education of men and women diverges, and that there are certain things which after that time women ought particularly to learn."[44]

Home economics in some form became institutionalized in most urban school districts, but the actuality scarcely resembled the dream of social redemption. Home economics reformers believed that their subject was so important that it should be required of all girls—one could not leave social salvation to the vagaries of the marketplace of elective courses. By and large, educators chose to locate required courses in the last grades of elementary school or in urban junior high schools. A survey in the 1930s found that about four-fifths of districts with junior high schools required girls to take home economics. A study in 1926–27 of high schools, however, found that only 18 percent of students enrolled in home economics courses were required to take the subject. In 1928 about 70 percent of high-school girls were not enrolled in domestic science courses. When polled about their reasons for not enrolling, girls said that they wanted to prepare for college or work and that they could learn domestic skills at home. Across the country, elective home economics courses were far less popular than commercial or academic subjects. There were significant racial differences, however, in policies requiring girls to take home economics. In the South in 1931, 85 percent of black high-school girls were required to take home economics, compared to only 30 percent of white girls. In some communities young black women resented being funneled into such courses, presumably designed to train them for domestic service and menial labor in laundries. It is likely that they attended school in the hope of escaping the drudgery and potential sexual harassment they faced in domestic service. But in Winston-Salem the school board threatened to dismiss black girls who refused to take cooking and laundry classes.[45]

As has often been the case in educational reform, bureaucratization brought marginalization. The rhetoric of justification shifted in the 1920s to more mundane claims, and home economics secured a place on the periphery of the academic core. In 1926 George Counts reported that girls in high schools spent only 4.7 percent of their time in home economics and that the field continued to consist primarily of cooking and sewing classes rather than more ambitious courses in household science, household management, and child care.[46]

For high-school administrators, however, this peripheral subject did have advantages. Like shop for boys, it was a place to put girls who did not fare well in academic work, and for many of these girls the classes were a welcome change from the traditional curriculum. Girls could cook and sew while boys took manual training or trade courses, thereby solving scheduling problems. And perhaps most important, home economics was a visible sign that schools were doing something about the "woman question" and addressing a need that the Progressive reformers had identified: buttressing the family through deliberate instruction of future mothers. Another campaign, not vocational but confronting similar issues about the purity and health of the family, was more controversial and less visible by design. This was the movement for instituting sex education programs in the school.

Desexualizing Society

Reformers pressing for home economics wanted the public school to bolster the family values in a world that threatened the stability of the home and hence of all society, a concern also shared by many early advocates of sex education. In both cases—home economics and sex education—reformers believed that families were failing to do their jobs: preparing girls to be homemakers and counseling youth about their sexuality. By shifting the burden of these forms of instruction to the school, one might argue, they were weakening the family by invading its jurisdiction. The advocates of sex education claimed, however, that the aim of controlling sexuality and limiting it to the family dovetailed well with the concerns of the age about strengthening the home, although it clearly called for a more cautious and quiet strategy than other more visible changes in the curriculum: vocational education, home economics, and physical education and sports.

In 1913 members of "social purity" groups, doctors, eminent educators, social reformers, and philanthropists joined to form the American Social Hygiene Association to promote sex education in the schools. Proper "social hygiene" required, they believed, an end to the reticence that had characterized the subject of sexuality, the most intimate part of family life. In the nineteenth century, groups of women and men had banded together in organizations to combat prostitution, abolish double standards in male and female morality, raise the age of consent for young women, and promote the idea that chastity was as "natural" for men as it was for women. Now sex educators wanted the public school to promote a unisex form of continence.[47]

A health crisis—the threat of venereal disease—added urgency to the movement. Among the most influential early advocates of sex education were doctors in public health. In the early twentieth century there was basically no cure for syphilis, which errant husbands might communicate unknowingly to their innocent wives (or vice versa, but that was rarely mentioned). Doctors turned to education as the best way to prevent the spread of the disease, much as people have recently used education to combat AIDS. The message these public-health experts wanted to convey to youth was "don't," and they phrased it in the languages of Victorian morality and science. Reformers who had crusaded against prostitution and the double standard that condoned male extramarital sex also saw in schooling a vehicle for advancing their cause.[48]

Some of the educators who were seeking to expand the role of the school in solving all kind of social problems also responded to this new demand. In 1909 the National Society for the Study of Education devoted its yearbook to the topic of "Education with Reference to Sex." In the age of "social efficiency" in education, reformers tended to believe that the school could do practically anything, even tame the hormones of the young. One educator asserted that "at best, law, police, government can do little more than affect the external conduct; they do not reach the springs of action. . . . We must look to some influence far deeper and more pervasive for the ultimate self-regulation of life in accordance with the laws of social welfare and of the noblest life." The answer "is education, and therefore we now turn . . . to that profession which deals with the character, the will, the moral nature in the most direct and persuasive way."[49]

These reformers wanted to convince youth that abstinence was not only safer but more moral than sexual indulgence and were determined to end the "conspiracy of silence" that had surrounded sexuality during the nineteenth century. "The traditional method of educating children concerning sex was not to educate them at all," Brian Strong observes, "and to allow the silence regarding sex to indicate the necessity of repressing its expression." William T. Harris had praised coeducational schools as a "desexualized" environment where boys and girls took little erotic interest in one another. Many of the proponents of sex purity viewed sex education as a way to desexualize society, except in the marriage bed. The school, in their opinion, was the best agency for this ambitious undertaking.[50]

Because they wanted to discourage sexual activity among the young and to preserve the purity of the family, the sex educators of the early twentieth century faced a dilemma: how to teach moral and scientific lessons about sexuality without promoting interest in the very behavior they were trying to suppress, especially in an era when, as Strong argues, "the dominant ideology of sex as restraint was being challenged increasingly by the hitherto radical doctrine of sex as pleasure." According to G. Stanley Hall, it was necessary "to guard the rising generation against sex dangers without any allusion to sex." Convinced that the prevalence of prostitution and venereal disease made action imperative, one educator wrote that even the "wise and skillful" parent was "inadequate to the full task, and the ordinary parent is hardly able to make a beginning." But, he cautioned, "the first principle of our school work in relation to sex is that it be not lugged in obtrusively."[51]

One approach, Strong argues, was "to de-eroticize sexuality by transforming it into an instrument for achieving socially prescribed ends rather than its own instinctual end of pleasure." Like sports, which had originally been played for fun and were later adopted into the curriculum for their positive effect on character, sex became a matter of ulterior motive. By stressing that continence led to achievement and conjugal sex to procreation, sex educators revived Victorian morality in Progressive garb. In teaching "sex hygiene," they used their version of science in the service of the older morality—for example, warning against venereal disease, discouraging masturbation, or denying the "sexual necessity" argument that males would lose their sexual powers if they did not use them.[52]

Given the delicacy of their mission, sex educators proceeded cautiously, as Michael Imber has shown. Unlike the advocates of vocational and physical education, they did not lobby for state legislation or advocate separate courses; they sought to build support for their controversial project by canvasing eminent people for endorsements, enlisting help from local parents, and educating teachers in preferred methods. Most of them approved of teaching about sex in existing courses—for example, in biology or physiology—rather than highlighting the subject in a separate course. One point was clear: in any but the vaguest forms of sex education, boys and girls should be taught separately and were best instructed by teachers of their own sex. As one sex educator put it, male teachers, even doctors, should never teach girls unless accompanied by women teachers who could "help with attitude." He considered it dangerous for boys to be "frankly instructed by attractive young women" but thought that possibly "very mature women" might be safe, adding, "Note that I have said, 'very mature women.'" Physical education courses offered a logical site for sex education, for boys and girls were typically separated and taught by their own sex in this area of the curriculum. In New York State, for example, a 1917 law decreed that all boys and girls receive fifteen minutes of instruction in hygiene each week in their physical training classes.[53]

Since they did not believe in offering sex education as a distinct course, school officials tried to teach students about sexuality through special lectures or as part of regular courses in biology, health, physiology, physical education, and even literature. At first some sex educators used scare tactics, employing pictures and descriptions of advanced stages of venereal disease, but that strategy quickly lost favor as being too "sensational." In 1913 St. Louis included sex hygiene as one of a series of lectures on "sanitation and other matters of health." That year Superintendent Ella Flagg Young of Chicago, an advocate of sex education, tried a bolder experiment. She convinced her school board to appoint physicians who were well trained in physiology and displayed "a high moral tone" to give lectures on sex hygiene in all city high schools to separate groups of boys and girls. Although few parents or pupils objected, the program became a national *cause célèbre* and attracted more negative than positive editorial attention. A Philadelphia newspaper, for example, headlined its article "Teaching Vice to Little Children." The post office banned the lectures from the mails. Before the year was out the school board, bowing to local opposition, canceled the series. Young almost lost her job over the issue. But the Chicago experiment succeeded in raising the public's awareness of sex education, thus ending the "conspiracy of silence."[54]

Most educators proceeded more cautiously than Young—as indeed the American Social Hygiene Association had urged. Yet the idea that a socially efficient school should somehow promote sex education became more and more compelling around the time of World War I, when attention was being focused on health and physical education and troops were being taught about venereal diseases. Reflecting disagreement among its members, the National Education Association waffled on the issue but made vaguely approving noises in its resolutions. After the war, the U.S. commissioner of education mailed to high schools a curriculum in social hygiene developed by New York biology teachers. In 1920 the U.S. Public Health Service and Bureau of Education distributed more than twelve thousand questionnaires to high schools across the nation to find out how they handled the subject; only 54 percent responded. It is likely that in the postwar climate of educational activism about social problems, the administrators who answered thought that they should be doing something about the issue of social hygiene. The replies showed that 85 percent of the principals approved of sex education. Eighty percent of these said they were satisfied with their programs. Some kind of sex education was offered in 41 percent of the high schools. Of these, 60 percent gave special lectures, and 40 percent had integrated sex education into existing courses, such as biology, physiology, hygiene, sociology, physical education, or home-making.[55]

Seven years later the agencies conducted a follow-up study and elicited a considerably cooler response. Only 34 percent of the high schools responded, and this time they reported more dissatisfaction and fewer programs in place. By then almost two-thirds of the schools that were teaching social hygiene were not offering special lectures but instead were incorporating sex education into regular courses. From the data in the later report and from a comparative silence about sex education in the professional journals, Imber infers that by the 1920s the initial postwar enthusiasm for sex education had waned. It is probable that in many schools programs in sex education were more nominal than substantial and avoided controversial topics. In Middletown this seems to have been the case: when they interviewed 600 high-school students in Middletown, Robert and Helen Lynd discovered only 25 who had learned about sex from teachers.[56]

Although sex education initially enjoyed support from influential

Girls in a health education class in a high school in Washington, D.C., in 1943. It was customary for school districts to assign sex education to such sex-segregated classrooms. (Esther Bubley, Office of War Information, Library of Congress.)

A teacher in a junior high school in Oregon, 1948, using a slide to teach about human reproduction in a mixed class of girls and boys. (Library of Congress.)

groups and individuals outside the schools and from some bold pedagogical pioneers, it tended to create problems for school people. Because
of the common policy of incorporating social hygiene into regular courses,
the movement did not create a new constituency of sex education teachers
comparable to that of the physical education teachers. Teachers in sex
education had no distinct professional niche in school bureaucracies and no
easy way to mobilize support, unlike the active lobbies for vocational
education. The topic of sex was not something school people wanted to
discuss openly, as they might discuss jobs or the latest baseball game.
Although some dedicated teachers continued to teach about sexuality from
a sense of duty, the sensitivity of the issue made the practice hazardous in
many local communities.[57]

While many principals apparently welcomed the idea of sex hygiene
when it became fashionable after World War I, their enthusiasm diminished
when religious groups and conservative parents went on the offensive.
Teaching about the evils of alcohol and the virtues of teetotalism as mandated by temperance groups did not arouse much opposition, except from
some liberals who found scientific temperance instruction neither scientific
nor temperate nor instructive. But teaching about sex, except in the most
muted way, proved divisive. Many of the teachers who tried to teach the
subject felt isolated and vulnerable, for the public high school as an institution seemed bent on denying the existence of hormones. The apostles of
adrenaline on the playing fields, however, won public acclaim.[58]

The contrast between the status of sex education and that of home
economics or sports was striking. As we have suggested, the introduction
of domestic science was a low-cost and minimally disruptive way to assure
traditionalists that schools were not seducing women away from the home
by training them for work. Competitive athletics promised to alleviate
major institutional problems: the high male dropout rates and the difficulty
of disciplining energetic boys, especially those from the working class.
Sports events focused the attention of one important constituency of the
schools—the lay public—on an exciting spectacle that featured heroes and
villains, suspense and triumph, valor and skill. Whether sports improved
character or enhanced learning was almost irrelevant; boys were the heroes
of this newly adopted school activity, and the masculine character of the
school was proclaimed to all. Laws that mandated physical education protected the market for the services of physical educators, and their associations proved to be effective lobbyists for greater support. To some degree,
sex education was a clandestine addition to the curriculum; it could not be

publicly celebrated, as sports were, or exalted in millenial rhetoric, as home economics was.[59]

Reforms that addressed gender issues stood a better chance of becoming incorporated into school systems when they met institutional needs as well as serving broader social purposes. While the schools certainly responded to the agenda of outside groups, they had their own dynamics that transformed or marginalized the reforms as these were being institutionalized. This process raises the question of how much the gender-based reforms we have been analyzing in these two chapters actually altered the mainstream of coeducation in American public schools.

How Much Did Coeducation Actually Change?

Policy talk about differentiating public schools by gender clearly underwent a sea change in the Progressive Era. Americans translated their general anxieties and hopes about gender relationships—expressed in terms of the "boy problem" and the "woman question"—into proposals for educational reform, some of which became institutionalized in the schools. The politics of gender differentiation enlisted male and female reformers both outside and inside the schools. Different outside groups—businessmen, clubwomen, labor union leaders, and social reformers—had conflicting interests, concerns, and agendas for reform. There was even some sexual division of labor in the reform movement: men did most of the lamenting about the "boy problem," while women's organizations often focused more on issues such as equalizing trade education for girls or training them in home economics. Inside the schools, the new sex-segregated programs created niches in school bureaucracies for the men and women who administered and taught in them. The reforms expanded in part because these specialists and their political allies proved to be skillful lobbyists.[60]

The "boy problem" and the "woman question" were names attached to a bewildering variety of phenomena. Although the general mandate to differentiate education by gender won widespread assent, controversies arose over almost every specific proposal for change. Even reforms, such as home economics, that had the support of powerful constituencies often were only marginally incorporated into the schools. The older acceptance of identical coeducation eroded, but to what degree did everyday practice in standard classrooms change?

Most of the talk about gender differentiation focused on the high school. Two reports of the National Education Association sharply outline the change in conventional wisdom about the purposes and nature of secondary education, including its gender policies. In 1893 the Committee of Ten considered its task to be deciding what academic subjects to teach and how to teach them. It did not address the diverse needs of youth or the multiple demands of social efficiency, and it did not mention gender. The committee recognized that only a few graduates would go on to college but assumed that the best preparation for college was also the best preparation for life for those few students who had the ability and the resources to attend high school.[61]

By contrast, the committee that prepared the *Cardinal Principles of Secondary Education* in 1918 was skeptical about the value of academic subjects, at least as traditionally taught, and shifted the emphasis from academic to practical training in its recommendations for curriculum design. They believed that education should be calibrated to changes in society, the kinds of pupils attending school, and new understandings of developmental psychology. They argued that the school should take on a whole new array of duties: to train youth for health, family life, work, citizenship, leisure, ethical character, and "command of fundamental processes" (by which they meant the academic basics). Not surprisingly, they accepted gender differentiation as essential and wanted, for example, all girls to take home economics to prepare them to be efficient wives and mothers.[62]

The thinking represented in the *Cardinal Principles* became the stock-in-trade of up-to-date educators. As believers in social efficiency, educators thought it incongruous that adolescent boys and girls should be treated alike just as they were about to enter the gender-segregated workplace and the different duties of the sexes in the home. This disparity raised a problem of legitimacy for an institution that was coming to take up an ever-increasing proportion of the time and effort of youth and the taxes of citizens. Why should boys and girls be treated more or less alike in school when their future lives were so different? To remedy the problem, reformers wanted the institution itself to serve as a bridge to the gender-segregated order of the larger society—in other words, to adapt the high-school curriculum to the sexual division of labor in the adult workplace and the home. This line of reasoning led naturally to separate-sex courses. By imitating the sex segregation found in adult institutions, the schools could defuse criticism that they were not related to "life." The rhetoric of vocationalism became increasingly common among lay and professional leaders, even though most of the curriculum remained academic and enrollment in trade programs and home economics were comparatively small.

But it was not only adult reformers who shaped changes in gender practice in the schools. Students themselves took the lead in creating boys' interscholastic sports and the extracurricular activities that flourished in modern high schools. In the more informal world of the peer group, sex segregation and different gender roles played an important part. Progressive administrators and teachers came to regard such activities as a lively adjunct to the formal curriculum and recognized that the extracurriculum often enlisted more enthusiasm and interest from students than their academic studies did. While technically under the supervision of teachers, and often coordinated by a dean of girls or a vice-principal, the social clubs, service societies, sports teams, dances, dramatic groups, and publication staffs were often started by the students themselves. Such organizations tended to reflect a self-contained middle-class youth culture that at times was only loosely connected to the institutional structure of the high school. As with sports, however, educators tried to exercise some control over these extracurricular activities and apply to them their own version of social efficiency.[63]

When they were allowed greater freedom in shaping their own social lives, students were more likely to be segregated by sex than they were in the official school curriculum, just as boys and girls were more likely to play in separate-sex groups at recess in the common school. In Quincy, Massachusetts, for example, when the last school bell rang in the high school on December 3, 1925, some of the girls went to the gymnasium to play intramural basketball, while others met with their friends in the Thalia club, a social group; the football team held its practice on the playing field; seniors of both sexes prepared for the class play and dance; and the staff of the school magazine conferred. In many high schools, extracurricular activities were frequently sex-segregated, as in Quincy, and in others, boys and girls adopted sex-stereotypes roles; in student government, for example, it was typical for a boy to be president and a girl secretary. In activities such as drama, music, and journalism, which were more likely to be under the direct sponsorship of teachers, there appears to have been less sex segregation. In P.S. 202 in Brooklyn, New York, in the 1930s, the upper-grade pupils were supervised by their teachers in their extracurricular activities. There were five all-boy groups involved with sports, scouting, and science. Seven all-girl groups learned dancing, dressmaking, first-aid, and "stunts." But there were twenty-eight mixed-sex groups engaged in music, drama, art, history, literature nature study, embroidery, and crafts.[64]

Progressive pedagogy—which stressed student initiative in learning, a

In 1942 the student council in Banneker Junior High School meets in the gymnasium. Note the sex-segregation in seating and the disproportionate number of boys. (Marjorie Collins, Office of War Information, Library of Congress.)

lessening of teacher-centered instruction, and sensitivity to peer groups—may have steered gender relationships in the same direction as the expanding extracurricular activities. Without necessarily being self-conscious about the gender issues, progressive teachers may have given more scope to the self-segregation of the sexes and to sex-distinct activities than was found in the standardized, teacher-led classroom characteristic of traditional education. To be sure, the work of Larry Cuban suggests that such progressive teaching practices were rare. But where there was more opportunity for students to choose their own activities and groups, it is plausible to suppose that boys and girls may have chosen to associate more with their own sex and to undertake more sex-typed tasks. In her examination of gender in the project method and core curriculum in progressive schools, Sari Knopp Biklen has documented that gender stereotypes played an important part in the student-centered curriculum. Just as childhood play was and is typically segregated by sex, so the pedagogical principle of socialization through play probably encouraged boys and girls to pursue different activities and follow the gender norms of their peers.[65]

The most clear-cut kind of segregated education was the separate-sex high school, but this institution was nearly extinct. Most of these schools were survivals from the nineteenth century, and some were academically selective schools like Boston Latin School, restricted to boys. Others, mostly new and in large cities, were trade or industrial schools designed to prepare students for jobs. Some of these had originally been fairly demanding technical schools that attracted middle-class boys, but increasingly they came to be seen as academically weak and blue-collar in orientation. As comprehensive coeducational high schools became the norm almost everywhere, the separate-sex, elite academic high schools and working-class industrial schools were charged with class bias.[66]

Winifred Richmond, an advocate of specialized education for girls, found that there were only twenty-eight separate girls' high schools in the whole United States in 1914. Over half the students in these schools were in New York and Pennsylvania. These institutions included both elite academic schools, like Girls' High School in San Francisco, and schools specializing in practical subjects, like Wadleigh High School in New York. Although the separate-sex trade schools enrolled many more boys than girls, most of them were located in big cities and accounted for a small percentage of the total male enrollment in vocational education. Most vocational training, then, took place in comprehensive and coeducational high schools, in which both boys and girls took a large number of their courses in academic subjects.[67]

Despite all the talk about the new sex-segregated subjects, these usually occupied only a fraction of the average student's time during the four years of high school. Where home economics, manual training, and physical education were required, they took up only a small amount of instructional time during the week. Where vocational courses were elective, they enrolled only a small number of students, with the important exception of commercial education. Courses in business education at first were almost entirely for males, but in time this area of the curriculum became increasingly identified as female. It is important to note, however, that business courses generally continued to enroll both boys and girls.[68]

If one were to compare the high schools of 1893 with those of 1918 or the 1920s, in the later period one would clearly find more evidence of the kind of sex differentiation the reformers advocated. In the average high school, however, this differentiation occurred on the periphery rather than at the center of the curriculum, in programs like vocational or physical education that were added to the traditional core of instruction and taught in self-contained classes or activities. Blueprints for new-model high schools typically showed the basement or first floor as the location of these segregated activities—in shops, cooking and sewing rooms, gymnasiums, and boys' and girls' shower rooms. Business classes often took place in conventional classrooms and were quickly assimilated into the conventional forms of instruction.[69]

Activities and classes peripheral to the mainstream academic curriculum—physical education, vocational programs, and extracurricular activities, for example—were more likely to be sex-segregated or differentiated by sex. Extra-curricular activities reflected the separate gender arrangements of youth groups outside the school, such as the Boy and Girl Scouts or the sex-segregated YMCA and YWCA. But how successful were the advocates of curricular differentiation by sex in reaching the core of the high-school's academic curriculum?

It is difficult to answer this question. No doubt there were many subtle forms of differential treatment of girls and boys of the sort we will discuss in the next chapter, but historical evidence on such behavior is hard to unearth. In any case, we are here interested less in subtle classroom interactions or sex-based messages in the curriculum than in standardized institutional gender arrangements in instruction, which were often simply taken for granted and thus not discussed. We suspect that the traditional forms of coeducation continued in most academic courses despite all the policy talk about adapting schooling to the two sexes. We do not mean to imply that educators thought that the product of schooling should be undifferentiated; one educator expressed a common attitude when he said that schools should turn out "manly, honorable, self-reliant boys and womanly, efficient girls." Instead, we think that differentiating by gender did not become so influential a principle of institutional organization in the high school as some reformers hoped it would or as visible but peripheral changes might have led outsiders to believe it was.

In other words, relatively undifferentiated coeducation probably continued to be the predominant gender practice in the public schools, not so much because educators had unanimously concluded that it was desirable—although people like Dewey continued to believe in coeducation as a matter of democratic principle—but because it was taken for granted as the only practical way to teach students in specialized academic courses in relatively small high schools. And as we mentioned in the last chapter, the great bulk of public-school pupils were in any case not in high schools but in elementary schools, where (as far as we can tell) the general pattern of coeducation in graded schools continued much as we described it in chapter 4.[70]

Table 15
Boys and Girls Enrolled in Various Subjects in the Last
Four Years of High School, 1900 and 1928

	1900		1928	
	Boys (%)	Girls (%)	Boys (%)	Girls (%)
Physics	19.5	18.7	9.4	4.5
Chemistry	8.2	7.4	8.0	5.7
Biology[a]	1.0	1.2	13.2	14.0
Physical Geography	23.6	23.2	2.7	2.6
Algebra	57.0	55.8	38.7	32.0
Geometry	27.0	27.7	22.4	17.4
Latin	47.1	53.1	20.6	23.2
French	6.6	8.7	12.6	15.3
History or Social Studies	58.3	61.0	17.4	18.2
English[b]	78.2	82.1	92.6	93.5

Source: John Francis Latimer, *What's Happened to Our High Schools?* (Washington, D.C.: Public Affairs Press, 1958), p. 149.
[a] 1900 data missing; figures given are for 1910.
[b] Percentage for 1900 combines English Literature and Rhetoric.

Table 15 gives a rough index of the ratio of boys to girls in various high-school subjects in 1900 and 1928. There are problems, of course, both with the validity and interpretation of such statistics on course enrollments. There was a good deal of incomplete and inaccurate reporting. One course name—say, "social studies"—may have disguised quite different subject matter, and a change in name may not have reflected much difference in actual content. The aggregated enrollments do not indicate if girls studied one kind of physics or chemistry and the boys another in separate classes. For our purpose of investigating the general pattern of course-taking by gender, however, the data are useful.

It is clear that there was a substantial change in course enrollments overall, if we stop looking for the moment at the sex ratios. The college-preparatory curriculum of 1900, reflecting the academic orientation of the Committee of Ten report and the absence of electives in the small high schools of the time, enrolled similar ratios of both sexes. By 1928 high-school enrollments had shifted in response to the new demands articulated in the *Cardinal Principles* and the growth of alternative courses. Physics, physical geography, history, algebra, geometry, and Latin, for example, showed considerable decline, while the percentages of students in English, biology, French, and vocational subjects discussed above showed significant increases. Such statistics indicate that the older academic course of study was broadening and serving new purposes. The steepest drops in proportional enrollments of girls appeared in physics and to a lesser extent in chemistry and mathematics. A higher ratio of girls than boys took languages, history and social studies, and English, but the disparities were not great.[71]

Overall, however, the discrepancies in the sex ratios in the regular academic subjects are less striking than the similarities. For a variety of reasons, we believe that in these courses the vast majority of boys and girls studied the same curriculum in the same room under the same teacher. First, most high schools were too small to offer separate academic classes for boys and girls. Although there were large high schools in some cities—even enormous ones in places like New York—small enrollments were far more common. As late as 1930, the average high school had only 216 students. Even large high schools, such as the ones in Chicago and Seattle that attempted sex segregation, abandoned their experiments. Smaller high schools had trouble enough offering a wide array of subjects at different levels of difficulty without dividing students by sex.[72]

Second, the strong force of institutional tradition and inertia anchored coeducation in the school system, and it would have taken a major counterforce to change it. Coeducation had been standard practice since the origins of the common school. Most of the teachers of the early twentieth century had been taught in coeducational public schools, and had learned how to teach in coeducational classrooms. While some teachers may have thought that separating students by sex was sensible in some of the new programs, as in physical and vocational education, very few argued that separate education was desirable in the academic mainstream. Indeed, most educators probably took coeducation for granted—it was just the way things were done.[73]

Still, the occasional calls to separate boys and girls in academic classes and to instruct them differently did provoke some educators to defend coeducation on principle. Creating separate academic courses for boys and girls and adapting the subject matter to each sex—as was common in Germany and as was attempted in some American schools—struck many

In the 1930s and 1940s—a time rich in images of public education—photographers were interested in portraying inequalities, in advertising progressive experiments, and in promoting their schools, among other agendas. But they probably did not intend to illustrate gender practices in schools. Thus photographs provide an unobtrusive measure of the variety of gender pattern in coeducational classrooms.

Boys and girls gather around their teacher to study butterflies in White Plains, Georgia, in 1941. On the board is written a universal "we": "We will know what we are to do." (Jack Delano, FSA, Library of Congress.)

Two girls in Caldwell, Idaho, demonstrate what was presumably a feminine skill: making a salad from string beans, cabbage, and carrots. Home economics and the algebra problems on the chalkboard seem to coexist comfortably in the picture. (Russell Lee, FSA, Library of Congress.)

In Greenbelt, Maryland, in 1939, young girls and boys cooperate in a sewing project. In later grades manual activities, like physical education, were typically sex-segregated. (Arthur Rothstein, FSA, Library of Congress.)

In this arithmetic lesson in a grade school in San Augustine, Texas, in 1939 girls and boys stand side by side as they put their sums on the board. It hardly seems likely that this was by chance; did the teacher find that this aided in class discipline? (Russell Lee, FSA, Library of Congress.)

In this algebra class in Woodrow Wilson High School in Washington, D.C., only boys line up to write their equations on the board. Why this gender segregation? (Esther Bubley, OWI, Library of Congress.)

In San Augustine, Texas, a teacher helps a girl while the other pupils do seatwork. One hand is raised for help while another (top right) reaches out to touch a boy while the teacher is occupied. The girls and boys appear to be clumped together rather than randomly distributed. (Russell Lee, FSA, Library of Congress.)

Two boys and four girls in Concho, Arizona, in 1940, get ready to play a game: "hunting the little squirrels." (Russell Lee, FSA, Library of Congress.)

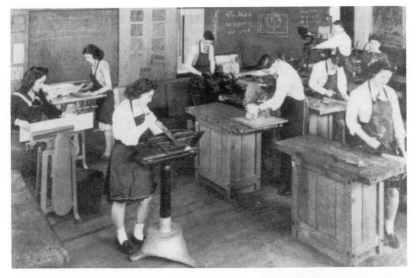

During world War II, girls were often admitted to trade training programs previously limited to boys in order to prepare them for wartime industrial jobs. (*Baltimore Report for 1945*, p. 100.)

In Springfield, Missouri, a mixed group of boys and girls engage in a discussion in a high school English class— a technique common in progressive classrooms. (Library of Congress.)

In the Brooklyn Industrial High School for Girls in 1935 apprentice beauticians practice their skills on their classmates. (*New York City Report for 1934–35*, p. 64.)

Under the eye of his teacher, a boy in a high school science class in Penasco, New Mexico, peers through a microscope while four girls and a boy look on. (John Collier, OWI, Library of Congress.)

For boys only: military training in Armstrong Technical High School in Washington, D.C., 1942. (Marjorie Collins, OWI, Library of Congress.)

In 1939 in San Augustine, Texas, young boys and girls in the center practice somewhat self-consciously for a school play while other students, clumped more or less in same-sex groups, look on. (Russell Lee, FSA, Library of Congress.)

people not as progressive but as silly. John Dewey, for example, wrote in the *Ladies Home Journal* in 1911 that " 'female botany,' 'female algebra'—and, for all I know, a female multiplication table—have been conceived, adapted to the 'female mind.' " Such talk he deemed "sheer mythology; upon no subject has there been so much dogmatic assertion [his target was G. Stanley Hall] based on so little scientific evidence, as upon male and female types of mind. . . . it is scientifically demonstrable that the average difference between men and women is much less than the range of *individual* differences between men or women by themselves." For these reasons, he wrote, "the argument is even stronger for abolition of all class instruction than it is for separation of men and women.[74]

Dewey repeated Harris's claim of a half-century earlier, that coeducation improved morals and manners as well as academic performance, to which he added his own, that coeducation was "an intellectual and moral necessity in a democracy." Like class segregation, sex segregation undermined the social and political purposes of the common school. Dewey justified coeducation on the grounds that it was fundamental to cooperative democracy: "the significant tasks of society—remedial and constructive—are to be performed by both men and women. Whatever increases their capacity to perform these tasks cooperatively must be cherished, for it increases the prospects the community has of making a success of its life."[75]

Many feminists of the Progressive Era rejected the notion that women and men were fundamentally different or needed a differentiated education. They applauded coeducation and wanted it to enlarge, not confirm, the condition of women. A few hoped that a genuinely identical coeducation might hasten the time when men and women could redesign and share domestic duties and thus make equality of careers a possibility for both sexes. The WTUL wanted to extend coeducation into the trades in order to give girls the same opportunities for blue-collar advancement as boys. To such feminists, the coeducational public school, with all its defects, was already more egalitarian than the workplace or the family. It was an essential part of the solution to the "woman question," as they understood it. But in the 1960s and 1970s, a new feminist movement arose that exposed the hidden injuries of coeducation and indicted the public schools as a source of gender injustice.[76]

Feminists Discover the Hidden Injuries of Coeducation

By the second decade of the twentieth century a few feminists were dreaming of a world in which traditional gender distinctions would wither away as a result of truly identical coeducation. One of these visionaries, a New York teacher named Henrietta Rodman, argued in 1915 that "coeducation is one of the essentials of civilization. This mixing makes the girls brave and resourceful and the boys courteous and helpful." Boys might play with dolls and dishes if they wanted, and "girls would not be told that they can't play vigorous games because they must keep their dresses clean and they must be ladylike." The cultural division into masculine and feminine was artificial, she said: "there is no quality good in one sex that is not good in the other." True coeducation could lead to a world in which women and men would have equal opportunity in all aspects of life.[1]

Another radical feminist, Crystal Eastman, argued in 1920 that the passage of the Nineteenth Amendment granting women the vote was only the beginning of women's liberation. She defined the task ahead in this way: "how to arrange the world so that women can be human beings, with a chance to exercise their infinitely varied gifts in infinitely varied ways, instead of being destined by the accident of their sex to one field of activity—housework and child-raising." Such a project would require "a revolution in the early training of both boys and girls. It must be womanly as well as manly to earn your own living, to stand on your own feet. And it must be manly as well as womanly to know how to cook and sew and clean and take care of yourself in the ordinary exigencies of life. I need not add that the second part of this revolution will be more passionately resisted than the first."[2]

Rodman and Eastman won few converts to their point of view in their day. They wanted a transformation—a thorough blending—of the traditional roles of men and women. Their pleas fell mostly on deaf ears in a period when many educational reformers wanted more, not less, gender differentiation in schools and when advocates of woman's rights often stressed the female virtues. But their vision of coeducation would be reborn a half-century later. Under the scrutiny of the new feminists, the coeducational school that had supposedly served girls rather well suddenly seemed rife with bias. The word *sexist,* applied to schools with increasing frequency in the 1970s, symbolized a major new departure in thinking about equality of the sexes in public education.[3]

The starting point for these later feminists who fought to reform coeducational schools was not education itself; rather, it was the unequal station and opportunities of adult women in the economic, political, and social life of the nation. They believed that if adult women lacked power and opportunities, the schools had played a large part in their subordination. The quest for gender justice in education grew out of and drew much of its energy, strategies, and agenda from the broader women's liberation movement of the 1960s and 1970s.[4]

Again, as during the Progressive Era, a familiar pattern of reform emerged in efforts to change gender practices and policies in the schools: broad objective and ideological changes in gender patterns in the society as a whole prompted activists to generate an agenda for educational reform, and in turn educators institutionalized the changes in differing degrees.

A major reason for the impact of the new feminist movement, as William H. Chafe has observed, was the congruence of its program with major social trends. At a time when about half of all married women were employed in the paid labor force, the attitude that women's place was in the home was becoming implausible. Well-publicized reports showed that women college graduates earned less than men who had only completed elementary school. In a period of postponed marriages and declining birthrates, more women were seeking fulfillment through careers, yet they found themselves blocked by males who were entrenched at the top levels in business corporations, the media, and the prestigious professions. Working-class women found themselves shunted to low-paying, sex-segregated jobs. Women active in politics and government were regularly excluded from the arenas where policy was made and from positions of power and influence.[5]

But it was not only in the labor market or public life that women experienced frustration. Many homemakers found that Betty Friedan's best-selling book, *The Feminine Mystique* (1963), expressed their own unnamed discontent. In 1963 Brigid Brophy published an article in the *Saturday Evening Post* entitled "Women Are Prisoners of Their Sex." Women, she wrote, may feel free, "but in reality women in the western, industrialized world today are like the animals in a modern zoo. There are no bars. It appears that cages have been abolished. Yet in practice women are still kept in place just as firmly as the animals are kept in their enclosures. The barriers which keep them in now are invisible."[6]

Ninety percent of housewives surveyed by Gallup in 1962 "did not want their daughters to lead the same type of life they had led. They hoped their daughters would get more education and marry later." As the Gallup poll response indicated, attitudes toward women's roles in the home and in the workplace were already changing before the women's liberation movement gathered momentum in the late 1960s and 1970s. The transformation of women's attitudes owed quite as much to their everyday experience as to the ideological impact of feminism, for their attitudes showed the biggest changes before the media began publicizing feminism.[7]

The women's movement of the 1960s and 1970s might be construed says Kathleen M. Dalton, as an "equity earthquake." It constituted a sudden realignment of beliefs and values along a social fault line to match major changes in the objective conditions of women's lives. The women's movement gave voice and direction to new attitudes already half-formed, a public language in which women could describe their individual situations. Thus, when feminists redefined women's grievances as a public issue rather than as a personal problem, they found in some quarters a ready audience. And sexual discrimination in schools became one of their prime targets.[8]

If the Progressive Era was the time of the "boy problem," the 1970s was the decade of the "girl problem" (although some feminists also addressed issues of gender justice for males). By sex equity in education, they understood the elimination of sex bias and a reduction of sex stereotyping. Whereas opponents of coeducation in the nineteenth century had claimed that high schools were too virile to fit the girls, and the champions of masculinity had claimed that schools feminized the boys, the new feminist activists reversed the charge: public education made the girls too feminine and the boys too masculine. They argued that schools perpetuated male dominance and female subordination because boys and girls did not really learn the same things in coeducational schools. In the process, unequal schooling contributed to the asymmetrical distribution of power, income, and prestige among adult women and men.[9]

This reformulation of sex discrimination derived from a new conviction that schools could not be considered to be favoring girls over boys or even to be observing gender-neutral policies if their women graduates fared so poorly in adult life. Unconsciously or deliberately, schools played a part in the subordination of women. It was the job of feminist researchers to document and remedy the hidden inequities that blocked women's access to the same opportunities that men enjoyed. The education press shows a sharply rising number of publications on women's issues after 1969.[10]

Opposition to feminist reform in education took many forms, ranging from mild foot-dragging to active resistance. One common reaction was incredulity: Was there really a problem for girls? Most educators from 1930 to the early 1960s did not believe there was a serious problem of sex bias in coeducational classrooms. They regarded boys and girls as largely inter-changeable parts for institutional purposes. In theory, the public school was gender-blind, just as it was thought to be class-blind.

When educational researchers and policy advocates of this period did detect a gap between the ideal and the reality of gender-blind schooling, they usually focused on boys. Males, they claimed, did not get a fair shake. What was their evidence of discrimination? Their case would have been a familiar one to educators of the early twentieth century. Boys, researchers reported, were held back in grade far more often than girls and outnum-bered them in remedial classes in reading. Boys performed about the same as or better than girls on standardized achievement tests but earned lower grades. They were much more likely to present discipline problems or be referred to special classes or child-guidance clinics for learning or behavioral disorders. Women teachers, said some latter-day writers on the "boy prob-lem," scolded boys more and tried to make them conform to a female regime. In the process, they produced either rebels or feminized males. Critics accused textbook writers of feminizing the curriculum and called for stories in school readers that would appeal more to male interests (they showed that girls would be willing to read "boys'" stories, but not vice versa). In the 1960s scholars like Patricia Cayo Sexton and Daniel Levine argued that a "feminized" school especially hurt male blacks and His-panics.[11]

Opposition to the feminist educational agenda also came from people to whom "sex-stereotyping" seemed natural and desirable. Unlike racial discrimination, which had been written into law and conscious policy, much educational discrimination against girls and women was unconscious and thus invisible to people—both educators and the general public. What was the problem, they asked, if boys behaved like boys and girls like girls? The task of the school was to teach both sexes the same subjects in the same manner, and was this not what was happening? In 1972 *Nation's Schools* polled school administrators on this question:

> Recent studies report that many elementary-school textbooks present a "biased" and negative view of girls and women, i.e., girls generally portrayed as "passive and emotional," while boys are depicted as "aggressive and logical." Do you think this type of sex bias exists in curriculum materials?[12]

Only 16 percent answered yes and 84 percent answered *no*. A California schoolman described the whole idea as "hogwash," while a Virginia administrator declared sex discrimination "just a figment of some feminist's frustrated imagination."

To some public educators, the requirements of antidiscrimination statutes like Title IX and litigation about sex bias were simply bothersome and costly distractions from their real business—properly education, not some new kind of social engineering. Racism was a more obvious target than sexism, and skeptical officials in the Office of Civil Rights (OCR) needed steady prodding to enforce the laws against gender discrimination. Under the Reagan administration, believers in the God-given traditional gender order sought to derail the feminist campaign.

Convinced of the hidden injuries of coeducation, educational activists in the women's movement had several tasks: convincing people that there was a problem by documenting gender discrimination; devising legal and policy remedies; following up on implementation; and raising the consciousness of educators about bias in everyday activities that they took for granted.[13]

Like many other social movements, the women's movement was itself a massive educational agency and intellectual forum. By a variety of means—publications, demonstrations, legislation, litigation, consciousness-raising groups, guerrilla theater, activist research, and media attention—it sought to change minds. Reforming schools was only one of the feminists' goals and the coeducational public school only one of many forms of education they analyzed. Dialogue within the feminist movement assured constant recasting of issues; movement members were hardly rigid or uniform in their beliefs. Thus, it is not surprising that in the 1980s a new group of feminist theorists would question the diagnoses and solutions of the liberal feminists of the 1970s. Although the women's movement had historically represented a varied constituency and promoted a changing agenda, the attack on the hidden injuries of the coeducational public school represented a new departure in the long history of American education and of women's search for equal rights.[14]

Defining and Explaining Sexism in Education

The movement for women's liberation owed much of its inspiration and its legal and educational strategies to the civil rights movement. Feminism was not an isolated venture but part of a broader array of social movements that swept the nation in the 1960s. Like their nineteenth-century predecessors, many of whom had been abolitionists, a number of the leaders of the modern women's movement had taken part in the campaign to secure equality for blacks. That crusade had demonstrated that discriminatory attitudes and practices could be exposed and that the status quo could change.[15]

In many respects, sexual discrimination differed from racial bias in education. There were crucial distinctions in the way the law was used to oppress or liberate blacks and white women, for example. In the South and in some parts of the North, racial segregation in the school system and unequal resources for schooling resulted from clearly racist laws and deliberate public policy. Like the disenfranchisement of blacks, legalized educational inequality buttressed racial caste, and what law had helped to create, it could also undo, however difficult the process. But law and conscious policy had not been major contributors to sex inequity in public education. At the time of the *Brown v. Board of Education of Topeka* decision attacking racial discrimination in education, nearly all American schools were desegregated by sex, except for a few peripheral courses and activities. Statutes and district regulations of the Progressive Era that distinguished between the sexes in coeducational public schools were few in number and could trace their origins as reforms, not discrimination. These regulations became ready targets for a statute like Title IX that banned single-sex classes in vocational subjects, for example.[16]

In other ways, however, race was similar to sex. Beyond the bias built into law and clear policy, blacks also faced a more amorphous and less conscious kind of discrimination, which became labeled "institutional racism." Blacks found that civil rights laws did not dismantle many of the attitudinal, economic, and institutional hurdles they faced. In public education, civil rights groups targeted a number of forms of institutional racism: the omission of blacks and the use of negative stereotypes of African-Americans in textbooks; biased behavior of teachers toward people of color, arguably all the more potent in its impact when unconscious; the use of racially unfair tests; bias in counseling; the failure to appoint and advance black employees; and the tracking of blacks into slow lanes or dead-end vocational programs that blocked them from further education or white-collar jobs.[17]

The concept of sexism owed much to this discovery of institutional racism. In a 1970 article called "Woman as Nigger," which popularized the term "sexism," Gayle Rubin wrote that "people are more sophisticated about blacks than they are about women: black history courses do not have to begin by convincing people that blacks are not in fact genetically better suited to dancing than to learning." As we have said, sexism in public schools was not nearly as visible to most people as racism. Many educators thought gender distinctions natural and hence regarded sex stereotyping as a non-issue. They saw gender differences but not discrimination. Teachers who equated bias with conscious unfairness or dislike resented the accusation of "sexism"—it was an article of faith with most teachers that they should be and were fair in their dealings with students.[18]

Many educators who agreed that blacks were not well served by schools did not see any significant academic or social disabilities for girls. Differences of academic achievement by sex sometimes favored boys, sometimes girls; they were relatively slight—ranging from about 1 to 5 percent; and they were much smaller than racial or class differences. Gender cuts across all social classes, but disproportionate numbers of blacks were poor. Discrimination against blacks, therefore, was compounded by class bias. In addition, girls seemed to fit well into schools and were less often perceived to be educationally disadvantaged than were boys.[19]

The concept of institutional sexism caught on rapidly among feminists, however, for it defined the silent, subtle character of sex conditioning and the broad scope of the battle for sex equity. Feminist researchers on institutional sexism labored to expose the schools' hidden curriculum, in part to convince educators and parents that sex bias was a reality. The growth of women's studies programs and local consciousness-raising groups fueled the effort to document and remedy discrimination. Some investigators were based in universities, but much research was a grassroots effort on the part of teachers in elementary and high schools, NOW chapters in places like New York City, feminist writers and librarians, and parents and students. These groups found many disturbing signs of institutional sexism, systematic patterns of bias against females:[20]

- Textbooks proved to be riddled with bias. Investigators found that stories had many more male than female characters and illustrations; that history books ignored,distorted, or trivialized the role of women; that texts portrayed occupations in sex-stereotyped ways; and that even mathematics and science texts showed a consistent male bias.[21]
- Studies of classroom interactions between teachers and students revealed that instructors typically paid more attention to boys, criticizing them disproportionately but also rewarding them more for active thinking. Teachers often reinforced sex stereotyping of social behavior and aspirations.[22]
- Counselors often held sex-stereotyped notions of what courses or careers were appropriate for males and females; the tests they employed also were sex-typed.[23]
- Sports and extracurricular activities reinforced the image of boys as active, aggressive, and enterprising and of girls as passive or oriented to personal relationships rather than public activity. Funds spent on boys' athletics were grossly disproportionate to those available for girls' sports.[24]
- Teacher educators and the textbooks they wrote showed little awareness of the ways in which teachers perpetuated sex bias.[25]
- Although girls started out ahead of boys in their academic performance, by the end of high school boys had caught up with and were surpassing girls in subjects like mathematics and science. By the college years there were great disparities between men and women in enrollments in fields like engineering and science.[26]
- Since administrators were overwhelmingly male, pupils learned that men ran things. Subtle and overt forms of discrimination barred women from positions of influence in education even though they constituted two-thirds of all teachers. Men dominated the governance of education, vastly outnumbering women on school boards.[27]

Feminist researchers generally focused on three occasionally overlapping concepts to explain the origins of discriminatory policies: (1) patriarchy, which encompassed the whole of society as the unit of analysis and described universal male domination; (2) sex-role stereotyping, which stressed the individual's internalization of cultural gender roles; and (3) institutional sexism, which addressed the inequalities built into institutional structures and policies.

The patriarchal interpretation asserted that male domination characterized society as a whole. In this view, schools, like all other institutions, revealed a pattern of discrimination against women: men set educational policy and preempted the administration of schools; they determined what knowledge was considered most important; and their values permeated instruction. To dislodge patriarchy would require nothing less than a revolution in attitudes and a profound redistribution of power.[28]

Another approach that had greater currency in educational analysis—the sex-role socialization model—focused on how girls and boys were taught different gender roles. One reason for the popularity of this interpretation may be that psychological thinking has dominated educational research in fields like developmental psychology and in programs like compensatory education. It could also accommodate the peculiarly American self-help therapies, such as assertiveness training for women or Dale Carnegie's strategies for winning friends. Advocates of this position typically took a hierarchical view of sex-role socialization, according to which adults such as parents or teachers inculcated the stereotypes in the child. Underlying this approach was an individualist and pluralist ideal: that all pupils, if given the right help, could realize all their potential in a world in which people were no longer handicapped by faulty gender socialization.[29]

If the patriarchal interpretation took all of society as the unit of analysis and the sex-role socialization model focused on the individual, the institutional approach highlighted the school as intermediary between society and the individual. The tendency to shift responsibility onto the schools had been witnessed before in educational reform movements. Educators of the Progressive Era did not explain the poorer academic performance and higher dropout rates of boys in terms of boys' deficiencies but instead claimed that the school had become a feminized environment ill suited to boys. Activists in the black liberation movement attacked the notion that innate racial differences could account for black students' educational problems, arguing instead that the school was a white, middle-class institution that failed to meet the needs of black students. Likewise, feminists who developed the idea of institutional sexism treated the school itself as a key source of gender inequities, both in education and in the larger society.[30]

Why, in such diverse circumstances, did the blame fall on the institution?

Part of the answer to this question lies in the increased prominence of schools as institutions. In the nineteenth century, when the common school was more informal and occasional, educators and citizens usually attributed students' educational failings to the individuals' lack of character, not to defects in the schools. As bureaucratized educational systems began to occupy more of student's lives and have greater impact on their chances in future life, some reformers came to view the school as a quasi-independent and powerful agency in its own right. It became reasonable, then, to talk of institutional racism or institutional sexism.[31]

Advocates of institutional model of reform sought to change discriminatory policies or procedures imbedded in institutional structures and cultures. They attacked biased institutional practices through demands for policies explicitly requiring open enrollment for both sexes, equal funding, and affirmative action. This approach relied less on changing individual consciousness or behavior and more on changing the institutional rules of the game.[32]

As feminists gained momentum in their campaign against sexism in public education, they expressed optimism about the possibility of change as well as anger at the inequities they had discovered. Public schools seemed a logical target for reform. As public institutions, schools were expected to be more egalitarian than private organizations. In rhetoric at least, educators had espoused an ideology of equal opportunity that could be used to prick their consciences. For over a century the public had regarded schools as an appropriate domain for women, who constituted over two-thirds of all teachers. If these teachers could be alerted to the ways in which they were shortchanging the girls in their classes, they might be able to counteract the hidden injuries of coeducation. The civil rights movement had demonstrated that legislatures and courts, when pressed by protest groups, could alter some racist practices in public education. The feminist agenda was taking shape.

Strategies of Educational Reform

Just as they used different explanations of sexual inequities in the schools, feminists used different approaches to reform, ranging from national legislation to local consciousness raising. "Like its nineteenth-century counterpart," wrote activist Florence Howe, "the new feminism is a teaching movement. In addition to leaflets, pamphlets, magazines, newspapers, and a few books, the consciousness-raising group has made an important impact on our lives and has begun to be felt in classrooms." Howe pointed out that in colleges and universities feminism was an upswelling of change "*from the ground up*"; the number of women's studies courses increased, for example, from about 64 in 1970 to more than 1,200 in 1973. By contrast, she wrote, the "pattern of change . . . in public education is *from the top down*," through legislation and activities in national educational organizations. What was needed in public schools was also an unleashing of the same kinds of energy that had begun to transform women teachers' and students' experience in higher education.[33]

The political-legal strategies used by feminist organizations like NOW to eliminate sex bias in the schools resembled those of an earlier reform movement in education run by women: the campaign by the Women's Christian Temperance Union (WCTU) to require instruction in temperance. The WCTU was organized on the national, state, and local levels. This federated structure offered distinct advantages in enacting and policing legislation, for the national organization could shape policy and influence the federal government, state affiliates could lobby their legislatures, and local chapters could monitor and enforce laws. Such a three-pronged strategy offered special advantages in changing so decentralized and vast an enterprise as public education. While statutes provided leverage for reform, they were hardly self-enforcing. Community pressure persuaded local officials to enforce the laws.[34]

Working on these three levels, the WCTU achieved remarkable success. By the early twentieth century all the states had passed laws mandating "scientific temperance instruction" in the public schools, and Congress had done so for the District of Columbia and the Territories. Not content simply with passing laws, the WCTU asked its local branches to ensure that the statutes were obeyed. Furthermore, it created model curricular units, successfully pressured publishers to alter textbooks, and trained teachers in proper methods of temperance instruction (this special training was sometimes required by law). By working both from the top down and from the bottom up, the WCTU succeeded in making temperance instruction the one subject that was universally mandated in all American public schools. The General Federation of Women's clubs used similar techniques to install home economics in American schools.[35]

Although the goals of feminists who belonged to organizations like NOW in the 1960s and 1970s differed from those of their predecessors in the temperance movement, their methods were similar. They pressed for legislation at the federal and state levels but realized they would have to lobby local leaders in order to see these laws implemented. Liberals in the legislatures might be willing to pass symbolic statutes in order to satisfy feminist activists, but bureaucrats charged with enforcement often dragged their feet. Male-dominated governments and school districts were likely to ignore sex discrimination in the schools unless pressured and closely monitored.[36]

But even if successful, the political-legal strategy of reform could only touch the tip of the iceberg of institutional sexism in public education. It might make coeducation more egalitarian by attacking sex-separate vocational schools and classes, separate physical education programs and sports, or employment policies that discriminated against women. But these changes did not reach the subtler forms of sexism, such as biased textbooks and sex-stereotyped ways of teaching. More profound reforms would require the same strategies that the WCTU had employed: training teachers, rewriting curricular materials, and grassroots campaigns to arouse the public.

Activists in the feminist movement worked to write sex equity into legislation like the Equal Pay Bill of 1963 and Title VII of the Civil Rights Act of 1964. Such laws, however, were no stronger than their enforcement; in the beginning, some members of the Equal Employment Opportunity Commission regarded the sex provision of the Civil Rights Act of 1964 as a joke, deeming their real business to be promoting racial equality. The EEOC's neglect of women's issues impelled liberal feminists to work through NOW and other action groups, such as the Women's Equity Action League (WEAL), in order to publicize inequalities, bring sex-equity suits, lobby officials, testify at congressional hearings, and press for legislation. At its second national conference in 1967, NOW drew up a women's bill of rights that included this demand: "Equal and unsegregated education."[37]

Liberal feminists were in effect affirming the importance of truly identical coeducation and arguing at the same time that it did not exist. Their major legal tool in implementing equal coeducation was Title IX of the 1972 Education Amendments. Its controlling provision read as follows: "No person in the United States shall, on the basis of sex, be excluded from participation in, be denied the benefits of, or be subjected to discrimination under any education program or activity receiving Federal financial assistance." Since all but a tiny handful of public elementary and secondary schools were already coeducational, the law covered practically all students in public education. Despite its sweeping language, Title IX aroused little interest or controversy as it passed through Congress, which was being buffeted at the time by the storm over court-ordered racial busing. The bill was thin on particulars, beyond the threat of cutting off federal funds to schools that did not comply.[38]

Title IX can be interpreted as a symbolic gesture on the part of a Congress that delegated to the administrative branch the crucial task of devising regulations and modes of enforcement. Anne N. Costain argues that it was a typical strategy at the time for the "Congress to pass legislation responding to the grievances of [a disadvantaged] group, then for the bureaucracy to delay implementation of this legislation for prolonged periods of time. This has the effect of forcing the group to fight its most difficult political battles in bureaucratic settings, out of the public eye." The history of implementation of Title IX corroborates Costain's analysis and illuminates the strategies of the pressure groups that emerged on both sides of the campaign against sex discrimination.[39]

Passed by a Democratic Congress, the statute languished in the Republican administrations of Presidents Richard Nixon and Gerald Ford. "To get Title IX regulations was like pulling teeth with your fingers," complained Senator Birch Bayh, who was a key ally of feminists. The Department of Health, Education, and Welfare (HEW), charged with devising regulations, stalled for two years before finally issuing a tentative version in 1974 for congressional and public comment. This delay gave constituencies on both sides the chance to mobilize their forces.[40]

The lobby for strong enforcement of Title IX—called the Educational Task Force—was composed largely of sympathetic educational organizations and feminist research, legal, and political action groups. The most vocal opponents were representatives of college sports who feared that sex equity in athletics would endanger that citadel of masculinity, football. Costain reports that HEW officials were "not willing to view women or the Task Force as a constituency," whereas football coaches won easy access to President Ford's White House. Within Congress a number of conservatives tried to kill the regulations on affirmative action, the grievance process, integrated physical education programs, and revenue-producing sports. But by gaining the support of black congressmen concerned about the potential for a similar gutting of civil rights provisions, the women's lobby managed to save the Title IX regulations proposed by HEW. They finally went into effect three years after passage of the bill.[41]

Although the regulations for Title IX that were finally approved in 1975 did not contain all the provisions sought by feminists, they did provide a legal basis for making public elementary and secondary coeducation more identical for both sexes. They required every school system to evaluate its policies and alter them if they did not comply with the rules. Every district was to appoint a Title IX officer responsible for coordinating compliance and hearing complaints about sex discrimination. With some exceptions, regulations outlawed separate-sex classes in health, physical education, and vocational subjects as well as banning sex-segregated vocational programs and schools. The regulations outlined the general principle of equal treatment of boys and girls in athletics but exempted contact sports and shaded the mandate of sex equality in sports by ambiguous language that would later provide grist for lawyers. They banned discriminatory counseling and sex-biased guidance tests and materials. Districts were enjoined not to discriminate by sex in employment and compensation or to treat students or employees differently according to marital status or pregnancy.[42]

Rough legal tools were now available to combat explicit sex bias in public education of the sort that existed on the periphery of the system and to attack sexual discrimination in employment. Legal action against even obvious forms of sex bias was "stalled at the start," however. A report on enforcement by NOW's Project on Equal Education Rights (PEER) in 1977 told a depressing story: federal implementation of Title IX in public elementary and secondary schools was "indifferent, inept, ignorant of the law itself, or bogged down in red tape." The HEW civil rights office, the report claimed, had failed to publicize the law adequately, clarify disputed points in the regulations, train staff, conduct thorough investigations into non-complying districts, and resolve complaints within a reasonable period of time. As one insider put it, "it's not respectable to work on Title IX in the agency."[43]

PEER pointed out that most of the cases, by their nature, required prompt resolution, for justice delayed was often justice denied for students who were passing rapidly through school. The cases illuminate the kinds of discrimination practiced in local districts. Parents of girls in Louisiana complained in 1974 that their daughters in an all-girls high school could not take the Latin and advanced mathematics courses offered in the boys' school; in 1977 their case was still pending. A mother in Massachusetts wrote that her daughter had been denied access to a shop class; when HEW got around to calling her, the family had moved. When a NOW chapter in Pennsylvania asserted that three districts wee disobeying Title IX, HEW took twenty-two months to reply and reported two years later that it had lost the original report. A NOW member in that community observed:

"When we first filed the complaint, the school people were really nervous. Today, when you talk to someone in the school district, they just smile. They know nothing is going to happen."[44]

Other investigations by agencies inside and outside the federal government largely confirmed PEER's dismal account of enforcement in the early years of Title IX, although the record improved during the Carter administration. Despite a court order in 1977 stemming from a feminist suit against HEW for failing to enforce the law, the Civil Rights Commission reported in 1980 that the agency was still a Bermuda Triangle of unresolved complaints and that it was laggard in making compliance reviews in school districts. Although feminists, like blacks, had resorted to the federal government to secure rights not honored at the local level, both groups knew that reform from the top down could easily be stymied by a reluctant or inefficient bureaucracy. Despite the fact that some districts openly challenged Title IX, the federal government never imposed the ultimate sanction, the cutting off of federal funds. Indeed, in the case of *Grove City College v. Bell* in 1984, the U.S. Supreme Court, following the lead of the Reagan administration's brief, narrowed the coverage of Title IX to particular programs that discriminated, not to institutions as a whole, thereby further limiting whatever fiscal threat remained. Feminists united with other equity advocates to pass the Civil Rights Restoration Act in 1988 to undo some of the damage of *Grove*.[45]

Under the administration of President Ronald Reagan, feminist programs suffered not only the indifference or inefficiency of the federal bureaucracy but also direct attacks. A prime target was the Women's Educational Equity Act (WEEA). In 1974 Congress had passed this act to establish model educational programs to combat sex bias. Although a small program—its funding never exceeded $10 million—through demonstration projects it provided state and local education agencies with services that had previously been lacking in the implementation of Title IX. WEEA took the lead, for example, in developing programs to open scientific and technological courses and careers to girls and women, counteract sex stereotypes in vocational education, eliminate the barriers that kept women from administrative positions, and create sex-fair programs in physical education and athletics. It constituted the only action arm of a federal government that had otherwise taken a passive stance toward the implementation of Title IX. As such, it became a lightning rod for opponents of the feminist agenda.[46]

Conservative publications attacked WEEA as "an important resource for the practice of feminist policies and politics" and as a "money machine for a network of openly radical feminist groups." President Reagan first tried to abolish the agency and when that failed, to withhold funds. When this maneuver also failed, his Education Department tried another tack: appointing as field readers for WEEA-sponsored projects a number of people, some associated with Phyllis Schlafly's Eagle Forum, who were unsympathetic to feminist goals. One of these field readers wrote this appraisal of a grant proposal: "Do not see the need for project. Most girls and boys go into field because it is way parents bring them up and mostly they are born with certain desires." The director of WEEA was reassigned to another job, and a pro-feminist advisory council for WEEA was replaced by Reagan-appointed members who promptly fired the executive director and hired as her successor a member of Eagle Forum who had opposed appropriations for WEEA.[47]

Conservatives in Congress also assaulted the campaign against sex discrimination in education. In 1979 and again in 1981, senators introduced a Family Protection Act that was designed, in the words of Senator Paul Laxalt, to "withhold funds to any program that teaches children values that contradict demonstrated community beliefs or to buy any textbooks that denigrate, diminish, or deny the historically understood role differences between the sexes." These bills also left to the states or local districts "the right, with parental consultation, to limit or prohibit intermingling of the sexes in sports or other school-related activities, free of Federal interference." Promoted by the Moral Majority and applauded by *Conservative Digest,* the Family Protection Act shows that anti-feminists, too, tried to use the power of the federal government to serve their aims. Although this campaign was unsuccessful except in symbolic terms, it demonstrated that in some quarters anti-feminism was a potent cause.[48]

Fearful that the federal government was undermining the quest for sex equity, feminist activists turned to state governments for support in their attack on sex bias in the schools. In 1987 Phyllis W. Cheng reported that a total of twelve states (all but one of them in the North) had adopted comprehensive laws on sex equity similar to Title IX, nineteen had adopted fragmented statutes, and nineteen had passed no legislation on the subject (of these, fourteen were in the South). The timing of the state Title IX laws was revealing: Only one was passed before the federal statute; four were enacted during the period of ferment over the federal regulations from 1972 to 1975; none appeared in the period from 1976 to 1980 when feminists were focusing on federal implementation of the new regulations;

and seven, or over half, were adopted during the Reagan years, when feminists had reason to believe that the federal government was sabotaging their work.[49]

The new laws generally covered the same guarantees as the regulations of the federal Title IX, but half of them also banned sex discrimination in instructional materials such as textbooks. As in the case of the federal government, no state ever cut off funding because of non-compliance. Although the states that passed Title IX laws did demonstrate more sex-fair practices in the schools after enactment than before, it is obviously hard to disentangle the effects of federal and state laws or to assess the impact of changes that had little to do with the laws. Some states made rapid progress because influential and committed state educational officers or sex-equity coordinators worked in tandem with women's lobbies that monitored local districts.[50]

As in the case of the WCTU and local enforcement of temperance instruction, women's groups worked hard in local districts to publicize and correct sex discrimination. In community after community, feminists created grassroots coalitions to educate the educators about the federal and state laws and compel compliance. "The key to enforcement is community pressure," said an activist in the Iowa state department of education. "That is the only viable vehicle for enforcing the law." The key to success in such efforts, wrote PEER in a report on these campaigns, was to "set limited, concrete goals," build "a broad base of public support," and publicize "findings to the widest possible audience."[51]

The South, which had passed no sex-equity laws and was generally traditional in gender values, offered a somewhat unlikely case in point. In 1975 Winnifred Green, who had worked to end racial segregation as a worker for the American Friends Service Committee, shifted her attention to gender bias. She recruited volunteers to monitor violations of Title IX in twenty-one communities in six southern states. In a region already in turmoil over racial desegregation, the monitors encountered much hostility. In Arkansas a superintendent declared: "We'll comply the last minute of the last day." When Green had collected a massive array of Title IX violations, she presented a complaint to the regional offices of the Office of Civil Rights (OCR) in Atlanta and Dallas. The media broadcast her report, and this publicity galvanized the Atlanta OCR into action (pp. 10–12).

The federal courts came into play as well. A number of communities had responded to racial integration by establishing separate-sex high schools as a way of keeping black boys and white girls apart. As a result, girls found that they did not have access to advanced science, math, and language courses. A federal judge ended this policy, arguing that sex-segregation "results in a similar if not equivalent injury to school children as would occur if a racially segregated school system were imposed" (p. 12).

In Iowa, a state senator, Joann Orr, started another sex-equity campaign when she invited members of women's groups to a meeting to discuss enactment of a state law on sex bias. The women left the meeting determined to document the problems by monitoring their own communities. These women's groups—the League of Women Voters, the American Association of University Women, the PTA, NOW, and others—provided networks for recruiting volunteers. A PEER staff member from Washington, D.C., came to train the local monitors and provided press releases on Title IX to local media. The volunteers collected reports on twenty-three districts and provided documentation and publicity that helped persuade legislators to pass a sex-discrimination bill (pp. 16–18).

The volunteers also worked with local educators. In Pella, Iowa, activists interviewed the superintendent, teachers, and counselors, helping them analyze textbooks and their own practices. They believed that such an approach was more productive in a small town than confrontation. The superintendent, apprehensive at first, said "all in all it was a positive experience. And the people doing the monitoring were local. It wasn't like it was someone from outside the community." One volunteer wrote: "Teachers came to realize that the texts were, in fact, sex biased. . . . The long-range impact of our study will be through changing the consciousness of teachers." Some people might think the feminist concerns were silly, she said, but in the face of local pressure they stopped criticizing so loudly (pp. 16–18).

A campaign to monitor sex equality in twelve Michigan school districts illustrates how national organizations, state and local women's groups, the media, school districts, foundations, and local volunteers interacted. In 1979 a director from PEER, Elizabeth Giese, began by going from community to community, speaking to local groups, working through organizational newsletters, collaring volunteers at meetings, and meeting with local media people to explain sex equity. Foundations and corporations supported the effort. Giese urged local monitors to secure endorsements from local organizations and to take a cooperative approach, assuming that educators wanted equitable schools (pp. 32–34).

Detroit, facing a huge deficit and a desegregation order for a school population that was 87 percent minority, proved to be "a special challenge," Giese wrote. "You want to talk about the quality of their program . . . and they wonder if they'll have a program." Less than a third of the staff and only 13 percent of the students had ever heard of Title IX. Over two-thirds of the district's vocational classes were sex-segregated. "We don't have a problem with sex discrimination in my class," observed an aerospace teacher, "because we don't have any girls." Despite such obstacles, a PEER official and her blue-ribbon advisory board moved ahead, wrote a report that was distributed across the system, and won the endorsement of eighteen community groups. The strategy was one used in many other communities: documenting problems, creating community awareness, and generating pressure to change. "Because educators are busy people involved in running regular school programs," wrote PEER, "they tend to overlook suggestions for change unless there is evidence of widespread community support for them. That is why an organized campaign is important" (pp. 34–35, 37).

What Happened in the Schools?

Case studies of local campaigns, like those of the WEEA projects, were often success stories of Title IX implementation, while individual complaints to HEW, litigation, and compliance reviews by federal or state agencies told of failures to carry out the law. More difficult to assess is the degree to which approximately sixteen thousand local school districts actually complied with the mandate to make coeducation more identical for both sexes. In such a vast, decentralized system local attitudes toward gender mattered; both community expectations and school cultures differed greatly by region, by size of community, and by social class.

As in past attempts to reform gender relationships in the schools, policy talk and practice often diverged. Some changes were easier to make than others; some reforms were largely symbolic, others practical. And amid the campaigns in the past generation to root out sex inequities or to restore a partly mythical traditional order of sex differentiation, both feminists and their foes sometimes lost sight of the substantial gender parities built long ago into the structure of instruction in coeducational classrooms.

School districts responded in a variety of ways to Title IX and to the broader feminist campaign against institutional sexism. Some sought to meet the spirit as well as the letter of the law by addressing the subtler as well as the more obvious forms of institutional sexism. Most complied at least with the letter of the law—for example, by abolishing the sex-labeling of courses and by expanding sports programs for girls. Some districts remained ignorant of the requirements of Title IX or openly defied it.

Part of the difficulty in evaluating the effects of Title IX and programs like WEEA arises, as Rita Bornstein observes, from the ambiguity of the criteria used to determine compliance or success. Such diffuse goals "were both confusing and liberating. Confusing in that they provided few clear, specific guidelines for action; liberating because their very unclarity invited creative local definitions." Complicating this story still further is the fact that feminists themselves came to disagree about whether a gender-neutral approach—one that sought to expose girls and boys to identical coeducation—was preferable to a gender-sensitive strategy that recognized differences between males and females and attempted to honor feminine values and cognitive and behavioral styles.[52]

Another problem in assessing implementation is an absence of statistics on gender practices. Federal and state records on implementation are so spotty and incomplete that PEER found as late as the 1980s that it had to rely in part on data collected independently by private agencies.[53]

A sense of fair play and social justice motivated many school officials to comply with Title IX regulations. Compliance usually cost money—as in upgrading girls' athletics—and did not increase resources, because funds for sex desegregation in local districts were minuscule. The negative incentives for compliance were perhaps more compelling: a fear of bad publicity resulting from local or state monitoring of practices; the threat of state or federal investigations of complaints; and the prospect of costly and time-consuming lawsuits. Although not many Title IX cases entered the courts, the fear of litigation probably induced many administrators to comply, for potential lawsuits cast a long shadow on school districts. By the end of the 1970s all but the most uninformed or recalcitrant districts had probably implemented, at least in a formal way, the most explicit regulations of Title IX. But the gap between token and full compliance was enormous.[54]

The results of the campaign for sex equity were summed up in the title of a 1981 report prepared by the National Advisory Council on Women's Educational Programs: *Title IX: The Half Full, Half Empty Glass.* If complaints and lawsuits constituted the half-empty glass, the success stories in the report balanced the image:

- A man teaching auto mechanics in Kingstree, South Carolina, concluded that "the three girls in my first year class are doing just as well as the boys."
- A teacher in Kansas recalled that "if I went back to before '79, . . . we had boy lines and girl lines, . . . boy bubblers [drinking fountains] and girl bubblers. . . . If a boy would drink out of a girls'

bubbler, goodness sakes! . . . segregation doesn't solve a problem. You solve a problem through integration."
• A student in Louisiana said of her drafting teacher: "He has really helped me a lot to see what I can do now and later. He understands the female students can make a career based on skills learned in his class."
• A parent who served as a Title IX monitor said: "It is exciting to realize that individuals who care about equity and work toward that can truly make a change. . . . My daughter, in her first year of junior high school, is becoming an effective community advocate who knows her rights, the rights of others, and stands up for what she believes."[55]

The complaints and the successes convey the human side of the search for sex equity, but statistics, hard as they are to find, illuminate concrete institutional changes. Certain parts of the Title IX regulations lent themselves to statistical analysis: for example, data on girls' participation in athletics, on the number of girls in nontraditional vocational education courses or programs, and on the hiring of women administrators.[56]

In the federal government, state capitols, local districts, and the courts, the quest for sex-fair athletics initially aroused controversy and continued to generate debate and legal tangles. Sports had great symbolic importance in gender psychology and politics and had mobilized the public's interest in and support for public education. In the Progressive Era, school leaders welcomed competitive football and baseball because they made the high school seem virile. The prospect—rare, as it turned out—of girls playing on boys' teams aroused fears of a female invasion of a traditionally masculine domain. The panicky response of male administrators to boys with long hair or earrings—and the large number of cases involving the length of boys' hair but not girls'—suggests that many schoolmen were still anxious about the "feminization" of male students (in Salem, Alabama, the high-school principal suspended three boys for wearing earrings, complaining that "I feel that young men should dress like young men and young ladies should dress like young ladies").[57]

The inequalities between boys' and girls' athletics at the time of the passage of Title IX were blatant. The ratio of expenditures for girls' sports in comparison to boys' ranged from 1 : 8 to 1 : 450 in eight communities. In two states, public schools spent no funds on girls' sports, while in Minneapolis the district spent more on one football team than on all girls' sports in the eleven city high schools. Public opinion supported greater equality of athletic opportunity for girls, however, and the decade after Title IX was a time of rapid progress. In 1974 the Gallup poll found that 88 percent of all respondents and 89 percent of high-school juniors and seniors agreed that girls and boys should "have equal financial support for their athletic activities." In this case, "equal" typically meant separate: girls played on their own teams, and this practice generally did not disrupt the boy' programs. In 1971 girls constituted only 7 percent of all interscholastic athletes, but by 1980–81 the ratio of girls had increased to nearly 36 percent. The proportion of female athletes varied widely between states, ranging from 54 percent in Iowa to 24 percent in Alabama.[58]

During the 1970s there was a fivefold increase in high-school girls' participation in competitive sports. While this was a major gain—one that paralleled the greater recognition of women athletes in the society as a whole—boys' programs continued to be better funded and girls continued to be limited to fewer sports and to be excluded from contact sports. Women physical educators also raised important questions about whether the earlier philosophy of women's sports, which stressed participation and cooperation over commercialized competition among the star athletes, might be lost if girls' athletics were to become assimilated to male sports.[59]

Coeducational physical education—especially in the elementary school—aroused less resistance than the apparent threat posed by full coeducation to the male domains of contact sports and interscholastic athletics, yet it raised a number of questions about the nature of equity. In supposedly mixed classes resegregation often took place when students engaged in contact sports. Certain activities deemed appropriate to women—such as modern dance—were sometimes dropped from the coeducational physical education curriculum because they were not considered virile enough for the boys. As physical education departments became sexually integrated, women athletic directors and coaches were often replaced by men. By 1983–84, only 17 percent of coaches in senior high schools were women. The analogy with racial desegregation in the South is striking: there, as white and black schools were merged, large numbers of black principals lost their jobs to whites.[60]

Sports might be regarded as peripheral to the main academic purpose of the public schools, but their symbolic value propelled them into the limelight during the Title IX controversy. Similarly, relatively few students entered the elective vocational education programs, but the direct connection between such practical training and sex-typed jobs made sex bias and sex segregation in vocational education one of the primary targets of feminists. Activists argued that inadequate job training was one of the major reasons for the low status of women in the labor market. Similar reasoning lay behind the sex-equity provisions in the 1976 amendments to the Vocational Education Act (P.L. 94-482). Because advocates of vocational education had justified their programs as a way to prepare students for the adult workforce, it was natural to assume that changes in vocational training could improve the lot of women in the workforce.[61]

That connection between school training and a sex-stratified work force also made more than token compliance with the law difficult, however. In theory, enrollment in occupational programs was voluntary, but many factors influenced and constrained the choices of students, including the attitudes of fellow students, the advice of school staff and parents, interactions with teachers, and perceptions of opportunity after graduation. A school system might declare that all occupational classes were open to both sexes and still find that boys and girls continued to choose sex-typed programs. Only in required classes in subjects like home economics and shop could school systems prescribe mixing by sex, but these were usually regarded not as specific job preparation but rather as general education for all students.[62]

Before Title IX, prevocational and vocational classes were highly sex-segregated. In the middle grades of many school systems, boys and girls were separated in required home economics and shop classes. Another form of segregation was the separate-sex vocational school. New York City, for example, had thirteen schools for boys only and five for girls. The male schools offered a far wider range of courses, most of which led to higher-paying jobs than programs for girls. Separate vocational schools for girls mostly prepared them for work in the home or low-paying female jobs. In Boston, graduates of the girls' trade school could expect to earn 47 percent less than graduates of the boys' school. Title IX regulations banned such sex-segregated vocational schools and required integration of courses such as shop and home economics that had been limited to one sex.[63]

In comprehensive coeducational high schools that offered vocational programs and courses as electives, sex segregation was also widespread, either as a result of deliberate policy—as in the case of boys-only welding classes—or as a result of student choice (constrained, of course, by sex stereotyping). In 1972–73, 79 percent of all girls in vocational classes were enrolled in homemaking or office-business training programs. Eighty-eight percent of students in technical courses in high schools and 86 percent in trades-industry courses were boys. It was clearly not enough to declare—as required by Title IX—that all classes were open to girls and boys alike; active efforts were needed to recruit students for courses that were non-traditional for their sex and to institute sex-fair methods of teaching. When Congress attached sex-equity amendments to its funding of vocational education in 1976, it required states to appoint full-time sex-equity coordinators in their vocational departments and provided them with a list of duties explicitly designed to lessen sex segregation and discrimination.[64]

What were the results of these attempts to achieve sex equity in occupational training? There were improvements in some fields between 1972 and 1979: female enrollments in agriculture programs went from 5.3 percent to 19.2 percent and in technical programs from 9.7 percent to 17.5 percent; male enrollments in certain home economics specialties increased somewhat during those years. But a survey conducted in 1979 disclosed that almost half of vocational programs enrolled students of one sex only and that only 8.5 percent of students in apprenticeship programs were women. A 1980 study found that over 90 percent of students training to be nursing assistants and secretaries were women and between 94 and 96 percent of students in carpentry, auto mechanics, welding, and small-engine repair were men. Almost 70 percent of women were preparing for occupations that paid below-average wages. PEER reported that in 1982–83 only 13 percent of women were enrolled in non-traditional vocational programs—those previously defined as for men only—almost one percentage point lower than the 1978–79 school year figure. Clearly, severe problems persisted in the effort to make occupational training sex-fair. Despite some programs that attempted to redress the bias of vocational training, students were often reluctant to enter fields that were non-traditional for their sex. In general, enrollments reflected the sex segregation of the work force.[65]

Women have been historically underrepresented in the administration of public schools. Attempts to remedy this in equality directly challenged the dominant position of men and thus aroused opposition (usually not explicit but powerful nonetheless). Title IX and several other statutes and executive orders prohibited sex discrimination in employment, and securing more leadership positions has been a key item on the feminist education agenda. As table 16 indicates, the progress made in promoting women between 1972–73 and 1983–84 was mixed at best for a system in which women continued to constitute about two-thirds of all teachers. Data on the sex of school administrators are only approximate, for agencies that normally gather all sorts of statistics on them have been laggard in recording both sex and ethnicity. The greatest growth in the percentage of women

Table 16

Women in Various Administrative Positions (Estimated)

	1972–73 (%)	1983–84 (%)
Superintendent	0.1	6.8
High School Principal	1.4	6.1
Junior High School Principal	2.9	10.2
Elementary School Principal	19.6	26.5

Sources: Andrew Fishel and Janice Pottker, "Women in Educational Governance: A Statistical Portrait," in Janice Pottker and Andrew Fishel, eds., *Sex Bias in the Schools: The Research Evidence* (Rutherford, N.J.: Farleigh Dickinson University Press, 1977), p. 511; "The PEER Report Card: Update on Women and Girls in America's Schools—A State-by-State Survey," *PEER Policy Paper #4,* Autumn 1985, charts 3, 5–7.

administrators appears to have taken place in the 1980s, in part because women have entered administrative training programs in much greater numbers than before and in part because activists have worked hard to clear the obstacles in their path.[66]

Efforts to dislodge sex bias in physical education and athletics, vocational education, and the hiring of administrators to fulfill the requirements of Title IX produced mixed results. Certain kinds of mandates were clear and demanded institutional responses—that is, they called for definite changes in policy, regardless of the commitments and values of individual educators and students. It became illegal, for example, to limit courses to one sex only or to limit job descriptions to one sex, as in notices for administrative positions. Even in such cases, resistant staff might evade the intent of the law: for example, teachers might resegregate a coeducational class by assigning different activities to the two sexes, or school boards might tap the "old boy" network to screen candidates for an administrative position.

But even when the new policies were clear and enforced, and hence formal discrimination was absent, there was considerable leeway for differential gender practices that could be attributed to individual choice. A district could open a nursing-assistant class to boys and a carpentry class to girls, but strong pressures from parents, peers, and some school staff often kept all but the most intrepid students from making unorthodox choices. When student and public opinion was in line with new opportunities—as in the case of girls' sports—rapid change occurred. Boys' and girls' athletics, in which participation was voluntary, may have become more equal in funding and public support, but they continued to be segregated as a rule. But when men's traditional dominance was directly challenged, as in administrative hiring practices, changes in the law did not erase, though they did erode, the many informal barriers blocking women from leadership positions.

Feminists seeking to bring about change in sixteen thousand decentralized school districts have relied on a complex mix of federal and state legislation, model projects, and federated pressure groups operating at each level, including local communities. But one major target of feminist reform in education was not so decentralized and hard to reach: the large corporations that produced textbooks for the vast education market. Here reformers did not have to police thousands of local districts or change the choices of millions of students. Publishers sensitive to negative publicity that might hurt sales, responded to charges of sex bias by changing their products, at least in token ways. The knew, also, that several states had passed laws prohibiting the use of sex-stereotyped curricular materials. A number of states and publishers issued guidelines for non-sexist language. Five large states went beyond proscribing sex-stereotyping in textbooks to require social studies classes to include women's experience and contributions to American history. Publishers who did not adapt their textbooks faced the loss of lucrative markets. In any case, feminists on the editorial staffs of the publishing companies were committed to producing nonsexist books.[67]

Changes in the textbooks, unlike reforms in sports or vocational education, went to the core of the educational process: what millions of students learned in regular classrooms. The feminists' initial research on textbooks reported a deeply ingrained male bias: they found, among other things, highly unequal representation of the sexes in text and illustrations, blatant sex stereotyping, and generic use of male pronouns. Many companies adopted guidelines to eliminate these obvious forms of bias. Feminist educators welcomed these improvements but feared that textbook reform might stop at the surface of the problem. Cleaning up the pronouns, adding a few token women, and eliminating the more obvious forms of sex stereotyping—these were only the beginning of a much more thorough rethinking of the curriculum that feminists advocated.[68]

Since textbooks constituted the chief source of academic knowledge in public schools, they became the focus of a debate over what the common understanding of the world should be. Much of the reconceptualization of women's experience was related to the rapid growth of women's studies programs. In higher education, women's studies courses burgeoned in the 1970s. Researchers in fields like history and literature not only made invisible women visible but questioned the male canon of what should be taught and male paradigms of explanation.[69]

In 1986 Mary Kay Tetreault indicated what a feminist analysis might entail when she appraised a dozen high-school texts published between 1979 and 1982. Janice Trecker's earlier study of U.S. history textbooks of the 1960s revealed that they largely excluded women, in part because their experience was not directly relevant to the chief topics of traditional male history: politics, wars, and diplomacy. Tetreault found that although women were no longer invisible in the later textbooks, they still were far less prominent than men. She estimated that only about 5 percent of the prose and from 30 to 58 percent of the pictures described women. All the books discussed and illustrated a similar cast of famous women, especially those who most easily blended into political history, such as presidents' wives.[70]

This "contributionist" stance, though similar in tone to the early treatment of minorities in textbooks, was accompanied by the appearance of a new theme in the more recent books: the oppression of women (the limitation of their legal and political rights) and their efforts to liberate themselves. Some texts discussed women's participation in the paid labor force. But by and large, the texts stopped there in their treatment of women's experience, even though the illustrations offered more opportunity to analyze the everyday lives of women. Tetreault concluded that the "textbooks *have changed* since Trecker's analysis," but women were included mostly as contributors to major events of traditional (male) history or as the complements in oversimplified, dualistic (male versus female, public versus private) treatments of social issues. What was lacking was a new conceptualization that reflected the new questions and findings of feminist history—and, more generally, the social history of groups excluded from traditional textbooks—and did not simply shoehorn women into the existing frameworks of interpretation.[71]

To provide an accurate picture of the past, Tetreault argued, textbook authors should "pay attention to the content of women's everyday lives by including women's reproductive work within the home—childbearing, childrearing, and housework. Textbooks must document women's efforts to break out of their traditional sphere of the home in a way that uses women's activities, not men's, as the measure of historical significance." Tetreault's recommendations were aimed at creating a curriculum that would legitimate women's experience as different from but of equal importance to men's.[72]

On the other side, conservatives complained that feminist revision of textbooks had gone too far and that textbooks no longer promoted traditional sex roles. One of these critics, Paul V. Vitz, analyzed stories used in basal readers from the third through the sixth grade in Texas and California. "By far the most noticeable ideological position in the readers is a feminist one," he concluded. Striking for their absence were stories celebrating romance, marriage, or motherhood, and stories or pictures showing girls with dolls. Instead, he found many stories in which heroines acted like and outshone boys: the new girl on the block who wins at "King of the Hill"; a girl in a dog sled race who turns back to help a boy but wins the race nonetheless; and a princess who agrees to marry a dragon-prince "only if her new kingdom has lots of dragons in it for her to slay and lots of drawbridges for her to fix."[73]

An oblique corroboration of Vitz came from a feminist sociologist, Mary Jo Neitz, who argued that students resisted feminist analysis in women's studies classes that stressed "persistent, structural inequality of men and women in our society." Part of the reason, according to her, was that young women believed their education had been on the whole a sex-fair enterprise and had "experienced much of their schooling through reformed textbooks." In the sanitized world of the textbooks students picked up the message that "the unequal position of women has largely been ameliorated."[74]

As Vitz's attack suggests, publishers and public-school educators in the 1980s have been caught in a crossfire of opinion about gender lessons in textbooks. Fundamentalists have protested in court against reversals of traditional sex roles in textbooks, which corrupt their children and violate their religious convictions; in a highly publicized Tennessee case, they objected to a story in which a girl read to a boy while he was cooking. Some advocates of academic freedom argued that guidelines on sex equity constituted censorship. Whether changes in textbooks represented progress, regress, or inept cosmetic responses, then, depended on the eye of the beholder.[75]

Gender in Classrooms

If it is difficult to assess the impact of the women's liberation movement on textbooks, it is even harder to appraise changing gender practices in the classrooms where children and young adults learn academic subjects. Yet it is there, and not in the peripheral arenas of sports or vocational education, that most schooling takes place. These academic classrooms are over-whelmingly desegregated by sex. To what degree have girls and boys in such settings been treated differently by teachers?

In the last generation there have been many studies of classroom interactions between teachers of both sexes and boys and girls in coeducational classrooms. The questions, methods, and conclusions have changed over time. Those who adopted the hierarchical view of sex-role socialization—something done by adults to children—have often downplayed the pupils' influence on each other. By focusing only on the behavior of the teacher, investigators also often overlooked the interactive character of relations between pupils and teachers. The search for discriminatory behavior often obscured the degree to which boys and girls had similar experiences in coeducational classrooms. And studies rarely distinguished between different styles of pedagogy—"progressive" or "traditional"—and the degree to which these contributed to sex segregation and sex-typing.[76]

In the 1960s scholars studied sex interactions in elementary classrooms mainly to figure out why boys had more trouble learning to read. Some scholars thought that there were too many women teachers, that teachers had lower expectations of boys, or that the passive student role was too feminine. But researchers found in general that the sex of the teacher made no difference in student achievement, that reading instruction was about the same for both sexes, and that there was little evidence of teachers feminizing boys. In his review of the research Jere Brophy concluded that "elementary school teachers and their students are focused on teaching and learning the curriculum, which tends to be sexually neutral. . . . Compared to other roles common in the lives of children, the student role is more neutral or androgynous than sex-typed." There were some differences in the way teachers treated boys and girls, but these could "more accurately be construed as student effects on teachers than as teacher effects on students." In other words, boys were more boisterous than girls and for that reason the teachers (both male and female) tended to criticize them more often and in harsher tones than they used with girls.[77]

The focus in studies of classroom interaction shifted in the 1970s to girls as the high-risk group and to the role of teachers in perpetuating sex stereotyping. Underlying much of this research was a conviction that teachers treated boys and girls differently and that over time this inequality produced differences in school achievement (with boys performing better than girls in the upper grades), lowered girls' self-concept and career aspirations, and accentuated stereotypical behavior and beliefs. By treating boys and girls differently, the argument went, teachers increased female passivity and male dominance. Such inequalities in the classroom directly contributed to the larger inequities women faced as adults.[78]

Three problems, however, complicate the interpretation of studies of teachers' interactions with and influence on girls and boys. One is the point made by Brophy about the earlier research that presupposed teachers' prejudicial treatment of boys: to what degree is the behavior of the teachers a response to the behavior of individual boys and girls? Another is determining the degree to which teachers do—or can—influence or alter the sex-role socialization that students have already undergone. The third issue is the degree to which children themselves reinforce each other's sex-typed attitudes and behavior. In other words, how accurate is a hierarchical interpretation of socialization?

In considering the first problem, it is helpful to think of the classroom institutionally. As Larry Cuban has shown in his history of instruction, there has been remarkable continuity over the last century in the basic methods of instruction in coeducational classrooms. Students, fellow teachers, principals, and parents have expected teachers to do two things above all: to maintain order and to instruct pupils in the standard curriculum.[79]

Almost all studies of classrooms, old and new, have found boys more aggressive and disruptive in school than girls. It is not surprising to find that in order to maintain discipline, teachers interacted more with boys, especially with those who misbehaved. Nor should it be surprising to learn that both male and female teachers, in Brophy's words, "preferred conforming and obedient students over the independent and assertive students" and gave better grades to girls, who were more likely to follow the rules and complete their assignments. But in assuring that the more independent or refractory boys attended to the academic tasks at hand, teachers also may have thought it necessary to criticize them, praise them, and push them more intellectually.

If this model is plausible, the institutional context and the behavior of individual children can be considered more significant in shaping the actions of teachers than the teachers' own preexisting sex bias. The result may be the same—unequal treatment of the two sexes—but the source of the inequity in the interactive model is different. The institutional context constrained both students and teachers (this is not to say, of course, that teachers made aware of their different responses to boys and girls could not change their behavior).[80]

To move to the related second and third questions on sex-role socialization, recent studies have stressed that children already come to school with strong gender identities and that altering these in a classroom context may be very difficult. The hierarchical view of sex-role socialization treats adults such as parents and teachers as conferring gender roles on relatively passive children—wax to be impressed. But this is an oversimplification, as any feminist parent or teacher knows. The influence of children's peer groups and the broader culture on concepts of gender and appropriate behavior is very powerful.

Research by psychologists Eleanor Maccoby and Carol Jacklin on the origins of sex segregation in young children shows how powerfully children affect each other's behavior, producing a sharp sense of distinctive gender group membership at an early age. Ethnographies of school playgrounds by sociologists Barrie Thorne and Zella Luria vividly illustrate how gender differentiation in informal activities results from rules of interaction or exclusion that girls and boys of elementary-school age develop on their own. When they are free of the adult-dominated formal requirements of the classroom, children structure distinct patterns of behavior according to their own gender norms. Even in the classroom, students do not passively receive messages from teachers but also resist them or transform them into their own forms of meaning; Jean Anyon has shown that fifth-grade girls, for example, accommodate to or resist contradictory gender values taught in school in part according to their social class. Most are "not passive victims of sex-role stereotyping and expectations but are active participants in their own development."[81]

Two anthropologists, Cynthia A. Cone and Berta E. Perez, found that the students themselves "used gender as a major organizational feature of their social relationships and in their classroom's physical arrangements." They studied an "open school" in Minneapolis that sought to eradicate sexist practices by integrating boys and girls in all activities and by avoiding gender stereotyping. At the same time, the school had a progressive philosophy that promoted student initiative and sought to make them "partners in the teaching-learning process." The researchers used two methods to study gender behaviors. They observed "cooperation and conflict in how classroom spaces and furniture were used," and they asked a sample of the pupils to draw maps of the classroom.[82]

Both strategies revealed that the students themselves divided the class-

These photographs indicate the same pattern of voluntary gender segregation on school playgrounds fifty years ago that researchers document today.

Recess at the black Veysey school in Greene County, Georgia, 1941. (Jack Delano, FSA, Library of Congress.)

A boys' and a girls' slide in Greenhills, Ohio, 1938. (John Vachon, FSA, Library of Congress.)

A rousing game of ball at the Booker T. Washington School in Louisville, Kentucky, ca. 1940. (Library of Congress.)

Players and spectators, Breathitt County, Kentucky, 1940. (Marion Post Wolcott, FSA, Library of Congress.)

room by gender whenever they had a chance. In three of the four class-rooms, the teacher allowed the pupils to arrange their own desks, but in the fourth the teacher assigned seating in a desegregated pattern. In the first classroom, students divided the space into a boys' section and a girls' section where the desks of each sex were congregated, and boys' and girls' maps generally showed their own side on a larger scale and in more detail. In the second room, the sixteen children who had desks of their own segregated them by sex, and even in common spaces, boys and girls generally associated with the same sex. The third room had lofts for private work spaces, and students identified these as male and female territories. Only one girl placed her desk in a boys' space, and a boy complained that she was hostile to boys, "refusing to allow boys to sit on or at her desk" while allowing her girlfriends that privilege. In the fourth room, where the teacher was more traditional, the teacher-enforced desegregation of the sexes in formal seating arrangements dissolved into separate-sex groupings when the students had free choice of activities.[83]

When the researchers asked all the boys and girls to place three animals—a tiger, a pig, and a monkey—on their maps of the classroom, in two of the rooms the children placed the positive ones (tiger and monkey) in their own territory (except for one boy who put the tiger in the girls' space to frighten them), and the pig (which they thought of as smelly and undesirable) in the territory of the opposite sex.[84]

The "open" classroom approach gave pupils more social autonomy than the more traditional class. When they could apply their own rules of gender interaction to the classroom as they did on the playground, the children tended to segregate themselves by sex, despite the nonsexist philosophy of the school. When the researchers pointed out to the teachers what was happening, two of them decided to integrate the seating of boys and girls but gave it up because it produced disruption. "The general response of the teachers," wrote Cone and Perez, "was to accept the students' wishes in regard to sex segregation of space and to encourage integrated activities" such as a mock trial and a business project.[85]

Even when teachers have learned to monitor their own behavior in order to treat girls and boys more equally, they encounter obstacles in altering sex-typed attitudes and behavior of students. Peer pressures among students, societal gender norms, and expectations about traditional teacher roles complicate the attack on sex stereotyping and sex segregation. Even with little children, it is no easy task to change basic gender patterns, writes an expert on preschools: "There probably is little teachers can do to change children's sex-typed behavior unless they are actually to get down on the floor and actively intervene in their play. It is doubtful that many teachers would really want to do this or that school systems would support such interventions."[86]

If one looks only for the negative results of teachers' sex bias, one may overlook the possibility that teachers have neither diminished nor increased very much the strong sense of sex distinctions that children bring to school. A six-year study in more than fifty elementary and junior high schools by psychologists Jacqueline S. Eccles and Phyllis Blumenfeld illuminates this issue. They investigated ways in which sex-differentiated socialization in the classroom "might yield sex differences in students' attitudes toward school and toward themselves as learners." They expected to find "rather blatant sex differences in children's school experience" that would be linked to students' attitudes. Instead, they found only small differences in teachers' treatment of boys and girls, inconsistent across the classrooms they studied, that did not strongly predict "any of the student attitudes and beliefs that have been found to be sex-differentiated."[87]

This research led Eccles and Blumenfeld to believe "that teachers play a rather passive role in the maintenance of sex-differentiated achievement patterns." Boys and girls come into school with gender-distinct goals and attitudes, they wrote, which "appear to consolidate into sex-differentiated beliefs regarding math and scientific abilities some time around early adolescence." Although teachers did not do much to create the beliefs, they did little to challenge them either. Thus they contributed passively to sex-stereotyped decisions about academic work and careers. "If teachers are guilty of sexism," they observed, "it is [in] their failure to get students to reconsider" the self-limiting cultural beliefs they bring to school.[88]

Much research on the interaction of boys and girls also suggests, as Brophy noted, that the student role may be more sex-neutral than young people's behavior in more informal settings. If one considers how strongly children segregate themselves by sex on the playground, for example, adult-led instruction in a coeducational classroom may seem relatively egalitarian by comparison. A hierarchical model of socialization that stresses the behavior of teachers may blame them for sex differences that are chiefly created and reinforced by other children and the gender norms found in the larger society.[89]

The search for the hidden injuries of coeducation, however, did uncover many forms of subtle as well as blatant sex bias, and the campaign against discrimination produced impressive, if mixed, results. Public schools proved to be a more responsive target for feminist reformers than many other institutions, in part because both the public and educators themselves expected them to be fair and in part because schooling has been increasingly viewed as a path to adult equality of opportunity. As an educational agency in its own right, the women's liberation movement opened citizens' eyes to the unfinished business of social justice both in the schools and the larger society. But in the 1980s both conservatives and feminists began to reformulate the liberal agenda of the 1970s.[90]

⇒ *Conclusion* ⇐

Controversy over gender policy in the schools has a complex history, in part because Americans have long used debate over schooling as a way of projecting preferred gender futures for the society as a whole. Rather than attempting to change the behavior or attitudes of adults or to redistribute power directly, they have often talked about changing the young. Frequently, actual practice in the schools has changed little in response to such policy talk. And it is by no means clear how directly the changes that did occur in the education of girls and boys actually translated into major shifts in adult experience, despite the adage that "as the twig is bent, so grows the tree," popular since the time of Horace Mann.

In no period of their history have Americans debated gender issues in public schools more ardently than during the last generation. Convinced that sexual stereotyping produced gender differentiation, liberal feminists of the 1970s argued that a truly identical coeducation of boys and girls would open freedom of choice and equality of opportunity for adult women and men. Traditionalists opposed such attempts to treat girls and boys alike. Echoing the old concept of separate spheres, they claimed that God or a stable social order demanded not a unisex education and interchangeable adult opportunities but distinct paths in life for the two sexes.

This controversy over gender policy in the United States took place in a world in which coeducation has spread rapidly since World War II. Practically all nations that have had a socialist revolution adopted coeducation as a template for egalitarian schooling, no matter what their earlier practice had been. Under American occupation, Japan created coeducational schools. But in many countries coeducation came about in what UNESCO called a "slow evolution" that reflected not only indigenous conditions

279

but also the influence of the superpowers and institutional patterns of a spreading world culture. Across the globe, as Francisco O. Ramirez has shown, coeducation became the dominant gender practice in national systems of education, and with it, the curriculum for boys and girls became less differentiated.[1]

To policymakers in new nations, "coeducation often seems almost axiomatically to be an egalitarian measure," concluded the authors of a UNESCO report in 1970. Coeducation, they asserted, "in itself tends to favour participation by girls and to raise the level of their educational and occupational aspirations." Beyond providing greater access to schooling, "one of the consequences of coeducation was to arouse in girls a greater ambition, a preference for a longer course of studies on more varied subjects, and far greater ease and naturalness in their relations with boys and with other people in general." If fully developed, "coeducation might then play its true part, which is to train together, according to their aptitudes and needs, responsible and equal men and women for a common occupational and social life."[2]

As European nations sought to remedy inequalities in schooling based on differences of class or gender, they also moved toward mixing the sexes and the social classes. In Great Britain, for example, where separate-sex schools had been common for the middle and upper classes, educators deliberately emulated the American model of coeducational and socially comprehensive schools. By 1982, only 449 English comprehensive schools were single-sex, whereas 2,634 were coeducational. Coeducation also spread to Europe's religious schools. The Catholic church had long regarded coeducation as a violation of the fundamental separation of the sexes, but in Council Vatican II it softened its doctrine somewhat. An increasing proportion of Catholic schools became coeducational, a decision often justified by economic expedience.[3]

In the United States, private schools remained a last bastion of sex segregation in education. During the 1960s and 1970s, the number of single-sex private educational institutions dropped sharply at all levels. In the twenty-year period from 1966 to 1986, the proportion of single-sex colleges and universities declined from 25 to 6 percent (all Ivy League universities, for example, became coeducational). During this period, the number of all-male colleges dropped from 236 to 99, and the number of all-female colleges, from 231 to 102. By 1980, only 2.3 percent of all college women were attending all-female institutions. Among the membership of the National Association of Independent Schools, the percentage of coeducational schools increased from 38 to 76 from 1963–64 to 1986–87, while the proportion of girls' schools dropped from 24 to 12 percent and that of boys' schools, from 37 to 11 percent.[4]

In the 1980s, at the very time when coeducation was becoming the standard pattern worldwide and was virtually universal in the school systems of United States—the pioneer, exemplar, and exporter of the policy—a number of feminists were coming to doubt whether coeducation truly benefited girls. Some began to redefine the 1970s liberal agenda of gender reform in education. Coeducational schools, they held, were basically male in control, values, pedagogy, and the knowledge they taught. Simply assimilating girls more thoroughly into such a system deprived them of their own heritage and perpetuated male domination.[5]

In the 1980s, a number of scholars have argued that while coeducation may be good for boys, single-sex schools are better for girls. Some have claimed that girls taught separately perform better academically and have more positive attitudes and leadership experience. Graduates of separate girls' schools, they conclude, go on to more distinguished careers than those of coeducational institutions. And other feminist activists have suggested that girls need their own school because coeducational schools are fundamentally patriarchal.[6]

At a time when coeducation was becoming increasingly entrenched as the standard practice, then, the dialogue about its worth persisted, sometimes reintroducing old issues in new garb and sometimes creating new meanings. Educators and feminists reexamined the issue of the similarities and differences between the sexes and the education appropriate to each, the merits of separate schools, and the fundamental values taught in coeducational institutions. In the process, they demonstrated once again that the debate over the schooling of girls and boys reflected fundamental disagreements about social goals as well as educational means.

Sex Similarities and Differences in Coeducation

In the nineteenth century almost all proponents of coeducation and probably all its opponents agreed on one matter: girls and boys had different natures and would pursue different paths in later life as adults. They disagreed, however, in their interpretations of the meaning of these differences. People like William T. Harris believed that mixing boys and girls in school would not accentuate the sexes' negative traits but rather blend their distinctive virtues. Critics argued that girls and boys were so different morally and academically that mixing them was a recipe for disaster.

In the Progressive Era some feminist psychologists and educators at-

tacked the notion—common in social science as well as in lay opinion—
that females were different from (i.e., inferior to) males in intelligence and
temperament. They argued that men and women were basically the same
and that apparent gender differences resulted from disparities of upbringing and opportunity. They claimed that identical coeducation was not only
academically appropriate but also socially just.[7]

When feminists of the 1970s redefined the problem of sex equity, they
reaffirmed the ideas of the feminist psychologists of the Progressive Era:
girls and boys were identical in intelligence and abilities and needed the
same education. But they asked, if males and females were intellectual
equals, how could it be that men dominated the positions of power and
prestige as adults, that women earned only three-fifths of male salaries, and
that in most domains females were a suppressed majority? One answer they
advanced was that girls and boys did not in fact receive identical educations.

Implicit if not always explicit in the feminist educational critique and
program of reform of the 1970s was a set of liberal assumptions: that
schools could be made gender-neutral institutions; that individual boys and
girls would discover and develop their fullest potential in school and beyond, once sex stereotyping and biased instruction were abolished; and
that mental capacities, tastes, and character traits should not be sex-typed
but portrayed as human, so that schools could foster more androgynous
people—"assertive as well as yielding, ambitious and compassionate, self-
sufficient yet able to sooth hurt feelings, forceful but understanding."[8]

Although there are important continuities between the outlooks of
liberal feminists of the 1970s and feminist educational theorists of the
1980s, some writers—Nel Noddings, Carol Gilligan, and Jane Roland
Martin, among others—have begun to view sex differences and identical
coeducation in a new light. They make two claims. First, the experiences of
women are different from those of men and have produced differences of
moral and intellectual perspective. Second, the school reflects male hege-
mony not only in its administration and curriculum but also in sanctioning
a male epistemology and morality. The task of changing education, as these
writers see it, is far more complex and difficult than in the liberal paradigm,
which is predicated on an integrationist model that appeals to universal
norms of fairness. If males and females have fundamental differences, if
schools basically reflect male outlooks, and if men are securely in charge of
education, how can or should schooling be transformed?[9]

These new feminists hold that women's experience gives them qualities
of character and ethical outlooks that are different from those of men. They

suggest that it is not just a stereotype but a cultural fact that on average females are more caring, concerned about human relationships, and nurturing than men. Yet male-oriented schools do not reinforce or validate such qualities; they ignore or distort women's achievements, activities, values, and indeed the crucial duty of bearing and nurturing children. Instead, schools stress abstract thought instead of subjectivity and interrelatedness, competitiveness instead of cooperation, assertiveness instead of compassion. Male perspectives permeate the whole curriculum, which is not gender-neutral but based on a male epistemology and abstract ethic of justice. And some feminist writers argue that when traditionally female domains, such as home economics or girls' physical education, become sexually integrated, they run the risk of losing the distinctive character that once expressed and ratified female values.[10]

Accordingly, merely giving girls equal access to the male-defined school and assimilating them into the system does them (and boys) a disservice. The school does not feminize girls or turn them into androgynous graduates. Instead, it integrates them into a world of male values: the "successful" women are those who have learned to compete in a male world. Such a coeducational school does not teach girls to find their own moral voice or to appreciate and develop their own valuable qualities and activities. Martin states the problem this way: "In a society in which traits are genderized and socialization according to sex is common, an educational philosophy that tries to ignore gender in the name of equality is self-defeating." By seeming to ignore such stereotypes and injustices, "it makes invisible the very problems it should be addressing. . . . We must constantly be aware of the workings of sex and gender because in this historical and cultural moment, paradoxically they sometimes make a big difference even if sometimes they make no difference at all."[11]

The ultimate educational goal of many of these 1980s feminists is what Martin calls a "gender-sensitive" and Mary Kay Tetrault calls a "gender-balanced" education that promotes the full range of human values and intellectual perspectives for all students, female and male. In the end, they hope "to reintegrate the productive and reproductive processes of society, liberal and vocational education, reason and emotion, rationality and connectedness, and self and others."[12]

An analysis that stresses the differences between the sexes and the maleness of the school raises problems, however. The argument that certain qualities and virtues grow out of sex-specific experience—nurturance (female) versus aggressiveness (male), abstract rationality (male) versus subjectivity and connectedness (female)—runs the risk of obscuring the enormous overlap of male and female experiences and attitudes. And if the school is so overwhelmingly male-defined and male-dominated—which we doubt—the politics of gender change in education faces serious obstacles. If men so dominate the schools, what will make them relinquish a measure of control, not to mention their educational priorities, to women? The concept of male domination has led some feminists to propose separate schools for girls in order to give them a place in which to explore and develop their own values and intellectual perspectives.[13]

As one looks back at the debate over coeducation, certain patterns seem to recur over time. Those who stress differences between boys and girls have been more likely to characterize the school environment as either male or female, while those who emphasize the sexes' similarities or complementarity have tended to view the school as more gender-neutral. The debate over differences and similarities has not progressed in a linear fashion to a consensual resolution but has zigzagged to this day. Even the question of coeducational versus separate schools, which seemed to have been settled in practice in American public education by the late nineteenth century, has resurfaced in the 1980s.

Single-Sex or Coeducational Schools?

As in the nineteenth century, feminists in the late twentieth century have often worked to transform public single-sex schools into coeducational institutions. One means to this end was through legislation, as in the banning of single-sex vocational public high schools under Title IX. Another was litigation. The constitutional issues involved in sex segregation—which were not even raised until the 1960s—were more complex and disputable than those at stake in race segregation. But because girls' high schools typically received less funding than boys' schools and had a less extensive curriculum, lawyers successfully brought suits on grounds on non-comparable resources, thereby opening the doors of the male schools to girls. Faced with the fact or prospect of litigation, a number of large school districts made venerable boys' high schools (like Boston Latin School) coeducational in the 1970s and 1980s. Thus, single-sex, academically selective high schools have nearly vanished, partly as a result of the campaigns of feminists.[14] But did separate mean unequal?

Feminists were hardly of one mind about the advantages of coeducation over single-sex schooling. For some, it was only a small step from criticizing coeducational schools to advocating single-sex girls' schools. In the 1970s and 1980s, a number of feminists began to question the massive shift to coeducation worldwide. Having concluded that the education of girls and women in coeducational institutions was far from equal, some feminists decided that young women would be better served by single-sex schools.[15]

Feminist research on coeducational public schools revealed the kinds of inequalities discussed in chapter 9. Similar studies of higher education showed that simple access to coeducational institutions did not guarantee equality of treatment for females. Women students in coeducational colleges encountered discriminatory admissions procedures or financial-aid policies. They clustered in curricular programs that led to sex-stereotyped and low-paying jobs. On occasion women encountered hostility from male students and sexual harassment from faculty. Coeducational colleges typically had few women professors or administrators. Feminists complained that the male-oriented curriculum ignored or distorted women's issues and created women's studies courses to solve the problem.[16]

Some advocates of separate-sex secondary schools and colleges argued that young women would learn better in sex-segregated classrooms and thus be more likely to succeed in a mixed-sex world after graduation. Women in single-sex schools, they claimed, would enjoy the full range of leadership opportunities that were often denied them in coeducational institutions. Teachers in math and science classes had no choice but to focus on their female students, and one result was that girls in separate-sex schools scored higher on standardized achievement tests in these subjects. Researchers reported that girls in single-sex schools studied harder, displayed fewer sex-typed attitudes and aspirations, and received more academic support from peers and teachers. Investigating the careers of graduates of the prestigious Seven Sisters colleges, some scholars theorized that the women's institutions did a better job of preparing women for rewarding work than coeducational institutions. The evidence marshaled to support this hypothesis was complicated and contested. It was difficult to sort out the influence of the schools' sex composition from other factors such as family background, cognitive ability, and motivation. Comparisons of schools also proved problematic because of the great diversity of single-sex and coeducational institutions.[17]

Other feminist advocates of separate girls' schools were less interested in measuring the value of education according to the conventional criteria of test scores and success in male-defined careers. They believed that women were different from men in moral and intellectual orientation and wanted to provide girls with a separate education in which they could freely develop their distinctive talents and outlooks. Nineteenth-century advocates of women's education such as Emma Willard, Mary Lyon, and Catharine Beecher would have found some of these views familiar, but not the radical political opposition to male domination accompanying them.[18]

Some feminists doubted that they could counter the patriarchal character of coeducational schools. In Great Britain, where there was a strong tradition of separate-sex girls' schools staffed entirely by women, some radical feminists argued, writes Madeleine Arnot, "forcefully against mixed schools on the basis that they are the main means of reproducing the patriarchal relations of domination. . . . It is the presence of boys which affects girls' low self-perception, low academic performance and narrow traditional feminine interests after school." These feminists asserted that the only way "to prevent such gender reproduction is through single-sex schools where the 'subversive potential' of schools can be appropriated for feminist practice."[19] This view assumes no neutral ground in the contest of the sexes. Cleaning up textbooks, hiring more women administrators, and diminishing sex-typing would not be sufficient to eradicate the bias underlying the institution of coeducation.

But, as Arnot observes, the solution of single-sex schools for girls does not address the question of how to educate boys and change *"male prejudicial attitudes* to women. The question remains, are patriarchal and sexist attitudes a female or a male problem? A separate strategy for one sex does not . . . challenge the overall reproduction of dominant gender relations." She further notes that small single-sex schools for girls are unlikely to receive equal funding or to be equal in curriculum or status to boys' schools "unless the economic and political basis of patriarchal relations is challenged, since within such relations what is 'female' will always be defined as inferior." Feminists should seek to create, Arnot believes, "coeducational comprehensive schools that will have the resources to offer a more equal education to boys and girls" and that will bring "to the fore the issue of gender discrimination and prejudice, for both male and female pupils and teachers."[20]

The topic of single-sex schools for young women has recently reappeared in feminist policy talk and research about coeducation, in part because separate-sex school leaders have been determined to preserve their niche in the educational ecology and in part because feminists have continued to stress the defects of mixed-sex schools. As Deborah Rhode writes, "separatist education, like other forms of separatist affiliation, offers the vices and virtues of a ghetto; it provides support, solidarity, and self-esteem for subordinate groups." In such institutions, however, "it is more difficult to challenge the underlying cultural attitudes that perpetuate subordination; by definition, many of those most in need are absent." But by illuminating the ways in which coeducation has failed to serve females adequately and by proposing alternate models of gender-sensitive schooling, the current debate over separate-sex schools may prompt a new vision of gender-balanced learning in mixed schools.[21]

Another reason to focus on reforming coeducation is that it is here to stay. There is little chance that Americans will change the basic institutional contours of so deeply ingrained a gender practice as coeducation in public elementary and secondary schools. Many public schools have changed from single-sex to coeducational; few have gone the other way. Earlier challenges did not substantially undermine coeducation. Cost, custom, institutional inertia, and now the fear of litigation virtually guarantee the permanent survival of coeducation in the public schools.[22]

The School Through the Lens of Gender

Coeducation became a defining characteristic of American public schools very early in their history. This central gender practice began with the one-room rural school of the nineteenth century, continued in the graded urban schools, and still endures in almost all public schools, from the most elegant suburbs to the plains of Nebraska. The template of the coeducational classroom—the one-room school later aggregated into a cellular mass of separate classes in a complex school system—corroborates an observation made by Arthur Stinchcombe, that institutions often preserve through time the distinctive characteristics acquired at their time of origin. Despite vast social, ideological, political, and economic changes in the society and the development of a far more complex educational system, the coeducational classroom has persisted.[23]

Over time, schools were linked in various ways to the ecology of institutions that surrounded them, taking on some of the features of other social agencies. This was especially true at the beginning and end of schooling, the points of entry and exit, when the public might have been most aware of the relation of schools to society. We have shown how the practice of coeducation moved almost imperceptibly from the family to the common school. From the colonial period on, women were entrusted with the instruction of the young, first in the home or dame school, then in summer and winter

A kindergarten class eating lunch in Jefferson county, Arkansas, 1939. The photograph captures the homelike atmosphere characteristic of many kindergartens. (Russell Lee, FSA, Library of Congress.)

schools taught at public expense. The entry of women into public-school teaching, justified in part by likening the role of teacher to that of mother, made the idea of educating girls with boys in the school seem as natural as teaching brothers and sisters in the home. The coeducational school thus cloaked itself in the reassuring aura of the family. Even in complex urban systems, kindergartens were promoted as part of a smooth transition from family to graded school. As city schools became more complex, educators established other kinds of institutional connections at the point of exit by adapting the curriculum to the future high-school graduate's occupation.

Thus, at the beginning and end of the educational process, the blurring of institutional boundaries lent a kind of protective coloration to the unusual gender arrangement of the coeducational classroom, which represented the pedagogical norm in the middle grades. In those sex-mixed classes boys and girls by and large learned the same subjects, obeyed the same rules, earned similar rewards, and achieved nearly identical results. Race and class were far more important predictors of performance than sex, and age and proficiency counted much more in school regulations and organization than gender.

Despite the fact that girls and boys studied the same subjects together, people have at times labeled coeducational public schools as male or female. Those who describe the public school as a "feminine" environment—from the critics of the Progressive Era to Redding Sugg, author of the recent tract *Motherteacher*—accuse women of weakening the curriculum, turning the students into passive conformists, and feminizing the boys. Some of those who see the school today as male attack it as a harsh and hierarchical institution that rewards competition and assertiveness. These opposing views of the coeducational school have in common their insistence that the problems of the school stem from its domination by one sex or the other.[24]

We are skeptical about any absolute characterization of the school as male or female. It is true that the upper reaches of school administration have been and are clearly male-dominated. Arenas such as sports and training for trades, similarly, were fostered in part to create niches for boys to call their own, while other fields such as home economics or girls' physical education had a distinctively female cast. The further students go in the educational system, particularly in higher education, the more likely they are to find sex differences in program enrollments. But the basic unit of public schooling—the graded classroom stemming from the old one-room school—is hard to categorize as distinctively male or female.

From its origins, the practice of "identical coeducation" did not imply a desire to equalize adult roles. On the contrary, coeducation appeared at a time when Americans were busily drawing lines between adult spheres. But coeducation did provide an economical, convenient, and standardized pattern of discipline and instruction. The graded school and bureaucratized city system fixed coeducation into uniform operating procedures. Although this system of "identical coeducation" in everyday classrooms, inherited from the past and embedded in institutional structures and routines capable of resisting formal challenges, did manifest sex bias, it also provided a fairly sex-neutral pedagogical model in theory and in practice. Girls received more egalitarian treatment in their coeducational classrooms than in many other parts of their lives.

For over a century, many educators have regarded the coeducational classroom as not only organizationally and pedagogically efficient but also essential in realizing gender equality in a democratic society. John Dewey, for example, considered coeducation to be a laboratory of social democracy in which boys and girls could learn to participate in a common life by learning together in school. "Steady, frank, effective cooperation in the many interests men and women have in common," he wrote, "upon whose successful realization all social advances depend, cannot be achieved without a sympathetic and practically instinctive understanding by each of the point of view and method of the other."[25]

Dewey dreamed that the coeducational school could become a microcosm and model of a future democratic and egalitarian gender order. What has happened to this hope? Comparing gender practices in public schools with those in other institutions, Patricia Cayo Sexton states that "despite some conspicuous problems, females are probably treated in a more egalitarian way in schools than in other institutions, including religious, familial, economic, and political institutions." If it is true that the public school has been more gender-neutral than most other institutions—and we suspect that it is—it may not be wise to place too much of the burden for rectifying gender injustices in the larger society on the schools alone. Despite the American belief in the redemptive power of the public school, it is quite possible that adult institutions would continue to be highly gendered-stratified even if schools were to become sex-fair or gender-sensitive environments. Improving education is one essential means of achieving gender equality, but sex equity in education must be combined with other strategies designed to correct the sex discrimination deeply imbedded in American political, economic, and social structures.[26]

We have been looking at public schools through the lens of gender. Now we would like to raise another, necessarily speculative question: How does gender appear when viewed through the lens of the school, using the institutional approach we outlined in the introduction? Do people experience their gender in some uniform way, or does gender have quite different meaning and salience in different settings? We suspect the latter to be true and agree with Barrie Thorne, who argues that instead of emphasizing "oppositional dichotomies" in thinking about children and gender, scholars should strive "for an alternative, more fluid and situated, approach."[27]

In the public school, the meanings of gender may be more fluid and contextual than fixed and monolithic. Children know what their sex is at an early age and typically segregate themselves by sex when quite young. But they may experience the meaning of being male or female in quite different ways in different situations in the school. In informal contexts—on the playground or in the lunchroom—they usually organize themselves in separate groups and have elaborate cultural rules that govern their behavior. In gender-segregated, official activities of the school, such as certain vocational classes and sports, students show a strong sense of what is appropriate behavior for each sex. But they also participate in common activities in sex-mixed settings such as the graded classroom as if that, too, were normal. In school they thus learn to navigate through a variety of gender practices, some of which are decreed by adults, some by their peers, some typical of high school, others of kindergarten. The requirements of the different gender practices of the school may seem as natural to them as the fact of their own sex.[28]

If one could compare gender maps of different institutions—families, churches, or various kinds of workplaces, for example—one might understand better how adults and children negotiate the transitions between the different gender expectations and patterns of each setting. Contemporary theories of personality suggest that there is not one stable self in all social settings. This means that people may experience gender, not as a uniform pole in a male-female field, but in changing and diverse ways depending not only on institutional context but also on age, class, ethnicity, and race. The various ways in which young people adapt to different gender practices in the schools may have their parallels in adult life. While this might seem confusing, the process of adjusting to different institutional gender practices could be construed as liberating, as it becomes obvious that, instead of one hegemonic gender order in all contexts, there are many formal and informal gender practices and many possible responses to each. As Barrie Thorne has observed, "in some contexts gender is highly salient; in others, much less so. . . . Furthermore, the meanings of gender are not fixed or unitary, but are multiple and sometimes contradictory."[29]

An institutional analysis of coeducation also suggests an ambiguous historical relationship between silence, policy talk, and gender practices. Here as well, conflicting categories may mask the variety and complexity of gender relations that flourish within school settings. Ironies and unintended results abound in the history of gender policy and practice in education. This suggests keeping a wary eye for positive consequences of changes adopted for reasons that no longer appeal to advocates of sex equity; discrepancies between policy talk about gender and actual practice; the unnoticed persistence of institutional practices that may promote or hinder equal opportunity; negative by-products of well-intended reforms; and the gender implications of reforms adopted without regard to sex.

Many gender practices deeply ingrained in the institutional structure of public schools at their time of origin, such as coeducation, have continued despite major changes in educational purposes and gender attitudes in society. Institutional convenience, the preference of educators for familiar ways, and demographic and economic pressures often have had more to do with the introduction or retention of gender practices in the schools than conscious reforms or gender ideology. Institutional reforms introduced without attention to gender have also had far-reaching consequences for sex equity. High-school-reform reports in the 1980s, for example, have largely ignored the gender gap in education and have paid scant attention to sex equity, but by advocating more required mathematics and science courses for high-school graduation, they may unwittingly serve the 1970s feminist agenda by reducing enrollment in sex-typed electives and giving female students the necessary background for science majors in college.[30]

Over the past 150 years gender policy in public education has been shaped by diverse groups that had quite disparate notions about the ideal gender order in society and about how schools should respond to new conditions. The first campaign sought to pry open the doors of the common school, then the high school, so that girls as well as boys could become educated in roughly equal ways. To a large degree that crusade succeeded, but its major aim was to better prepare women for their separate destinies as wives and mothers. In the Progressive Era, a major purpose of reformers was to better adapt the upper levels of the public schools to boys, while differentiating schooling for girls as well. Again, those who attended to gender policy in public education did not generally question the gender order of adult life. But the recent campaigns to create sex equity or gender-sensitive learning in public education, originating outside the schools, have raised fundamental questions about the relations of women and men in the whole society and have set a new agenda, full of promise and conflict, for the next century.

→ Appendix ←
Using Photographs
as Evidence of Gender
Practices in Schools

The written sources we have consulted are very often silent on everyday gender practices in the schools, though at times they are prodigal in prescriptions. Because of this silence, we have found photographs taken during the last century especially helpful in elucidating gender practices that were so taken for granted that few people bothered to comment on them. The major advantage of pictures, we think, is that they are unobtrusive measures of what interests us: whatever their other purposes, neither the photographers nor their subjects were usually interested in recording gender patterns in education.

Historians must be cautious in using photographs as evidence, but they should, of course, be critical about all kinds of evidence, written as well as visual, statistical as well as qualitative.

No photograph can be an unmediated transcript of "reality," not even one that through modern high-speed technology purports to be "candid." The researcher needs to be aware of a variety of mediating influences: the purpose and aesthetic eye of the photographer; the conventions of the times; the self-conscious behavior of subjects who may, in Christopher Lyman's words, "alter

In thinking about these issues we are indebted to three colleagues: Christopher Lyman, a photographer and photo researcher who helped us find our way through some collections, and Joseph and Wanda Corn.

their behavior to conform more closely to what they imagine to be the ideal for the activity in which they are engaged"; the bias that dictates which scenes are worth recording; and the judgment that determines which pictures will be preserved in archives.

In the early days of school photography, the need for abundant light and lengthy exposures meant that active children were posed as still lifes. Common examples were the portraits of rural schoolchildren and their teacher posed outside the one-room school, dressed in their Sunday best. Photographers often aimed to create the effect of a solemn portrait, formal and stereotypical. The very deliberativeness of their compositions reveals a great deal about cultural beliefs and hierarchies of power and hence has its own uses in historical interpretation.

Even when formal posing became technically unnecessary, cultural beliefs continued to shape images, despite the possibility of producing "candid" photographs that seemed less consciously posed. Pupils grouped informally about a teacher, all examining a guinea pig, might seem more "natural" than children sitting stiffly in rows with hands folded, but both images no doubt expressed a pedagogical ethos that the teacher wanted to convey. In both the nineteenth and twentieth centuries, teachers commonly supervised the students while they were being photographed. School pictures thus more faithfully recorded the teachers' notions of an acceptable image than the pupils' sense of themselves, although irreverent schoolchildren could subvert the enterprise by mugging or sticking out their tongues.

The artistic eye of the photographer and the photographic conventions of the time also shaped images of schools. Photographers, for example, frequently focused on patriotic rituals, such as pupils saluting the flag. The compelling image, like the telling phrase, may bend historical interpretation, for the vivid part may come to seem representative of the whole and thus exerts its own tyranny over the imagination. Pictorial icons, while they may be fascinating in their own right and provide rich sources for historians of culture, probably do not capture typical life in schools.

Photographers often wanted to convey a specific message and selected scenes to suit the purpose. Reformers such as Jacob Riis, educators surveying school systems, and the Farm Security Administration photographers of the 1930s wanted to demonstrate how cramped and inadequate the classrooms were. In her photographs of schoolchildren in Washington, D.C., Frances Benjamin Johnston intended to illustrate the "new education" (or what is now called "progressive education") for the Paris Exposition of 1900. In the 1930s and 1940s the New York public schools used photographs in their annual reports as part of a public-relations effort to show what a fine job they were doing. Pictures purporting to record "what is" can be made to serve a variety of purposes ranging from muckraking to self-promotion.

Just as photographs record a skewed sample of school experiences, another kind of selectivity is at work in the process that determines which pictures end up in archives. A large set of photographs of education in the superb collections of the Library of Congress, for example, deal with a rather idiosyncratic form of education, the "open air" schools for sickly and handicapped children. The same problem of representativeness arises with manuscripts in archives and published books and articles in libraries. Indeed, many of the same problems we have discussed with respect to images apply to written sources as well: the biases apparent in self-presentation and self-justification, the special agendas of authors and agencies, and the artistic conventions that obscure as well as reveal the ordinary.

The need for critical interpretation is inescapable, whether one uses visual or written sources. Pictures frame certain scenes, and often one can only guess at what is not portrayed. Inferences from photographs about gender practices can only be cautious and provisional, for all the reasons we have suggested above. When an outside picture of a one-room school shows two entrances, one for boys and one for girls, for example, one can only speculate as to whether this gender consciousness translated into separating the sexes inside the classroom. A floor plan of a large high school, by contrast, may indicate that girls and boys not only had separate entrances but also occupied separate spaces for activities such as vocational training and physical education.

We have arrived at some tentative inferences from the visual evidence about common gender practices. Photographs depicting free play on school grounds show far more sex segregation when students have been allowed to group themselves than one finds in scenes of classrooms supervised by teachers, although even in classrooms there are different configurations of boys and girls depending on time and place. More varied in gender pattern are the in-between activities involving the authority of the school but allowing some student discretion, such as field trips, assemblies, and some extracurricular clubs. Photographs tend to confirm written evidence that sex segregation in the formal activities of the school increased as one moved up the age-graded ladder of the organizational structure of the school.

More than written documents, photographs can be mined for evidence on topics that were not part of the conscious intent of their producers. This is the chief reason we find images valuable: they document gender practices that were largely taken for granted. Thus, we include photographs to supplement a variety of other materials, such as school reports, life histories, statistics, normative writings, floor plans, and studies by social scientists. We have scattered some photographs to illustrate specific points raised in the text, whereas we combined others in clusters of evidence on general themes.

➤ Notes ◄

City, state, and federal school reports are
cited in this abbreviated form:
St. Louis Report for 1870
Vermont Report for 1840
U.S. Com. Ed. Report for 1900
Annual reports of the National Education
Association are cited thus:
NEA Addresses and Proceedings

Introduction

1. Carl Degler, "What the Women's Movement Has Done to American History," in Elizabeth Langland and Walter Gove, eds., *A Feminist Perspective in the Academy* (Chicago: University of Chicago Press, 1983), 72, 67–85.

2. On school policy as an arena of symbolic discourse, see David Cohen and Bella Rosenberg, "Functions and Fantasies: Understanding Schools in Capitalist America," *History of Education Quarterly* 17(1977): 113–37. For useful discussions of coeducation, see John Clinton Maxwell, "Should the Education of Boys and Girls Differ? A Half-Century of Debate, 1870–1920" (Ph.D. diss., University of Wisconsin, 1966), and Arnold Jack Keller, "An Historical Analysis of the Arguments for and against Coeducational Schools in the United States" (Ed.D. diss., Teachers College, Columbia University, 1971).

3. For discussions of the cultural construction of gender and theories of sex differences, see Sylvia J. Yanagisako and Jane F. Collier, "Toward a Unified Theory of Gender and Kinship," in Collier and Yanagisako, eds., *Gender and Kindship: Toward a Unified Analysis* (Stanford: Stanford University Press, 1987), 14–50, and Joan W. Scott, "Is Gender a Useful Category of Historical Analysis?" *American Historical Review* 91(1986): 1053–75; Cynthia Fuchs Epstein, *Deceptive Distinctions: Sex, Gender, and the Social Order* (New Haven/New York: Yale University Press/Russell Sage Foundation, 1988); R. W. Connell, "Theorising Gender," *Sociology* 19(1985): 260–72; Barrie Thorne, "Children and Gender: Constructions of Difference," in Deborah L. Rhode, ed., *Theoretical Perspectives on Sexual Difference* (New Haven: Yale University Press, 1990), 100–113.

4. For data on the enormous contemporary variations in schooling and literacy by sex, which also reflect in part great differences in the status of women in different countries, see Jeremy D. Finn, Loretta Dulberg, and Janet Reis, "Sex Differences in Educational Attainment: A Cross-National Perspective," *Harvard Educational Review* 49 (1979): 477–503.

5. Adrienne Rich, *On Lies, Secrets, and Silence: Selected Prose, 1966–1978* (New York: W. W. Norton, 1979), 35. On the history and historiography of gender and education, see Thomas Woody, *A History of Women's Education in the United States* (New York: Octagon Books, 1974; orig. ed. 1929), and Willystine Goodsell, *The Education of Women: Its Social Background and Its Problems* (New York: Macmillan, 1924); Sally Schwager, "Educating Women in America," *Signs* 12(1987): 333–354; Geraldine Jonçich Clifford, "Shaking Dangerous Questions from the Crease: Gender and American Higher Education," *Feminist Issues* 3(1983): 3–62; Patricia Albjerg Graham, "So Much to Do: Guides for Historical Research on Women in Higher Education," *Teachers College Record* 76(1975): 421–29; John Rury, "Education in the New Women's History," *Educational Studies,* 17(1986): 1–15; Jill K. Conway, "Perspectives on the History of Women's Education in the United States," *History of Education Quarterly* 14(1974): 1–12; Joan Jacobs Brumberg and Nancy Tomes, "Women in the Professions: A Research Agenda for American Historians," *Reviews in American History* 10(1982): 275–96; Joan N. Burstyn, "Women in the History of Education" (Paper presented at the American Educational Research Association [AERA], April 1983); Maxine Seller, "The Education of the Immigrant Woman, 1900–1935," *Journal of Urban History* 4(1978): 307–30; and Ellen Condliffe Lagemann, "Women's History," in John H. Best, ed., *Historical Inquiry in Education* (Washington, D.C.: AERA, 1983), 251–64.

6. John D. Philbrick, superintendent of schools in Boston and an active opponent of coeducation, thought that urban schools, at least, might emulate Europe and reverse the trend toward coeducation: "Coeducation of the Sexes," American Institute of Instruction, *Lectures and Proceedings 1880,* 122; John D. Philbrick, *City School Systems in the United States,* U.S. Bureau of Education, Circular of Information, no. 1, 1885 (Washington, D.C.: GPO, 1885), 8, 10–11, 57–59.

7. The most influential justification of coeducation by a school superintendent was the one written by William T. Harris, later U.S. commissioner of education, in *St. Louis School Report for 1870,* esp. pp. 19–20.

8. Patricia Sexton wrote in 1976 that "despite some conspicuous problems, females are probably treated in a more egalitarian way in schools than in other institutions." She notes that boys and girls attend the same classes, take similar courses of study, and compete "on an equal footing. . . . Virtually nowhere in the adult working world is so little sex segregation present." Sexton, *Women in Education* (Bloomington, Ind.: Phi Delta Kappa, 1976), 5.

9. We recognize that other approaches to the topic would illuminate other

features of the educational landscape, pose different questions, and use different kinds of evidence. We do not examine very much, for example, the subjective meaning of attending coeducational schools, a subject which life histories could illuminate.

10. For examples of the sex-role socialization model, see many of the projects in *Sex Equity in Education: NIE-Sponsored Projects and Publications* (Washington, D.C.: NIE, 1980). For a sophisticated review of previous theories of sex-typing and a broader "gender schema theory," see Sandra Lipsitz Bem, "Gender Schema Theory and Its Implications for Child Development: Raising Gender-Aschematic Children in a Gender-Schematic Society," *Signs: Journal of Women in Culture and Society* 8(1983): 598–616. For criticisms of sex-role socialization and the concept of sex roles, see Judith Stacey and Barrie Thorne, "The Missing Feminist Revolution in Sociology," *Social Problems* 32(1985): 301–316; Epstein, *Deceptive Distinctions;* Connell, "Theorising Gender," 263, 268; and Dale Spender, "Education: The Patriarchal Paradigm and the Response to Feminism," in *Men's Studies Modified: The Impact of Feminism on the Academic Disciplines* (Oxford: Pergamon Press, 1981), chap. 11. For a critical discussion of patriarchy in historical analysis, see Scott, "Is Gender a Useful Category?"

11. Elisabeth Hansot and David Tyack, "Gender in American Public Schools: Thinking Institutionally," *Signs* 13(Summer 1988): 741–60; "Institutions," *International Encyclopedia of the Social Sciences,* ed. David L. Sils (New York: Macmillan, 1968), 409–21; Thomas Bender et al., "Institutionalization and Education in the Nineteenth and Twentieth Centuries," *History of Education Quarterly* 20(1980): 449–72; and George M. Thomas et al., *Institutional Structure: Constituting State, Society, and the Individual* (Newbury Park, Calif.: Sage Publications, 1987).

12. James G. March and Johan P. Olsen, "The New Institutionalism: Organizational Factors in Political Life," *American Political Science Review* 78(1984): 734–49; and James W. Fesler, "The State and Its Study: The Whole and the Parts," *PS: Political Science and Politics* 21(1988): 891–900.

13. For constancy in patterns of instruction, see Larry Cuban, *How Teachers Taught: Constancy and Change in American Classrooms, 1890–1980* (New York: Longman, 1985).

14. March and Olsen, "The New Institutionalism," 738–39; Barrie Thorne, "Girls and Boys Together . . . But Mostly Apart: Gender Arrangements in Elementary Schools," in Willard W. Hartup and Zick Rubin, eds., *Relationships and Development* (Hillsdale, N.J.: Erlbaum, 1986), 167–84.

15. Robert Dreeben, *On What Is Learned in School* (Reading, Mass.: Addison-Wesley, 1968), 63–64.

16. Ibid.

17. Florence Howe, ed., "Education and the Feminist Movement," *Phi Delta Kappan* 60(1973): 99–139, with summary by Howe, "Sexism and the Aspirations of Women," 99–104; Susan S. Klein, ed., *Handbook for Achieving Sex Equity*

Through Education (Baltimore: Johns Hopkins University Press, 1985); David B. Tyack and Myra Strober, "Jobs and Gender: A History of the Structuring of Educational Employment by Sex," in Patricia A. Schmuck, W. W. Charters, Jr., and Richard G. Carlson, eds., *Educational Policy and Management: Sex Differentials* (New York: Academic Press, 1981), 131–52.

18. Myra Pollack Sadker and David Miller Sadker, *Sex Equity Handbook for Schools* (New York: Longman, 1982); Janice Pottker and Andrew Fishel, *Sex Bias in the Schools: The Research Evidence* (Cranbury, N.J.: Associated University Presses, 1977); Nancy Frazier and Myra Sadker, *Sexism in School and Society* (New York: Harper & Row, 1973); Stephen Walker and Len Barton, eds., *Gender, Class, and Education* (New York: Falmer Press, 1983).

19. We are indebted to Larry Cuban, Harvey Kantor, and Michael Kirst for conversations that influenced this interpretation. On the politics of school reform in relation to the larger political economy, see Richard Rubinson, "Class Formation, Politics, and Institutions: Schooling in the United States," *American Journal of Sociology* 92(November 1986): 519–48, and Ira Katznelson and Margaret Weir, *Schooling for All: Class, Race, and the Decline of the Democratic Ideal* (New York: Basic Books, 1985).

20. Jane Bernard Powers, "The 'Girl Question' in Education: Vocational Training for Young Women in the Progressive Era" (Ph.D. diss., Stanford University, 1986), chaps. 2, 6, 8.

21. Horace Mann spoke of the creation of coeducation as "smuggling in the girls" in *A Few Thoughts on the Powers and Duties of Woman* (Syracuse: Hall, Mills, 1853), 57–58; Keller, "Arguments for and against Coeducational Schools"; Maxwell, "Half-Century of Debate"; Edward D. Clarke, *Sex in Education* (Boston: Osgood, 1874); F. E. Chadwick, "The Woman Peril in American Education," *Educational Review* 47(1914): 115–17; G. Stanley Hall, *Adolescence* (New York: D. Appleton, 1907), vol. 2, chap. 17.

22. Harris, *St. Louis School Report for 1870;* Klein, *Handbook for Achieving Sex Equity.*

23. Today some conservatives echo earlier arguments. See *Family Protection Act,* (27 September 1979, *Congressional Record,* 96th Cong., 1st sess., 125, pt. 20:26435–36); Eve Cary and Kathleen Willert Peraltis, *Woman and the Law* (Skokie, Ill.: ACLU, 1977), chap. 4. For the mixed accounting on sex equity in the Reagan years, see Susan Shurberg Klein, "Education," in Barbara Haber, ed., *The Woman's Annual, Number 4, 1983–84* (Boston: G. K. Hall, 1984), 8–30. For shifts in perspectives among feminists in the 1980s, see, for example, Mary Kay Thompson Tetreault, "The Journey from Male-Defined to Gender-Balanced Education," *Theory into Practice* 25(1986): 227–34; Carol Gilligan, *In a Different Voice* (Cambridge: Harvard University Press, 1982); and Nel Noddings, *Caring: A Feminine Approach to Ethics & Moral Education* (Berkeley: University of California Press, 1984).

24. David Tyack, Thomas James, and Aaron Benavot, *Law and the Shaping of Public Schools, 1785–1954* (Madison: University of Wisconsin Press, 1987).

Chapter 1. *"Smuggling in the Girls"*

1. Horace Mann, *A Few Thoughts on the Powers and Duties of Woman* (Syracuse: Hall, Mills, 1853), 57.

2. Barbara E. Lacey, "Women and the Great Awakening in Connecticut" (Ph.D. diss., Clark University, 1982).

3. William Gouge, *Of Domestical Duties,* 1622, as quoted in John Demos, *Past, Present, and Personal: The Family and the Life Course in American History* (New York: Oxford University Press, 1986), 27 (emphasis added).

4. Ruth H. Bloch, "American Feminine Ideals in Transition: The Rise of the Moral Mother, 1785–1815," *Feminist Studies* 4(1978): 102; and Laurel Thatcher Ulrich, "Vertuous Women Found: New England Ministerial Literature, 1668–1735," in Janet Wilson James, ed., *Women in American Religion* (Philadelphia: University of Pennsylvania Press, 1978), 82.

5. Nathaniel B. Shurtleff, ed., *Records of the Governor and Company of Massachusetts Bay in New England* (Boston: William White, 1853), 2:6–7; Marcus W. Jernegan, "Compulsory Education in the American Colonies," *School Review* 26(1918): 740–41 (contractions of words have been expanded for easier reading). On the role of the family in education, see Bernard Bailyn, *Education in the Forming of American Society* (Chapel Hill: University of North Carolina Press, 1960); Lawrence Cremin, *American Education: The Colonial Experience, 1607–1783* (New York: Harper & Row, 1970); and Edmund S. Morgan, *The Puritan Family: Religion and Domestic Relations in Seventeenth-Century New England* (New York: Harper & Row, 1966).

6. *Records and Files of the Quarterly Courts of Essex County, Massachusetts, 1636–1671* (Salem: Essex Historical Society, 1911–14), 4:212; and John Winthrop, "A Modell of Christian Charity," *The Winthrop Papers* (Boston: Massachusetts Historical Society, 1931), 2:94–95.

7. Kenneth A. Lockridge, *Literacy in Colonial New England: An Enquiry into the Social Context of Literacy in the Early Modern West* (New York: W. W. Norton, 1974), 38–39; and N. Ray Hiner, "The Cry of Sodom Enquired Into: Educational Analysis in Seventeenth-Century New England," *History of Education Quarterly* 13(1973): 12–13.

8. Gerald F. Moran and Maris A. Vinovskis, "The Great Care of Godly Parents: Early Childhood in Puritan New England," in Alice B. Smuts and John W. Hagen, eds., *History and Research in Child Development* (Monographs of the Society for Research in Child Development, vol. 50, nos. 4–5), 34–35. Not all families could fulfill their legal and religious obligations to teach children to read, and in Connecticut a law of 1690 fining parents and masters for not teaching boys and

girls to read made an exception for those adults who were themselves illiterate and did not have relatives or neighbors who could instruct the young; see Linda Auwers, "The Social Meaning of Literacy: Windsor, Connecticut, 1660–1775," *Newberry Papers in Family and Community History*, no. 77-4A, 15.

9. Watertown record quoted in Walter H. Small, "Girls in Colonial New England," *Education* 22(1902): 533. The evidence on wills appears in Walter H. Small, *Early New England Schools* (Boston: Ginn, 1914), 278.

10. Law of 1647 in Shurtleff, *Records*, 2:203. Because the General Court, in its law of 1648, issued the following year, did not refer to schools in its requirement of universal literacy, it is clear that the Puritans still placed the major duty of educating children on the family and not the school. James Axtell, *The School upon a Hill: Education and Society in Colonial New England* (New Haven: Yale University Press, 1974), 169–75.

11. Shurtleff, *Records*, 2:203; Small, *Early New England Schools*, 275–77; Hopkins regulation in Thomas Davis, Jr., *Chronicles of Hopkins Grammar School, 1660–1935* (New Haven: Yale University Press, 1938), 157. George H. Martin ("The Early Education of Girls in Massachusetts," *Education* 20(1900): 323–27) reaches conclusions similar to Small's but does not provide such rich examples from town records and town histories. On the concern for orthodox thought and civil behavior, see Hiner, "Cry of Sodom."

12. Axtell, *School upon a Hill*; Cremin, *American Education*.

13. Axtell, *School upon a Hill*, chap. 5; Stephen W. Sellers, "Family Background and Social Origins of Schoolmasters: Massachusetts, 1635–1800" (unpublished paper, University of Illinois/Chicago Circle, 1981).

14. Joseph Wightman, comp., *Annals of the Boston Primary School Committee from Its First Establishment in 1818 to Its Dissolution in 1855* (Boston: George C. Rand, 1860), 18–35.

15. Kathryn Kish Sklar, "Public Expenditures for Schooling Girls in Massachusetts, 1750–1800" (Paper presented at the History of Education Society, Cambridge, October 1976); Small, *Early New England Schools*, chap. 6, contains rich documentation on dame schools from town records and shows that the dame school was incorporated into the public primary school (p. 162).

16. Small, *Early New England Schools*, chap. 6; quote on Northfield teacher appears on pp. 162–63. For a comparison with English dame schools, see D. P. Leinster-Mackay, "Dame Schools: A Need for Review," *British Journal of Educational Studies* 24(1976): 33–48. Alison Prentice has observed that "the movement of elementary teaching into public schools [from dame schools taught in the home] eventually meant the gradual loss of an important source of income for the traditional woman teacher working in the home"; see "Towards a Feminist History of Women and Education," in David C. Jones et al., eds., *Approaches to Educational History* (Winnipeg, Manitoba: Education Department, University of Manitoba, 1981), 48. The negative stereotype of dame schools perpetuated by

historians who have focused only on public institutions and the professionalization of teaching may reveal a male bias.

17. Quote about fire and water is from J. H. Higginson, "Dame Schools," *British Journal of Educational Studies* 22(1974): 167; Mary Beth Norton, *Liberty's Daughters: The Revolutionary Experience of American Women, 1750–1800* (Boston: Little, Brown, 1980), 259; Adolph B. Benson, ed., *Peter Kalm's Travels in North America* (New York: Dover Publications, 1934), 1:204.

18. Small, *Early New England Schools*, 166–76; Maris A. Vinovskis, "Family and Schooling in Colonial and Nineteenth-Century America" (Essay presented at Conference on the Family in Historical Perspective, Clark University, Worcester, Massachusetts, November 14–16, 1985).

19. Small, *Early New England Schools*, 176–82; Thomas Woody, *A History of Women's Education in the United States* (New York: Science Press, 1929), 1:137–49.

20. Small, *Early New England Schools*, 180; Carlos Slafter, comp., *A Record of Education: The Schools and Teachers of Dedham, Massachusetts, 1644–1904* (Dedham: Dedham Transcript Press, 1905), 62–63.

21. Kathryn Kish Sklar, "The Founding of Mount Holyoke College," in Carol Ruth Berkin and Mary Beth Norton, eds., *Women of America: A History* (Boston: Houghton Mifflin, 1979), 181.

22. Moran and Vinovskis, "Godly Parents," 35–36; Vinovskis, "Family and Schooling". Bloch, in "American Feminine Ideals," dates the transition to mothers as ideal teachers somewhat later but provides rich evidence on the glorification of women as mothers. On the Puritans' evaluation of women's role as pious teachers, see Ulrich, "Vertuous Women."

23. Lacey, "Women and the Great Awakening," 64–69; Demos, *Past, Present, and Personal*, 29. On changes in the sex composition of churches, see Mary Maples Dunn, "Saints and Sisters: Congregational and Quaker Women in the Early Colonial Period," and Gerald F. Moran, "'Sisters' in Christ: Women and the Church in Seventeenth-Century New England," in James, ed., *Women in American Religion*, 27–66.

24. Kathryn Kish Sklar, "Sources of Change in the Schooling of Girls in Massachusetts, 1750–1810" (unpublished paper, University of California at Los Angeles, n.d.). On seating and social status in churches, see Robert J. Dinkin, "Seating the Meeting House in Early Massachusetts," *New England Quarterly* 43(1970): 450–64.

25. Legislator quoted in Axtell, *School upon a Hill*, 180–84.

26. Sklar, "Sources of Change."

27. Ibid., 10.

28. Sklar, "Public Expenditures for Schooling Girls"; William A. Benedict and Hiram A. Tracy, *A History of the Town of Sutton, Massachusetts, from 1704–1876* (Worcester: n.p., 1878), 498–99.

29. Sellers, "Schoolmasters," 13–14; Sklar, "Public Expenditures for Schooling Girls"; Small, *Early New England Schools,*" chap. 6.

30. Lucy Lane Allen, "Female Education—Pupil and Teacher," *American Journal of Education* 30(1889): 581.

31. Sklar, "Sources of Change"; Vinovskis, "Family and Schooling"; Linda K. Kerber, *Women of the Republic: Intellect and Ideology in Revolutionary America* (Chapel Hill: University of North Carolina Press, 1980), 201.

32. For a discussion of the problems of assessing different levels of literacy, see William J. Gilmore, "Elementary Literacy on the Eve of the Industrial Revolution: Trends in Rural New England, 1760–1830," *Proceedings of the American Antiquarian Society* 92(1982): 87–178.

33. Lockridge, *Literacy,* 4, 38–42; Auwers, "Social Meaning of Literacy," 1, 3; Gilmore, "Elementary Literacy," 125–28.

34. Robert F. Seybolt, *The Private Schools of Colonial Boston* (Cambridge: Harvard University Press, 1935).

35. Small, *Early New England Schools,* 278–89.

36. Plymouth man quoted in Small, *Early New England Schools,* 281; Mary Sumner Benson, *Women in Eighteenth-Century America: A Study of Opinion and Social Usage* (New York: Columbia University Press, 1935), 148–49; William B. Fowle, "Memoir of Caleb Bingham," *American Journal of Education* 5(1858): 325–29.

37. Norton, *Liberty's Daughters,* 263.

Chapter 2. Why Educate Girls?

1. On the role of Protestant-republican ideology in the common-school movement, see David Tyack and Elisabeth Hansot, *Managers of Virtue: Public School Leadership in America, 1820–1980* (New York: Basic Books, 1982), pt. 1.

2. Emma Willard, *A Plan for Improving Female Education* (reprint of 1819 edition; Middlebury, Vermont: Middlebury College, 1918), 15. John W. Meyer and his colleagues note that even such basic social categories as "person" or "self" are constructed and problematic "cultural accounts"; see John W. Meyer, John Boli, and George M. Thomas, "Ontology and Rationalization in the Western Cultural Account," and John W. Meyer, "Self and Life Course: Institutionalization and Its Effects," in George M. Thomas et al., *Institutional Structure: Constituting State, Society, and the Individual* (Beverly Hills: Sage Publications, 1987), 12–38, 242–60.

3. Horace Mann, *A Few Thoughts on the Powers and Duties of Woman* (Syracuse: Hall, Mills, 1853), preface; Barbara Welter, "She Hath Done What She Could: Protestant Women's Missionary Careers in Nineteenth-Century America," *American Quarterly* 30(1978): 624–638; Joan Jacobs Brumberg, *Mission for Life: The Story of the Family of Adinoram Judson, the Dramatic Events of the First Foreign Mission,*

and the Course of Evangelical Religion in the Nineteenth Century (New York: Free Press, 1980).

4. Edward D. Mansfield, *American Education: Its Principles and Elements, Dedicated to the Teachers of the United States* (New York: A. S. Barnes, 1851), p. 296, chap. 14.

5. Ibid.; Barbara Welter, "The Cult of True Womanhood, 1820–1860," *American Quarterly* 18(1966): 151–74; Mann, *Duties of Woman*; Alma Lutz, *Susan B. Anthony: Rebel Crusader, Humanitarian* (Boston: Beacon Press, 1959), 69–70, passim.

6. Alexis de Tocqueville, *Democracy in America*, ed. Phillips Bradley (New York: Vintage Books, 1954), 2:222–23, 210; Mary P. Ryan, *The Empire of the Mother: American Writing about Domesticity, 1830–1860*, Women and History, nos. 2–3 (Binghamton, N.Y.: Haworth Press, 1982).

7. Tocqueville, *Democracy in America*, 2:212, 223.

8. Kathryn Kish Sklar, *Catharine Beecher: A Study in American Domesticity* (New Haven: Yale University Press, 1973).

9. Henry Barnard, *Rhode Island Report for 1848*, 280.

10. Nancy Cott, *The Bonds of Womanhood: "Woman's Sphere" in New England, 1780–1835* (New Haven: Yale University Press, 1977); Carl N. Degler, *At Odds: Women and the Family from the Revolution to the Present* (New York: Oxford University Press, 1980). John E. Craig notes that in developed countries women continue "to put more more emphasis on the nonmonetary returns to education"; see John E. Craig, "The Expansion of Education," in *Review of Research in Education*, vol. 9 edited by David C. Berliner (Washington, D.C.: American Educational Research Association, 1981), 160–61.

11. Linda K. Kerber, *Women of the Republic: Intellect and Ideology in Revolutionary America* (Chapel Hill: University of North Carolina Press, 1980), chap. 7; Benjamin Rush, "Thoughts upon Female Education, Accommodated to the Present State of Society, Manners, and Government in the United States," in Frederick Rudolph, ed., *Essays on Education in the Early Republic* (Cambridge: Harvard University Press, 1965), 230, 25–40.

12. Mary Sumner Benson, *Women in Eighteenth-Century America: A Study of Opinion and Social Usage* (New York: Columbia University Press, 1935), 148–49, 154; Janet Wilson James, *Changing Ideas about Women in the United States, 1776–1825* (New York: Garland Publishing, 1981), 171–204; Susan McIntosh Lloyd, *A Singular School: Abbot Academy, 1828–1973* (Hanover, N.H.: University Press of New England, 1979), p. 5, chap. 1; Kerber, *Women of the Republic*, chap. 7.

13. Judith Sargent Murray, "On the Equality of the Sexes," *The Massachusetts Magazine* (March 1790): 132–35.

14. Ibid.; Mary Beth Norton, *Liberty's Daughters: The Revolutionary Experience of American Women, 1750–1800* (Boston: Little, Brown, 1980), 271; Kerber, *Women of the Republic*, 204.

15. Rush, *Thoughts upon Female Education*, 27–40.

16. Ibid. For an intriguing description of the academy, see Ann D. Gordon, "The Young Ladies Academy of Philadelphia," in Carol Berkin and Mary Beth Norton, eds., *Women of America* (Boston: Houghton Mifflin, 1979), 68–91.

17. Benjamin Rush, *A Plan for the Establishment of Public Schools and the Diffusion of Knowledge in Pennsylvania; to Which Are Added, Thoughts upon the Mode of Education, Proper in a Republic, Addressed to the Legislature and Citizens of the State*, reprinted in Rudolph ed., *Essays*, 22.

18. Mann, *Duties of Woman*, 97–99.

19. Ibid. Mann quotes Wendell Phillips's criticism of Mann himself for limiting women's political role: "she should be book-taught for some dozen years, *and then return to private life*" (p. 125).

20. For a discussion of Quaker schools and how their purposes differed from Rush's patriotic agenda, see Joan M. Jensen, "Not Only Ours But Others: The Quaker Teaching Daughters of the Mid-Atlantic, 1790–1850," *History of Education Quarterly* 24(1984): 3–19.

21. William Woodbridge, "Reminiscences of Female Education," *American Journal of Education* 16(1866): 137–40; John P. Cowles, "Miss Z. P. Grant—Mrs. William B. Banister," *American Journal of Education* 30(1880): 611–24; Anonymous, "George B. Emerson," *American Journal of Education* 5(1858): 420–23; Joseph Emerson, *Female Education: A Discourse Delivered at the Dedication of the Seminary Hall in Saugus, Jan. 15, 1822* (Boston: Samuel T. Armstrong, 1822); Lloyd, *Singular School*, chap. 1; Thomas Woody, *A History of Women's Education in the United States* (New York: Science Press, 1929), vol. 1, chaps. 8–9; Catherine Clinton, "Equally Their Due: The Education of the Planter Daughter in the Early Republic," *Journal of the Early Republic* 2(1982): 39–60.

22. Frances W. Knickerbocker, "Mary Moody Emerson," in Edward T. James, Janet Wilson James, and Paul S. Boyer, eds., *Notable American Women: A Biographical Dictionary* (Cambridge: Harvard University Press, 1971), 580–81.

23. Merchant quoted in Clarence P. McClelland, "The Education of Females in Early Illinois," *MacMurray College Bulletin* 34(1944): 17–18; Anne M. Boylan, "Growing Up Female in Young America, 1800–1860," in Joseph M. Hawes and N. Ray Hiner, eds., *American Childhood: A Research Guide and Historical Handbook* (Greenwich, Conn.: Greenwood Press, 1985), 153–84; Degler, *At Odds*; Mary P. Ryan, *Cradle of the Middle Class: The Family in Oneida County, New York, 1790–1865* (New York: Cambridge University Press, 1981).

24. For more radical views of the role of schooling than those provided by these three educators, see Thomas Woody, "Emancipation [of women] and Education," in *Women's Education*, vol. 2, chap. 8.

25. Mann, *Duties of Woman*, 67–68; Carl F. Kaestle, *Pillars of the Republic: Common Schools and American Society, 1780–1860* (New York: Hill and Wang, 1983), chap. 5; Cott, *Bonds*, 2. Cf. Mansfield, *American Education*, 290–330.

26. Willard, *Female Education*, 15; Phillida Bunkle, "Sentimental Womanhood

and Domestic Education, 1830–1870," *History of Education Quarterly* 14(1974): 13–30.

27. Willard, *Female Education,* 15; Anne Firor Scott, "The Ever-Widening Circle: The Diffusion of Feminist Values from the Troy Seminary, 1822–1872," *History of Education Quarterly* 19(1979): 16–17; Cott, *Bonds,* chap. 4; Mary Ryan, "A Woman's Awakening: Evangelical Religion and the Families of Utica, New York, 1800–1840," in James, ed., *Women in American Religion,* 89–110.

28. For a sample of such pamphlets and addresses, see Joseph Emerson, *Female Education*; Rev. Joseph Muenscher [Brookfield Female Seminary], "Maternal Instruction," *American Journal of Education* 3(1828): 689–90; "South Carolina Female Institute," *American Journal of Education* 3(1828): 583–94; James M. Garnett, *Lectures on Female Education, Comprising the First and Second Series of a Course Delivered to Mrs. Garnett's Pupils, at Elm-wood, Essex County, Virginia* (Richmond: Thomas W. White, 1825); Catharine McKeen [Mount Holyoke], "Mental Education of Woman," *American Journal of Education* 1(1856): 567–78; R. W. Cushman [Mount Vernon Ladies School], *American Female Education: What? And by Whom?* (Boston: John P. Jewitt, 1855); Anna C. Embury, "Female Education: An Address Delivered at the Brooklyn Collegiate Institute for Young Ladies," in Anna Brackett, *Woman and Higher Education* (New York: Harper & Brothers, 1893), 47–64; Julius Rockwell, *Address Delivered at the Pittsfield Young Ladies Institute, July 5, 1847, on the Education of American Women* (Pittsfield: A. Hanford, 1847); Mann, *Duties of Woman,* 57–69; and Horace Mann, *Massachusetts Report for 1844,* 427–29. Barnard's *American Journal of Education* is a rich source of reports advocating women's education.

29. Willard, *Female Education;* Catharine E. Beecher, *Suggestions Respecting Improvements in Education, Presented to the Trustees of the Hartford Female Seminary and Published at Their Request* (Hartford: Packard & Butler, 1829).

30. Sklar, *Beecher,* 74–77, and "Mount Holyoke College"; Catharine E. Beecher, "Educational Reminiscences," *American Journal of Education* 28(1878): 65–96; Catharine E. Beecher, *An Essay on the Education of Female Teachers* (New York: Van Nostrand & Dwight, 1835); Henry Fowler, "The Educational Services of Mrs. Emma Willard," *American Journal of Education* 6(1859): 125–68; Mary Lyon, "Principles and Design of the Mt. Holyoke Female Seminary," in Edward Hitchcock, "Mary Lyon," *American Journal of Education* 10(1861): 67–78, 649–80.

31. Henry Tappan, *A Discourse on Education, Delivered at the Anniversary of the Young Ladies Institute, Pittsfield, Mass., October 2, 1846* (New York: Roe, Lockwood & Son, 1846), 38; Rev. Samuel Harris, *A Report Presented to a Convention of the Friends of Education, Assembled March 31, 1853, at the Chapel of the Young Ladies Institute, Pittsfield, Mass.* (New Haven: T. J. Stafford, 1853), 7; Ray Palmer, *Address on the Education of Woman, Delivered at the Anniversary of the Pittsfield Ladies Institute, September 30, 1852* (Albany: Gray, Sprague, 1852), 5.

32. "Motives to Study in the Ipswich Female Seminary," *American Annals of*

Education 3(1833): 75–80; Willard, *Female Education;* Cowles, "Grant"; Hitchcock, "Lyon"; Catharine E. Beecher, *A Treatise on Domestic Economy for the Use of Young Ladies at Home, and at School* (New York: Harper & Brothers, 1850); Nancy Green, "Female Education and School Competition, 1820–1850," *History of Education Quarterly* 18(1978): 129–42.

33. Woody, *Women's Education,* 1:418.

34. Stearns quoted in Alice Felt Tyler, "The Education of a New England Girl in the Eighteen-Twenties," *New England Quarterly* 17(1944): 165–66.

35. Beecher quoted in *Godey's Lady's Book,* January 1853, 177; Catharine E. Beecher, *The True Remedy for the Wrongs of Women; with a History of an Enterprise Having That for Its Object* (Boston: Phillips, Sampson, 1851), 52–60; Grant quoted in Cowles, "Grant," 615.

36. Bunkle, "Sentimental Womanhood"; Glenda Riley, "Origins of the Argument for Improved Female Education," *History of Education Quarterly* 9(1969): 455–70.

37. "George B. Emerson"; Woodbridge, "Female Education"; Emit Duncan Grizzell, *Origin and Development of the High School in New England before 1865* (New York: Macmillan, 1923).

38. Willard, *Female Education,* 27–28.

39. Ibid.; Mann, *Duties of Woman,* 27, 82; Woody, *Women's Education,* 1:416.

40. David F. Allmendinger, Jr., "Mount Holyoke Students Encounter the Need for Life-Planning, 1837–1850," *History of Education Quarterly* 19(1979): 27–46; Beecher, *True Remedy*; Lyon letter quoted in Woody, *Women's Education,* 1:321.

41. Keith Melder, "Women's High Calling: The Teaching Profession in America, 1830–1860," *American Studies* 13(1972): 19–32, and "Training Women Teachers: Private Experiments" (Paper delivered at the American Educational Research Association, San Francisco, April 1978); Woody, *Women's Education,* 1:416.

42. Scott, "The Ever-Widening Circle," 16–17; Allmendinger, Jr., "Mount Holyoke Students," 40; Cowles, "Grant."

43. Anne Firor Scott, "What, Then, Is the American: This New Woman?" *Journal of American History* 65(1978): 698–701; Woody, *Women's Education,* vol. 2, chap. 9.

44. "Female Common School Association in the East District of Kensington, Conn.," *American Journal of Education* 15(1865): 612–16; Fowler, "Willard," 160–64.

45. Ira Mayhew was the superintendent—*Annual Report of the Superintendent of Public Instruction of the State of Michigan* (Detroit: Bagg and Harmon, 1848), 39–40; Scott, "This New Woman."

46. Scott, "This New Woman"; Sklar, *Beecher.*

47. Lutz, *Anthony,* 69–70 and passim; Elizabeth Griffen, *In Her Own Right: The Life of Elizabeth Cady Stanton* (New York: Oxford University Press, 1984), 17, 19, 164, 202.

Chapter 3. Coeducation in Rural Common Schools

1. In a pioneering study, Maris A. Vinovskis and Richard M. Bernard suggested the importance of studying shifts in female school attendance and literacy: "Beyond Catharine Beecher: Female Education in the Antebellum Period," *Signs* 3(1978), 856–69; in another pathbreaking study, Kathryn Kish Sklar takes as a point of departure the rapid increase in literacy from colonial levels: "Public Expenditures for Schooling Girls in Massachusetts Towns, 1750–1800" (Paper delivered at the meeting of the History of Education Society, Cambridge, October 1976), 2–3.

2. *Rhode Island Report for 1848,* 280; *Rhode Island Report for 1845*, 35. William Fowle, a pioneer in the education of women, wrote that everywhere in Massachusetts except for Boston, in the late eighteenth century "the girls of every town in the state were allowed and expected to attend the village schools"; see William Fowle, "A Memoir of Caleb Bingham," *American Journal of Education* 5(1858): 327. Daniel Putnam notes that some towns there were willing to educate girls only if no additional expense was involved, but in rural communities boys and girls customarily attended school together (where the population was scanty, the cost of adding the girls was minimal); see *The Development of Primary and Secondary Education in Michigan: A Historical Sketch* (Ann Arbor: George Wahr, 1904), 185–89. State education laws were mostly silent on policy relating to gender; see David Tyack, Thomas James, and Aaron Benavot, *Law and the Shaping of Public Schools, 1785–1954* (Madison: University of Wisconsin Press, 1987).

3. Even John D. Philbrick, the archenemy of coeducation, wrote that, where the population was sparse, the sexually mixed school was the only "expedient solution"; see "Coeducation of the Sexes," American Institute of Instruction, *Lectures and Proceedings, 1880,* 118.

4. J. W. Buckley, "The Education of Boys and Girls Together," *New York Teacher* 5(1855): 131.

5. *Vermont Report for 1850,* 20; Maris A. Vinovskis and Richard M. Bernard, "Women in Education in Ante-Bellum America," Center for Demography and Ecology, University of Wisconsin-Madison, Working Paper 73-7, 12; Willard S. Elsbree, *The American Teacher: Evolution of a Profession in a Democracy* (New York: American Book, 1939), 207; Thomas Woody, *A History of Women's Education in the United States* (New York: Science Press, 1929), 1:488–98; *U.S. Com. Ed. Report for 1900–1901,* lxxxiv.

6. David B. Tyack and Myra H. Strober, "Jobs and Gender: A History of the Structuring of Educational Employment by Sex," in Patricia A. Schmuck, W. W. Charters, Jr., and Richard O. Carlson, eds., *Educational Policy and Management: Sex Differentials* (New York: Academic Press, 1981), 131–52.

7. James H. Blodgett, *Report on Education in the United States at the Eleventh Census: 1890* (Washington, D.C.: GPO, 1893), 26, 49 (on p. 3 Blodgett observes that by 1890 school officials took gender so much for granted that in twenty states

they did not even report the number of pupils by sex); *U.S. Bureau of Education, Coeducation of the Sexes in the Public Schools of the United States,* Circular of Information, no. 2-1883 (Washington, D.C.: GPO, 1883), p. 8. On the predominance of the rural school, see David Tyack and Elisabeth Hansot, *Managers of Virtue: Public School Leadership in America, 1820–1980* (New York: Basic Books, 1982), chap. 2.

8. Vinovskis and Bernard, "Beyond Catharine Beecher"; Blodgett, *Education,* pp. 26, 49; Thomas L. Webber, *Deep Like the Rivers: Education in the Slave Community, 1831–1865* (New York: W. W. Norton, 1978).

9. Vinovskis and Bernard, "Beyond Catharine Beecher"; Blodgett, *Report on Education,* 26, 49; Woody, *Women's Education,* vol. 1, chaps. 8–9. See Carl F. Kaestle, *Pillars of the Republic: Common Schools and American Society, 1780–1860* (New York: Hill and Wang, 1983), chap. 3, on the importance of the entry of girls in the early period. Lee Soltow and Edward Stevens found in their studies of school attendance in Ohio from 1840 to 1869 that despite some variations "sex, by itself, was not a significant factor in determining attendance"; see Lee Soltow and Edward Stevens, *The Rise of Literacy and the Common School in the United States: A Socioeconomic Analysis to 1870* (Chicago: University of Chicago Press, 1981), 108–10. Maris Vinovskis and Carl F. Kaestle make a similar finding in *Education and Social Change in Nineteenth-Century Massachusetts* (Cambridge, England: Cambridge University Press, 1978).

10. For a historiographical analysis of studies of literacy, see Carl F. Kaestle, "The History of Literacy and the History of Readers," in Edmund Gordon, ed., *Review of Research in Education* (Washington, D.C.: American Educational Research Association [AERA], 1985), 11–55.

For a summary of literacy differentials in Europe, see John E. Craig, "The Expansion of Education," *Review of Research in Education,* vol. 9 (Washington, D.C.: AERA, 1981), 170–71; Kenneth Lockridge, *Literacy in Colonial New England: An Inquiry into the Social Context of Literacy in the Early Modern West* (New York: Norton, 1974), 39–40, 97, and passim.

For contrasting views on the measurement and meaning of literacy, see Lawrence Stone, "Literacy and Education in England, 1640–1900," *Past and Present* 42(1969): 61–139; Harvey J. Graff, *The Literacy Myth: Literacy and Social Structure in the Nineteenth-Century City* (New York: Academic Press, 1977); and reviews of Lockridge's book in *The Review of Education* 1(1975): 517–21 (Lawrence A. Cremin); *William and Mary Quarterly* 32(1975): 638–40 (Kevin Kelly); *History of Education Quarterly* 15(1975): 467–74 (Harvey Graff); and *American Historical Review* 81(1976): 203–4 (David Cressy).

11. U.S. Bureau of the Census, *Illiteracy in the United States,* Bulletin 26, 1905 (Washington, D.C.: GPO, 1905), 11–12; Charles Warren, *Illiteracy in 1870 and 1880,* U.S. Office of Education, Circular of Information, no. 2, 1884 (Washington, D.C.: GPO, 1884), 248–49; Sterling G. Brinkley, "Growth of School Attendance and Literacy in the United States since 1840," *Journal of Experimental Education* 26(1957): 51–66; Vinovskis and Bernard, "Beyond Catharine Beecher."

12. U.S. Bureau of the Census, *Illiteracy in the United States,* 11–12; Warren, *Illiteracy in 1870 and 1880,* 248–49; *New York City Report for 1874,* 223; Henry C. Kinney, "Sex in Education," *Indiana School Journal* 23(1878): 20, 18–21; *Cincinnati Report for 1859,* 36.

13. Richard A. Easterlin, "Factors in the Decline of Farm Family Fertility in the United States: Some Preliminary Research Results," *Journal of American History* 63(1976): 602. On the connection between literacy and schooling, see Gilmore, "Elementary Literacy"; Lockridge, *Literacy;* Lee Soltow and Edward Stevens, "Economic Aspects of School Participation in Mid-Nineteenth-Century United States," *Journal of Economic History* 8(1977): 221–43.

14. Anna Julia Cooper, "The Higher Education of Women," in Bert James Loewenberg and Ruth Bogin, eds., *Black Women in Nineteenth-Century American Life: Their Words, Their Thoughts, Their Feelings* (University Park: Pennsylvania State University Press, 1976), 330, 317–31. Black women had long been active, even before emancipation, in this "uplifting." See Linda Perkins, "Black Women and Racial 'Uplift' Prior to Emancipation," in Filomina Chioma Steady, ed., *The Black Woman Cross-Culturally* (Cambridge: Schenkman Publishing, 1981), 317–34; and Bette Collier-Thomas, "The Impact of Black Women in Education: An Historical Overview," *Journal of Negro Education* 51(1982): 173–80.

15. Webber, *Deep like the Rivers;* James D. Anderson, *The Education of Blacks in the South, 1860–1935* (Chapel Hill: University of North Carolina Press, 1988), chap. 1; Jacqueline Jones, *Soldiers of Light and Love: Northern Teachers and Georgia Blacks, 1865–1873* (Chapel Hill: University of North Carolina Press, 1980), chap. 5.

16. Jones, *Soldiers of Light and Love;* Cooper, "Higher Education of Women," 330.

17. David Tyack and Robert Lowe, "The Constitutional Moment: Reconstruction and Black Education in the South," *American Journal of Education* 94(1986): 236–56.

18. Anderson, *Education of Blacks,* chap. 1; James D. Anderson, "The Historical Development of Black Vocational Education," in Harvey Kantor and David B. Tyack, eds., *Work, Youth, and Schooling: Historical Perspectives on Vocationalism in American Education* (Stanford: Stanford University Press, 1982), 180–222; Paula Giddings, *When and Where I Enter: The Impact of Black Women on Race and Sex in America* (New York: William Morrow, 1984), 72, 100–101, 329, chap. 6; W. E. Burghardt Dubois, *Dark Water: Voices from within the Veil* (New York: Harcourt, Brace, and Howe, 1920), 170–86; Jeanne L. Noble, *The Negro Woman's College Education* (New York: Teachers College, 1958), 45; Linda M. Perkins, "The Impact of the 'Cult of True Womanhood' on the Education of Black Women," *Journal of Social Issues* 39(1983): 17–28.

19. On the replacement of black male teachers by black women in Jamaica and the "marginalization" of black men in white-collar jobs, see Errol Miller, *Marginalization of the Black Male: Insights from the Development of the Teaching Profession* (Jamaica: University of the West Indies, 1986); census reports on occupations,

1890, 1900, and 1920; Thomas Jesse Jones, *Negro Education: A Study of the Private and Higher Schools for Colored People in the United States,* Bureau of Education, Bulletin no. 38, 1916 (Washington, D.C.: GPO, 1916), 1:71; Bond, *Education of the Negro,* 296–97; Ambrose Caliver, *Secondary Education for Negroes,* Bureau of Education, Bulletin no. 17, 1932 (Washington, D.C.: GPO, 1933), 61–65; Noble, *Negro Woman,* chap. 2.

20. Warren Burton, *The District School as It Was* (Boston: T. R. Marvin, 1852); David Tyack, *The One Best System: A History of American Urban Education* (Cambridge: Harvard University Press, 1974), pt. 1; Alonzo Potter, *The School and the Schoolmaster* (Boston: W. B. Fowle & N. Capen, 1843), 210; *Rhode Island Report for 1848,* 295; U.S. Bureau of Education, *Coeducation of the Sexes,* 8.

21. For coeducational parish schools in Wisconsin, see *Sadlier's Catholic Directory, Almanac and Ordo for the Year of our Lord 1883* (New York: D. & J. Sadlier, 1883), 136–38; U.S. Bureau of Education, "Coeducation of the Sexes."

22. Clifton Johnson, *Old-Time Schools and Schoolbooks* (New York: Macmillan, 1904), chap. 4; Polly Welts Kaufman, *Women Teachers on the Frontier* (New Haven: Yale University Press, 1984).

23. Hale quoted in Kaestle, *Pillars,* 14. See chap. 2 in the same work for a general discussion of rural education.

24. Dean May and Maris A. Vinovskis, "A Ray of Millennial Light: Early Education and Social Reform in the Infant School Movement in Massachusetts," in Tamara Hareven, ed., *Family and Kin in American Urban Communities, 1800–1940* (New York: Watt, 1977), 89, 62–99; Anne M. Boylan, "Growing Up Female in Young America, 1800–1860," in Joseph Hawes and N. Ray Hiner, eds., *American Childhood: A Research Guide and Historical Handbook* (Greenwich: Greenwood Press, 1985), 131.

25. The records of the Ashland, Oregon, District School in the 1860s, deposited in the O. C. Applegate Papers of the Library of the University of Oregon, contain many student themes, declamations, and student newspapers that demonstrated the high quality of the work students demonstrated at "exhibitions" to their parents and neighbors; Barbara Jean Finkelstein, "Reading, Writing, and the Acquisition of Identity in the United States: 1790–1860," in Barbara Finkelstein, ed., *Regulated Children/Liberated Children: Education in Psychosocial Perspective* (New York: Psychohistory Press, 1979); Johnson, *Old-Time Schools;* Willard Hall, "Schools as They Were Sixty Years Ago," *American Journal of Education* 16(1866): 127–29; Kaestle, *Pillars,* chap. 2.

26. Timothy Smith, "Protestant Schooling and American Nationality, 1800–1850," *Journal of American History* 53(1967): 679–95; David Tyack, "The Kingdom of God and the Common School: Protestant Ministers and the Educational Awakening in the West," *Harvard Educational Review* 36(1966): 447–69. On analogies between Sunday schools and common schools, see Tyack and Hansot, *Managers of Virtue,* chap. 4.

27. David Tyack, "The Tribe and the Common School: The District School in Ashland, Oregon, in the 1860s," *The Call Number* 27(1966): 13–23; Barbara Finkelstein, "Pedagogy as Intrusion: Teaching Values in Popular Primary Schools in Nineteenth-Century America," *History of Childhood Quarterly* 2(1975): 350–78. Observer quoted in U.S. Bureau of Education, *Coeducation of the Sexes,* 8; this study also contains an excellent summary of educators' views on coeducation.

28. Kaufman, *Women Teachers;* Joanna Stratton, *Pioneer Women: Voices from the Kansas Frontier* (New York: Simon and Schuster, 1981), 158–65; Maris Vinovskis, "Family and Schooling in Colonial and Nineteenth-Century America" (Paper delivered at the Conference on the Family in Historical Perspective, Clark University, Worcester, Mass., November 1985), 16–18.

29. Iowa legislator quoted in Thomas Morain, "The Departure of Males from the Teaching Profession in Nineteenth-Century Iowa," *Civil War History* 26 (1980): 165; John M. Bernard and Maris A. Vinovskis, "The Female School Teacher in Ante-Bellum Massachusetts," *Journal of Social History* 10(1977): 336; Walter R. Burgess, *Trends of School Costs* (New York: Russell Sage Foundation, 1920); John K. Folger and Charles P. Nam, *Education of the American Population,* 1960 Census Monograph (Washington, D.C.: GPO, 1967), chap. 3.

30. Bernard and Vinovskis, "Female School Teacher," 333, 343; Geraldine Jonçich Clifford, "'Daughters into Teachers': Educational and Demographic Influences on the Transformation of Teaching into 'Women's Work' in America," *History of Education Review* 12(1983): 17; S. H. White, "The Means of Providing the Mass of Teachers with Professional Instruction," *U.S. Com. Ed. Report for 1870,* 396; Lotus D. Coffman, *The Social Composition of the Teaching Profession* (New York: Teachers College, 1911), 28. Coffman found that women teachers in city schools had an average tenure of seven years and men twelve, but other studies have found much longer tenure for urban women teachers; see, for example, Victoria MacDonald Huntzinger, "A Portrait of Late-Nineteenth-Century Schoolteachers: The Case of Providence, Rhode Island" (unpublished manuscript, Harvard University, 1984).

31. Wayne E. Fuller, *The Old Country School: The Story of Rural Education in the Middle West* (Chicago: University of Chicago Press, 1982), chap. 9; Morain, "Departure of Males". For the importance of looking at local job markets in rural areas, see the study of Canada by Marta Danylewycz, Beth Light, and Alison Prentice, "The Evolution of the Sexual Division of Labour in Teaching: A Nineteenth-Century Ontario and Quebec Case Study," *Histoire Sociale—Social History,* 15(1983): 81–109.

32. Cott, *Bonds,* chap. 1.

33. Medicus, Letter to the Editor, *Common School Journal* 5(1843): 353–58; T. H. G., "What Can Be Done to Improve the Common Schools this Winter?" *Connecticut Common School Journal* 2(1839): 53–55; "Teachers," *Connecticut Common School Journal* 3(1841): 248–50. On centralized state decisions about the sex of teachers in other nations, see, for example, Helen Corr, "The Sexual Division of

Labor in the Scottish Teaching Profession, 1872–1914," in W. Hines and H. Peterson, eds., *Scottish Culture and Scottish Education* (Edinburg: John Donato, 1983), 136–53; Noeline Williamson, "The Feminization of Teaching in New South Wales: A Historical Perspective," *The Australian Journal of Education* 27(1983): 33–44; Kaufman, *Women Teachers;* and "Selections from the Report of the School Committee of Ware," *Common School Journal* 1(1840): 277–80.

34. Hall, "Schools Sixty Years Ago," 127; *Michigan Report for 1845–46*, p. 39; *Connecticut Report for 1839*, p. 37; Vinovskis and Bernard, *Women in Education in Ante-Bellum America*, table A-9.

35. Alonzo Potter, *The School and the Schoolmaster: A Manual for the Use of Teachers, Employers, Trustees, Inspectors, & of Common Schools* (Boston: W. B. Fowle & N. Capen, 1843), 205; "Report of Ware," p. 278.

36. *Vermont Report for 1849*, 42; *Massachusetts Report for 1841*, 87–91; Finkelstein, "Pedagogy as Intrusion."

37. Deborah Fitts, "Una and the Lion: The Feminization of District School-Teaching and Its Effects on the Roles of Students and Teachers in Nineteenth-Century Massachusetts," in Finkelstein, ed., *Regulated Children/Liberated Children*, 145, 140–57; quote from woman teacher in Anna Callendar Brackett, *Women and Higher Education* (New York: Harper & Brothers, 1893), 150.

38. *Report for Massachusetts, 1841*, pp. 87–91; Fitts, "Una and the Lion," 144–46; town report of 1838 quoted on p. 147; *Rhode Island Report for 1848*, 168.

39. Potter, *The School*, 204–6.

40. Carlos Slafter, *The Schools and Teachers of Dedham, Massachusetts, 1644–1904* (Dedham: Dedham Transcript Press, 1905), 11; quote from man on discipline in Fitts, "Una and the Lion," 148–49.

41. Mary Abigail Dodge, *Our Common School System* (Boston: Estes & Lauriat, 1880), 165, as quoted in Fitts, "Una and the Lion," 149.

42. Fitts, "Una and the Lion," 142.

43. Geraldine Jonçich Clifford, "'Marry, Stitch, Die, or Do Worse': Educating Women for Work," in Kantor and Tyack, eds., *Work, Youth, and Schooling*, 227. It appears to have been common to seat boys and girls separately in district schools during the early nineteenth century. William Woodbridge wrote that near Hartford, Connecticut, "girls had no separate classes, though generally sitting on separate benches"; see his "Female Education prior to 1800," *American Journal of Education* 27(1877): 273.

44. *Indiana Report for 1852*, 59; *Connecticut Report for 1850*, 64; Henry Barnard, "Schools of Connecticut," *American Journal of Education* 1(1856): 687; Fuller, *Old Country School*, 69, 75–76.

45. *Connecticut Report for 1850*, 64; Barnard, "Schools of Connecticut"; Fuller, *Old Country School*, 69, 75–76. See Andrew Gulliford, *America's Country Schools* (Washington, D.C.: Preservation Press, 1984), 50, on playgrounds, and passim for pictures.

46. For a sampling of the most influential textbook series of the nineteenth

century, which is a useful index of differentiated adult gender roles, see Stanley W. Lindberg, ed., *The Annotated McGuffey: Selections from the McGuffey Readers, 1836–1920* (New York: Van Nostrand, 1976); Warren Burton, *Your Family, Your School, and Your Neighborhood* (Boston: n.p., 1853), 3; Alonzo Potter, *The School,* 50–52.

47. Taylor picture in Gulliford, *Country Schools,* 34; Patricia Cline Cohen, *A Calculating People: The Spread of Numeracy in Early America* (Chicago: University of Chicago Press, 1982), 139–49; Lucy Lane Allen, "Female Education,—Pupil and Teacher," *American Journal of Education* 30(1889): 581.

48. John Swett, *Methods of Teaching: A Hand-book of Principles, Directions, and Working Models for Common-school Teachers* (New York: Harper & Brothers, 1885), chap. 10, p. 21.

49. Swett quoted in *U.S. Com. Ed. Report for 1870,* 94.

50. Samuel R. Hall, *Lectures on School-Keeping* (Boston: Richardson, Lord and Holbrook, 1829), 66, 63; letter of B. Million to Oliver Cromwell Applegate, n. d., O. C. Applegate Papers, Library of the University of Oregon.

51. *Vermont Report for 1849,* 42. For two of the rare late instances of gender segregation, see Ethel M. Johnson, "Country School Ma'am of the Olden Days," *South Atlantic Quarterly* 48(1949): 375, and Amanda M. Chase, *All in the Pioneer Teacher's Day* (n.p., 1934), 23; Bernard and Vinovskis, "Women in Education," 8.

52. *Cambridge Report for 1846,* 21–22.

53. Gulliford, *Country Schools.* The Michigan superintendent of schools wrote in 1847 that "all the scholars should face the teacher, but none of them should face each other. This is particularly important where both sexes attend the same schools"; see *Michigan Report for 1848,* 123.

Chapter 4. Coeducation in Urban Public Schools

1. E. E. White, "Coeducation of the Sexes," *National Teacher* 2(1872): 674, 674–78. In 1852 the word *coeducation* was used in an article entitled "Coeducation of the Sexes," in *Pennsylvania School Journal* 1(1852): 9–10, and the word was also used in Michigan and New York during that decade; see Arnold Jack Keller, "An Historical Analysis of the Arguments for and against Coeducational Public Schools in the United States," (Ed.D. diss., Teachers College, Columbia University, 1971).

2. *Majority and Minority Reports Made to the School Committee of the City of Charlestown, May 24, 1848, upon the Petition of William Eager and Others for the Separation of the Sexes in the Harvard School* (Boston: Tuttle & Dennett, 1848).

3. John D. Philbrick, "Coeducation of the Sexes," American Institute of Instruction, *Lectures and Proceedings, 1880,* 122, 124. Mrs. I. M. E. Blandin observed that "the Southern people were . . . opposed to coeducation, hence girls were not admitted to the [male] academies and colleges"; see I. M. E. Blandin, *History of Higher Education of Women in the South prior to 1860* (New York: Neale Publishing, 1909), 18.

4. John D. Philbrick, *City School Systems in the United States,* U.S. Bureau of

Education, Circular of Information, no. 1, 1885 (Washington, D.C.: GPO, 1885), 8, 10–11, 57–59.

5. David B. Tyack, *The One Best System: A History of American Urban Education* (Cambridge: Harvard University Press, 1974), 104–9.

6. Barnard, *Rhode Island Report for 1848,* 281; James H. Blodgett, *Report on Education in the United States in the Eleventh Census, 1890* (Washington, D.C.: GPO, 1893), 21–22. J. W. Rust rejected a family analogy as apt for the school, arguing that there were so many ill-ordered families whose children were vicious that conscientious parents would not let their children attend mixed schools; see his "Mixed Schools," *New York Teacher* 5(1856): 453–55.

7. *School Report for Boston, 1857,* 137–38; Richard P. DuFour, "The Exclusion of Female Students from the Public Secondary Schools of Boston, 1820–1920" (Ed.D. diss., Northern Illinois University, 1981).

8. Carl F. Kaestle, *The Evolution of an Urban School System: New York City, 1750–1850* (Cambridge: Harvard University Press, 1973); Stanley K. Schultz, *The Culture Factory: Boston Public Schools, 1789–1860* (New York: Oxford University Press, 1973); Tyack, *One Best System,* pt. 2. For the evolution of school organization in Providence, Rhode Island, see "Public Schools of Providence," *Rhode Island Report for 1848,* 35, 41, 94–96.

9. Henry Barnard, "Gradation of Public Schools, with Special Reference to Cities and Large Villages," *American Journal of Education* 2(1856): 456–58; John D. Philbrick, "Report of the Superintendent of Schools to the General Assembly [of Connecticut], May, 1856," *American Journal of Education* 2(1856): 263.

10. William J. Shearer, *The Grading of Schools* (New York: H. P. Smith, 1898), 21; Frank F. Bunker, *Reorganization of the Public School System,* U.S. Bureau of Education, Bulletin of Education, no. 8, 1916 (Washington, D.C.: GPO, 1916), 19–24, 35.

11. Blodgett, *Education in the United States,* 52, 134–40.

12. James Boykin, "Women in the Public Schools," *Educational Review* 18 (1899): 138; Lewis Solmon, "Estimates of the Cost of Schooling in 1880 and 1890," *Explorations in Economic History,* Supplement, 7:539, 557, 574–76; Tyack, *One Best System,* 59–65.

13. Boykin, "Women in the Public Schools," 141–42; "Public Schools of Providence," *Report for Rhode Island, 1848,* 53.

14. Willard S. Elsbree, *The American Teacher: Evolution of a Profession in a Democracy* (New York: American Book, 1939), 431–35.

15. David B. Tyack and Myra H. Strober, "Jobs and Gender: A History of the Structuring of Educational Employment by Sex," in Patricia A. Schmuck, W. W. Charters, and Richard O. Carlson, eds., *Educational Policy and Management: Sex Differentials* (New York: Academic Press, 1981), 131–52; Myra H. Strober and Audri Gordon Langford, "The Feminization of Public School Teaching: Cross-Sectional Analysis, 1850–1880," *Signs* 11(1986): 212–35.

16. Philbrick, "Report of the Superintendent," 261–64; Barnard, "Gradation of Public Schools," 461, 459.

17. Mary Abigail Dodge, *Our Common School System* (Boston: Estes & Lauriat, 1880), 90; Madeline Grumet, "Pedagogy for Patriarchy: The Feminization of Teaching," *Interchange* 12(1981): 165–84; Michael Apple, "Teaching and 'Women's Work': A Comparative Historical Analysis," in Edgar B. Gumbert, ed., *Expressions of Power in Education* (Atlanta: Georgia State University, 1984), 29–49.

18. Boykin, "Women in the Public Schools," 140–41.

19. "The School Mistress," *Harper's New Monthly Magazine* 57(1878): 607–11; "Women as Teachers," *U.S. Com. Ed. Report for 1891*, 360.

20. National Education Association, *Report on the Committee on Salaries, Tenure, and Pensions of Public School Teachers in the United States to the National Council of Education, July, 1905* (Winona, Minn.: NEA, 1905), 52; *U.S. Com. Ed. Report for 1892*, 2:669–71.

21. Dodge, *Common School System*, 316–17; David Wilbur Peters, *The Status of the Married Woman Teacher* (New York: Teachers College, 1934); Kathleen C. Berkeley, "The Ladies Want to Bring about Reform in the Public Schools: Public Education and Women's Rights in the Post–Civil War South," *History of Education Quarterly* 24(1984): 45–57.

22. Howard N. Rabinowitz, "Half a Loaf: The Shift from White to Black Teachers in the Negro Schools of the Urban South, 1865–1890," *Journal of Southern History* 40(1974): 565–94; Blodgett, *Education in the United States*, 134–40.

23. *Charlestown Report for 1848*, 27, 23–29.

24. *Majority and Minority Reports, Charlestown, 1848*. The majority report of the subcommittee of the board, which proposed a return to separate classes, was published as an article "Separation of the Sexes in Schools" in *The Massachusetts Teacher* 6(1848): 247–52.

25. *Majority and Minority Reports, Charlestown, 1848*, 11–13.

26. Ibid.

27. Ibid. Similar fears about mixing boys and girls surfaced in 1838 in Bristol, Rhode Island, where the school committee wanted to have separate rooms for all boys and girls. When lack of funds precluded this arrangement, the teachers discouraged any conversation between the sexes, even on lessons, "and so strict a watch was kept upon them, that they were virtually kept apart from each other"; see *Bristol, Rhode Island, Report for 1876*, xv.

28. *Majority and Minority Reports, Charlestown, 1848*, 14–16. The passages quoted in the paragraphs that follow derive from the same source and will be identified by page references in the text only.

29. *Charlestown Report for 1848*, 23–24.

30. Ibid., 22–23, 25–26. The Charlestown school reports for 1849 through 1852 show that the reorganization into all-coeducational classes continued and that far more girls than boys applied to and attended the high school. The admission

exams were numbered rather than giving names of the pupils, presumably to ensure objectivity, but the sex of the applicants was indicated by the letters B and G; see *Annual Report of the School Committee of the City of Charlestown* (Charlestown: William W. Wheeler, 1849), 5–9. In 1849 the chairman of the committee reported that "there has been no single year of our acquaintance with the schools, in this city, when resort to punishments has been so infrequent, and the occasions for them so rare, as during the year which has just closed" (p. 23).

31. *Majority and Minority Reports of the Boston School Committee on the Subject of Coeducation of the Sexes* (Boston: Blackwell & Churchill, 1890), 60.

32. *San Francisco Report for 1868,* 33–34; Swett quoted in *U.S. Com. Ed. Report for 1870,* 93.

33. *Memphis Report for 1869–70,* 14–15; *Memphis Report for 1870–71,* 47.

34. Philbrick, "Coeducation of the Sexes," 124; Anonymous, "A Colored Woman, However Respectable, Is Lower than a White Prostitute," *The Independent* 54(September 18, 1902): 2221–24, as quoted in Gerda Lerner, ed., *Black Women in White America: A Documentary History* (New York: Vintage Books, 1973), 167.

35. *Bertonneau v. The Board of Directors of City Schools et Al.,* 1878, La. 177, 180.

36. U.S. Bureau of Education, *Coeducation of the Sexes in the Public Schools of the United States,* Circular of Information, no. 2-1883 (Washington, D.C.: GPO, 1883), 25. In Louisville, Ky., the average per-pupil cost of the white boys' high school was $71 compared with a per-pupil cost of $41 for both white girls and for blacks (of both sexes in one school); see *Louisville Report for 1902,* 7. On the grossly unequal funding of separate girls's schools in Montreal, see Marta Danylewycz and Alison Prentice, "Teachers, Gender, and Bureaucratizing School Systems in Nineteenth-Century Montreal and Toronto," *History of Education Quarterly* 24(1984): 88–91.

37. Blandin, *Higher Education of Women,* 18.

38. *Washington, D.C., Report for 1850,* 12, 44; *Washington, D.C. Report for 1870–71,* 32–33; *Savannah Report for 1868–69,* 15.

39. *Majority and Minority Reports of the Boston School Committee on Coeducation,* pp. 5, 22, 1–105; DuFour, "Exclusion of Female Students," chap. 5. In the Puritan churches in the colonial period, the sexes were separated, as Laurel Thatcher Ulrich has shown in *Good Wives: Image and Reality in the Lives of Women in Northern New England, 1650–1750* (New York: Knopf, 1982), 9, 34.

40. *Majority and Minority Reports of the Boston School Committee on Coeducation,* 41–42, 60–62, 7–104; DuFour, "Exclusion of Female Students," chap. 5; Louisa Parsons Hopkins, "Coeducation of the Sexes in Boston Public Schools," *Educational Review* 1(1891): 46–48.

41. Philbrick, "Coeducation of the Sexes," 116, 120–21, 122, 115–131.

42. Letter from Harris to Dr. Voss, quoted in *U.S. Com. Ed. Report for 1900–1901,* 2:1268, fn 2. For a sample of professional writings on coeducation, see ibid., 1240–52.

43. White, "Coeducation of the Sexes"; "Separate Education of Boys and Girls," *Common School Journal* 13(1851): 87–90; J. W. B., "The Education of Boys and Girls Together," *New York Teacher* 5(1855): 131–33; "Description of a Good School," *Common School Journal* 8(1846); 347; National Council of Education, Committee on the Education of Girls, "Coeducation of the Sexes," *NEA Addresses and Proceedings, 1890,* 338–39. For elaborate laws on race, see Charles P. Mangum, Jr., *The Legal Status of the Negro* (Chapel Hill: University of North Carolina Press, 1940), chap. 4.

44. *Michigan Report for 1857–58,* 17, 53–55, 445, 447, 452–54, 457, 460–61, 465, 467; J. P. Wickersham and James Thompson, "On the Coeducation of the Sexes," *Pennsylvania School Journal* 3(1854): 90–91; J. W. B., "Girls' Rights," *New York Teacher* 1(1860): 266–68; A. T., "Female Education," *Pennsylvania School Journal* 2(1854): 370–71; Caroline Davis, "Female Education," *Pennsylvania School Journal* 1(1852–53): 431–32; Thomas H. Burrowes, "Coeducation of the Sexes," *Pennsylvania School Journal* 5(1856): 27–32.

45. Wickersham and Thompson, "On the Coeducation of the Sexes," 89, 87–92. For a minority report of the association the next year, see J. H. Brown, P. W. Gegembre, and W. V. Davis, "Report on the Co-Education of the Sexes," *Pennsylvania School Journal* 3(1855): 211–15.

46. Wickersham and Thompson, "On the Coeducation of the Sexes," 90–91.

47. *Dedham Report for 1852,* 12; *West Cambridge Report for 1852–53,* 5.

48. *Cincinnati Report for 1859,* 36; *New York City Report for 1874,* 223; Henry C. Kinney, "Sex in Education," *Indiana School Journal* 23(1878): 20, 18–21 [reporting on Washington and other cities]; For an excellent discussion of mathematics gender stereotypes in this period, see Patricia Cline Cohen, *A Calculating People: The Spread of Numeracy in Early America* (Chicago: University of Chicago Press, 1982), 139–49. On the superiority of girls as readers, see George A. Walton, *Report of Examinations of Schools of Norfolk County, Massachusetts* (Boston: Lee and Shepard, 1880), 139. For perceptive discussions of male-female differences in academic achievement in this period, see Daniel Calhoun, *The Intelligence of a People* (Princeton: Princeton University Press, 1973), 95–96, 100, 102, 131, and passim.

49. William T. Harris, "Coeducation," *Educational Foundations* 20(1908–1909): 111–15; *St. Louis Report for 1870.* When he became U. S. commissioner of education, Harris publicized his views in his annual reports; his 1870 report was reprinted in the *Mississippi Educational Journal* 1(1872), 393–96, and his report for 1872–73 was quoted approvingly, among other places, in the *Chicago School Report for 1874* (Chicago: Bryant & Walker, 1875), 104–106, and J. T. Valentine, "The Coeducation of the Sexes," *Pennsylvania School Journal* 24(1875): 184. The National Council of Education's Report, "Coeducation of the Sexes," was practically a transcript of Harris's ideas.

50. *St. Louis Report for 1870,* 19–20.

51. Ibid.

52. Ibid.; *St. Louis Report for 1872–73,* 106; Carl Lester Byerly, *Contributions of William Torrey Harris to Public School Administration* (Chicago: University of Chicago Press, 1946), 22–26.

53. U.S. Bureau of Education, *Coeducation of the Sexes,* 19, 16, 16–23.

54. National Council of Education, "Coeducation of the Sexes," 338–39.

55. Ibid., 341–42, 339.

56. Anna Tolman Smith, "Coeducation of the Sexes in the United States," in *U.S. Com. Ed. Report for 1891–92,* 2:783–91; see also her more extensive survey of the same title in *U.S. Com. Ed. Report for 1900–1901,* 2:1217–27.

57. Burrowes, "Coeducation of the Sexes," 29; Valentine, "Coeducation"; Wickersham and Thompson, "On the Coeducation of the Sexes"; Anon., "Female Education"; J. W. Buckley, "The Education of Boys and Girls Together," *New York Teacher* 5(1855): 131; U.S. Bureau of Education, *Coeducation of the Sexes,* 17; and see other citations above. Harris was to some degree an exception among professional educators, for he did see a new stage of civilization emerging in which "directive intelligence" would become important and in which women would greatly expand their sphere beyond the home. They might become leaders in the arts and social services and have an opportunity to enter the trades and professions. See William T. Harris, "The Relation of Woman to the Trades and Professions," *Educational Review* 20(1900): 217–29.

58. Edward H. Clarke, *Sex in Education; Or, A Fair Chance for Girls* (Boston: James R. Osgood, 1874); Elizabeth Duffey, *No Sex in Education; Or An Equal Chance for Both Girls and Boys* (Philadelphia: J. M. Stoddart, 1874).

59. Brown, Gegembre, and Davis, "Report on Co-education," 213.

60. Ibid., 214.

61. "Declaration of Sentiments and Resolutions, Seneca Falls, 1848," in Miriam Schneir, ed., *Feminism: The Essential Historical Writings* (New York: Vintage Books, 1972), 79; Caroline H. Dall, *The College, the Market, and the Court; Or, Woman's Relation to Education, Labor, and Law* (Boston: Memorial Edition, 1914; orig. ed. 1867), 3–4, 8, chap. 1; Keller, "Coeducation," pp. 97–108.

62. "Seneca Falls Declaration," 79; Dall, *The College,* 3–4, 8, chap. 1; Elizabeth Griffen, *In Her Own Right: The Life of Elizabeth Cady Stanton* (New York: Oxford University Press, 1984), 17, 93, 164, 202; H. B. B., "Coeducation Vindicated," *Woman's Journal* 4(1873): 20; R. T. B., "Coeducation—Its History and Significance," *Woman's Journal* 3(1872): 229; "Suffrage and Education," *The Woman's Journal* 46(1915): 142.

63. Per A. Siljestrom, *Educational Institutions of the United States* (London: John Chapman, 1853); Smith, "Coeducation of the Sexes, 1901." Smith's and other federal surveys of coeducation in 1883 and 1891 were conducted in part to answer questions from foreign educators about coeducation in America. For a sample of European views, see Alice Woods, ed., *Coeducation: A Series of Essays by Various Authors* (London: Paternoster, Green, 1903); L. B. Pekin, *Coeducation in Its Histor-*

ical and Theoretical Setting (London: Hogarth Press, 1939); Dudley Campbell, *Mixed Education of Boys and Girls in England and America* (London: Irvington's, 1874); and Alice Zimmern, *Methods of Education in the United States* (London: Swan Sonnenschein, 1894).

64. Dugard quoted in Smith, "Coeducation of the Sexes, 1901," 1269; Siljestrom, *Educational Institutions*, 197; Woods, ed., *Coeducation: Essays*; Pekin, *Settings of Coeducation*; Campbell, *Mixed Education*.

Chapter 5. The Rising Tide of Coeducation in the High School

1. U.S. Bureau of Education, *Coeducation of the Sexes in the Public Schools of the United States*, Circular of Information, no. 2-1883 (Washington, D.C.: GPO, 1883), 12, 24; *U.S. Com. Ed. Report for 1900–1901*, 1221.

2. *U.S. Com. Ed. Report for 1888–89*, 2:775; *Report for 1889–90*, 2:1388; John Francis Latimer, *What's Happened to Our High Schools?* (Washington, D.C.: Public Affairs Press, 1958), 144–46.

3. James M. Greenwood, "Report on High School Statistics," *NEA Addresses and Proceedings, 1900*, 347, and citations on achievement given below.

4. U.S. Bureau of Education, *Biennial Survey of Education, 1918–20* (Washington, D.C.: GPO, 1923), 497; *U.S. Com. Ed. Report for 1889*, 2:775.

5. Apart from some first-rate case studies of individual schools—several of them cited below—there have been few comparative or comprehensive studies of public high schools in the era before 1880. For an excellent introduction to the issues such a history might address, see William J. Reese, "Common and Exclusive Inheritance: A Social History of the American High School, 1821–1880" (unpublished paper, Indiana University, 1986). We are also indebted to John L. Rury's unpublished "Women at School: The Feminization of American High Schools, 1870–1900," a chapter in a forthcoming book, and pleased to find that both his research on gender in early high schools and ours have led independently to similar conclusions.

6. Kasuya Yoshi, *A Comparative Study of the Secondary Education of Girls in England, Germany, and the United States* (New York: Teachers College, 1933). Many of the arguments for and against coeducation treated in the previous chapter applied equally to grammar and high schools.

7. M. Carey Thomas quoted in International Federation of University Women, Bulletin no. 1 (Report of the First Conference, July 1920), 56–57; M. Carey Thomas, *Education of Women*, Monographs on Education in the United States, no. 7 (Washington, D.C.: GPO, 1899), 5–6. On feminist support for coeducation, see William Leach, *True Love and Perfect Union: The Feminist Reform of Sex and Society* (New York: Basic Books, 1980), 61–62, 76–77, 80, 124, 152, 166, 283, 312, 314.

8. *U.S. Com. Ed. Report for 1873*, xliii–xliv; see below for data on attrition.

9. Some of these themes are skillfully developed by David F. Labaree, *The*

Making of an American High School: The Credentials Market and the Central High School of Philadelphia (New Haven: Yale University Press, 1988); see also case studies below and local school reports for the rationale of the high school.

10. David B. Tyack, *The One Best System: A History of American Urban Education* (Cambridge: Harvard University Press, 1974), 56–59. For an anguished complaint when the high school did not operate in this meritocratic manner, see *Lowell, Mass., Report for 1851,* 56–58.

11. Charles W. Eliot, "The Gap between the Elementary Schools and the Colleges," *NEA Addresses and Proceedings, 1890,* 522–33. For arguments about the purposes of the early high school, see David Tyack, ed., *Turning Points in American Educational History* (Waltham, Mass.: Blaisdell Publishing, 1967), 352–411; for the post–1880 period, a standard work is Edward A. Krug, *The Shaping of the American High School, 1880–1920* (New York: Harper & Row, 1964).

12. Principals quoted in Henry Barnard, "Public High School," *Rhode Island Report for 1848,* 258; Labaree, *American High School,* 41, 45; Michael B. Katz, *The Irony of Early School Reform: Educational Innovation in Mid-Nineteenth Century Massachusetts* (Cambridge: Harvard University Press, 1968), 271, 39; Joel A. Perlmann, *Ethnic Differences* (Cambridge, England: Cambridge University Press, 1988); Selwyn K. Troen, *The Public and the Schools: Shaping the St. Louis School System, 1838–1920* (Columbia, Mo.: University of Missouri Press, 1975), 232; Krug, *Shaping the American High School,* 12–13.

On the complexity of motives of the proponents and opponents of high schools in one community, see Maris A. Vinovskis, *The Origins of Public High Schools: A Reexamination of the Beverly High School Controversy* (Madison: University of Wisconsin Press, 1985). Vinovskis has provided evidence that high-school attendance in Essex County, Mass., and specifically in Newburyport, was higher than earlier estimates: "Have We Underestimated the Extent of Antebellum High School Attendance?" (Paper presented at the History of Education Society Annual Meeting, New York, October 1987).

13. Principal quoted in *Oakland Report for 1881,* 82–84; David Tyack, Thomas James, and Aaron Benavot, *Law and the Shaping of Public Education, 1785–1954* (Madison: University of Wisconsin Press, 1987), 102–4; State of California, *Debates and Proceedings of the Constitutional Convention of the State of California, 1878–79,* 3 vols. (Sacramento: State Printer, 1880–81).

14. *Oakland Report for 1881,* 73; editor quoted in David B. Tyack, "Bureaucracy and the Common School: The Example of Portland, Oregon, 1851–1913," *American Quarterly* 19(1967): 489.

15. Mary Abigail Dodge, *Our Common School System* (Boston: Estes & Lauriat, 1880), 21–44; Carl Kaestle, *Pillars of the Republic: Common Schools and American Society, 1780–1860* (New York: Hill and Wang, 1983); Vinovskis, *Beverly High School.*

16. One report of the U.S. Office of Education that attempted to explain coed-

ucation to foreign critics was U.S. Bureau of Education, *Coeducation of the Sexes.*

17. Our estimate that 90 percent of public high schools were coeducational is computed from *U.S. Com. Ed. Report for 1873,* table 5, pp. 586–617.

18. Emit Duncan Grizzell, *Origin and Development of the High School in New England Before 1865* (New York: Macmillan, 1923); Arnold Jack Keller, "An Historical Analysis of the Arguments for and against Coeducational Public High Schools in the United States" (Ed.D. diss., Teachers College, Columbia University, 1971).

19. E. A. Miller, "High Schools in Ohio Prior to 1850," *School Review* 28(1920): 454–69; Paul E. Belting, *The Development of the Free Public High School in Illinois to 1860* (Springfield, Ill.: Illinois State Historical Society Journal, 1919); Theodore Sizer, *The Age of the Academy* (New York: Teachers College, 1964).

20. *U.S. Com. Ed. Report for 1873,* 586–643; James H. Blodgett, *Report on Education in the United States at the Eleventh Census, 1890* (Washington, D.C.: GPO, 1893), 26–33; Theodore R. Sizer, *Secondary Schools at the Turn of the Century* (New Haven: Yale University Press, 1964), 21–22, 39.

21. *U.S. Com. Ed. Report for 1873,* xxxvi–xlii; *U.S. Com. Ed. Report for 1874,* xlviii–lv; "Statistics of Schools," *Census of 1870,* table 13, 461–70; Blodgett, (*Report on Education in the United States,* pp. 3–11) is vitriolic and vivid on the parlous state of school statistics.

22. For the highly diverse character of secondary schools, see *U.S. Com. Ed. Report for 1873,* table 5, pp. 586–613; *Philadelphia Report for 1894,* 16–18; Franklin Spencer Edmonds, *History of the Central High School of Philadelphia* (Philadelphia: J. B. Lippincott, 1902); Sizer, *Secondary Schools,* 39; and city school reports cited below.

23. Barnard, "Public High School," 253.

24. Ibid., 253, 254–59.

25. Ibid., 254–55.

26. Ibid., 254.

27. Barnard, "Public High School," 255; Labaree, *The Making of an American High School;* Jane Hunter, "Victorian Schoolgirls and Their Diaries: A Perspective on American Adolescence" (unpublished paper, Colby College, 1987).

28. Alexander James Inglis, *The Rise of the High School in Massachusetts* (New York: Teachers College, 1911), 15–17.

29. Ibid.; Grizzell, *Origin and Development of the High School,* 43–44.

30. Report of the Boston School Board on attrition and several documents on the girls' high school are conveniently reprinted in "Girls in the Public Schools of Boston," *American Journal of Education* 13(1863): 248–49, 258; Grizzell, *Origin and Development of the High School,* 43–44; Labaree, *The Making of an American High School,* chap. 3.

31. *Providence Report for 1828,* 4.

32. "Girls in the Public Schools of Boston," 243–44, 245–47. The first public school for girls opened in 1824 in Worcester, Mass. The Worcester school commit-

tee had considered a plan to open all its schools to both boys and girls, but when the plan failed, the committee opened a high school for girls parallel to the boys' Latin Grammar School.

33. "Girls in the Public Schools of Boston," 252–58.

34. Ibid., 248, 246–47, 252–58; Richard P. DuFour, "The Exclusion of Female Students from the Public Schools of Boston, 1820–1920" (Ed.D. diss., Northern Illinois University, 1981), 52–58, 72.

35. DuFour, "The Exclusion of Female Students," 59–94.

36. "Girls in the Public Schools of Boston," 249–50.

37. Ibid., 249–51.

38. Ibid., 255–58; also see *Annual Report of the School Committee of Boston, 1903* (Boston: Municipal Press, 1904), 43–49; "Boston High School for Girls," *American Journal of Education* 1(1826): 96–105.

39. *Philadelphia Report for 1846,* 104–8; *Newburyport Report for 1842–43,* 12–14, as quoted in Maris Vinovskis, "Patterns of High School Attendance in Newburyport, Massachusetts, in 1860" (Paper presented at the American Historical Association in New York City, December 28, 1985); statistics on male and female graduation rates, ibid., 23–24. For a vivid account of the eagerness of girls in Newburyport for secondary education, see Norma Kidd Green, *A Forgotten Chapter in American Education: Jane Andrews of Newburyport* (Framingham, Mass.: Alumnae Association of the State College at Framingham, 1967), 20–26; Rury, "Women at School," 48–51; Keller, "Arguments for and against Coeducation," 64–90.

40. *Washington, D.C., Report for 1856,* 25; *Washington, D.C., Report for 1875–76,* 14; Keller, "Arguments for and against Coeducation," 87–88.

41. *Baltimore Report for 1860,* 84–85; Grizzell, *Origin and Development of the High School.*

42. *Baltimore Report for 1855,* 10, 100.

43. *Louisville Report for 1902,* 7; Thomas, *Education of Women;* DuFour, "The Exclusion of Female Students."

44. *Boston Report for 1866,* 186.

45. *Louisville Report for 1902,* 7; Law of 1827 quoted in Inglis, *Rise of the High School,* pp. 27–28.

46. Inglis, *Rise of the High School,* 27–28; Vinovskis, *Origins of Public High Schools,* chap. 3; Grizzell, *Origin and Development of the High School,* 48–53, 73–82; *Springfield Report for 1858,* 60–62. Chelsea had a coeducational high school even though its grammar schools were sex-segregated; *Chelsea Report for 1846–47,* 6–7. In *Dorchester Report for 1853,* p. 12, the committee announced that the founding of its coeducational high school was a "fixed fact."

47. *Cambridge Report for 1846,* 18–21.

48. Ibid.; *Cambridge Report for 1852,* 49–50.

49. Henry Barnard, *School Architecture* (New York: A. S. Barnes, 1849), 108–9;

Per A. Siljestrom, *Educational Institutions of the United States* (London: John Chapman, 1843), 302–3.

50. Anna Tolman Smith, "Coeducation," *U.S. Com. Ed. Report for 1901*, 2:1053–54.

51. Andrew Freese, *Early History of the Cleveland Public Schools* (Cleveland: Robison, Savage, 1876), 32–33, 34–39; William J. Akers, *Cleveland Schools in the Nineteenth Century* (Cleveland: Wm. Bayne Printing House, 1901), 46–47; principal, E. E. White, quoted in Anna Tolman Smith, "Coeducation," 1054; Akers, *Cleveland Schools,* 39, 47–48. For comparison with coeducation in Columbus, see *Columbus Report for 1845–46,* 6–8, 22–23, and *Columbus Report for 1848–49,* 22–23.

52. Rufus King, "Report on the Cincinnati Public Schools," in *Ohio Report for 1859,* 135–36; *Cincinnati Report for 1854,* 33–34; *Cincinnati Report for 1859,* 36; *Cincinnati Report for 1838,* 5; *Cincinnati Report for 1846,* 24–29. For statistics on single-sex and coeducational private secondary schools, see *U.S. Com. Ed. Report for 1873,* 586–613.

53. *Chicago Report for 1854,* 12; *Chicago Report for 1856,* 12–14; *Chicago Report for 1858,* 34–35; John Wesley Bell, "The Development of the Public High School in Chicago" (Ph.D. diss., University of Chicago, 1939), 8; Shepard Johnston, *Historical Sketches of the Public School System of Chicago* (Chicago: Clark & Edwards, 1880), 48–50. For a sampling of reports on other midwestern coeducational high schools where girls and boys took similar courses, see *St. Paul, Minn., Report for 1875,* 61–64; *Milwaukee Report for 1869,* 43–54, and *Milwaukee Report for 1874,* 139–42; and *Lawrence, Kansas, Report for 1872,* 20–24.

54. *Census of 1870,* table 13, pp. 461–70.

55. Blodgett, *Report on Education in the United States,* 123; U.S. Bureau of Education, *Biennial Survey of Education, 1918–1920,* 497; *U.S. Com. Ed. Report for 1903,* 2:1818.

56. *U.S. Com. Ed. Report for 1889–90,* 2:1388–89; *U.S. Com. Ed. Report for 1893–94,* 1:65, 75; Krug, *Shaping the American High School,* 13–14; *Historical Statistics of the United States,* 1:397; Sizer, *Secondary Schools,* 53–54.

57. See, for example, reports cited above and *Fresno, California, Report for 1900,* 54–55; *Los Angeles Report for 1885,* 46–47; *Course of Study for Arizona Schools* (Phoenix: H.H. McNeil, 1899), 60–63; *Little Rock Report for 1896,* 266–67; *Birmingham Report for 1899,* 76–77; *Berkeley Report for 1890,* 23–27; *Oakland Report for 1892,* 32–35.

58. Latimer, *What's Happened to Our High Schools?* 149–50.

59. David Labaree found that while social class served as a filter for entrance to Central High School, once a student was enrolled, a rough form of meritocracy prevailed inside the institution. The best predictor of graduation was not class background but grades in courses; see Labaree, *The Making of an American High*

School, chap. 3. See also the meritocratic assumptions underlying the report by the Committee of Ten on Secondary School Studies, *Report* (New York: American Book, 1894), 41.

60. On valedictorians, see Reed T. Ueda, "Avenues to Adulthood: Urban Growth and the Rise of Secondary Schools in Somerville, Massachusetts, 1800–1930" (Ph.D. diss., Harvard University, 1981), 248–49; Rury, "Women at School," 57–58; James M. Greenwood, "Report on High School Statistics," *NEA Addresses and Proceedings, 1900,* 347; Walter S. Monroe, "Progress and Promotion of Pupils in Certain Indiana City and Rural Schools," *Indiana University Studies* 5(1918, no. 39): 43, 39.

61. Patricia Cline Cohen, *A Calculating People: The Spread of Numeracy in Early America* (Chicago: University of Chicago Press, 1982), 139–49; W. A. Fox and Edward T. Thorndike, "The Relationships between the Different Abilities Involved in the Study of Arithmetic and Sex Differences in Arithmetical Ability," in Edward T. Thorndike, ed., *Heredity, Correlation, and Sex Differences in School Abilities* (New York: Macmillan, 1903), 34, 38. In 1925 two other scholars summarized a series of studies on achievement in mathematics and found conflicting results; most favored boys by a small margin, although girls did better in some tasks—Thomas Buswell and Charles H. Judd, *Summary of Educational Investigations Relating to Arithmetic,* Supplementary Educational Monographs, no. 27 (Chicago: University of Chicago Press, 1925), 131–34.

62. *Philadelphia Report for 1904,* 23–30; John D. Philbrick, *City School Systems in the United States,* U. S. Bureau of Education, Circular of Information no. 1-1885 (Washington, D.C.: GPO, 1885), 41–47; *Sketch of the Philadelphia Normal School for Girls* (Washington, D.C.: GPO, 1882); *San Francisco Report for 1898,* 13–16.

63. Letter of Joan Jacobs Brumberg to authors, November 30, 1983; Hunter, "Victorian Schoolgirls".

64. Krug, *Shaping the American High School,* 12–13; Troen, *The Public and the Schools,* 127; Labaree, *The Making of an American High School,* 42.

65. Joseph F. Kett, *Rites of Passage: Adolescence in America, 1790 to the Present* (New York: Basic Books, 1977), 138; Sara Burstall, *Impressions of American Education in 1908* (London: Longmans, Green, 1909), 57; *Atlanta Report for 1894,* 16.

66. *Alameda Report for 1900,* 27.

67. We are indebted to two former students for insightful papers on this subject: Shelby Baetz, "The Preponderance of Girls in U.S. Public Schools, 1890–1920" (History Honors Project, Stanford University, 1975); and Joseph E. Devine, "The Preponderance of Girls in American Secondary Schools, 1890–1920" (Seminar Paper, History 401, Stanford University, 1974). *Statistical Abstract of the United States* (Washington, D.C.: GPO, 1974), 109; Blodgett, *Report on Education in the United States,* 124–26.

Chapter 6. King Canutes Attack the Perils of Coeducation

1. Edward H. Clarke, *Sex in Education; Or, A Fair Chance for Girls* (Boston: Houghton Mifflin, 1873); G. Stanley Hall, *Adolescence: Its Psychology and Its Relations to Physiology, Anthropology, Sociology, Sex, Crime, Religion and Education* (New York: D. Appleton, 1907), vol. 2, chap. 17; Adm. F. E. Chadwick, "The Woman Peril in American Education," *Educational Review* 47(1914): 109, 115–16.

2. Chadwick, "The Woman Peril"; Edward H. Clarke, "The Building of a Brain," *NEA Addresses and Proceedings, 1874,* 101; Janice Law Trecker, "Sex, Science and Education," *American Quarterly* 26(1974): 352–66.

3. For a sample of feminists' responses to Clarke, see Julia Ward Howe, *Sex and Education: A Reply to Dr. E. H. Clarke's "Sex in Education"* (Boston: Roberts Brothers, 1874). For Harris's reply to Clarke, see *St. Louis Report for 1874,* 109–10; and Arnold Jack Keller, "An Historical Analysis of the Arguments for and against Coeducational Public Schools in the United States" (Ed.D. diss., Teachers College, Columbia University, 1971), 228–32. On concepts of women's mental inferiority and feminist opposition, see Patricia Smith Butcher, "More than Just a Parlor Ornament: Women's Rights Periodicals and Women's Higher Education, 1849–1920" (Ed.D. diss., Rutgers University, 1986), chap. 4.

4. While stressing the danger to girls, in *Sex in Education,* p. 125, Clarke did write that if schools ignore the natural polarity between the sexes, coeducation "emasculates the boys, stunts the girls". G. Stanley Hall, "Coeducation in the High School," *NEA Addresses and Proceedings, 1903,* 446–60.

5. Clarke, *Sex in Education,* 125; G. Stanley Hall, "Feminization in School and Home: The Undue Influence of Woman Teachers—the Need of Different Training for the Sexes," *World's Work* 16(1908): 10237–44.

6. Rosalind Rosenberg, *Beyond Separate Spheres: Intellectual Roots of Modern Feminism* (New Haven: Yale University Press, 1982), xv. One clear institutional response to the talk about the poor health of girls was the creation of physical education programs. See Thomas Woody, *A History of Women's Education in the United States* (New York: Science Press, 1929), vol. 2, chap. 3.

7. Clarke, *The Building of a Brain* (Boston: Osgood, 1874), 53; Trecker, "Sex, Science and Education," 353; Rosenberg, *Beyond Separate Spheres.* For an account of similar debates in England about the education of middle-class girls, see Joan N. Burstyn, *Victorian Education and the Ideal of Womanhood* (London: Croom Helm, 1980; reprinted Totowa, N.J.: Barnes & Noble Books, 1980).

8. Clarke, *Sex in Education,* 149; Clarke, "Building a Brain," 101; John Clinton Maxwell, "Should the Educations of Boys and Girls Differ? A Half-Century of Debate, 1870–1920" (Ph.D. diss., University of Wisconsin, 1966), 33, 24–27; Rosenberg, *Beyond Separate Spheres,* 11; Trecker, "Sex, Science and Education."

9. Clarke, *Sex in Education,* 123, 127, 41, 120–28; Clarke focused on colleges in

his objections to coeducation, but his reasoning about maturation applies to female secondary-school students perhaps more than to those of college age. Burstyn, *Victorian Education,* chap. 5.

10. Clarke, *Sex in Education,* 79–80, 114–15; T. S. Clouston, "Woman from a Medical Point of View," *Popular Science Monthly* 24(December 1883): 224.

11. M. Carey Thomas, "Present Tendencies in Women's Education," *Educational Review* 25(1908): 68; Butcher, "Women's Rights Periodicals," 118–19.

12. Anna C. Brackett, *The Education of American Girls, Considered in a Series of Essays* (New York: G. P. Putnam's Sons, 1874), 91–92.

13. Ibid., 93, 94.

14. Woody, *Women's Education,* vol. 2, chap. 3.

15. Brackett, *Education of American Girls;* E. B. Duffey, *No Sex in Education; Or, an Equal Chance for Both Girls and Boys* (Philadelphia: J. M. Stoddard, 1874); Howe, *Sex in Education: A Reply to Dr. E. H. Clarke;* Butcher, "Women's Rights Periodicals," 120–30; Rosenberg, *Beyond Separate Spheres,* 20.

16. Butcher, "Women's Rights Periodicals," 122–24; Woody, *Women's Education,* vol. 2, chap. 3.

17. *St. Louis Report for 1872–73,* 108–10.

18. Ibid., 111–12. For an opposing view by a veteran schoolman, see John D. Philbrick, "Coeducation," *American Institute of Instruction, Lectures and Proceedings, 1880,* 115–19.

19. "Coeducation," *National Teacher's Monthly* 1(Nov. 1874): 17–19; "Review of Books," *National Teacher's Monthly* 2(Jan. 1875): 89, as quoted in Keller, "Arguments for and against Coeducation," 230–31.

20. Hall, *Adolescence,* 561, 640, 562.

21. G. Stanley Hall, "The Question of Coeducation," *Muncey's Magazine* 35(February 1908): 589.

22. Hall, *Adolescence,* 2:636, 645, 636–647.

23. Thomas, "Present Tendencies," 65; Willystine Goodsell, *The Education of Women: Its Social Background and Its Problems* (New York: Macmillan, 1924), 62–68. For a discussion of Hall's personal sexual confusions, see Dorothy Ross, *G. Stanley Hall: The Psychologist as Prophet* (Chicago: University of Chicago Press, 1972), 9–11, 255–59 (Hall's parents referred to his genitals as "the dirty place").

24. Chadwick, "The Woman Peril," 109, 115–16.

25. Woody, *Women's Education,* 1:505–14.

26. John Higham, "The Reorientation of American Culture in the 1890s," in John Weiss, ed., *The Origins of Modern Consciousness* (Detroit: Wayne State University Press, 1965), 25–48.

27. Mark C. Carnes, "The Making of the Self-Made Man: The Emotional Experience of Boyhood, 1860–1900" (Paper presented at the annual meeting of the Organization of American Historians, April 1985); Joseph F. Kett, *Rites of Passage: Adolescence in America, 1790 to the Present* (New York: Basic Books, 1977), 173–74.

28. Higham, "American Culture," 27, 32, 25–48.

29. Professor Henry E. Armstrong, quoted in Luther H. Gulick, "The Alleged Feminization of Our American Boys," *American Physical Education Review* 10 (1905): 212; Ross, *G. Stanley Hall*, 255; John Dewey quoted in Woody, *Women's Education* 1:514; W. J. Osburn, *Foreign Criticism of American Education*, U.S. Bureau of Education, Bulletin no. 8-1921 (Washington, D.C.: GPO, 1922), 107–111. For a more positive view of the effects of women teachers on boys, see Sara A. Burstall, *Impressions of American Education in 1908* (London: Longmans, Green, 1909), chap. 9.

30. Joan N. Burstyn, "American Society during the Eighteen-Nineties: 'The Woman Question,'" *Studies in History and Society* 4(Spring 1973): 34–40; David Tyack and Elisabeth Hansot, *Managers of Virtue: Public School Leadership in America, 1820–1980* (New York: Basic Books, 1982), 181–201.

31. David B. Tyack, *The One Best System: A History of American Urban Education* (Cambridge: Harvard University Press, 1974), 255–58; Ella Flagg Young quoted in anonymous article, "The Highest Salaried Woman in the World," *Western Journal of Education* 14(1909): 10; Tyack and Hansot, *Managers of Virtue*, 181–201; Louise Connolly, "Is There Room at the Top for Women Educators?" *The Woman Citizen* (8 March 1919): 840; Margaret Gribskov, "Feminism and the Woman School Administrator," in Sari Knopp Biklen and Marilyn B. Brannigan, eds., *Women and Educational Leadership* (Lexington, Mass.: Lexington Books, 1980), 77–92.

32. "Women as Teachers," *Educational Review* 2(1891): 358–62.

33. Philadelphia Public Schools, *Report for 1894*, 14; Maxwell, "Boys and Girls," 101–2; Woody, *Women's Education*, 1:507–9. Dissent about the value of women teachers appeared in an NEA discussion in 1886, when a schoolman argued that Horace Mann's assertion that 90 percent of teachers should be women was "one of his greatest mistakes"; see E. A. Sheldon, "Report of the Discussion," *NEA Addresses and Proceedings, 1886*, 302.

34. F. E. DeYoe and C. N. Thurber, "Where Are the High School Boys?" *School Review* 7(1900): 7; Willard Waller, *The Sociology of Teaching* (New York: Russell & Russell, 1961; reprint of 1932 ed.), chap. 5; Carter Alexander, *Some Present Aspects of the Work of Teachers' Voluntary Associations in the United States* (New York: Teachers College, 1910).

35. Male Teachers' Association of New York City, "Are There Too Many Women Teachers?" *Educational Review* 28(1904): 100–101, 98–105.

36. Ibid., 101–2, 103. It is interesting to contrast the negative characterization of women teachers with the current interest in feminine approaches to moral reasoning and pedagogy discussed in our concluding chapter.

37. Grace C. Strachan, *Equal Pay for Equal Work: The Story of the Struggle for Justice Being Made by the Women Teachers of the City of New York* (New York: B. F. Buck, 1910).

38. C. W. Bardeen, "The Monopolizing Woman Teacher," *Educational Review*

43(January 1912): 19–20, 26–27, 17–40; C. W. Bardeen, "Why Teaching Repels Men," *Educational Review* 35(April 1908): 351–59; Frederick Burk, "The Withered Heart of the Schools," *Educational Review* 34(December 1907): 448–58; William L. Howard, "Feminization of the High School," *Arena* 35(June 1906): 593–96; William L. Howard, "Helpless Youths and Useless Men," *American Magazine* 67(June 1906): 51–56; Earl Barnes, "The Feminizing of Culture," *Atlantic Monthly* 109(June 1912): 770–76; Josephine Conger-Kaneko, "The 'Effeminization' of the United States," *World's Work*, 12(August 1906): 7521–24; William D. Lewis, "The High School and the Boy," *The Saturday Evening Post* 184(April 6, 1912): 8–9, 77–78.

39. Hall, "Feminization in School and Home," 10238, 10240, 10237–44; Hall, "The Question of Coeducation," 590, 588–92; Hall, "Coeducation in the High School," 538–42.

40. Roosevelt letter quoted in Ross, *G. Stanley Hall*, 318, fn. 18; M. V. O'Shea "Masculinity in the Schools," *Wisconsin Journal of Education* 41(March 1909): 81.

41. Sanford Bell, "Influence of Men and Women Teachers," *NEA Addresses and Proceedings, 1903*, 809–11.

42. John Dewey, "Is Coeducation Injurious to Girls?" *Ladies Home Journal* 28(June 11, 1911): 22, 60–61; J. H. Tufts, "Feminization," *School Review* 17(January 1909): 55–58; Gulick, "Alleged Feminization," 216, 213–220; David Starr Jordan, "The Question of Coeducation," *Muncey's Magazine* 34(1909): 683–88. For women's responses to Chadwick, see *Educational Review* 47(1914): 411–15, 507–12.

43. Edward L. Thorndike, "The Influence of the Number of Men Teachers upon the Enrollment of Boys in Public High Schools," *Educational Review* 37(January 1909): 71, 80, 71–85. In 1912 Thorndike indicated that he did not consider the question of the women teachers settled; he wrote that the hiring of so many women teachers was "odious to many intelligent men and some women in this country and . . . directly contrary to the practice in other large nations whose devotion to education is most notable." See Edward L. Thorndike, *Education, A First Book* (New York: Macmillan, 1912), 154.

44. Fosdick quoted in "Discussion," *NEA Addresses and Proceedings, 1903*, 451, 453, 451–60.

45. Edward L. Thorndike, *The Teaching Staff of Secondary Schools in the United States*, U.S. Bureau of Education, Bulletin no. 4-1909 (Washington, D.C.: GPO, 1909), 20–21.

Chapter 7. Differentiating the High School: The "Boy Problem"

1. William D. Lewis, "The High School and the Boy," *The Saturday Evening Post* 184(April 6, 1912): 8, 8–9, 77–78.

2. Ibid., 8.

3. Ibid., 9, 77–78.

4. The first use of the phrase "dropping out" we have discovered occurs in a talk given in 1900 by James M. Greenwood, superintendent of the Kansas City, Mo., schools; "Report on High School Statistics," *NEA Addresses and Proceedings, 1900,* 340–51.

5. J. E. Armstrong, "The Advantages of Limited Sex Segregation in the High School," *School Review* 18(1910): 337–38.

6. Ellwood P. Cubberley, *Changing Conceptions of Education* (Boston: Houghton Mifflin, 1909); Edward A. Krug, *The Shaping of the American High School* (New York: Harper & Row, 1964); Lawrence A. Cremin, *The Transformation of the School: Progressivism in American Education* (New York: Knopf, 1961).

7. On the Protestant-republican ideology that animated the common school reformers and their design for the common school, see David Tyack and Elisabeth Hansot, *Managers of Virtue: Public School Leadership in America, 1820–1980* (New York: Basic Books, 1982), pt. 1.

8. Carl Kaestle, *Pillars of the Republic: Common Schools and American Society, 1780–1860* (New York: Hill and Wang, 1983); Michael B. Katz, *The Irony of Early School Reform: Educational Innovation in Mid-Nineteenth-Century Massachusetts* (Cambridge: Harvard University Press, 1968); David Nasaw, *Schooled to Order: A Social History of Public Schooling in the United States* (New York: Oxford University Press, 1979); Tyack and Hansot, *Managers of Virtue,* chaps. 6–7.

9. For studies of this impulse to design the economy and society more generally, see David Noble, *America by Design: Science, Technology, and the Rise of Corporate Capitalism* (New York: Knopf, 1979); in educational history, see Krug, *Shaping the American High School.*

10. Cubberley, *Changing Conceptions;* Joel H. Spring, *Education and the Rise of the Corporate State* (Boston: Beacon Press, 1972); David B. Tyack, *The One Best System: A History of American Urban Education* (Cambridge: Harvard University Press, 1974), pts. 4–5; Michael B. Katz, *Class, Bureaucracy, and Schools* (New York: Praeger, 1971); Paul D. Chapman, "Schools as Sorters: Lewis M. Terman and the Intelligence Testing Movement, 1890–1930" (Ph.D. diss., Stanford University, 1979); Geraldine Jonçich Clifford, "'Marry, Stitch, Die, or Do Worse': Educating Women for Work," in Harvey Kantor and David Tyack, eds., *Work, Youth, and Schooling: Historical Perspectives on Vocationalism in American Education* (Stanford: Stanford University Press, 1982), 223–68.

11. Clarence J. Karier, Paul C. Violas, and Joel H. Spring, *Roots of Crisis: American Education in the Twentieth Century* (Chicago: Scott, Foresman, 1973); Walter Feinberg and Henry Rosemont, eds., *Work, Technology, and Education: Dissenting Essays in the Intellectual Foundations of American Education* (Urbana, Ill.: University of Illinois Press, 1976); Robert A. Carlson, *The Quest for Conformity: Americanization through Education* (New York: John Wiley & Sons, 1975); Judy Jolley Mohraz, *The Separate Problem: Case Studies of Black Education in the North, 1900–1930* (West-

port, Conn.: Greenwood Press, 1979); Guadalupe San Miguel, *"Let Them All Take Heed": Mexican Americans and the Campaign for Educational Equality, 1929–1981* (Austin: University of Texas Press, 1987).

12. Winifred Richmond, "Present Practices and Tendencies in the Secondary Education of Girls," *Pedagogical Seminary* 23(June 1916): 193; Ellen R. Rushmore, "The Secondary Education of Girls" (M.A. thesis, Columbia University, 1910); Jane Bernard Powers, "The 'Girl Question' in Education: Vocational Training for Young Women in the Progressive Era" (Ph.D. diss., Stanford University, 1986).

13. Leta S. Hollingsworth, "Comparison of the Sexes in Mental Traits," *The Psychological Bulletin* 15(1918): 428; Helen Thompson Wooley, "The Psychology of Sex," *The Psychological Bulletin* 11(1914): 363–65; Lewis M. Terman, "Were We Born That Way?" *The World's Work* 44(1922): 660. Terman believed, however, that the I.Q. tests had proved the mental inferiority of blacks, Mexicans, and southern Europeans. A professor at the University of Washington, A. H. Yoder, voiced in 1903 what was at the time an unusual opinion, that many supposed sex differences were really individual differences, and that many supposed sex differences were really the result of different socialization and economic opportunities; see A. H. Yoder, "Sex Differentiation in Relation to Secondary Education," *NEA Addresses and Proceedings, 1903,* 786–87.

14. Wooley, "Psychology of Sex," 365.

15. "Report on Massilon Union Schools," in *Ohio Report for 1858,* 115. On the predominance of girls as high-school valedictorians, see Reed T. Ueda, "Avenues to Adulthood: Urban Growth and the Rise of Secondary Schools in Somerville, Massachusetts, 1800–1930" (Ph.D. diss., Harvard University, 1981), 248–49; Reed T. Ueda, *Avenues to Adulthood* (Cambridge, England: Cambridge University Press, 1987).

16. Leonard P. Ayres, *Laggards in Our Schools: A Study of Retardation and Elimination in City School Systems* (New York: Charities Publications Committee, 1909), 7.

17. On ethnic differences in the sex ratio of teenage students (only some of whom would have been in high school), see John L. Rury, "Urban Enrollment at the Turn of the Century: Gender as an Intervening Variable" *Urban Education* 28 (1988): 68–87; and for a later period in Bridgeport, Conn., George Counts, *The Selective Character of American Secondary Education* (Chicago: University of Chicago Press, 1922), 113; A. Caswell Ellis, "The Percentage of Boys Who Leave the High School, and the Reasons Therefore," *NEA Addresses and Proceedings, 1903,* 793–94; Joseph King Van Denburg, *Causes of the Elimination of Students in Public Secondary Schools of New York* (New York: Teachers College, 1911).

18. Harvey Kantor, *Learning to Earn: School, Work, and Vocational Reform in California, 1880–1930* (Madison: University of Wisconsin Press, 1988), 132–34, 114; Selwyn K. Troen, "The Discovery of the Adolescent by American Educational Reformers, 1900–1920: An Economic Perspective," in Lawrence Stone, ed., *School-*

ing and Society: Studies in the History of Education (Baltimore: Johns Hopkins Press, 1976), chap. 10.

19. *Digest of Educational Statistics 1980* (Washington, D.C.: GPO), 44; and from *Historical Statistics of the United States from Colonial Times to 1970* (Washington, D.C.: GPO, 1975), pt. 1, pp. 379, 381; *U.S. Com. Ed. Report for 1917,* 2:38; Willystine Goodsell, *The Education of Women: Its Social Background and Its Problems* (New York: Macmillan, 1924), 175; Kantor, *Learning to Earn,* 130.

20. James Russell Parsons, "High School Attendance," *School Review* 10(March 1904): 293–98; J. K. Stapleton, "How to Increase the Attendance of Boys at the High School," *NEA Addresses and Proceedings, 1903,* 801–9; David Tyack and Michael Berkowitz, "The Man Nobody Liked: Toward a Social History of the Truant Officer, 1840–1940," *American Quarterly* 29(1977): 31–54. For a useful summary of studies of child labor in relation to schooling, see W. Carson Ryan, *Vocational Guidance and the Schools,* U.S. Bureau of Education, Bulletin no. 24–1918 (Washington, D.C.: GPO, 1919), 38–58.

21. F. E. DeYoe and C. N. Thurber, "Where Are All the High School Boys?" *School Review* 8(1900): 234, 240.

22. Daniel T. Rodgers and David B. Tyack, "Work, Youth, and Schooling: Mapping Critical Research Areas," in Kantor and Tyack, eds., *Historical Perspectives,* 280–81; Leslie Woodcock Tentler, *Wage-Earning Women: Industrial Work and Family Life in the United States, 1900–1930* (New York: Oxford University Press, 1979), chap. 4; Ryan, *Vocational Guidance,* 38–58.

23. Ellis, "Boys Who Leave the High School," 795; George E. Gay, "Why Pupils Leave the High School without Graduating," *Education* 22(1902): 302.

24. William F. Book, "Why Pupils Drop Out of School," *Pedagogical Seminary* 13(June 1904): 209–211, 231. It would be interesting to duplicate Book's strategy of collecting student themes today.

25. Ibid., 212–14.

26. Ibid., 215–16.

27. Ibid., 218–19, 221.

28. Lewis, "High School and Boy," 9.

29. Caroline F. Ware, *Greenwich Village, 1920–1930* (New York: Harper & Row, 1935), 145; Paul Willis, *Learning to Earn: How Working Class Kids Get Working Class Jobs* (Farnborough, England: Saxon House, 1977).

30. Ware, *Greenwich Village,* 145–46, 319, chap. 11.

31. Ibid., 337, 455, chap. 11.

32. Ellis, "Boys Who Leave the High School," 797–78; DeYoe and Thurber, "High School Boys," 236–43; Stapleton, "Attendance of Boys," 801–7; Reuben Post Halleck, "What Kind of Education Is Best Suited to Boys?" in National Education Association, *Fiftieth Anniversary Volume, 1857–1906* (Washington, D.C.: NEA, 1906), 58–65.

33. J. E. Armstrong, "Limited Segregation," *School Review* 14(December 1906):

726, 729–34; Armstrong, "Advantages," 339, 341–42; *U.S. Com. Ed. Report for 1907*, 1:422.

34. J. E. Armstrong, "Limited Segregation," *School Review* 14(December 1906): 726, 729–34; Armstrong, "Advantages," 339, 341–42.

35. Armstrong, "Advantages," 345–47. Stuart A. Courtis found that teachers did show some subjectivity in grading, for they gave boys generally lower grades than they gave girls, but boys scored higher on certain objective tests. In Baltimore, school officials noted the discrepancy between boys' and girls' promotions and grades, and drawing on Courtis's study, called for greater objectivity in grading, *Baltimore Report for 1925*, 108–9.

36. Armstrong, "Limited Segregation," 732–34; Richmond, "Present Practices," p. 189; Arnold Jack Keller, "An Historical Analysis of the Arguments for and against Coeducational Public High Schools in the United States" (Ed.D. diss., Teachers College, Columbia University, 1971), 347–50.

37. Thomas R. Cole, "Segregation at the Broadway High School, Seattle," *School Review* 22(1915): 550, 551–52, 553.

38. John Clinton Maxwell, "Should the Educations of Boys and Girls Differ? A Half-Century of Debate—1870–1920" (Ph.D. diss., University of Wisconsin, 1966), 194.

39. U.S. Bureau of Education, *Features in City School Systems*, Bulletin no. 31-1913 (Washington, D.C.: GPO, 1913), 52–53. Richmond ("Present Practices," p. 187) reported that partial segregation of girls in coeducational schools also took place in Richmond, Indiana; Hackensack, New Jersey; Muskogee, Oklahoma; Columbus, Ohio; Fresno, California; and Clinton, Iowa, in addition to Seattle and Chicago. In these eight cities, four districts separated the sexes in all science and mathematics classes, and three separated them in physiology, manual training, and physical culture classes.

40. Edward L. Thorndike, "A Neglected Aspect of the American High School," *Educational Review* 33(1907): 254; *U.S. Com. Ed. Report for 1907*, 422. For an illuminating case study of sex differentiation of courses in science in San Jose, California, see Millicent Rutherford, "Feminism and the Secondary School Curriculum, 1890–1920" (Ph.D. diss., Stanford University, 1977), chap. 6.

41. Rutherford, "Feminism," 151; E. R. Breslich, "The Girl and Algebra," *School Review* 22(October 1914): 562–64.

42. Rutherford, "Feminism," 130–31; *U.S. Com. Ed. Report for 1907*, 422.

43. Carroll G. Pearce, "Study of Traits Desirable in an American Citizen—A Preliminary Report," *NEA Addresses and Proceedings, 1930*, 230, 562–64; W. L. Steele, "Elective Studies in the High School," *Galesburg Republican Register*, January 3, 1901; E. H. Elmendorf, "Some Things a Boy of Seventeen Should Have Had an Opportunity to Read," *Review of Reviews* 28(December 1903): 713–17; S. Thurber, "English Literature in Girls' Education," *School Review* 2(June 1894): 321–36.

44. Sol Cohen, "The Industrial Education Movement, 1906–17," *American Quarterly* 20(1968): 95–110; David K. Cohen and Marvin Lazerson, "Education and the Corporate Order," *Socialist Revolution* 2(1972): 47–72; John Rury, "Vocationalism for Home and Work: Women's Education in the United States, 1880–1930," *History of Education Quarterly* 34(1984): 21–45.

45. Edith Waterfall, *The Day Continuation School in England: Its Functions and Future* (London: George Allen and Unwin, 1923), 154–55; Helen Todd, "Why Children Work: The Children's Answer," *McClure's Magazine* 40(1913): 38–59; Kantor, *Learning to Earn*, chap. 2.

46. Daniel T. Rodgers, *The Work Ethic in Industrial America, 1850–1920* (Chicago: University of Chicago Press, 1978); Marvin Lazerson and Norton Grubb, eds., *American Education and Vocationalism: A Documentary History* (New York: Teachers College Press, 1974), 18–19, 88–100; Philip R. V. Curoe, *Educational Attitudes and Policies of Organized Labor in the United States* (New York: Teachers College, 1926); Kantor, *Learning to Earn*, 18–25; Paul H. Douglas, *American Apprenticeship and Industrial Education* (New York: Columbia University Press, 1921).

47. Charles W. Eliot, "The Value during Education of the Life Career Motive," in Meyer Bloomfield, ed., *Readings in Vocational Guidance* (Boston: Ginn, 1915), 4. On the middle-class concept of career, see Burton J. Bledstein, *The Culture of Professionalism: The Middle Class and the Development of Higher Education in America* (New York: W. W. Norton, 1976).

48. Edward L. Thorndike, "The University and Vocational Guidance," in Bloomfield, ed., *Vocational Guidance,* 100.

49. Selwyn K. Troen, *The Public and the Schools: Shaping the St. Louis System, 1838–1920* (Columbia: University of Missouri Press, 1975), 196; James D. Anderson, "The Historical Development of Black Vocational Education," in Kantor and Tyack, eds., *Work, Youth, and Schooling,* 180–222; William H. Dooley, *The Education of the Ne'er-Do-Well* (Cambridge: Houghton Mifflin, 1916).

50. Edward C. Elliott, "Equality of Opportunity Can Be Secured Only by Proper Recognition of (a) Individual Differences in Native Capacities and in Social Environment, (b) The Requirements of Vocational Efficiency as Well as of (c) General Intelligence and Executive Power," *NEA Addresses and Proceedings, 1908,* 159–61; Arthur Wirth, *Education in the Technological Society: The Vocational-Liberal Studies Controversy in the Early Twentieth Century* (Scranton, Pa.: Intext Educational Publishers, 1972); Paul Violas, *The Training of the Urban Working Class: A History of Twentieth-Century American Education* (Chicago: Rand McNally, 1978).

51. David Cohen and Bella Rosenberg, "Functions and Fantasies: Understanding Schools in Capitalist America," *History of Education Quarterly* 17(1977): 113–37; Rodgers and Tyack, "Critical Research Areas," 292–94.

52. Counts, *Selective Character;* Joseph F. Kett, "The Adolescence of Vocational Education," in Kantor and Tyack, *Work, Youth, and Schooling,* 79–109.

53. *Providence Report for 1828,* 4; Rodgers and Tyack, "Critical Research Areas," 273–75; Troen, *Public and Schools,* 189.

54. *Digest of Educational Statistics 1980* (Washington, D.C.: GPO), 44; *Historical Statistics of the United States from Colonial Times to 1970* (Washington, D.C.: GPO, 1975), pt. 1, pp. 379, 381; *U.S. Com. Ed. Report for 1917,* 2:38; Goodsell, *Education of Women,* 175; Kantor, *Learning to Earn,* 130.

55. William T. Harris, "Elementary Education," in Nicholas M. Butler, ed., *Monographs on Education in the United States* (Albany: J. B. Lyon, 1900), 32–34; *U.S. Com. Ed. Report for 1889–90,* 2:1351–56.

56. John Francis Latimer, *What's Happened to Our High Schools?* (Washington, D.C.: Public Affairs Press, 1958), 150. Latimer shows that in 1900 almost one-third of the students in high-school manual training classes were girls. Kantor, *Learning to Earn,* 47–59; Goodsell, *Education of Women,* 110–20; Marvin Lazerson, *Origins of the Urban School: Public Education in Massachusetts, 1870–1915* (Cambridge: Harvard University Press, 1971), chap. 4; Clifford, "Educating Women for Work," 242.

57. Lazerson and Grubb, eds., *American Education and Vocationalism,* 32.

58. Since the courses usually enrolled only boys and Latimer's figures are percentages of all students, boys and girls, we have doubled his figures; see Latimer, *What's Happened to High Schools,* 38; Kantor, *Learning to Earn,* 138.

59. John D. Russell et al., *Vocational Education* (Washington, D.C.: GPO, 1938); Percy E. Davidson and H. Dewey Anderson, *Occupational Mobility in an American Community* (Stanford: Stanford University Press, 1937); Kantor, *Learning to Earn,* chap. 8; Kett, "Adolescence."

60. Latimer, *What's Happened to High Schools,* 145, 150, 36; Kantor, *Learning to Earn,* 59–64.

61. Richard Rubinson, "Class Formation, Politics, and Institutions: Schooling in the United States," *American Journal of Sociology* 92(1986): 521, 519–48.

62. Ibid., 521–23.

63. Kantor, *Learning to Earn,* chap. 7.

64. *New York City Report for 1909,* 475; W. J. S. Bryan, "Principals' Conference," *NEA Addresses and Proceedings, 1902,* 485–89; Arthur L. Trester, "The Answer to High School Athletics: What One State Is Doing," *Journal of Education* 98(1923): 268–70; *Quincy Report for 1919,* 32–34; J. M. Garver, "Inter-School Athletics," *Education* 22(1902): 420-25; Timothy P. O'Hanlon, "School Sports as Social Training,: The Case of Athletics and the Crisis of World War I," *Journal of Sports History* 9(1982): 5–29.

65. Jeffrey Mirel, "From Student Control to Institutional Control of High School Athletics: Three Michigan Cities, 1883–1905," *Journal of Social History* 16(1982): 83–100; Joel Spring, "Mass Culture and School Sports," *History of Education Quarterly* 14(1974): 485; Frederick Cozens and Florence Stumpf, "The Rise of the School in the Sports Life of America," in *Sport and American Society:*

Selected Readings (Reading, Mass.: Addison-Wesley, 1974), 104–6; C. W. Hacken-smith, *History of Physical Education* (New York: Harper & Row, 1966), 392–93; Thomas W. Gutowski, "Student Initiative and the Origins of the High School Extracurriculum: Chicago, 1880–1915," *History of Education Quarterly* 28(1988): 49–72.

66. "Symposium on Physical Training in the Public Schools," *NEA Addresses and Proceedings, 1897*, 898–909.

67. M. V. O'Shea, "Physical Training in the Public Schools," *Atlantic Monthly* 75(1895): 246–54; *U.S. Com. Ed. Report for 1889–90*, 603–11.

68. Rebecca Stoneroad, "How Far Should Physical Training Be Educational and How Far Recreative in Grammar Schools?" *NEA Addresses and Proceedings, 1905*, 771. Stoneroad was not a killjoy (she wanted more "joy and happiness" in the gymnastics), but she was a realist about what was possible in crowded schools.

69. Pictures of the Washington, D.C., schools in 1899 by Frances Johnston (in the Library of Congress) show both sexes doing their calisthenics together and "yawning and stretching." On play, see, for example, George E. Johnson, "Play in Physical Education," *NEA Addresses and Proceedings, 1898*, 948–58.

70. J. H. McCurdy, "A Study in the Characteristics of Physical Training in the Public Schools of the United States," *American Physical Education Review* 10(1905): 206, 211, 202–13.

71. William Orr, "The Place of Athletics in the Curriculum of Secondary Schools for Girls and Boys," *American Physical Education Review* 12(1907): 50; Trester, "High School Athletics," 268; A. H. Maurer, "Football in the High School," *Educational Review* 40(1910): 132–37; Alfred E. Stearns, "Athletics and the School," *Atlantic Monthly* 113(1914): 148–53 (Stearns argued that football had developed a code of ethics that was "nothing less than base, deceitful, and dishonorable," and that the coaches were quite as much to blame as the boys); McCurdy, "Physical Training," 212–13; Luther H. Gulick, "Athletics for School Children," *Lippincott's Magazine* 88(1911): 201.

72. Trester, "High School Athletics"; Orr, "The Place of Athletics."

73. Bryan, "Principals' Conference," 485, 486, 488.

74. Ibid., 486, 488; D. A. Sargent, "Athletics in Secondary Schools," *American Physical Education Review* 8(1903): 57–69; "The Question of School and College Athletics," *School Review* 10(1902): 4–8; *Quincy Report for 1910*, 33.

75. Gulick quoted on p. 269 of *New York City Report for 1904;* Luther H. Gulick, "Games and Gangs, *Lippincott's Magazine* 88(1911): 84–89; Jacob A. Riis, "Fighting the Gang with Athletics: Stopping Bad Habits by Substituting What the Girls and Boys Like Better," *Colliers,* February 11, 1911, p. 17; J. Thomas Jable, "The Public Schools Athletic League of New York City: Organized Athletics for City Schoolchildren, 1903–1914," in Wayne M. Ladd and Angela Lumbkin, eds., *Sport in American Education: History and Perspectives* (Washington, D.C.: American Alliance for Health, Physical Education, Recreation and Dance, 1978), 1–18.

76. Roosevelt quoted in Jable, "Public Schools Athletic League," 5; Luther H. Gulick, "Team Games and Civic Loyalty," *School Review* 14(1906): 676–78; "School Athletics," *World's Work* 44(1922): 242. Not all school people agreed with Roosevelt about the value of football; because of injuries and deaths, the New York schools abolished football in 1909, though other sports continued (see *New York City Report for 1909,* 439-40).

77. Spring, "School Sports," 493–94; McCurdy, "Physical Training," 213.

78. In the 1960s, when attention focused on poor and minority students, the charge arose again that such boys did poorly in school in part because the schools were feminized environments. See Daniel Levine, "Coeducation—A Contributing Factor in Miseducation of the Disadvantaged," *Phi Delta Kappan* 46(1964): 126–28; Gary L. Peltier, "Sex Differences in the School: Problem and Solution," *Phi Delta Kappan* 50(1968): 182–86; Thomas B. Lyles, "Grouping by Sex," *National Elementary School Principal* 46(1966): 38–41; William Goldman and Anne May, "Males: A Minority in the Classroom," *Journal of Learning Disabilities* 3(1970): 39–41; Patricia Cayo Sexton, *The Feminized Male: Classrooms, White-Collars, and the Decline of Manliness* (New York: Random House, 1969).

Chapter 8. Differentiating the High School: The "Woman Question"

1. M. Carey Thomas, "A New-Fashioned Argument for Woman Suffrage" (Speech delivered to the National College League for Woman Suffrage, October 17, 1908), as quoted in Eleanor Flexner, *Century of Struggle: The Woman's Rights Movement in the United States* (Cambridge: Harvard University Press, 1975), 238, 243.

2. Marguerite Stockman Dickson, *Vocational Guidance for Girls* (Chicago: Rand McNally, 1919), 3–4; W. Elliott Brownlee and Mary M. Brownlee, *Women in the American Economy: A Documentary History, 1675 to 1929* (New Haven: Yale University Press, 1976), 3; Thomas Woody, *A History of Women's Education in the United States* (New York: Science Press, 1929), vol. 2, chap. 1; Flexner, *Century of Struggle,* chaps. 18-22; William L. O'Neill, "Divorce in the Progressive Era," in Michael Gordon, ed., *The American Family in Social-Historical Perspective* (New York: St. Martin's Press, 1973), 252; Richard Jensen, "Family, Career, and Reform: Women Leaders of the Progressive Era," in Gordon, ed., *American Family,* 267–80; Mary P. Ryan, *Womanhood in America: From Colonial Times to the Present,* 2d ed. (New York: New Viewpoints, 1979), chap. 4.

3. Carolyn C. Lougee, "Noblesse, Domesticity, and Social Reform: The Education of Girls by Fenelon and Saint Cyr," *History of Education Quarterly* 15(1974): 87; John L. Rury, "Vocationalism for Home and Work: Women's Education in the United States, 1880–1930," *History of Education Quarterly* 24(1984): 21–44.

4. Robert W. Smuts, *Women and Work in America* (New York: Schocken Books, 1971), 111, chap. 4; Flexner, *Century of Struggle,* 255.

5. Edward O'Donnell, "Women as Breadwinners—The Error of the Age,"

American Federationist 4(1897), as quoted in Rosalyn Baxandall, Linda Gordon, and Susan Reverby, eds., *America's Working Women* (New York: Vintage Books, 1976), 167–69; Brownlee and Brownlee, *Women in the Economy,* chap. 4.

6. Woody, *Women's Education,* 2:40; O'Neill, "Divorce"; Carl N. Degler, *At Odds: Women and the Family in America from the Revolution to the Present* (New York: Oxford University Press, 1980), chaps. 13–14; George MacAdam, "Feminist Apartment House to Solve Baby Problem," as quoted in June Sochen, ed., *The New Feminism in Twentieth-Century America* (Lexington, Mass.: D.C. Heath, 1971), 50–58; Flexner, *Century of Struggle,* 236, 239–40.

7. Mary Putnam-Jacobi, *"Common-Sense" Applied to Woman Suffrage* (New York: G. P. Putnam and Sons, 1894), 17–18; Rose Schneiderman quoted in Wage Earners' Equal Suffrage League of New York, "Senators Versus Working Women," March 20, 1912, p. 5, as reproduced in Flexner, *Century of Struggle,* 267.

8. San Jose High School, *Bell* (June 1908): 39, as quoted in Millicent Rutherford, "Feminism and the Secondary School Curriculum, 1890–1920" (Ph.D. diss., Stanford University, 1977), 133; Ryan, *Womanhood in America,* 148–49; Susan B. Anthony and Ida Husted Harper, eds., *The History of Woman Suffrage,* 6 vols. (Rochester: Susan B. Anthony, 1902), 4:171; Ida Husted Harper, ed., *The History of Woman Suffrage* (New York: National American Woman Suffrage Association, 1922); Flexner, *Century of Struggle,* 271; Degler, *At Odds,* chap. 13.

9. Rutherford, "Feminism and the Secondary School Curriculum," 35; the mentions of suffrage are in NEA Committee on Resolutions, "Ratification of Suffrage Amendment," *NEA Addresses and Proceedings, 1920,* 25; Mrs. G. Howland Shaw and Mrs. Francis M. Scott, "Woman Suffrage in the United States," *Educational Review* 38(1909): 405.

10. Anna J. Hamilton, "What Kind of Education Is Best Suited for Girls?" *NEA Addresses and Proceedings, 1906,* 72; "Teachers Want Votes—Kansas State Teachers' Association Unanimous for Woman's Ballot," *The Woman's Journal* (November 25, 1911): 369; "Boston Teachers Out in Favor, Say if Justice and Proper Pay Are to Be Won, Must Have Ballot," *The Woman's Journal* (April 24, 1915): 134; Alice Stone Blackwell, "Do Teachers Need the Ballot?" *The Woman's Journal* (October) 174; Degler, *At Odds,* 347.

For discussions of activists among women teachers and administrators, see Margaret Gribskov, "Feminism and the Woman School Administrator," in Sari Knopp Biklen and Marilyn B. Brannigan, eds., *Women and Educational Leadership* (Lexington, Mass.; Lexington Books, 1980), 65–75; Geraldine Jonçich Clifford, "The Female Teacher and the Feminist Movement" (unpublished paper, University of California, Berkeley); Jensen, "Women Leaders," p. 173; David Tyack and Elisabeth Hansot, *Managers of Virtue: Public School Leadership in America, 1820–1980* (New York: Basic Books, 1982), chap. 13.

11. Annie G. Porritt, "The Feminization of Our Schools and Its Political Consequences," *Educational Review* 44(1911): 441, 442–43, 448.

12. Ibid., 445, 448.

13. C. W. Bardeen, "The Monopolizing Woman Teacher," *Educational Review* 43(1912): 27; Frederick Burk, "The Withered Heart of the Schools," *Educational Review* 34(1907): 448–56; Margaret Haley, "Why Teachers Should Organize," *NEA Addresses and Proceedings, 1904,* 145–52; Margaret Haley, *Battleground,* ed. Robert Reid (Urbana: University of Illinois Press, 1982); Patricia Anne Carter, "A Coalition Between Women Teachers and the Feminist Movement in New York City, 1900–1920" (Ed.D. diss., University of Cincinnati, 1985).

14. Jane Bernard Powers, "The 'Girl Question' in Education: Vocational Training for Young Women in the Progressive Era" (Ph.D. diss., Stanford University, 1986), chaps. 2, 6, 8; Willystine Goodsell, *The Education of Women: Its Social Background and Its Problems* (New York: Macmillan, 1924), 110–121.

15. Geraldine Jonçich Clifford, "'Marry, Stitch, Die, or Do Worse,': Educating Women for Work," in Harvey Kantor and David B. Tyack, eds., *Work, Youth, and Schooling: Historical Perspectives on Vocationalism in American Education* (Stanford: Stanford University Press, 1982), 223–68; Rury, "Vocationalism"; Powers, "Girl Question."

16. Clifford, "Educating Women for Work," 265, 261–68; Eli Ginzberg, "Introduction," in Smuts, *Women and Work,* ix; Kantor, *Learning to Earn,* chap. 7.

17. Brownlee and Brownlee, *Women in the Economy,* 25–31; they note that this middle-class model was also one that native-born reformers urged immigrant mothers to adopt.

18. Joan W. Scott and Louise A. Tilly point out that much confusion has resulted from a middle-class model that presupposes that "women at home are assumed to be non-productive, the antithesis of women at work"; see Joan W. Scott and Louise A. Tilly, "Women's Work and the Family in Nineteenth-Century Europe," *Comparative Studies in Society and History* 17(1975): 36, 36–64; Smuts, *Women and Work,* 6–11; John Dewey, *The School and Society* (Chicago: University of Chicago Press, 1899); Ellwood P. Cubberley, *Rural Life and Education: A Study of the Rural-School Problem as a Phase of the Rural-Life Problem* (Boston: Houghton Mifflin, 1914).

19. Smuts, *Women and Work,* 9–10; Gerda Lerner, ed., *Black Women in White America: A Documentary History* (New York: Vintage Books, 1973).

20. Smuts, *Women and Work,* 38; Baxandall, Gordon, and Reverby, eds., *Working Women,* 406–87. For explorations of the experience of assimilation from the immigrants' perspective, see Maxine Schwartz Seller, ed., *Immigrant Women* (Philadelphia: Temple University Press, 1981); Corinne Azen Krause, "Urbanization Without Breakdown: Italian, Jewish, and Slavic Women in Pittsburgh, 1900 to 1945," *Journal of Urban History* 4(1978): 291–306; Janice Reiff Webster, "Domestication and Americanization: Scandinavian Women in Seattle, 1888 to 1900," *Journal of Urban History* 4(1978): 275–90.

21. Edith A. Abbott, *Women in Industry* (New York: D. Appleton, 1910); Harriet Hazen Dodge, *Survey of Occupations Open to the Girl of Fourteen to Sixteen Years*

(Boston: Girls' Trade Education League, 1912); Albert H. Leake, *The Vocational Education of Girls and Women* (New York: MacMillan, 1918), 265; Goodsell, *Education of Women,* chap. 6; Flexner, *Century of Struggle,* chaps. 17–18; Alice Kessler-Harris, *Women Have Always Worked: A Historical Overview* (Old Westbury, Conn.: Feminist Press, 1981), chap. 3.

22. Margaret Dreier Robins, *Life and Labor* (August 1913), p. 231, as quoted in Powers, "Girl Question," p. 107; Powers quoted p. 105. On the often uneasy relation between unionized working women and their elite allies, see Robin Miller Jacoby, "The Women's Trade Union League and American Feminism," and Nancy Schrom Dye, "Creating a Feminist Alliance: Sisterhood and Class Conflict in the New York Woman's Trade Union League, 1903–1914," in Milton Cantor and Bruce Laurie, eds., *Class, Sex, and the Woman Worker* (Westport, Conn.: Greenwood Press, 1977), 203–24, 225–45.

23. Powers, "Girl Question," 118–19, 74–75.

24. Goodsell, *Education of Women,* 105–8; Leake, *Vocational Education,* 6–7.

25. Ruth Milkman, "Organizing the Sexual Division of Labor: Historical Perspectives on 'Women's Work' and the American Labor Movement," *Socialist Review* 49(1980): 95–159; James D. Anderson, "The Historical Development of Black Vocational Education," in Kantor and Tyack, eds., *Work, Youth, and Schooling,* 180–222.

26. Winifred Richmond, "Present Practices and Tendencies in the Secondary Education of Girls," *Pedagogical Seminary* 23(June 1916): 193–4; Goodsell, *Education of Women,* 178; Elizabeth W. Burbank, "Profitable Training for Girls," *Vocational Education Magazine* 1(1923): 610; Powers, "Girl Question," 146–50, 163–64, chap. 9.

27. Richmond, "Present Practices," 193; Rury, "Vocationalism," 29–34.

28. Kantor, *Learning to Earn,* xiii, 59–63; Powers, "Girl Question," chaps. 3 and 10.

29. Janice Weiss, "Educating for Clerical Work: The Nineteenth-Century Private Commercial School," *Journal of Social History* 14(1981): 407–23; John Francis Latimer, *What's Happened to Our High Schools?* (Washington, D.C.: Public Affairs Press, 1958), 35–37. Latimer points out that the percentage of boys in commercial courses was 96 in 1871 and 72 in 1890. Nancy S. Jackson and Jane S. Gaskell trace the middle-class origins of commercial education in Canada in "White-Collar Vocationalism: The Rise of Commercial Education in Ontario and British Columbia, 1870–1920," *Curriculum Inquiry* 17(1987): 177–201.

30. Powers, "Girl Question," 80; Latimer, *What's Happened to High Schools?* 145; Baxandall, Gordon, and Reverby, eds. *Working Women,* 407.

31. Elyse J. Rotella, *From Home to Office: U.S. Women at Work, 1870–1930* (Ann Arbor: UMI Research Press, 1981); Margery W. Davies, *Woman's Place Is at the Typewriter: Office Work and Office Workers, 1870–1930* (Philadelphia: Temple University Press, 1982).

32. Powers, "Girl Question," 210; Robert S. and Helen M. Lynd, *Middletown: A Study in Modern American Culture* (New York: Harcourt, Brace and World, 1956; reprint of 1929 ed.), 49; George S. Counts, *The Selective Character of American Secondary Education* (Chicago: University of Chicago Press, 1922), 57; Miriam Cohen, "Italian-American Women in New York City, 1900–1950: Work and School," in Cantor and Laurie, eds., *Class,* 120–43; Jackson and Gaskell, "White-Collar Vocationalism."

33. Letter in *Jewish Daily Forward* (August 8, 1905), as quoted in Powers, "Girl Question," 212. John L. Rury, "Education and Women's Work: Female Schooling and the Division of Labor in American Life, 1870–1930" (MS, DePaul University, June 1988), 246–47; immigrant student quoted in Nona Goodwin, "Socializing Influences in a Part-Time School for Girls," *Chicago Schools Journal* 5(September 1922): 5, as quoted in Lisa Fine, "Commercial Education in Chicago" (MS, History Department, University of Wisconsin-Madison, 1984); letter in *Jewish Daily Forward* (August 8, 1905), as quoted in Powers, "Girl Question," 212. Rury gives rich detail on class and ethnic issues in women's work.

34. Kantor, *Learning to Earn,* 61; Powers, "Girl Question," 203; Rury, "Education and Women's Work," 399.

35. Susan B. Carter and Mark Prus, "The Labor Market and the American High School Girl, 1890–1928," *Journal of Economic History* 42(1982): 163–71.

36. Rury, "Vocationalism," 33–34.

37. As Jackson and Gaskell show in "White-Collar Vocationalism," there was considerable covert or unconscious ideological baggage in the form of sex stereotyping in commercial education, as in the whole educational enterprise. This is especially apparent in the textbooks preparing women to be clerical workers, which stress their feminine subordination to male bosses.

38. William J. Reese discusses women school reformers in *Power and the Promise of School Reform: Grassroots Movements during the Progressive Era* (Boston: Routledge & Kegan Paul, 1986), chap. 2.

39. Rury, "Vocationalism," 23, 22–29; Powers, "Girl Question," chap. 2—senator quoted on pp. 33–34; Ellen Richards, "The Social Significance of the Home Economics Movement," *Journal of Home Economics* 3(1911): 116–22; Hamilton, "Education for Girls"; J. McKeen Cattell, "The School and the Family," *Popular Science Monthly* 124(1909): 84–95.

40. Powers, "Girl Question," 157–66, 130–31; Kate Brew Vaughn, "Some Colored Schools of the South," *Journal of Home Economics* 8(1916): 583–89.

41. Mary Leal Harkness, "The Education of the Girl," *Atlantic Monthly* 113(1914): 324.

42. Ibid., 325, 328–29.

43. Catharine Beecher, *Treatise on Domestic Economy for the Use of Young Ladies at Home and at School* (Boston: T. H. Webb, 1843); Karen J. Blair, *The Clubwoman as Feminist: True Womanhood Redefined, 1868–1914* (New York: Holmes and Meier, 1980). For a discussion of the value of "female institution building" and creating a

"strong, public female sector," see Estelle Freedman, "Separatism as Strategy: Female Institution Building and American Feminism, 1870–1930," *Feminist Studies* 5(1979): 512–29.

44. Powers, "Girl Question"; senator is quoted pp. 145–46, chap. 6; Rutherford, "Feminism," chaps. 3, 5.

45. Powers, "Girl Question," 163–65, 175–78; Rury, "Vocationalism," 28–29; Vaughn, "Colored Schools," 588; Lerner, ed., *Black Women,* chap. 3; Paula Giddings, *Where and When I Enter: The Impact of Black Women on Race and Sex in America* (New York: Bantam Books, 1984), 33, 101, 204.

46. George S. Counts, *The Senior High School Curriculum* (Chicago: University of Chicago Press, 1926), 104; Powers, "Girl Question," 174–75; Rury, "Vocationalism," 28–29; Kantor, *Learning to Earn,* 72.

47. Michael Imber, "Analysis of a Curriculum Reform Movement: The American Social Hygiene Association's Campaign for Sex Education, 1900–1930" (Ph.D. diss., Stanford University, 1980, chaps. 2–3); Degler, *At Odds,* chap. 12; John D'Emilio and Estelle Freedman, *Intimate Matters: A History of Sexuality in America* (New York: Harper & Row, 1988), 153–57, 176–77.

48. Imber, "Curriculum Reform Movement," chaps. 2–3; also see Michael Imber, "Toward a Theory of Curriculum Reform: An Analysis of the First Campaign for Sex Education," *Curriculum Inquiry* 12(1982): 339–61; Michael Imber, "Toward a Theory of Educational Origins: The Genesis of Sex Education," *Educational Theory* 34(Summer 1984): 275–86; Michael Imber, "The First World War, Sex Education, and the American Social Hygiene Association's Campaign against Venereal Disease," *Journal of Educational Administration and History* 16(January 1984): 47–56.

49. Charles Richmond Henderson, "Education with Reference to Sex," in National Society for the Study of Education, *Eighth Yearbook, Part I* (Chicago: NSSE, 1909), 74.

50. Brian Strong, "Ideas of the Early Sex Education Movement in America, 1890–1920," *History of Education Quarterly* 12(1962): 135, 129–61.

51. Ralph E. Blount, "The Responsibility of the Teacher with Regard to the Teaching of Sex Hygiene," *NEA Addresses and Proceedings, 1914,* 470; Strong, "Sex Education," p. 129 (Hall quoted on p. 148); William Byron Forbush, *The Boy Problem: A Study in Social Pedagogy* (Boston: Pilgrim Press, 1901), 140–43; John C. Burnham, "The Progressive Era Revolution in American Attitudes toward Sex," *Journal of American History* 59(March 1973): 885–908.

52. Strong, "Sex Education," 142.

53. Imber, "Curriculum Reform Movement," chaps. 4 and 6; sex educator quoted in Strong, "Sex Education," 150; Benjamin C. Gruenberg, "What Girls Want to Know," *School Review* 26(1918): 750.

54. Imber, "Curriculum Reform Movement," 66–67; Mary Beard, *Woman's Work in Municipalities* (New York: A. Appleton, 1915), 6–8, 15.

55. Newell W. Edson, *The Status of Sex Education in High Schools* (Washington,

D.C.: GPO, 1922), 3–12; Imber, "Curriculum Reform Movement," 97, 100–101.

56. Imber, "Curriculum Reform Movement," 101–5, 112–14; Lynds, *Middletown,* 146.

57. Imber, "Curriculum Reform Movement," chap. 8.

58. Ibid.

59. On community reluctance to teach about sex and eagerness to glorify sports, see Willard Waller, *The Sociology of Teaching* (New York: John Wiley and Sons, 1932).

60. Beard, *Woman's Work in Municipalities,* chap. 1; James L. Leloudis, II, "School Reform in the New South: The Woman's Association for the Betterment of Public School Houses in North Carolina, 1902–1919," *Journal of American History* 69(March 1983): 886–909; Laura Drake Gill, "Service of Organized Women to the Public School," *Sierra Educational News* 5(August 1909): 25–29. The National Education Association had a special department to represent these women's groups; see E. E. Brown, "The Work of Women's Organizations in Education: Suggestions for Effective Co-Operation," *NEA Addresses and Proceedings, 1908,* 1218–22. For earlier discussions of women's role in reforms, see "Woman's Work in Education," *NEA Addresses and Proceedings, 1884,* 167–76, and *U.S. Com. Ed. Report for 1897–98,* 1:666–72.

61. Committee of Ten on Secondary School Studies, NEA, *Report* (New York: Published for NEA by American Book Company, 1893).

62. Commission on the Reorganization of Secondary Education, *Cardinal Principles of Secondary Education,* U.S. Bureau of Education Bulletin no. 35-1918 (Washington, D.C.: GPO, 1918).

63. Barbara Brenzel, Cathy Roberts-Gersh, and Judith Wittner, "Becoming Social: School Girls and Their Culture between the Two World Wars," *Journal of Early Adolescence* 5(1985): 479–88; Thomas W. Gutowski, "Student Initiative and the Origins of the High School Extracurriculum: Chicago, 1880–1915," *History of Education Quarterly* 28(1988): 49–72; Nancy Green, "Gender Differences in the High School Experience: Chicago, 1920–1940" (Paper delivered at the History of Education Society, Chicago, Ill. October 19, 1984); Romiet Stevens, "The Adviser of Girls in High School," *Teachers College Record* 20(1919): 301–23; Sarah M. Sturtevant, "The Dean of Girls in the Secondary School," *News-Bulletin of the Bureau of Vocational Education* 2(1924): 145–47, 150.

64. Warren Leon, "High School: A Study of Youth and Community in Quincy, Massachusetts" (Ph.D. diss., Harvard University, 1979), 78–93.

65. Biklen, "Progressive Education," 321–25; Larry Cuban, *How Teachers Taught: Constancy and Change in American Classrooms, 1890–1980* (New York: Longman, 1985).

66. Edward A. Krug, *The Shaping of the American High School* (New York: Harper & Row, 1964); Kantor and Tyack, *Work, Youth, and Schooling.*

67. Richmond, "Present Practices," 185; Goodsell, *Education of Women,* 178–79.

68. Latimer, *What's Happened to High Schools?* 149–50; Elon G. Salisbury, *Recent State Legislation for Physical Education,* U.S. Bureau of Education, Bulletin 1-1922 (Washington, D.C.: GPO, 1922), 15.

69. Fletcher B. Dresslar, *American Schoolhouses,* U.S. Bureau of Education, Bulletin no. 5-1910 (Washington, D.C.: GPO, 1911) plates 72–81. On regularities in the structure of teaching, see Larry Cuban, *How Teachers Taught.*

70. P. W. Horn, *Report of Supplementary Survey of Portland Public Schools* (Portland, Oreg.: Jefferson High School Press, 1917), 7.

71. For general studies in enrollment trends (mostly without regard to sex), see George E. Van Dyke, "Trends in the Development of the High School Offering," *School Review* 39(November and December 1931): 657–64, 737–47; and U.S. Office of Education, *Offerings and Registrations in High-School Subjects, 1933–34,* Bulletin no. 6-1938 (Washington, D.C.: GPO, 1938).

72. National Center for Education Statistics, *Digest of Educational Statistics, 1974* (Washington, D.C.: GPO, 1974), 7, 54.

73. Arthur Stinchcombe, "Social Structure and Organizations," in James March, ed., *Handbook of Organizations* (Chicago: Rand McNally, 1965), 143–60.

74. John Dewey, "Is Coeducation Injurious to Girls? What Coeducation Has Done," *Ladies Home Journal* 28(June 11, 1911): 22, 60–61. Dewey's colleague at Chicago, J. H. Tufts, also ridiculed the idea that academic subjects could be gendered; see "Editorial Notes," *School Review* 17(January 1909): 56. On sex differences in the teaching of academic subjects in Germany, see Yoshi Kasuya, *A Comparative Study of Secondary Education of Girls in England, Germany, and the United States, with a Consideration of the Secondary Education of Girls in Japan* (New York: Teachers College, 1933), 131–34.

75. Dewey, "Coeducation," 61.

76. For the views of one feminist—a New York teacher—who did want to erase sex stereotyping, see George MacAdam, "Feminist Apartment House to Solve Baby Problem," *New York Times,* January 24, 1915, pt. 5, p. 9, as reprinted in June Sochen, ed., *The New Feminism in Twentieth-Century America* (Lexington, Mass.: D. C. Heath, 1971), 56.

Chapter 9. Feminists Discover the Hidden Injuries of Coeducation

1. Rodman quoted in George MacAdam, "Feminist Apartment House to Solve Baby Problem," *New York Times,* January 24, 1915, pt. 5, p. 9, in June Sochen, ed., *The New Feminism in Twentieth-Century America* (Lexington, Mass.: D. C. Heath, 1971), 56.

2. Crystal Eastman, "Now We Can Begin," *The Liberator* 3(1920), 23–24, as quoted in Sochen, ed., *New Feminism,* 65–66. For an analysis of this broader kind of feminism, which had little influence until recently in education, see Nancy F. Cott, *The Grounding of Modern Feminism* (New Haven: Yale University Press, 1987).

3. Nancy Frazier and Myra Sadker, *Sexism in School and Society* (New York: Harper & Row, 1973). On p. 2 they quote a definition of "sexism" by Kathleen Shortridge: "(1) A belief that the human sexes have a distinctive make-up that determines their respective lives, usually involving the idea that one sex is superior and has the right to rule the other; (2) a policy of enforcing such asserted right; (3) a system of government and society based upon it." The term "sexism," derived from "racism," was used by Prof. Margaret Feldman during the fall of 1968 and gained currency at a conference on women at Cornell in 1969; letter from Dr. Feldman to David Tyack, January 29, 1989.

4. Caroline Bird, *Born Female: The High Cost of Keeping Women Down* (New York: Pocket Books, 1971); Terry Saario, Carol Nagy Jacklin, and Carol Tittle, "Sex-Role Stereotyping in the Public Schools," *Harvard Educational Review* 43(1973): 386–418.

5. William Chafe, *Women and Equality: Changing Patterns in American Culture* (New York: Oxford University Press, 1977), chap. 5; Kirsten Amundsen, *The Silenced Majority* (Englewood Cliffs, N.J.: Prentice-Hall, 1971), 70, 78–80.

6. Betty Friedan, *The Feminine Mystique* (New York: Dell, 1963); Brigid Brophy, "Women Are Prisoners of Their Sex," *Saturday Evening Post,* November 2, 1963, p. 10; David M. Potter, "American Women and the American Character" (written in 1962), in Don E. Fehrenbacher, ed., *History and American Society: Essays of David M. Potter* (New York: Oxford University Press, 1973), 277–303.

7. Barbara Sinclair Deckard, *The Women's Movement: Political, Socioeconomic and Psychological Issues* (New York: Harper & Row, 1979) 341; Therese L. Baker, "Changes in the Educational and Career Plans of American High School Senior Women in the Past Quarter-Century: A Comparative Cohort Study of National Samples of Women Seniors in 1960, 1972, and 1980" (unpublished manuscript, Department of Sociology, DePaul University, tables 1 and 3); Karen Oppenheim Mason, John L. Czaja, and Sara Arber, "Change in U.S. Women's Sex-Role Attitudes, 1964–1974," *American Sociological Review* 41(1976): 589, 573–96.

8. Kathleen M. Dalton, *A Portrait of a School: Coeducation at Andover* (Andover, Massachusetts: Phillips Academy, 1986), 1.

9. Janice Pottker and Andrew Fishel, eds., *Sex Bias in the Schools: The Research Evidence* (Rutherford, N.J.: Farleigh Dickinson University Press, 1977).

10. Ellen Carol DuBois et al., *Feminist Scholarship: Kindling in the Groves of Academe* (Urbana: University of Illinois Press, 1985) analyzes feminist scholarship in education and other fields; the authors point out (pp. 175–77) that there was not much feminist scholarship in mainstream research journals in education, but there were many articles after 1969 in policy-oriented and practitioner journals, a number of which devoted special issues to feminist scholarship.

11. Walter B. Waetgen and Jean D. Grambs, "Sex Differences: A Case of Educational Evasion?" *Teachers College Record* 65(1963): 261–71; E. S. Carter, "How Valid Are Marks Assigned by Teachers?" *Journal of Educational Psychology* 43(1952):

218–28; Earl H. Hansen, "Do Boys Get a Square Deal in School?" *Education* 79(1959): 597–98; Jean Stockhard, "Sex Differences in Behavior, Learning Problems, and Attitudes" in Jean Stockhard et al., *Sex Equity in Education* (New York: Academic Press, 1980), chap. 2; Jerome Kagan, "The Child's Sex-Role Classification of School Objects," *Child Development* 35(1964): 1051–56; Daniel Levine, "Coeducation—A Contributing Factor in Miseducation of the Disadvantaged," *Phi Delta Kappan* 46(1964): 126–28; Gary L. Peltier, "Sex Differences in the School: Problem and Proposed Solution," *Phi Delta Kappan* 50(1968): 182–85; Patricia Cayo Sexton, *The Feminized Male: Classrooms, White Collars, and the Decline of Manliness* (New York: Random House, 1969); F. C. Ellenburg, "Elementary Teachers: Male or Female?" *Journal of Teacher Education* 26(1975): 329–34. For a recent call for male teachers for inner-city schools, see Spencer H. Holland, "A Radical Approach to Educating Young Black Males," *Education Week,* March 28, 1987.

12. "Schoolbook Sex Bias," *Nation's Schools* 91(1972), as reprinted in Pottker and Fishel, *Sex Bias,* 529–30.

13. Frazier and Sadker, *Sexism;* in her introduction to the book, Florence Howe discusses the gap between rapid progress in instituting women's studies in higher education and the slower pace of feminist changes in the public schools. One of the earliest and most perceptive articles linking sex stereotyping in schools with gender stratification was Alice S. Rossi, "Equality Between the Sexes: An Immodest Proposal," in Robert Jay Lifton, ed., *The Woman in America* (Boston: Beacon Press, 1967; reprint of *Daedalus,* Spring 1964), 88–143.

14. Jo Freeman, ed., *Social Movements of the Sixties and Seventies* (New York: Longman, 1983); Florence Howe, *The Myths of Coeducation: Selected Essays, 1964–1983* (Bloomington, Ind.: Indiana University Press, 1984).

15. Flexner, *Century of Struggle,* chaps. 4–6; Chafe, *Women and Equality,* chaps. 3–4; Jo Freeman, "The Women's Liberation Movement: Its Origins, Structure, Activities, and Ideas," in Jo Freeman, ed., *Women: A Feminist Perspective* (Palo Alto, Ca.: Mayfield Publishing, 1984), 543–56.

16. David Tyack, Thomas James, and Aaron Benavot, *Law and the Shaping of Public Schools, 1785–1954* (Madison: University of Wisconsin Press, 1987), chap. 5, epilogue.

17. E. R. Feagin and Clairece Booher Feagin, *Discrimination American Style: Institutional Racism and Sexism* (Englewood Cliffs, N.J.: Prentice-Hall, 1978), chaps. 1–2, 5.

18. Gayle Rubin, "Woman as Nigger," *Argus,* March 28–April 11, 1970, as quoted in Amundsen, *Silenced Majority,* 44.

19. For data on school performance by sex, see Marcia C. Linn and Anne C. Petersen, "Facts and Assumptions about the Nature of Sex Differences," in Susan S. Klein, ed., *Handbook for Achieving Sex Equity through Education* (Baltimore: Johns Hopkins Press, 1985), 53–90; for analyses of the relation between class and gender,

see Stephen Walker and Len Barton, eds., *Gender, Class, and Education* (New York: Falmer Press, 1983).

20. For an example of one local investigation into sexist practices in schools, see Education Committee, New York Chapter of NOW, *Report on Sex Bias in the Public Schools,* 4th ed. (New York: NOW, 1977). For a handbook aimed at educators, see Myra Pollack Sadker and David Miller Sadker, *Sex Equity Handbook for Schools* (New York: Longman, 1982).

21. Marjorie U'Ren, "The Image of Women in Textbooks," in Vivian Gornick and Barbara Moran, eds., *Woman in Sexist Society* (New York: Basic Books, 1971), 218–25. Janice Pottker, "Psychological and Occupational Sex Stereotypes in Elementary School Readers"; and Janice Law Trecker, "Women in U.S. History High-School Textbooks," in Pottker and Fishel, eds., *Sex Bias,* 111–162. Women on Words and Images, "Look, Jane, Look: See Sex Stereotypes," in Judith Stacey, Susan Bereaud, and Joan Daniels, eds., *And Jill Came Tumbling After: Sexism in American Education* (New York: Dell, 1974), 159–77.

22. Pauline Sears and David Feldman, "Teacher Interaction with Boys and Girls," *National Elementary Principal* 46(1966): 30–35; Betty Levy and Judith Stacey, "Sexism in the Elementary School: A Backward and Forward Look," *Phi Delta Kappan* 55(1973): 105–23; Raphaela Best, *We've All Got Scars: What Boys and Girls Learn in Elementary School* (Bloomington: University of Indiana Press, 1983); Jere Brophy, "Interactions of Male and Female Students with Male and Female Teachers," in Louise Cherry Wilkinson and Cera B. Marrett, *Gender Influences in Classroom Interaction* (New York: Academic Press, 1985), 115–42.

23. John J. Pietrofesa and Nancy K. Scholsberg, "Counselor Bias and the Female Occupational Role," and Carol Kehr Tittle, Karen McCarthy, and Jane Faggen Steckler, "Women and Educational Testing," in Fishel and Pottker, eds., *Sex Bias,* 217–220, 256–74.

24. Celeste Ulrich, "She Can Play as Good as Any Boy," *Phi Delta Kappan* 60(1973): 113–17.

25. David Sadker and Myra Sadker, "The Treatment of Sex Equity in Teacher Education," in Klein, ed., *Handbook for Sex Equity,* 145–62.

26. Marcia C. Linn and Anne C. Petersen, "Facts and Assumptions about the Nature of Sex Differences," and Elizabeth K. Stage et al., "Increasing the Participation and Achievement of Girls and Women in Mathematics, Science, and Engineering," in Klein, ed., *Handbook for Sex Equity,* 53–90, 237–58; Elizabeth Fennema, "Girls, Women, and Mathematics," in Elizabeth Fennema, ed., *Women and Education: Equity or Equality* (Berkeley: McCutchan, 1984), 137–65.

27. Suzanne S. Taylor, "Educational Leadership: A Male Domain?" *Phi Delta Kappan* 70(1973): 124–28; Catherine Dillon Lyon and Terry N. Saario, "Women in Public Education: Sexual Discrimination in Promotions," *Phi Delta Kappan* 60(1973): 120–23; Suzanne Estler, "Women as Leaders in Public Education," *Signs* 1(1975): 363–86; Andrew Fishel and Janice Pottker, "Women in Educational

Governance: A Statistical Portrait," in Pottker and Fishel, eds., *Sex Bias,* 505–13.

28. Dale Spender, *Invisible Women: The Schooling Scandal* (London: Writers and Readers Publishing Cooperative Society, 1982); Dale Spender, *Men's Studies Modified: The Impact of Feminism on the Academic Disciplines* (Oxford: Pergamon, 1981), chap. 11. For a discussion of the patriarchal paradigm, see Joan Scott, "Is Gender a Useful Category of Historical Analysis?" *American Historical Review* 91(1986): 1053–75.

29. The 1970s produced a plethora of self-help books for women. On problems with the sex-role socialization model, see R. W. Connell, "Theorising Gender," *Sociology* 19(1985): 260–72; Judith Stacey and Barrie Thorne, "The Missing Feminist Revolution in Sociology," *Social Problems* 32(1985): 301–16.

30. William Ryan, *Blaming the Victim* (New York: Pantheon, 1971); Larry Cuban and David Tyack, "Mismatch: Schools and Children Who Don't Fit Them" in Henry Levin, ed., *Accelerated Schools,* forthcoming.

31. From her analysis of descriptions of nineteenth-century classrooms, Barbara Jean Finkelstein concludes that "teachers treated academic failure, not as a reflection of their own inabilities as instructors, but as evidence of the students' personal and moral recalcitrance"; see Barbara Jean Finkelstein, "Governing the Young: Teacher Behavior in American Primary Schools, 1820–1880: A Documentary History" (Ed.D. diss., Teachers College, Columbia University, 1970), 134–35.

32. This institutional approach was more a reform strategy than an articulated mode of analysis of gender; for a discussion of the latter, see Elisabeth Hansot and David Tyack, "Gender in American Public Schools: Thinking Institutionally," *Signs* 13(1988): 741–60.

33. Florence Howe, "Introduction: The Teacher and the Women's Movement," in Frazier and Sadker, *Sexism,* xi, xiii, xv, xi–xv. An example of combining models of explanation and strategies for change is Stockhard et al., *Sex Equity in Education.*

34. Tyack, James, and Benavot, *Law and the Shaping of Public Schools,* chap. 6.

35. Ibid. Even without the vote, women had access to decision-makers (the President of the General Federation of Women's Clubs, for example, was the wife of the U.S. senator who pushed to include home economics in Smith-Hughes), and clubwomen were skilled in networking and lobbying at different levels of the federated political system; see Jane Bernard Powers, "The 'Girl Question' in Education: Vocational Training for Young Women in the Progressive Era" (Ph.D. diss., Stanford University, 1986), chaps. 6, 8.

36. For a general analysis of strategies and action, see Nancy E. McGlen and Karen O'Connor, "An Analysis of the U.S. Women's Rights Movements: Rights as a Public Good," *Women and Politics* 1(1986): 65–85. For a summary of national politics, see Andrew Fishel and Janice Pottker, *National Politics and Sex Discrimination in Education* (Lexington, Mass.: Lexington Books, 1977).

37. NOW bill of rights in Deckard, *Women's Movement,* 348, and see also 342–49.

38. Title IX, Education Amendments of 1972, Public Law 92-318, 92d Cong., S. 659, June 23, 1972; Andrew Fishel and Janice Pottker, "Sex Bias in Secondary Schools," in Pottker and Fishel, eds., *Sex Bias,* 92; Anne N. Costain, "Eliminating Sex Discrimination in Education: Lobbying for Implementation of Title IX," *Policy Studies Journal* 7(Winter 1978): 189–95; Fishel and Pottker, *National Politics;* U.S. Congress, House Committee on Education, *Discrimination against Women: Hearings before the Special Subcommittee on Education of the Committee on Education and Labor on Section 805 of H.R. 16098,* pt. 1, 91st Cong., 2d sess., 1970, and pt. 2, 91st Cong., 2d sess., 1971; United States Commission on Civil Rights, *Enforcing Title IX* (Washington: CCR, October, 1980).

39. Costain, "Lobbying for Title IX," 189, 189–95.

40. Bayh quoted in Project on Equal Education Rights, NOW Legal Defense and Education Fund, *Stalled at the Start: Government Action on Sex Bias in the Schools* (Washington: PEER, 1977), 33–35.

41. Costain, "Lobbying for Title IX," 189–95.

42. Title IX regulations reprinted in U.S. Commission on Civil Rights, *Enforcing Title IX,* 63–70.

43. PEER, *Stalled at the Start,* 38, 5, 33–39. An internal report in the U.S. Office of Education noted that the office itself was doing a bad job of appointing women to professional positions; Commissioner's Task Force on the Impact of Office of Education Programs on Women, *A Look at Women in Education: Issues and Answers for HEW* (Washington, D.C.: Photocopied Report, November 1972). PEER reviewed 858 complaints of sex discrimination filed with the HEW civil rights investigators by private citizens from June 1972 to October 1976. The largest number, 564, alleged bias in employment, followed in order by athletics, access to classes, procedural regulations, student rules, and then a miscellaneous set of grievances. PEER found that HEW had resolved only 7 percent of these cases within six months and that only one in five had been resolved by 1976 (complaints still on the docket in 1976 had been at HEW for an average of 16 months).

44. PEER, *Stalled at the Start,* 21, 21–25; Appendix E.

45. U.S. Commission on Civil Rights, *Enforcing Title IX;* Order, *Adams v. Califano,* Civ. No. 3095-70, and *Weal v. Califano,* Civ. No. 74-1720 D.D.C., filed December 29, 1977 (commonly referred to as the *Adams* case and order); General Accounting Office, Report no. HRD-77-78, March 30, 1977; *Grove City College v. Bell* (1984) 465 U.S. 104 S. Ct. 1211 No. 82-792; Nancy Duff Campbell et al., *Sex Discrimination in Education: Legal Rights and Remedies* (Washington, D.C.: National Women's Law Center, 1983).

46. Patricia A. Schmuck et al., "Administrative Strategies for Institutionalizing Sex Equity in Education and the Role of Government," in Klein, ed., *Handbook for Sex Equity,* 96–100; Citizens Council on Women's Education, *Catching Up: A Review of the Women's Educational Equity Act Program* (Washington, D.C.: National Coalition for Women and Girls in Education, 1984).

47. Theresa Cusick, *A Clash of Ideologies: The Reagan Administration Versus the*

Women's Educational Equity Act (Washington, D.C.: PEER, 1983); PEER, "The New Women's Educational Equity Act: Still Alive and Making a Difference," *PEER Policy Paper,* no. 3, Spring 1985; Citizens Council on Women's Education, *Catching Up,* 2, 39.

48. Paul Laxalt, *Family Protection Act,* (27 September 1979, *Congressional Record,* 96th Cong., 1st sess., 125, pt. 20:26435–36); "Protecting the American Family," *Conservative Digest* 5(1979): 31–32; S. 1378, 97th Cong., 1st sess., June 17, 1981.

49. Phyllis W. Cheng, "The Second Wave: State Title IX Laws and the New Federalism" (unpublished paper presented at AERA Convention, Washington, D.C., April 22, 1987—a report on the Project on State Title IX Laws sponsored by WEEA), 10–12, 21.

50. Ibid., 14–15, 19; Susan Bailey and Rebecca Smith, *Policies for the Future: State Policies, Regulations, and Resources Related to the Achievement of Educational Equity for Females and Males* (Washington, D.C.: Resource Center for Sex Equity, Council of Chief State School Officers, 1982).

51. PEER, *Campaigns for Equal Education* (Washington, D.C.: PEER, 1982), 16, 5. The passages quoted in the paragraphs that follow derive from the same source and will be identified by page references in the text only.

52. Rita Bornstein, "Ambiguity as Opportunity and Constraint: Evolution of a Federal Sex Equity Education Program," *Educational Evaluation and Policy Analysis* 7(1985): 103, 99–114. For an evaluation of the project in Miami that Bornstein discusses, see B. E. Stake et al., *Evaluation of the National Sex Equity Demonstration Project, Final Report* (Urbana, Ill.: Center for Instructional Research and Instructional Evaluation, University of Illinois, 1983).

53. National Advisory Council on Women's Educational Programs, *Title IX: The Half Full, Half Empty Glass* (Washington, D.C.: GPO, 1981); PEER, "The PEER Report Card: Update on Women and Girls in America's Schools—A State-by-State Survey," *PEER Policy Paper,* no. 4, Autumn 1985, 1–4.

54. Glen Harvey and Leslie F. Hergert, "Strategies for Achieving Sex Equity in Education," *Theory into Practice* 25(Autumn 1986): 295, 290–99; Kathleen B. Boundy, "Sex Inequities in Education," *Clearinghouse Review* 14(February 1981): 1048–56, esp. 1052–53, and Campbell et al., *Sex Discrimination,* chaps. 1–3 (chapter 6 indicates grounds for action other than Title IX). In a survey of 1,631 cases dealing with students in state courts from 1976 to 1981, researchers found 14 cases involving sex discrimination, 10 of which concerned sports—as opposed to 765 involving the education of the handicapped, for example; see Thomas B. Marvell, Armand Galfo, and John Rockwell, *Court Selection: Student Litigation in State and Federal Courts* (Williamsburg, Va.: National Center for State Law Courts, 1982), 52–53.

55. National Advisory Council on Women's Educational Programs, *Title IX,* 9, 15, 20, 16.

56. PEER, "PEER Report Card."

57. Alabama principal quoted in *Los Angeles Times,* January 9, 1986, p. 16; Janice C. Wendt and John M. Carley, "Resistance to Title IX in Physical Education: Legal, Institutional, and Individual," *Journal of Physical Education, Recreation, and Dance* 54(1983): 54–59; David Monahan, "The Failure of Coed Sports," *Psychology Today* 17(March 1983): 58–63; Michael Brown, "Hair, the Constitution, and the Public Schools," *Journal of Law and Education* 1(1972): 371–82.

58. Fishel and Pottker, "Sex Bias in Secondary Schools," 97–103; George H. Gallup, "Participation in Sports by Girls," in Pottker and Fishel, eds., *Sex Bias,* p. 531; National Advisory Council on Women's Educational Programs, *Title IX,* 41; "PEER Report Card," 2, charts 1 and 2.

59. "Should Interscholastic Athletics Be Provided for High School Girls and College Women?" *Journal of Health, Physical Education and Recreation* 33(May 1962): 7–8; Julia M. Brown, "Women in Physical Education: The Dribble Index of Liberation," in Joan I. Roberts, ed., *Beyond Intellectual Sexism: A New Reality* (New York: David McKay, 1976), 365-80; Cheryl M. Fields, "Title IX at X," Ann Uhlir, "The Wolf is Our Shepherd: Shall We Not Fear?" and Jay J. Coakley and Marcia Westkott, "Opening Doors for Women in Sport: An Alternative to Old Strategies," in D. Stanley Eitzen, ed., *Sport in Contemporary Society: An Anthology* (New York: St. Martin's Press, 1984), 368–73, 374–84, 385–400.

60. Patricia L. Geadelmann, with Judy Bishoff, Mary Hoferek, and Dorothy B. McKnight, "Sex Equity in Physical Education and Athletics," in Klein, ed., *Handbook for Sex Equity,* 319–37; "PEER Report Card," 2; National Advisory Council on Women's Educational Programs, *Title IX,* 40–42; Brown, "Women in Physical Education"; Uhlir, "The Wolf Is Our Shepherd"; Coakley and Westkott, "Opening Doors for Women in Sport."

61. Helen S. Farmer and Joan Seliger Sidney, with Barbara A. Bitters and Martine G. Brizius, "Sex Equity in Career and Vocational Education," in Klein, ed., *Handbook for Sex Equity,* 338–59.

62. Ruth S. Barnhart, "Children's Sex-typed Views of Traditional Occupational Roles," *School Counselor* 31(November 1983): 167–70; Geraldine Jonçich Clifford, "'Marry, Stich, Die or Do Worse': Educating Women for Work," in Harvey Kantor and David B. Tyack, eds., *Work, Youth, and Schooling: Historical Perspectives on Vocationalism in American Education* (Stanford: Stanford University Press, 1982), 233–68.

63. Fishel and Pottker, "Sex Bias in the Secondary School," 94–96; Farmer and Sidney, "Sex Equity in Career and Vocational Education."

64. Donna Mertens, "Federal Policy for Sex Equity in Vocational Education," *Educational Evaluation and Policy Analysis* 6(1984): 401–9; Fishel and Pottker, "Sex Bias in the Secondary School," 94–96.

65. Mertens, "Federal Policy for Sex Equity," 405–6; Farmer et al., "Sex Equity," 342–43; "PEER Report Card," 3, chart 15; Learita Garfield-Scott and Paul LeMahieu, "Targeting Nontraditional Students: A Study of Change Process in

Vocational Education," *Vocational Guidance Quarterly* 33(December 1984): 157–68.

66. On the problem of obtaining adequate statistics and some additional estimates of numbers of women administrators in the years between 1972 and 1984, see Effie H. Jones and Xenia P. Montenegro, *Recent Trends in the Representation of Women and Minorities in School Administration and Problems in Documentation* (Arlington, Va.: Office of Minority Affairs, American Association of School Administrators, 1982); Charol Shakeshaft, "Strategies for Overcoming the Barriers to Women in Educational Administration," in Klein, ed., *Handbook for Sex Equity*, 124–44. Jacqueline Clement (*Sex Bias in School Leadership* [Evanston, Ill.: Integrated Education, 1976] speaks of a "conspiracy of silence" on gender statistics in administration. William Gerritz, Julia Koppich, and James Guthrie, *Preparing California School Leaders: An Analysis of Supply, Demand, and Training* (Berkeley, Calif.: PACE, 1984); articles on "Women in Administration," *Phi Delta Kappan* 67(1985); 281–301. Sakre Kennington Edson, in *Pushing the Limits: The Female Administrative Aspirant* (Albany: State University of New York Press, 1988) reports fewer women superintendents in 1984–85 (3 percent) than the PEER report card cited in table 16.

67. Susan Bailey and Rebecca Smith, *Policies for the Future*, 75–76. On the tendency of publishers to respond to criticism, see Frances Fitzgerald, *America Revised* (Boston: Little, Brown, 1979). Like textbook publishers, corporations that produced tests, which had come under severe criticism for bias, faced similar legal and commercial pressures to change. Title IX banned the use of separate-sex tests for appraisal purposes. The Strong Vocational Interest Blank, which had been issued in separate blue and pink versions, for example, was remade into a uniform integrated format. For continuing problems in testing, see Esther E. Diamond and Carol Kehr Tittle, "Sex Equity in Testing," in Klein, ed., *Handbook for Sex Equity*, 167–188.

68. See, for example, Women on Words and Images, "Sex Stereotypes."

69. On the impact of feminist research and women's studies programs on conceptualizations of women's experience, see Florence Howe, *Myths of Coeducation: Selected Essays, 1964–1983* (Bloomington, Ind.: Indiana University Press, 1984); Peggy McIntosh and Elizabeth Kamarck Minnich, "Varieties of Women's Studies," *Women's Studies International Forum* 7(No. 3, 1984): 139–48.

70. Mary Kay Tetreault, "Thinking about Women: The Case of United States History Textbooks," *The History Teacher* 19(February 1986): 211–62.

71. Ibid., Tetreault, "The Journey from Male-Defined to Gender-Balanced Education," *Theory into Practice* 25(Autumn 1986): 230.

72. Tetreault, "Thinking about Women"; Tetreault, "Gender-Balanced Education"; Maxine Greene, *Landscapes of Learning* (New York: Teachers College Press, 1978), chaps. 15–17.

73. Paul C. Vitz, "Religion and Traditional Values in Public School Textbooks," *The Public Interest* 84(Summer 1986): 88–89.

74. Mary Jo Neitz, "Resistances to Feminist Analysis," *Teaching Sociology* 12(April 1985): 339, 346–47, 339–53.

75. Kathryn P. Scott and Candace Garrett Schau, "Sex Equity," 226. On the question of censorship, see the exchange between Robert B. Moore and Lee Burgess in *English Journal* 70(September 1981): 14–19. On the influence of advocacy groups over textbook publishers, and the generally cosmetic and partial responses the publishers make, see Frances Fitzgerald, *America Revised,* and Harriet Tyson-Bernstein, *A Conspiracy of Good Intentions: America's Textbook Fiasco* (Washington, D.C.: Council for Basic Education, 1988), 17–18.

76. Jere Brophy, "Interactions of Male and Female Students with Male and Female Teachers," in Louise Cherry Wilkinson and Cera B. Marrett, eds., *Gender Influences in Classroom Interaction* (New York: Academic Press, 1985), 115–42; Marlaine E. Lockheed, "Sex Segregation and Male Preeminence in Elementary Classrooms," in Fenema and Ayer, eds., *Women and Education,* 117–35.

77. Brophy, "Interactions," 120, 115–23; Sears and Feldman, "Teacher Interactions," 31.

78. Frazier and Sadker, *Sexism,* chaps. 5–6; Lockheed, "Sex Segregation and Male Preeminence"; Myra and David Sadker, "Sexism in the Schoolroom of the '80s," *Psychology Today* 19(March 1985): 54, 54–57.

79. Larry Cuban, *How Teachers Taught* (New York: Longman, 1982).

80. Brophy, "Interactions," 121.

81. Eleanor Maccoby and Carol Jacklin, "Gender Segregation in Childhood," in H. Reese, ed., *Advances in Child Development and Research,* vol. 20 (New York: Academic Press, 1987); Barrie Thorne and Zella Luria, "Sexuality and Gender in Children's Daily Worlds," *Social Problems* 33(1986): 170–76; Jean Anyon, "Intersections of Gender and Class: Accommodation and Resistance by Working-Class and Affluent Females to Contradictory Sex-Role Ideologies," in Stephen Walker and Len Barton, eds., *Gender, Class and Education* (Sussex: Falmer Press, 1983), 33, 19–37.

82. Cynthia A. Cone and Berta Perez, "Peer Groups and Organization of Classroom Space," *Human Organization* 45(Spring 1986): 80–87.

83. Ibid., 81–85.

84. Ibid.

85. Ibid., 86.

86. Stockard, "Sex Inequities," 73.

87. Jacqueline S. Eccles and Phyllis Blumenfield, "Classroom Experiences and Student Gender: Are There Differences and Do They Matter?" in Wilkinson and Marrett, eds., *Gender Influences,* 79–81.

88. Ibid., 81, 87.

89. Brophy, "Interactions," 120, 115–23.

90. Some studies of adolescent girls in the 1980s found that they had higher career aspirations than boys, and in general they had similar employment goals

while in high school. The enrollment of women in colleges soared in the 1970s, outpacing that of men for the first time in 1979; women entered graduate and professional schools in rapidly growing numbers (female enrollments in law schools, for example, jumped from 10 percent in 1971–72 to 34 percent in 1980–81, and in medical schools from 11 percent to 26 percent). Farmer and Sidney, "Career Education," p. 341; National Advisory Council on Women's Educational Programs, *Title IX,* 27, 30.

Conclusion

1. UNESCO, *Comparative Study of Co-Education* (Paris: UNESCO, 30 October 1970, ED/MD/15), 119, 57, 120, 13–22, 33–35; Francisco O. Ramirez and Yun-kyung Cha, "Citizenship and Gender: Western Educational Development in Comparative Perspective," *Research in Sociology of Education and Socialization,* forthcoming, table 2; John W. Meyer and Michael T. Hannan, *National Development and the World System: Educational, Political, and Economic Change, 1950–1970* (Chicago: University of Chicago Press, 1979).

2. UNESCO, *Co-Education,* 119, 57, 120, 13–22, 33–35. For sex disparities in education cross-nationally, see Jeremy D. Finn, Loretta Dulberg, and Janet Reis, "Sex Differences in Educational Attainment: A Cross-National Perspective," *Harvard Educational Review* 49(1979): 480, 485, 477–503; Sita van Bemmelen and Maaike van Vliet, "Coeducation versus Single-Sex Schooling: A Comparison between Western and Third World Perspectives," Centre for the Study of Education in Developing Countries, The Hague, December, 1985.

3. Margaret B. Sutherland, "Whatever Happened to Coeducation? *British Journal of Educational Studies* 33(1985): 156–57, 155–63; Marcel deGrandpre, *La Coéducation dans les Ecoles de 45 Pays* (Québec: Editions Paulines, 1973); Didi Massell, "The Rise and Spread of Coeducation: A Comparative History" (unpublished MS, Stanford University, December, 1988). We thank Suk-ying Wong for her assistance in gathering international information on coeducation.

4. Deborah L. Rhode, "Association and Assimilation," *Northwestern Law Review* 81(1986): 107, fn. 6; Lee A. Daniels, "Women at Princeton, 20 Years Later," *New York Times* (April 5, 1989) B9; Carol Lasser, "Introduction," in Carol Lasser, ed., *Educating Men and Women Together: Education in a Changing World* (Urbana: University of Illinois Press, 1987), 1–2. Data on independent schools supplied by the National Association of Independent Schools from a study completed in April, 1989; *Education Week* (February 10, 1988), 1, 16; Lynn Olson, "Girls in Independent Schools: 'Equality of Access Is Not Enough,' *Education Week* (March 27, 1985), 5, 12.

5. Mary Kay Thompson Tetreault, "The Journey from Male-Defined to Gender-Balanced Education," *Theory into Practice* 25(1986): 227–34; Anne Bennison et al., "Equity or Equality: What Shall It Be?" in Elizabeth Fennema and M. Jane

Ayer, eds., *Women and Education: Equity or Equality?* (Berkeley: McCutchan Publishing, 1984), 1–17; Charol Shakeshaft, "A Gender at Risk," *Phi Delta Kappan* 67(1986): 499–503.

6. Madeleine Arnot, "A Cloud over Coeducation: An Analysis of the Forms of Transmission of Class and Gender Relations," in Stephen Walker and Len Barton, eds., *Gender Class & Education* (New York: Falmer Press, 1983), 86, 69–92.

7. Rosalind Rosenberg, *Beyond Separate Spheres: Intellectual Roots of Modern Feminism* (New Haven: Yale University Press, 1982).

8. Androgyny ideal characterized by Bennison et al., "Equity or Equality?" 5.

9. Nel Noddings, *Caring: A Feminine Approach to Ethics & Moral Education* (Berkeley: University of California Press, 1984); Carol Gilligan, *In a Different Voice: Psychological Theory and Women's Development* (Cambridge: Harvard University Press, 1982); Jane Roland Martin, *Reclaiming a Conversation: The Ideal of the Educated Woman* (New Haven: Yale University Press, 1985); Madeline R. Grumet, *Bitter Milk: Women and Teaching* (Amherst: University of Massachusetts Press, 1988); Tetreault, "Gender-Balanced Education"; Ann L. Sherman, "Genderism and the Reconstitution of Philosophy of Education," *Educational Theory* 34(Fall 1984): 321–25. For an early criticism of "economic feminists" and a call for increased attention to the importance of nurture, see Gene P. Agre and Barbara Finkelstein, "Feminism and School Reform: The Last Fifteen Years," *Teachers College Record* 80(December 1978): 307–15.

10. In "Beyond Gender: Equity Issues for Home Economics Education," *Theory into Practice* 25(Autumn 1986): 276–83, Patricia J. Thompson argues for a new paradigm for the domestic education of women that contrasts with the ideas of some of the early advocates of domestic "science" who wanted to wrap the new field in the prestige of (male) science. For an exchange of opinions on whether girls' sports should be competitive, see "Should Interscholastic Athletics Be Provided for High School Girls and College Women?" *Journal of Health, Physical Education, and Recreation* 33(May 1962): 7–9. Another reason for second thoughts about making home economics and physical education coeducational was that such integration endangered the positions women had won in separate programs; see previous chapter.

11. Martin, *Conversation*, 195.

12. Tetreault, "Gender-Balanced Education," 229.

13. Ibid., 228, 232–33; Martin, *Conversation*, 198; Arnot, "Coeducation."

14. Title IX, Education Amendments of 1972, Public Law 92-318; *Vorchheimer v. School District of Philadelphia*, 532 F.2d 880 (1976); Rhode, "Association and Assimilation," 136–41; *Newberg v. Board of Public Education*, 9 Pa. D. & C. 3rd 536, 565–66, 570 n. 124 (1983). A petition by students and graduates of Girls' High School to intervene in defense of their school through a legal appeal was denied, raising the question of who was actually represented in the original class action suit; *Newberg v. Board of Public Education*, 478 A.2bd 1352 (Pa. Super. 1984). The

fundamental philosophical and pedagogical issues involved in separate-sex education—a weighing of benefits and costs—have not received sensitive scrutiny in the courts, as Rhode observes.

15. For critiques of coeducation, see Florence Howe, *Myths of Coeducation: Selected Essays, 1964–1983* (Bloomington: Indiana University Press, 1984) and Roberta M. Hall and Bernice R. Sandler, *The Classroom Climate: A Chilly One for Women?* (Washington, D.C.: Association of American Colleges Report on the Status and Education of Women, 1982). On the benefits of single-sex education, see Jill K. Conway, "Coeducation and Women's Studies: Two Approaches to the Question of Woman's Place in the Contemporary University," *Daedalus* 103(1974): 239–49.

16. Sally Schwager, "Educating Women in America," *Signs* 12(Winter 1987): 333–36, 362–65; Jill K. Conway, "Perspectives on the History of Women's Education in the United States," *History of Education Quarterly* 14(Spring 1974): 1–12; Peggy McIntosh and Elizabeth Kamarck Minnich, "Varieties of Women's Studies," *Women's Studies International Forum* 7(no. 3, 1984): 139–48.

17. Valerie E. Lee and Anthony S. Bryk, "Effects of Single-Sex Secondary Schools on Student Achievement and Attitudes," *Journal of Educational Psychology* 78(1986): 381–95; Emmanuel Jimenez and Marlaine E. Lockheed, "The Relative Effectiveness of Single-Sex and Coeducational Schools in Thailand," The World Bank, *Working Papers,* August 1988; Patricia A. Palmieri, "Here Was Fellowship: A Social Portrait of Academic Women at Wellesley College, 1895–1920," *History of Education Quarterly* 23(Summer 1983): 195–214; M. Elizabeth Tidball, "Women's Colleges and Women Achievers Revisited," *Signs* 5(Spring 1980): 504–17; Mary J. Oates and Susan Williamson, "Women's Colleges and Women Achievers," *Signs* 3(Summer 1978): 795–806; van Bemmelen and van Vliet, "Coeducation."

18. Arnot, "Coeducation." For discussions of the neglect and distortion of women's issues in traditional scholarship and the emergence of new feminist ways of seeing, see Ellen Carol DuBois et al., *Feminist Scholarship: Kindling in the Groves of Academe* (Urbana: University of Illinois Press, 1985).

19. Arnot, "Coeducation," 86, 69–92.

20. Ibid., 88. For a discussion of feminist educators, see Kathleen Weiler, *Women Teaching for Change: Gender, Class & Power* (South Hadley, Mass.: Bergin & Garvey, 1988). A further problem with the single-sex solution is that boys in single-sex independent schools show more sex-stereotyped attitudes toward women's roles than those in coeducational schools, and if many girls are in single-sex schools, there aren't enough females to desegregate the remaining coeducational ones; Marcia K. Gilroy, "The Effects of Single-Sex Secondary Schooling: Student Achievement, Behavior, and Attitudes" (Paper delivered at American Educational Research Association, San Francisco, March 28, 1989).

21. Rhode, "Association and Assimilation," 143–44; Adrienne Rich, *On Lies, Secrets, and Silence: Selected Prose, 1966–1978* (New York: W. W. Norton, 1979), 125–55.

22. Although the new research on the benefits of single-sex private schools and colleges provides a good case for preserving at least the all-girls institutions, the chief reason why large numbers of private schools shifted to coeducation seems to have been the market for students: many single-sex schools were not attracting the kinds of students they wanted. For an insightful study of one school's transition to coeducation, see Kathleen M. Dalton, *A Portrait of a School: Coeducation at Andover* (Andover, Mass.: Phillips Academy, 1986).

23. Arthur L. Stinchcombe, "Social Structure and Organizations," in James G. March, ed. *Handbook of Organizations* (Chicago: Rand McNally, 1965).

24. Redding S. Sugg, Jr., *Motherteacher: The Feminization of American Education* (Charlottesville: University of Virginia Press, 1978).

25. John Dewey, "Is Co-education Injurious to Girls? What Co-education Has Done," *The Ladies Home Journal* 28(June 11, 1911): 61. For a critical interpretation of this essay and Dewey's concept of women, see Susan Laird, "Women and Gender in John Dewey's Philosophy of Education," *Educational Theory* 38(1988): 111–29. For a positive interpretation of Dewey's feminism, see Jo Ann Boydston, "John Dewey and the New Feminism," *Teachers College Record* 76(1975): 441–48.

26. Patricia Cayo Sexton, *Women in Education* (Bloomington, Ind.: Phi Delta Kappa, 1976), 6; David L. Kirp, Mark G. Udof, and Marlene Strong Franks, *Gender Justice* (Chicago: University of Chicago Press, 1986).

27. Barrie Thorne, "Children and Gender: Constructions of Difference," in Deborah L. Rhode, ed., *Theoretical Perspectives on Sexual Difference* (New Haven: Yale University Press, 1990), 100–113.

28. Raphaela Best, *We've All Got Scars* (Bloomington: Indiana University Press, 1983); Eleanor Maccoby and Carol Jacklin, "Gender Segregation in Childhood," in H. Reese, ed., *Advances in Child Development and Research,* vol. 20 (New York: Academic Press, 1987); Vivian Gussin Paley, *Boys & Girls: Superheroes in the Doll Corner* (Chicago: University of Chicago Press, 1984).

29. Thorne, "Children and Gender."

30. Tetreault notes the absence of attention to gender in recent reform reports; see her "Gender-Balanced Education," 232.

⇒ *Index* ⇐

15 12/94